Extraordinary USES for ordinary things

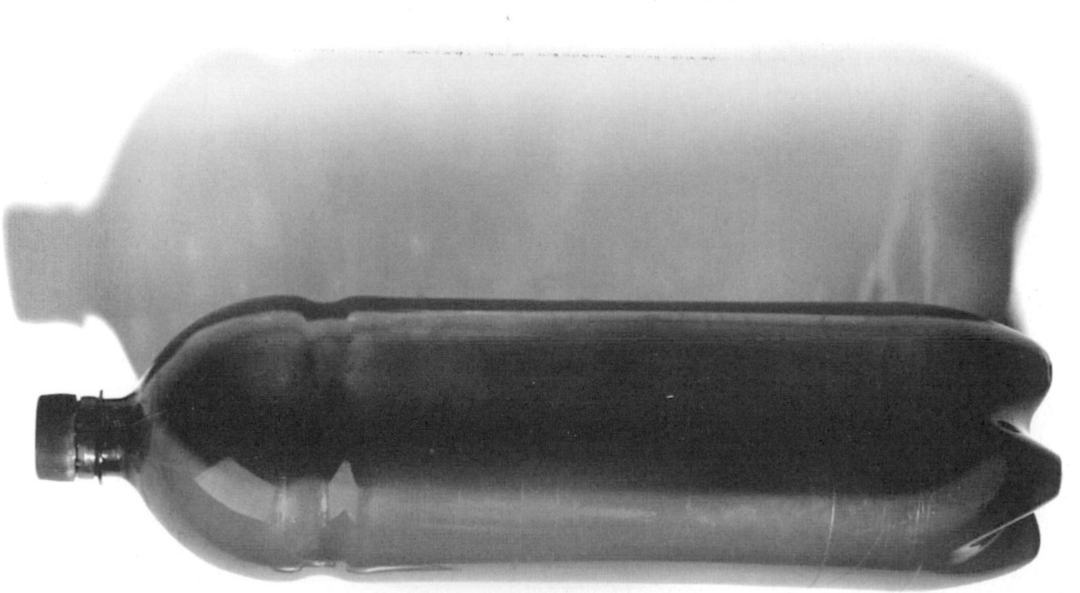

OVER 2000 WAYS TO **SAVE MONEY** AND **TIME**
USING 202 COMMON HOUSEHOLD ITEMS

Contents

Your complete A-Z guide

✱ Denotes a **SUPER ITEM**: A household item with an amazingly large number of uses.

A

B

C

D

Discover what's hiding in your cupboard

Not that long ago, in the days before computers, cable television, mobile phones and robots that can do the housework for you, washing windows was a simple job. Our grandparents poured a little vinegar or ammonia into a bucket of water, took an old rag and in no time had a clear view of the outside world through gleaming glass.

Then they would use the same combination to banish grime and grit from worktops, walls, shelves, floors and much of the rest of the house.

Some things, like window cleaning, shouldn't ever be more complicated than this. But supermarket shelves are laden with a dazzling array of cleaning products, each with a unique use, a special formula, and a multi-million-pound advertising campaign. Window cleaners alone take up acres of shelf space. The bottles are filled with colourful liquids and have labels touting their orange power or lemon scent. Ironically, many boast the added power of vinegar as their 'secret' ingredient.

This overwhelming choice applies to every aspect of modern life. Every problem, mess, hobby and daily task seems to require special tools, unique products, and extensive know-how. Why use a knife to chop garlic when there are 48 varieties of garlic press available? Why use a rag to clean when there are specialised sponges, wipes, magnetically charged dusters and HEPA-filter vacuums?

Which brings us to the point of this book: why *not* just use a solution of vinegar or lemon juice like our grandparents did to clean the windows? It works just as well as commercial products, if not better. And it costs only about a quarter as much, sometimes less.

202 everyday items with over 2000 uses

Making do with what you already have is an worthwhile, clever, money-saving approach to life. And in fact, it can even be fun. While you can buy a special lint brush to remove cat hairs from trousers, 1p worth of tape does the job even better. You can use strong kitchen chemicals to clean the inside of a vase. But it's easier – to use a couple of Alka-Seltzer tablets to fizz away the mess instead.

Welcome to *Extraordinary Uses for Ordinary Things*. We will show you more than 2000 ingenious ways to use 202 ordinary household products to restore, replace, repair or revive almost everything in and around your home or to pamper yourself or entertain your children. You'll save time, money – and shelf space because you won't need lots of different kinds of specialised commercial preparations. You will even save on petrol, because you won't need to speed off to the shops every time you run out of a staple such as air freshener, shampoo, oven cleaner or wrapping paper.

The household items featured in this book are not expensive commercial concoctions. They are everyday items that you are likely to find in your home: in the kitchen, medicine cabinet, desk, garage and even the dustbin. And you'll be amazed by how much you can actually accomplish using just a few of the most versatile of these items, such as bicarbonate of soda, gaffer tape, tights, salt, vinegar and WD-40. In fact, there's a popular maxim among handymen that pares the list down to a pair of basic necessities: 'To get through life', the saying goes, 'you only need two tools: WD-40 and gaffer tape. If it doesn't move, but should, reach for the WD-40. If it moves, but shouldn't, use the gaffer tape'.

Less toxic and more earth-friendly items

In addition to saving time and money, there are other, less tangible advantages to using these everyday household products. For one thing, many of the items are safer to use and considerably more environmentally friendly than their off-the-shelf counterparts. Consider, for example, using vinegar and bicarbonate of soda to clear a blocked bathroom or kitchen drain. It is usually just as effective as a commercial drain cleaner. The only difference is that the bicarbonate of soda and vinegar combination is far less caustic and therefore gentler on your plumbing. And, you won't have to worry about splashing it on your skin or in your eyes.

The hints in this book will also help you reduce household waste by giving you hundreds of delightful and surprising suggestions for re-using many of the items that you would otherwise throw in the dusbin or send for recycling. To name a few, these include lemon rinds and banana skins, used tea bags and coffee grounds, orphaned socks and worn-out tights and stockings, plastic bags, empty plastic bottles and jugs, cans and newspapers.

At the end of the day, you'll experience the distinct pleasure that can only come from learning creative, sometimes strange and occasionally eccentric new ways to use familiar objects around the house. Even if you never use Alka-Seltzer tablets to lure fish onto a fishing line or need to plug a hole in your car radiator with black pepper or fill a pair of old tights with dog hair to scare away deer and foxes or make a bath pillow out of a plastic sandwich bag or use cat litter as a face pack or make a sleeping bag out of bubble wrap isn't it great to know you can?

Folk wisdom for the 21st century

As we noted earlier, much of the advice you'll find in *Extraordinary Uses for Ordinary Things* is not really new – it's just new to us. After all, 'Waste not, want not' isn't merely a quaint adage from a bygone era; it actually defined a way of life for generations before us. In the days before mass manufacturing and mass marketing transformed most of the western world into a throwaway society, most people knew perfectly well that salt and bicarbonate of soda, had dozens and dozens of uses.

Now, as landfills swell and it is becoming increasingly clear that the earth's resources are not endless, there are signs that a shift back to a more economical, less wasteful approach to life is becoming more commonplace – and indeed may become a part of government policy on both a national and local level. From recycling programmes to energy - and water-efficient dishwashers and toilets to hybrid cars, we are constantly looking for new ways to stop wasting resources and find additional uses for existing materials.

People are designing and building houses to use resources more efficiently and even, in one recent case, actually constructing stylish homes using materials that would previously have been considered to be rubbish. On the simplest level, this book is an important part of that growing trend.

How we put this book together

To provide you with the most reliable information available, we conducted countless interviews with experts on everything from acne cures to garden care and scrutinised the latest research. We also performed numerous hands-on tests in our own kitchens, living rooms, bathrooms and other areas around the home.

The result, we believe, is the most comprehensive and dependable guide to alternative uses for ordinary household products available. We have combined some time-honoured, traditional tips (such as using apple cider vinegar to kill weeds) with new tips given to us by various reliable sources (such as recycling used fabric softener sheets to clean computer and television screens).

As in any comprehensive compilation such as this, the practical information contained in this book is as much art as it is science. So although we employed trial-and-error methods wherever possible to provide specific amounts and clear directions for using household products and objects to obtain the desired results, we can't guarantee that these solutions will work in all situations. In other words, your mileage may vary.

Moreover, while we are confident that every one of the 202 products used for all the tips included here is generally safe and effective when used as directed, please pay close attention to the 'Take Care' warnings about using, storing, and especially combining certain products.

What's on the following pages

The main part of this book is arranged like an encyclopedia, with the 202 product categories organized in A-Z fashion (running from Address labels to Zips), to provide instant access to information as well as entertaining reading. But before that, in the first part of this book, you'll find a guide to the items that are most useful for certain areas, such as the garden or for cooking.

Scattered throughout, you'll also find hundreds of fascinating asides and anecdotes. Some highlight specific warnings and safety precautions, or offer advice about buying or using certain items. But many are just meant to be fun – providing quirky historical information about the invention or origins of products. Haven't you always wondered who invented the sticking plaster or how who had the idea for cat litter or shampoo? We've also included dozens of engaging and enlightening activities and simple science experiments that you can do with your children or grandchildren (and not a single one requires a visit to a toy shop).

Whether you love discovering new ways to use everyday household items, or if you hate throwing things away, we're sure you'll find the ideas in this book entertaining and enlightening. So get ready to be dazzled by the incredible number of everyday problems that you will soon be able to solve with ease. We are confident this is a book you will return to over and over again for helpful hints, trustworthy advice, and even some good, old-fashioned inspiration.

—The Editors

Most useful items

for just about anything

If you have a special interest, such as cooking or health and beauty, you'll soon discover that certain household items are especially useful. There are, for example, close to a dozen uses for plastic bottles in the garden. On these following pages, you'll find these helpful items listed for most everyday areas of interest.

TOP

10

Most useful items for around the house

Pad a breakable package with a disposable nappy ...

p.136

Carpet remnants

{PAGE 103}

Make an exercise mat, car mat, or knee pad • Muffle noisy appliances • Protect the floor under plants • Cushion kitchen shelves • Give your car traction • Protect workshop tools.

Compact discs

{PAGE 125}

Use as holiday ornaments, driveway reflectors or to make a circle template • Catch candle drips • Make an artistic bowl, sun catcher or clock.

Fabric softener sheets

{PAGE 146}

Freshen air, cars, dogs, gym bags, suitcases and trainers • Pick up pet hairs • Repel mosquitoes • Stop static cling • Make sheets smell good • End tangled sewing thread.

Gaffer tape

{PAGE 160}

Remove lint and fluff from clothing • Repair toilet seats, screens, vacuum cleaner hoses and picture frames • Cover a book, wallet or gift • Make a bandage or a bumper sticker • Catch flies • Reinforce a book binding • Hem a pair of jeans • Hang Christmas lights • Make a fancy dress costume.

Nail varnish

{PAGE 212}

Mark hard-to-see items • Mark thermostat and shower settings and levels in measuring cups and buckets • Label sports equipment • Seal envelopes and labels • Stop shoes from scuffing and keep laces, ribbons and fabric from unravelling • Make needle-threading easier • Keep buckles and jewellery shiny • Stop a run in a stocking • Temporarily repair a pair of glasses • Fix small nicks in floors and glass • Repair lacquered items • Plug a hole in a cooler bag.

Paper bags

{PAGE 226}

Dust off a filthy mop • Carry laundry • Cover a textbook • Make a table decoration • Use as gift bags and wrapping paper • Reshape knitwear after washing • Use as a pressing cloth • Bag newspapers for recycling.

Plastic bags

{PAGE 248}

Keep a mattress dry at night • Add bulk to curtains • Stuff a cushion or soft toy • Drain bath toys • Hold items from pockets in the laundry • Make a temporary bib • Line a litter tray • Dispose of a Christmas tree.

Rubber bands

{PAGE 263}

Reshape a broom • Childproof cupboards • Keep threads from tangling • Make a holder for a car visor • Use to grip paper • Extend a tight shirt collar • Use as a bookmark • Cushion a remote control • Secure bed slats and tighten casters on furniture.

Sandwich and freezer bags

{PAGE 280}

Protect photographs • Dispense fabric softener • Carry baby wipes • Make new soap from old • Add stiffening to craft items • Feed birds • Make a funnel.

Tights

{PAGE 322}

Find and pick up small objects with a vacuum cleaner • Buff shoes • Keep a hairbrush clean • Remove nail varnish • Keep spray bottles from clogging • Organise a suitcase • Hang-dry a sweater • Secure a rubbish bag • Dust under fridge • Prevent soil erosion in houseplants.

TOP

12 Most useful items for the cook

Add vinegar to the water for perfect poached eggs …

p. 350

Aluminium foil {PAGE 40}

Bake a perfect piecrust • Soften brown sugar • Decorate a cake and create novelty cake tins • Keep rolls and bread warm • Make an extra-large salad bowl • Make a toasted cheese sandwich with an iron.

Apples {PAGE 50}

Keep a roast chicken juicy and cakes fresh • Ripen green tomatoes • Break up hardened brown sugar • Absorb excess salt in soups and stews.

Bicarbonate of soda {PAGE 66}

Clean fruit and vegetables • Soak away fishy smells • Reduce the acidity of coffee and tomato-based sauces • Reduce the gas-producing properties of beans • Make fluffy omelettes • Replace yeast in a recipe for bread.

Coffee filters {PAGE 120}

Cover food in microwave • Filter cork crumbs from wine or food remnants from cooking oil • Stop messy food from dripping.

Ice cube trays {PAGE 177}

Freeze eggs, pesto, chopped vegetables and herbs, chicken soup – even leftover wine – for future use.

Lemons
{PAGE 188}

Prevent potatoes from turning brown or rice from sticking • Keep guacamole green • Make soggy lettuce crisp • Freshen the fridge and clean a chopping board.

Paper towels
{PAGE 234}

Microwave bacon, clean sweetcorn and strain soup • Keep vegetables fresh and the fridge crisper clean • Prevent soggy bread and rusty pans.

Plastic bags
{PAGE 248}

Protect a cookbook • Keep phone clean when answering it while cooking • Crush biscuits or crackers for cooking • Use as mixing bowl or salad spinner • Ripen fruit.

Rubber bands
{PAGE 263}

Keep spoons from sliding into bowls • Secure casserole lids for travel • Anchor a chopping board • Get a better grip on twist-off lids and drinking glasses

Salt
{PAGE 268}

Prevent grease from splashing • Speed up cooking times • Shell hard-boiled eggs more easily • Test eggs for freshness and poach eggs perfectly • Wash spinach more effectively • Keep a salad crisp • Revive wrinkled apples and stop cut fruit from browning • Use to whip cream, beat eggs and keep milk fresh • Prevent mould on cheese.

Sandwich and freezer bags
{PAGE 280}

Make a pastry bag • Dispose of used cooking oil • Colour biscuit dough • Keep ice cream from forming crystals • Soften marshmallows, melt chocolate and save soft drinks • Grease pans.

Toothpicks
{PAGE 332}

Retrieve garlic cloves from a marinade • Prevent pans from boiling over • Microwave potatoes more quickly • Limit the quantity of salad dressing • Fry sausages more effectively

TOP

11 Most useful items for health and beauty

Soothe an aching back with a mustard bath ...

p. 206

Aspirin
{PAGE 52}
Dry up pimples • Treat callouses • Control dandruff • Soothe insect bites and stings • Restore hair colour after swimming in a chlorinated pool.

Baby oil
{PAGE 54}
Remove a sticking plaster painlessly • Treat cradle cap • Make your own bath oil.

Bicarbonate of soda
{PAGE 66}
Soothe minor burns, sunburn, nettle rashes, bee stings, nappy rash and other skin irritations • Combat cradle cap • Control dandruff • Use as gargle or mouthwash • Scrub teeth and clean dentures • Alleviate itching in casts and athlete's foot • Soothe tired, smelly feet • Remove built-up hair gel, spray or conditioner • Use as an antiperspirant.

Butter
{PAGE 89}
Make pills easier to swallow • Soothe aching feet • Remove tree sap from skin • Remove make-up • Use as shaving cream • Moisturise dry hair.

Chest rub
{PAGE 110}
Get rid of tough skin on your feet • Sooth aching feet • Stop insect-bite itch • Treat toenail fungus • Repel biting insects .

Lemons
{PAGE 188}
Disinfect cuts and scrapes • Soften rough hands and relieve sore feet • Remove warts • Lighten age spots • Create blonde highlights • Clean and whiten nails • Cleanse and exfoliate your face • Treat dandruff • Soften dry elbows.

Mayonnaise
{PAGE 199}
Relieve sunburn • Remove dead skin from feet and elbows • Condition hair • Make a facial • Strengthen fingernails.

Mustard
{PAGE 205}
Soothe aching back pain. • Relax stiff muscles. • Relieve congestion. • Make a facial mask.

Petroleum jelly
{PAGE 240}
Soothe windburn • Relieve nappy rash • Protect a baby's eyes during a shampoo • Moisturise dry lips • Remove make-up • Moisturise your face • Create emergency make-up • Strengthen the smell of a perfume • Soften hands • Ensure a professional manicure • Smooth eyebrows.

Tea
{PAGE 318}
Relieve tired eyes • Soothe bleeding gums • Cool sunburn • Stop the pain from a child's injection • Reduce razor burn • Condition dry hair and remove the grey • Make a fake tan • Drain a boil • Soothe nipples when breastfeeding • Relieve the pain of a mouth ulcer.

Vinegar
{PAGE 340}
Control dandruff and condition hair • Protect blonde hair from discoloration by chlorine • Apply as an antiperspirant • Soak aching muscles • Freshen breath • Ease sunburn and itching • Banish bruises • Soothe a sore throat • Clear congestion • Heal cold sores and athlete's foot • Pamper skin • Erase age or sun spots • Soften cuticles • Treat jellyfish or bee stings.

TOP

10 Most useful items for cleaning

Polish a patent leather handbag with a dab of petroleum jelly ...

242

Bicarbonate of soda

{PAGE 66}

Clean baby bottles, Thermos flasks, cutting boards, appliances, sponges and towels, coffeemakers, teapots, cookware and fixtures • Clear blocked drains • Deodorise rubbish bins • Boost washing-up liquid or make your own • Remove stains • Shine jewellery, stainless steel, chrome and marble • Wash wallpaper and remove crayon marks • Remove musty smells.

Bleach

{PAGE 80}

Remove mould • Clean chopping boards and wooden worktops • Brighten glass dishes and cookware • Brighten porcelain • Disinfect a rubbish bin • Sterilise garden tools.

Borax

{PAGE 83}

Clear a blocked drain • Remove stains from a sink • Clean windows and mirrors • Remove mildew from fabrics • Sterilise a waste disposal unit • Eliminate the smell of urine.

Fabric softener sheets

{PAGE 146}

Remove burned-on food from a casserole • Freshen drawers • Remove soap scum • Repel dust from a TV screen • Freshen laundry hampers and waste paper bins • Buff chrome • Keep dust off blinds • Renew the fur on stuffed toys.

Lemons
{PAGE 188}

Get rid of tough stains on marble • Polish metals • Clean the microwave • Remove a lingering smell from a chopping board, the fridge and a waste disposal unit.

Salt
{PAGE 268}

Clean vases, discoloured glass, flowerpots, artificial flowers, refrigerators, woks and wicker • Give brooms a longer life • Make cleaning up flour or ash easier • Make your own metal polish • Remove wine and grease from carpet, water marks from wood and lipstick from drinking glasses • Restore a sponge • Freshen the garbage disposal • Remove baked-on food • Soak up oven spills • Remove stains from pans and clean cast iron.

Surgical spirit
{PAGE 309}

Clean fixtures, venetian blinds, windows and telephones • Remove hair spray from mirrors • Prevent ring around the collar • Remove ink stains.

Toothpaste
{PAGE 330}

Clean piano keys and sinks • Polish metal and jewellery • Deodorise a baby bottle • Remove ink or lipstick from fabric, crayon from walls and water marks from furniture.

Vinegar
{PAGE 340}

Clean blinds, bricks, tiles, carpets, piano keys, computers, appliances and chopping boards • Clean china, crystal, glassware, coffeemakers and cookware • Banish grease in the kitchen • Deodorise drains and musty cupboards • Polish metal • Erase marks from ballpoint pen • Remove water rings and wax from furniture • Revitalise leather • Clean fixtures and get rid of insects.

WD-40
{PAGE 370}

Remove carpet stains and scuffs on flooring • Remove tea and tomato stains • Clean a toilet bowl • Condition leather furniture • Clean a blackboard • Remove marker and crayon from walls.

TOP

11 Most useful items for the garden

Keep aphids away from rose bushes with banana skins …

p. 60

Aluminium foil {PAGE 40}
Create a sun box for window plants or an incubator for seedlings • Mix with mulch to deter insects • Hang in strips to scare crows and other birds • Wrap tree trunks to keep nibbling mice and rabbits away • Keep cuttings from getting tangled.

Coffee cans {PAGE 118}
Make a sprinkler to spread seeds and fertiliser • Measure rainfall to ensure your garden is getting enough water • Make a bird feeder.

Milk cartons {PAGE 201}
Make a bird feeder • Use as a seed starter • Make a collar to protect growing vegetables • Collect kitchen scraps for compost.

Newspaper {PAGE 208}
Slowly ripen tomatoes in autumn • Use as mulch or add to compost to remove unpleasant smells • Block weeds in flower and vegetable beds • Get rid of earwigs.

Plastic bags
{PAGE 248}

Protect plants from frost and shoes from mud • Speed up the budding of seasonal plants • Keep insects away from fruit on trees • Store manuals for outdoor equipment • Bring a favourite, but cracked vase back into use • Make disposable work aprons.

Plastic bottles
{PAGE 254}

Make a bird feeder, a scoop for clearing a gutter, a watering can or an individual drip irrigator for a plant • Secure netting over flowerbeds • Isolate weeds when spraying • Cover seed-packet markers or make plant tags from cut strips • Use as a waste bin on a lawnmower • Use to space seeds • Trap insects.

Plastic containers
{PAGE 247}

Make traps for slug and wasps • Stop ants from crawling the legs of a picnic table • Use to start seedlings.

Salt
{PAGE 268}

Inhibit the growth of weeds in cracks in paths • Extend the life of cut flowers • Clean flowerpots.

Tea
{PAGE 318}

Spur the growth of rosebushes • Water acid-loving plants • Nourish houseplants • Prepare a planter for potting • Speed the rotting down of compost.

Tights
{PAGE 322}

Tie up tomatoes and beans • Fill with hair clippings to repel deer • Make a hammock for growing melons • Store onions and off-season bulbs • Prevent soil from being lost in houseplants • Fill with soap scraps for cleaning hands at a garden tap.

WD-40
{PAGE 370}

Keep animals out of flowerbeds and squirrels off bird feeders • Stop tool handles from splintering • Stop snow from sticking on shovel or snow thrower • Prevent wasps from building nests and repel pigeons • Kill thistles.

TOP

11 Most useful items for outdoors

Unblock a downpipe with a garden hose – without using any water ...

158

Aluminium foil

{PAGE 40}

Improve outdoor lighting • Keep wasps away from sweet drinks • Make an impromptu picnic platter or improvise a frying pan • Make a drip pan for your barbecue and clean the grill • Warm your toes when camping and keep your sleeping bag and matches dry • Make a fishing lure.

Bicarbonate of soda

{PAGE 66}

Keep weeds out of paving cracks • Clean plastic garden furniture • Use as plant food • Scour a barbecue grill.

Bubble wrap

{PAGE 86}

Keep soft drinks cold • Make a sleeping bag • Cushion hard seats and benches.

Buckets

{PAGE 88}

• Make a travelling food storage bin • Build an outdoor washing machine or shower when camping • Make a cooking pot.

Cat litter

{PAGE 105}

Give your car traction on ice • Prevent grease fires on a barbecue • Keep tents and sleeping bags smelling fresh • Remove grease spots from a driveway • Remove a foul smell from a dustbin.

Cooking spray
{PAGE 127}

Prevent grass from sticking to the lawn mower • Spray on a fishing line for easier casting • Stop snow from sticking to a shovel.

Gaffer tape
{PAGE 160}

Seal out ticks • Create a clothesline • Keep a secret car key • Patch a canoe or a pool • Repair outdoor cushions and replace webbing on garden • Make bike streamers • Tighten cricket shin pads and revive a hockey stick • Preserve sports shoes • Repair ski gloves or a tent • Waterproof footwear.

Plastic bottles
{PAGE 254}

Use to make a scoop or bailer for a boat • Turn into an anchor for your boat • Make a bird feeder • Keep a coolbag cold.

Sandwich and freezer bags
{PAGE 280}

Inflate to make valuables float when boating • Make a hand cleaner for travelling • Apply insect repellent with ease.

Vinegar
{PAGE 340}

Keep water fresh • Clean outdoor furniture and decks • Repel insects • Trap flying insects • Get rid of ants • Clean off bird droppings.

WD-40
{PAGE 370}

Repel pigeons and wasps • Waterproof shoes • Remove wax from skis and snowboards • Remove barnacles from a boat and protect it from corrosion • Untangle a fishing line and lure fish • Clean and protect golf clubs • Remove burrs from a horse's mane and protect its hooves in winter • Keep flies off cows.

TOP

13

Most useful items for storage

Keep valuables stored in a tennis ball while you are working out at the gym ...

313

Baby wipes containers

{PAGE 57}

Organise sewing supplies, recipe cards, coupons, craft supplies, old floppy disks, small tools, photos, receipts, bills and other items • Store plastic shopping bags • Store towels and rags in a workshop.

Cans

{PAGE 93}

Make a tool carrier with juice cans • Make a desk organiser • Create pigeonholes for storing silverware, nails, office supplies and other odds and ends.

Cardboard boxes

{PAGE 96}

Make magazine holders from detergent boxes • Make a home-office in-box • Store hoes, rakes and other long-handled garden tools • Protect glassware or lightbulbs • Store posters and artwork • Store Christmas ornaments • Organise dowels, mouldings, battens and metal rods.

Cardboard tubes

{PAGE 100}

Store knitting needles and fabric scraps • Keep Christmas lights tidy • Preserve children's artwork, important documents and posters • Keep linens and trousers crease-free and electrical cords tangle-free • Protect fluorescent lights • Store string.

Clothes pegs {PAGE 114} Keep snacks fresh • Organise a workshop, kitchen, bathroom or wardrobe • Keep gloves in shape.

Coffee cans {PAGE 118} Make a bank for children • Hold kitchen peelings • Carry toilet paper when camping • Store screws, nuts and nails • Organise and store belts • Collect items from pockets in the laundry.

Egg cartons {PAGE 139} Store and sort coins • Organise buttons, safety pins, threads, bobbins and fasteners • Store golf balls or Christmas ornaments.

Film canisters {PAGE 149} Make a label dispenser or a travel sewing kit • Organise pills • Store fishing flies • Carry spare change for tolls • Keep jewellery safe at the gym • Carry dressings, cooking spices and condiments when travelling • Carry nail varnish remover.

Plastic bags {PAGE 248} Store wipes to preserve their moisture • Collect used clothes • Protect clothes when doing messy jobs • Store skirts in drawers • Keep handbags in shape.

Plastic bottles {PAGE 254} Store sugar • Store small workshop items • Use as boot trees • Make a bag or string dispenser.

Sandwich and freezer bags {PAGE 280} Store breakables • Save sweaters from moths • Make a perfumed sachet • Add cedar to a closet • Make a pencil bag • De-clutter the bath.

Sweet tins {PAGE 311} Make an emergency sewing kit • Store broken jewellery • Prevent jewellery chains from tangling • Organise a sewing box • Store car fuses • Keep earrings together • Store workshop items.

Tights {PAGE 322} Store wrapping paper • Bundle blankets • Store onions or flower bulbs.

TOP

13 Most useful items for children

Make finger paints from yoghurt …

p. 378

Aluminium pie dishes {PAGE 48}
Use as mould for ice ornaments • Minimise the mess from glitter and spray paint • Make trays for craft supplies.

Bicarbonate of soda {PAGE 66}
Make watercolour paints or invisible ink • Clean crayon marks from walls and baby vomit from clothing • Combat cradle cap and nappy rash • Wash chemicals out of new baby clothes.

Cardboard boxes {PAGE 96}
Make a medieval castle, a puppet theatre or a sundial • Make a garage for toy vehicles • Store tennis rackets, fishing rods and other sporting equipment • Use as an impromptu sled.

Compact discs {PAGE 125}
Make artwork for a teenager's room • Create spinning tops.

Corks {PAGE 128}
Use burnt cork as face paint • Create a craft stamp • Make a bead curtain for a child's room.

Gaffer tape
{PAGE 160}
Make fancy dress costumes, a toy sword or hand puppets • Create bicycle streamers.

Jars
{PAGE 181}
Make a savings bank • Dry a child's mittens • Carry along baby treats and store baby-food portions • Create a miniature biosphere.

Margarine tubs
{PAGE 195}
Divide up ice cream into child-sized portions • Carry fast food for a baby • Make a coin bank • Give children variety in their lunch boxes.

Paper bags
{PAGE 226}
Cover a textbook • Make a kite • Create a life-size body poster.

Paper plates
{PAGE 233}
Make index cards and Frisbee flash cards • Make crafts, mobiles and seasonal decorations.

Pillowcases
{PAGE 244}
Make a wall hanging for a child's room • Protect stuffed animals in the washing machine.

Sandwich and freezer bags
{PAGE 280}
Make baby wipes • Make kitchen gloves for children • Make a pencil case • Keep spare children's clothes in the car for mishaps • Cure car sickness • Make pudding while playing football.

Tape
{PAGE 314}
Secure a baby's bib • Create instant childproofing • Make a multicolour pen • Make an unpoppable balloon.

TOP

13 Most useful items for DIY

Repair your garden hose with a toothpick ...

p 333

Aluminium foil {PAGE 40}
Make a flexible funnel for hard-to-reach places • Reattach a vinyl floor tile • Make an artist's palette • Prevent paint from skinning over • Line roller trays and keep paint off doorknobs.

Basters {PAGE 61}
Cure musty-smelling air conditioning unit • Safely transfer paints and solvents • Fix a leaky refrigerator.

Bicarbonate of soda {PAGE 66}
Clean car-battery terminals and remove tar from a car • Use as a de-icer for paths, patios and steps • Tighten cane chair seats • Give decking the weathered look • Clean air conditioner filters • Keep a humidifier odour-free.

Bubble wrap {PAGE 86}
Prevent condensation in a toilet cistern • Add insulation to windows • Cushion work surface and protect tools in a toolbox.

Buckets {PAGE 88}
Hold paint and supplies when painting on scaffolding or a ladder and use lids to contain paint drips • Make stilts for painting a ceiling • Organise extension cords • Make a Christmas tree stand.

Cardboard boxes

{PAGE 96}

Make a temporary roof repair • Protect fingers while hammering small nails • Make a drip pan for oil • Identify fluid leaking from your car • Organise your workshop • Keep upholstery tacks straight.

Clothes pegs

{PAGE 114}

Clamp thin objects • Make a clipboard • Grip a nail to protect fingers • Keep a paintbrush afloat when soaking in solvent.

Gaffer tape

{PAGE 160}

Temporarily fix a car tail light or hose • Make a temporary roof shingle • Create a clothesline • Hide a secret car key • Patch a canoe • Repair a dustbin.

Garden hose

{PAGE 158}

Protect a handsaw • Make a rounded sanding block • Make a comfortable grip for a can of paint.

Plastic bags

{PAGE 248}

Protect a ceiling fan or light fitting when painting the ceiling • Store paintbrushes for quick re-use • Contain paint when using a sprayer.

Plastic bottles

{PAGE 254}

Store paints • Make a workshop organiser • Use as a levelling device • Make an anchor for weighting tarpaulins and patio umbrellas.

Tights

{PAGE 322}

Test how smoothly you have sanded • Apply a stain in tight corners • Patch holes in screens • Strain lumpy paint.

Vinegar

{PAGE 340}

Wash concrete off skin • Remove paint fumes • Degrease grates, fans and air-conditioner grilles • Disinfect filters • Help paint adhere to concrete • Remove rust from tools • Peel off old wallpaper • Slow the rate of hardening of plaster • Revive a hardened paintbrush.

Your complete

A-Z guide

Address labels

Tag a bag Address labels aren't just for sticking on envelopes. They can be an effective, inexpensive way of making sure lost items stand a chance of finding their way home. Place an address label – covered with a small piece of sticky tape or clear packing tape to prevent wear – inside a laptop computer bag, glasses case, gym bag, rucksack and all items of luggage.

Label electronic equipment Few people bother to take out insurance on their collection of personal electronics equipment, but replacing an expensive digital camera, camcorder or MP3 player can cost serious money. A tape-covered address label conspicuously placed on your equipment may be sufficient to ensure its safe return.

Hang on to your umbrella A well-made umbrella can last for years, but that's no use if it gets left behind at the cinema or on a bus or train. Minimise the risk of your loss becoming someone else's gain by sticking an address label on the umbrella handle and wrapping it once around with clear packing tape. This will protect the label from the elements and general wear and tear and make it considerably more difficult to remove.

Secure school supplies It is one of the universal truths of parenthood: children are forever losing pencil cases, folders, markers, and other school supplies. You may be able to reduce the losses, by fixing address labels with a piece of transparent tape to the contents of your child's school bag and backpack.

Identify items for repair Do you feel anxious when you take stereo equipment or another precious item into a repair shop? You may feel better if you place an address label on the base or some other unobtrusive, undamaged area. Note: This practice is not recommended for all personal treasures – you may not want to label paper documents, paintings, photos and other personal items.

Adhesive plaster

Remove a splinter If a splinter is too tiny or too deep to remove with tweezers, avoid the agony of digging it out with a needle. Instead, cover the splinter with adhesive plaster. Leave for about three days, then remove the tape and the splinter should come out painlessly.

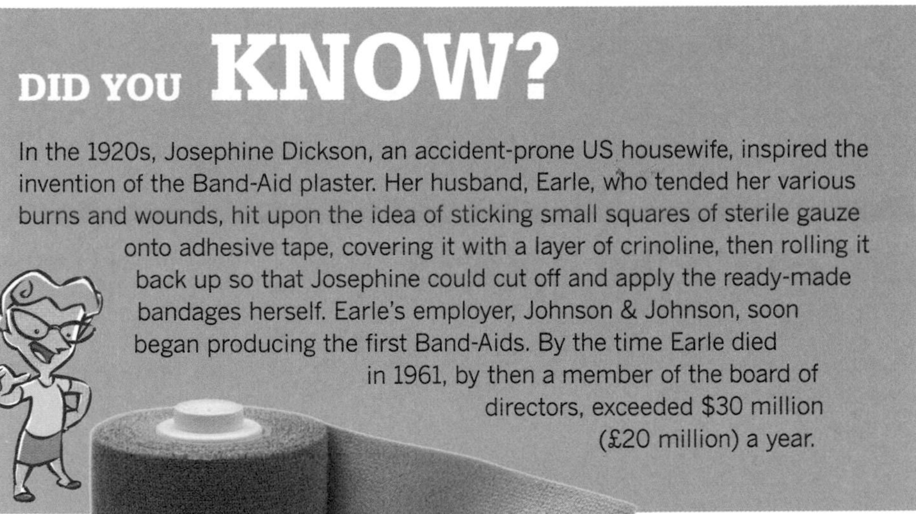

DID YOU KNOW?

In the 1920s, Josephine Dickson, an accident-prone US housewife, inspired the invention of the Band-Aid plaster. Her husband, Earle, who tended her various burns and wounds, hit upon the idea of sticking small squares of sterile gauze onto adhesive tape, covering it with a layer of crinoline, then rolling it back up so that Josephine could cut off and apply the ready-made bandages herself. Earle's employer, Johnson & Johnson, soon began producing the first Band-Aids. By the time Earle died in 1961, by then a member of the board of directors, exceeded $30 million (£20 million) a year.

Reduce your hat size Do you have a hat that's a bit too big for your head? Wrap adhesive plaster around the sweatband – it might take two or three layers depending on the size discrepancy – to ensure a perfect fit.

Get a grip on tools Adhesive plaster has just the right texture for wrapping around tool handles. It gives a positive, comfortable grip and it's highly absorbent so that the tool won't become slippery if your hand sweats. As you wrap the handle, overlap each winding by about half a tape width, using as many layers as needed to get the best grip. Here are some useful applications:

- Screwdriver handles are sometimes too narrow and slippery to grip well when you are driving in or removing stubborn screws. Wrap layers of adhesive plaster around the handle until the tool feels comfortable in your hand – this is especially useful if you have arthritis in your fingers as you won't have to grip so tightly.
- Take a tip from carpenters who wrap wooden hammer handles that can get slippery with sweat. Wrap the whole gripping area of the tool. A few wraps just under the head will also protect the handle from any damage caused by misdirected blows.
- Plumbers also keep adhesive plaster in their tool kits. When they want to cut a pipe in a spot that's too tight for their hacksaw frame, they make a mini-hacksaw by removing the blade and wrapping one end of the blade to form a handle.

Alka-Seltzer

Clean a coffeemaker Fill the water chamber of a coffeemaker with water and drop in four Alka-Seltzer tablets. When the Alka-Seltzer has dissolved, put the coffeemaker through a brew cycle to clean the tubes. Rinse the chamber two or three times, then run another cycle with plain water before making coffee again.

Clean a vase Stuck-on residue at the bottom of narrow-neck vases may seem impossible to get at, but you can easily bubble it away. Fill the vase halfway full of water and drop in two Alka-Seltzer tablets. Wait until the fizzing stops, then rinse the vase clean. The same trick works for cleaning glass Thermos flasks.

Clean glass cookware Don't scour stubborn stains off ovenproof glass cookware. Just fill the container with water, add up to six Alka-Seltzer tablets, and let it soak for an hour. The stains should easily scrub away.

Clean the toilet The citric acid in Alka-Seltzer combined with its fizzing action makes it an effective toilet bowl cleaner. Simply drop a couple of tablets into the bowl and leave for about 20 minutes. After a quick scrub with a toilet brush the bowl will be gleaming.

Clean jewellery Drop dull-looking jewellery in a glass of fizzing Alka-Seltzer for a couple of minutes. It will sparkle and shine when you pull it out.

Unblock the kitchen sink Get almost instant results by dropping a couple of Alka-Seltzer tablets down the plug hole, then pour in a cup of vinegar. Wait a few minutes and then run the hot-water tap at full force to clear the blockage. This is also a good way to eliminate unpleasant odours in the sink.

Soothe insect bites If a mosquito or other insect bite is persistently itchy, drop two Alka-Seltzer tablets into half a glass of water. Dip a cotton wool ball into the glass and apply it to the bite. Caution: don't do this if you are allergic to aspirin, which is a key ingredient in Alka-Seltzer.

Attract fish All avid anglers know that fish are attracted to bubbles. If you use a hollow plastic tube jig on the line, just break off a piece of Alka-Seltzer and slip it into the tube. The jig will produce an enticing stream of bubbles as it sinks.

{ SCIENCE FAIR }

AN ALKA-SELTZER ROCKET

The rocket gets its thrust from the gas created when you drop a couple of Alka-Seltzer tablets into a water-filled film canister. The type of film canister is critical: use a plastic canister that has a lid that fits tightly inside the canister. Canisters with lids that fit around an outside lip won't work. You'll also need stiff paper, sticky tape and scissors. To form the body of the rocket, wrap a piece of paper around the canister with the canister's open end facing out of the bottom end of the tube. Tape the paper in place. Form a piece of stiff paper into a nose cone. Trim it evenly along the bottom and tape it onto the top of the rocket body. To launch, fill the canister about half full with refrigerated water – vital to a successful lift off. Drop in two Alka-Seltzer tablets. Pop on the lid, set the rocket on the ground, and stand back. The gas will quickly build up pressure in the canister, causing the canister lid to pop off and the rocket to launch several feet into the air.

 Aluminium cans

Create a simple Chinese lantern Mark two lines around a clean empty can, about 2.5cm from the top and bottom. With a sharp craft knife, make vertical cuts about 1.5cm apart between the lines. Make a cut across the bottom of two adjacent strips to make an opening for a candle. Gently press down on the can to make the strips bend in the middle. Insert a tea-light through the opening, then tuck the cut ends of the opening strips inside the can. Finally attach a hanging loop. You can also spray paint the can before cutting if you like to make lanterns in different colours.

Create a decorative snowman Wrap an old soft drink can with white paper and tape it with transparent tape. For a head use a polystyrene foam ball and stick it to the top of the can. Cover the body with cotton wadding or cotton bandaging material and tape or glue it in place. Make a cone-shaped paper hat. Make eyes and a nose with buttons. To add arms, punch holes in the sides of the can and insert twigs. Use dots from a black marker pen to make buttons down the snowman's front. Finally, make a scarf from a long thin scrap of woolly fabric.

Make planters more portable Don't strain your back moving a planter loaded with heavy soil. Reduce the amount of soil and lighten the load by first filling a third to a half of the bottom of the planter with empty, upside-down aluminium cans. Finish filling with soil and add your plants. In addition to making the planter lighter, the rustproof aluminium cans also help it to drain well.

Protect young plants Remove both ends of an aluminium can and any paper label. Then push it into the earth to serve as a collar to protect young garden plants from cutworms (the caterpillars of noctuid moths). Use a soup can or a coffee can, depending on the size you need.

Keep track of bulbs and seedlings After removing the top and bottom of a can, cut plant labels from the remaining aluminium sheet. Write on them with a ballpoint pen or marker pen and attach them to the plant stakes or pots to identify the variety and colour of your plants, such as dahlias, orchids, bulbs and newly sown vegetable seeds.

Make Christmas decorations Use a craft knife or old scissors to cut the top and bottom from a number of empty cans, then slit and flatten the cylinder. Cut simple shapes, such as stars or circles and use a ballpoint pen to draw designs on the wrong side. Decorate with stick-on jewels or transparent glass paint and add a wire for hanging.

ALUMINIUM FOIL...

...in the kitchen

Bake a perfect piecrust Keep the edges of piecrusts from getting burnt by covering them with strips of aluminium foil. The foil will prevent the edges from getting overdone while the remainder of your pie gets perfectly browned.

Decorate a cake If you don't have an icing bag, form a piece of heavy-duty aluminium foil into a tube and fill it with soft icing. As a bonus, there's no icing bag to clean – just discard the foil when you have finished.

Make an extra-large salad bowl If you have invited lots of friends over for lunch or dinner, but don't have a bowl big enough to toss the salad to feed them all, simply line the kitchen sink with aluminium foil and you should have plenty of room to mix it up.

Keep rolls and bread warm How do you lock in the oven-fresh warmth of homemade rolls or bread for a dinner party or picnic? Before you fill the bread basket, wrap the freshly baked goods in a napkin and place a layer of aluminium foil underneath. The foil will reflect the heat to keep the bread warm and soft for quite some time.

Catch drips from an ice-cream cone Keep children from making a mess of their clothes or the house by wrapping the bottom of an ice-cream cone with a piece of aluminium foil before handing it to them.

Toast your own cheese sandwich Next time you pack for a trip, include a couple of cheese sandwiches wrapped in aluminium foil. If you check into a hotel after the kitchen has closed, you won't have to resort to the expensive mini-bar or room service. Instead, you can use the hotel room iron to press both sides of the wrapped sandwich and you will have a instant tasty hot snack.

Polishing silver If your best silverware has become dulled and blackened, try an ion exchange, a molecular reaction in which aluminium acts as a catalyst. Line a pan with a sheet of aluminium foil, fill it with cold water and add 2 teaspoons of salt. Drop the tarnished silverware into the solution, let it sit for 2-3 minutes, then rinse off and dry.

Stop silverware from tarnishing Store freshly cleaned silverware on top of a sheet of aluminium foil to stop it from tarnishing. For long-term storage of silverware, first tightly cover each piece in a clear plastic wrap – be sure to squeeze out as much air as possible – then wrap in foil and seal the ends.

Preserve steel-wool pads To stop a used steel-wool pad from turning into a rusty mess, wrap it in foil and place it in the freezer. You can also lengthen the life of steel-wool soap pads by crumpling up a sheet of foil and placing it under the steel wool in its dish or container. (Don't forget to periodically drain off the water that collects at the bottom of the dish.)

Scrubbing pots If you don't have a scrubbing pad or brush to hand, crumple up a handful of aluminium foil and use it to scrub pots and pans.

Keep the oven clean When baking a lasagna or casserole that's liable to bubble over, keep messy drips off the bottom of the oven by laying a sheet or two of aluminium foil over the rack below. But never line the bottom of the oven with foil as it could cause a fire.

Make novelty cake tins Make a teddy bear birthday cake, a Valentine's Day heart cake, a Christmas tree cake or whatever shaped cake the occasion may call for. Form a double thickness of heavy-duty aluminium foil into the desired shape inside a large cake tin.

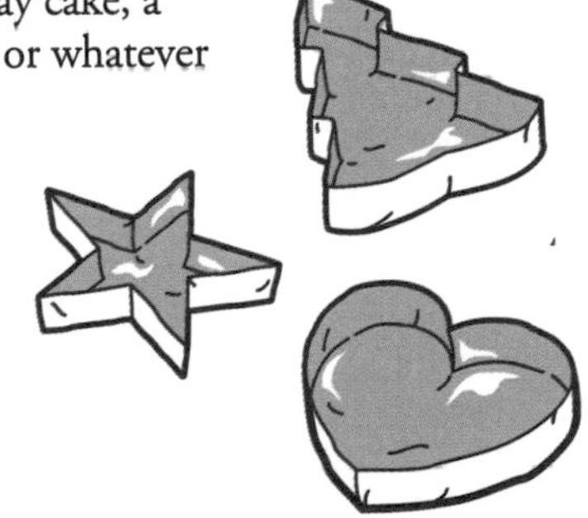

Soften up brown sugar To get hardened brown sugar flowing free again, chip off a piece, wrap it in aluminium foil, and bake it in the oven at 150°C (gas mark 2) for 5 minutes.

TIP* FOIL-EATING ACIDIC FOODS

Think twice before using aluminium foil to wrap left-over food, particularly if it is dripping with tomato sauce. Very acidic or salty foods such as lemons, grapefruits, ketchup and pickles accelerate the oxidation of aluminium and can actually 'eat' through foil with prolonged exposure. This can also leach aluminium into the food, which can affect its flavour and may pose a health risk. If you want to use foil for foods with acidic ingredients, cover it first with a layer or two of plastic wrap or greaseproof paper to prevent the sauce from coming into contact with the foil.

Super item
51 USES!

ALUMINIUM FOIL...

...around the house

Improve the efficiency of radiators Here is a simple way to get more heat out of radiators without spending a penny more on your gas or electricity bill. Make a heat reflector to put behind the radiators by taping heavy-duty aluminium foil onto a piece of cardboard with the shiny side of the foil facing out. The radiant heat waves will bounce off the foil into the room instead of being absorbed by the wall behind the radiator. If your radiators have covers, it is also helpful to attach a piece of foil under the top of the cover.

Keep pets off furniture If your cat or dog keeps jumping on the new sofa, place a piece of aluminium foil on the seat cushions. After one attempt at settling down on the noisy surface, your pet will no longer consider it a comfy place to snooze.

Protect a child's mattress As any parent of even a potty-trained youngster knows, accidents do happen. To spare the mattress, even if you don't have a plastic protector, lay several sheets of aluminium foil across the width of the mattress. Then cover them with a large beach towel. Finally, replace the mattress pad or mattress cover and the bottom sheet.

Hide worn spots on a mirror Sometimes a worn spot adds to the charm of an old mirror; sometimes it is a distraction. You can easily disguise small flaws on a mirror's reflective surface by putting a piece of aluminium foil, shiny side facing out, on the back of the glass. To hold the foil in place, attach it to the backing behind the mirror or to the frame with strips of masking tape. But don't tape the foil to the mirror itself.

Clean jewellery To brighten dull jewellery, line a small bowl with aluminium foil. Fill the bowl with hot water and mix in a tablespoon of bleach-free powdered laundry detergent (not liquid), such as Dreft. Put the jewellery in the solution and let it soak for a minute. Rinse well and air-dry. This procedure makes use of the chemical process known as ion exchange, which can also be used to clean silverware (see page 41).

Sharpening scissors What can you do with clean pieces of leftover foil? Use them to sharpen up a dulled pair of scissors. Smooth them out if necessary, and then fold the strips into several layers and start cutting against the 'pad' with the scissors. Seven or eight passes should be enough. (See page 44 to find out how you can use the resulting scraps of foil for mulching or keeping birds off fruit trees.)

Move furniture with ease To slide large pieces of furniture over a smooth floor, place small pieces of aluminium foil under each of the feet to increase traction. The dull side of the foil should face the floor as it is actually more slippery than the shiny side.

DID YOU KNOW?

Have you ever wondered why aluminium foil has one side that's shinier than the other? The answer has to do with how it is manufactured. The different shades of silver result from the final rolling process, when two layers of foil pass through the rolling mill simultaneously. The sides in contact with the mill's heavy, polished rollers come out shiny, while the inside layers retain a dull or matt finish. The shiny side is better for reflecting light and heat, but when it comes to wrapping food or lining grills, both sides are equally good.

Fix loose batteries If a torch, portable stereo or electric child's toy is working only intermittently, check the battery compartment. The springs that hold the batteries in place can lose their tension after a while, letting the batteries loosen. Fold a small piece of aluminium foil until you have made a pad that's thick enough to take up the slack. Place the pad between the battery and the spring.

Keep hair dye away from your glasses You may want to catch up on your reading during the time it takes to colour your hair. But you can't read without your specs, and if you put them on, you may worry that they'll get stained. For an easy solution, wrap the rim and sides of the glasses with aluminium foil.

Clean the fireplace Here's an easy way to clean the ashes out of a fireplace. Place a double layer of heavy-duty aluminium foil across the bottom of the fireplace or under the wood grate. The next day – or once you are sure all the ashes have cooled – simply fold it up and throw it away or, even better, use the ashes as described on pages 51-52.

...in the laundry

Speed up the ironing When you iron clothing, much of the iron's heat is sucked up by the board itself – so you may have to make several passes to remove creases. To speed up the process, place a piece of aluminium foil under the ironing board cover. The foil will reflect the heat back through the clothing, allowing you to smooth away creases more quickly.

Attach a patch An iron-on patch is an easy way to fix small holes in clothing. To stop the patch from sticking to the ironing board, put a piece of aluminium foil under the hole. It won't stick to the patch, and you can just slip it out when you have finished ironing.

Clean your iron Do you have a build-up of spray starch on the iron that is causing it to stick? To remove it, run the hot iron over a piece of aluminium foil.

ALUMINIUM FOIL...

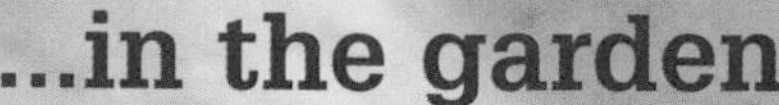

...in the garden

Put some bite in a mulch To keep hungry insects and slugs away from cucumbers and other vegetables, mix strips of aluminium foil in with the mulch. As an extra benefit, the foil will reflect light back up onto your plants.

Protect tree trunks Mice, rabbits and other animals often feed on the bark of young trees during winter, especially if you live in the country. A cheap and effective deterrent is to wrap lower tree trunks with a double layer of heavy-duty aluminium foil in late autumn. Be sure to remove the foil in spring.

Scare crows and other birds Are hungry birds eating all the fruit on your trees? Dangle strips of aluminium foil from the branches using monofilament fishing line. Even better, hang some foil-wrapped seashells, which will add a bit of noise to further startle them.

Grow untangled cuttings Help plant cuttings to grow up strong and uncluttered by starting them in a container covered with a sheet of aluminium foil. Make a few holes in the foil and insert the cuttings through the holes. As an added bonus, the foil slows evaporation, so you will need to add water less frequently.

Make a sun box for plants A sunny window is a great place for keeping plants that love a lot of light. However, since the light always comes from the same direction, the plants tend to bend toward it. To bathe your plants in light from all sides, make a sun box. Remove the top and one side from a cardboard box and line the other three sides and bottom with aluminium foil, shiny side out, taping or gluing it in place. Place plants in the box and place it close to a window.

Build a seed incubator To give plants grown from seed a head start, line a shoe box with aluminium foil, shiny side up, allowing about 5cm of foil to extend out over the sides. Make several drainage holes in the bottom, penetrating the foil, then fill the box to slightly more than halfway with potting compost and plant the seeds. The foil inside the box will absorb heat to keep the seeds warm as they germinate, while the foil outside the box will reflect light onto the young shoots. Place the box near a sunny window, keep the compost moist and watch them grow.

...in the great outdoors

Keep wasps away from sweet drinks You are about to relax in the garden with a cool glass of lemonade or cola. Suddenly a wasp starts buzzing around your drink. Keep wasps away by tightly covering the top of your glass with aluminium foil. Poke a straw through it and enjoy your drink in peace.

Lure a fish If fancy fishing lures aren't attracting the fish, you can make one quickly that just might do the trick. Wrap some aluminium foil around a fishhook. Fringe the foil so that it covers the hook and wiggles invitingly when you reel in the line.

TIP* PREVENT SUNSCALD ON TREES

Wrapping young tree trunks with a couple of layers of aluminium foil during the winter can help prevent sunscald, a condition that damages the bark of some young thin-barked trees – especially fruit trees, ashes, lindens, maples, oaks and willows. The problem occurs on warm winter days when the sun's rays reactivate dormant cells underneath the tree's bark. The subsequent drop in night time temperatures kills the cells and can injure the tree. In most areas, you can remove the aluminium wrapping in early spring.

Make a barbecue drip pan To keep meat drippings from falling onto barbecue coals, make a disposable drip pan out of a couple of layers of heavy-duty aluminium foil. Shape it freehand or use an inverted baking pan as a mould (remember to remove the pan once your creation is finished). Don't forget to make the drip pan slightly larger than the meat on the grill.

Clean a barbecue grill After the last steak is cooked through and while the coals are still red-hot, lay a sheet of aluminium foil over the grill to burn off any remaining food deposits. The next time you use the barbecue, crumple up the foil and use it to scrub off the burned food before you start cooking.

Improve outdoor lighting Brighten up the electrical lighting in a garden or at a campsite by making a foil reflector to put behind the light. Attach the reflector to the fixture with a few strips of electrical tape or gaffer tape – but do not apply tape directly to the bulb.

Make an impromptu picnic platter When you need a convenient disposable platter for a picnic or buffet supper, just cover a piece of cardboard with heavy-duty aluminium foil.

Improvise a frying pan If you don't want to take a frying pan along on a camping trip, make your own by placing a forked stick centrally over two layers of heavy-duty aluminium foil. Wrap the edges of the foil tightly around the forked branches but leave some slack in the foil between the forks. Invert the stick and depress the centre to hold food for frying.

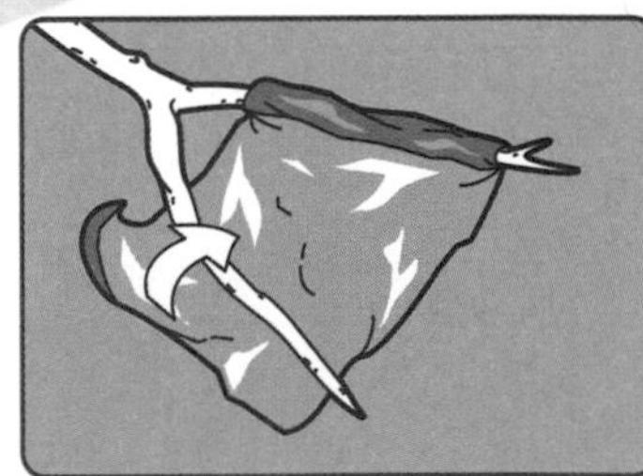

Keep your toes warm when camping Keep your feet warm at night even when camping in cold weather. Wrap some large stones in aluminium foil and heat them by the campfire. At bedtime, wrap the stones in towels and put them in the bottom of your sleeping bag.

Keep a sleeping bag dry Place a piece of heavy-duty aluminium foil under your sleeping bag to stop moisture seeping through.

Keep matches dry Soldiers and experienced campers swear by this useful trick. Wrap matches in aluminium foil to keep them from getting damp or wet on camping trips.

ALUMINIUM FOIL...

...for the DIY-er

Make a funnel Double up a length of heavy-duty aluminium foil and roll it into the shape of a cone. This impromptu funnel has an advantage over a permanent funnel – you can bend the aluminium foil to reach awkward holes, like the oil filler hole tucked against the engine of a lawnmower.

Re-attach a vinyl floor tile If a vinyl floor tile has become detached, reposition the tile on the floor, lay a piece of aluminium foil over it and run a hot clothes iron over it a few times until you can feel the glue melting underneath. Put a pile of books or bricks on top of the tile to weight it down while the glue resets. This technique also works well to smooth out unsightly bulges and straighten curled seams in sheet vinyl flooring.

Keep paint off doorknobs and handles When painting a door, use aluminium foil to wrap the doorknobs to keep paint away from them. Overlap the foil onto the door when you wrap the knob, then run a sharp craft knife around the base of the knob to trim the foil. In this way you can paint right up to the edge of the knob. In addition to wrapping knobs on the doors that you are painting, wrap all the doorknobs that are along the route to the sink where you clean your hands and brushes so that an accidental touch won't matter.

Reflect light for photography Professional photographers use reflectors to throw extra light on dark areas of their subject and to even out the overall lighting. To make a reflector, lightly coat a large piece of heavy cardboard with glue and cover it with aluminium foil, shiny side out. You can make one single reflector, as large as you want, but it is more useful to make three panels and join them together with gaffer tape. That way they will stand up by themselves and can be easily folded for handy storage and carrying.

Keep a paintbrush wet If you have finished painting for the day but want to continue painting the next morning, don't bother to clean the brush – just squeeze out the excess paint and wrap the brush tightly in aluminium foil (or plastic wrap). Use a rubber band to hold the foil tightly at the base of the handle. For extended wet-brush storage, you can place the wrapped brush in the freezer. But don't forget to defrost the brush for an hour or so before you paint.

Line roller trays Cleaning out paint roller trays is a pain, which is why many people dispose of plastic trays after use or buy liners. But lining a roller tray with aluminium foil works just as well – and can be a lot cheaper.

DID YOU KNOW?

Some people still ask for tinfoil when they want to wrap up leftovers. Household foil was made only of tin until 1947, when aluminium foil was introduced, eventually replacing tinfoil in the kitchen drawer.

Make an artist's palette Tear off a length of heavy-duty aluminium foil, crimp up the edges and you have a ready-to-use palette for mixing paints. For a more stylish solution, cut a piece of cardboard into the shape of a palette, complete with thumb hole and cover it with foil. Or if you already have a wooden palette, you can cover it with foil before each use and then simply strip off the used foil instead of having to clean the palette.

Prevent paint from forming a skin When you open a half-used can of paint, you will typically find a skin of dried paint on the surface. Not only is this annoying to remove, but dried bits can end up in the paint. You can prevent this by using a two-pronged attack when you close a used paint can. First, put a piece of aluminium foil under the can and trace around it. Cut out the circle and drop the aluminium foil disc onto the paint surface. Then take a deep breath, blow into the can, and quickly put the top in place. The carbon dioxide in your breath replaces some of the oxygen in the can, and helps to keep the paint from drying.

Give a shine to chrome For sparkling chrome on electrical appliances such as kettles and toasters, golf club shafts and older car bumpers, crumple up a handful of aluminium foil with the shiny side out and apply some elbow grease. If you rub really hard, the foil will even remove rust spots. Note: some 'chrome' on new cars is actually plastic – so check before you rub it with aluminium foil.

* Aluminium pie dishes

Make an instant colander A pan of spaghetti has almost finished cooking when you realise that you have forgotten to replace the broken colander. Take a large, clean aluminium pie dish and a small nail and poke holes in it. When you're finished, bend the dish to fit comfortably over a deep bowl. Rinse your new colander clean, place it over the bowl and carefully pour out the pasta.

Control splashes when frying Why risk burning yourself or anyone else with grease splashes from a hot frying pan? A safer way to fry is to poke a few holes in the bottom of an aluminium pie dish of a similar size to the frying pan and place it upside down over the food in the frying pan. Use a pair of tongs or a fork to lift off the pie dish and don't forget to wear an oven mitt.

Create a centrepiece Make a quick centrepiece for a special dinner party by securing a tall, thick candle or a few church candles to an aluminium pie dish by melting some wax from the bottom of the candles onto the dish. Add a thin layer of water or sand and cover it completely with rose petals or seashells.

Contain the mess from children's projects Glitter is notorious for turning up in the corners and crevices of your home long after a child's masterpiece has been discarded. Cut down on the mess by using an aluminium pie dish to enclose projects that involve working with glitter, beads, spray paint and feathers.

Make trays for craft supplies Bring some order to your children's – or your own – inventory of crayons, beads, buttons, sequins, pipe cleaners and other craft items by sorting them in aluminium pie dishes. To secure materials when storing the tin, cover each with a layer of plastic wrap.

Keep insects out of pet dishes Use an aluminium pie dish filled with about 1cm of water to create a metal moat around your pet's food dish. It should keep marauding ants and other small insects at bay.

Train your pet If Rover or Fluffy has a tendency to leap up on the sofa or kitchen worktop, leave a few aluminium pie dishes along the worktop edges or back of the sofa when you're not at home. The resulting loud rattling noise will give him a good scare when he jumps up on top of them and should stop him from doing it again.

{ KIDS' STUFF }

MAKING ICE ORNAMENTS

Keep children busy indoors on a cold, winter day by making ice ornaments that you can hang on a tree outside the house. All you need is an aluminium pie dish, some water, a piece of heavy string or a shoelace and a mix of decorative – preferably biodegradable – materials, such as dried flowers, dried leaves, pine cones, seeds, shells and twigs.

Let the children arrange the materials in the pie dish to their liking. Then fold the string or shoelace in half and place it in the dish. The fold should hang over the edges of the tin, while the two ends meet in the centre. Slowly fill the pan with water, stopping just below the rim. You may have to place an object on the string to keep it from floating to the top.

If the temperatures outside your home are indeed below freezing, you can simply put the pan on the doorstep to freeze. Otherwise just pop it into the freezer. Once the water has frozen solid, slide off the pie dish and let your children choose the best outdoor location to display their artwork in ice.

Keep squirrels and birds off fruit trees Are furry and feathered thieves stealing fruit from the garden? Scare them away with a few dangling aluminium pie dishes. String them up in pairs so they will make some noise and you shouldn't have to worry about finding any half-eaten apples or plums come autumn.

Make a mini-dustpan If you need a spare dustpan for a home office or bathroom, an aluminium pie dish cut in half is a cheap option.

Use as a drip catcher under a can of paint Next time you have a small item that needs painting, place an aluminium pie dish under the paint can as a ready-made drip catcher. You'll save a lot of time cleaning up, and you can just throw the dish in the bin when you have finished. Even better, rinse it off and recycle it for future paint jobs.

Store sanding discs and other items As they are highly resistant to corrosion, aluminium pie dishes are excellent for storing sanding discs, hacksaw blades and other hardware accessories in the workshop. Cut a dish in half and attach it (with staples or duct tape around the edges) open side up to a peg board.

Make an impromptu ashtray If there's no ashtray on hand when you're entertaining a smoker in your home, use an aluminium pie dish – or even a piece of heavy-duty aluminium foil folded into a square with the sides turned up – as a simple substitute.

Protect your fingers when cooking outdoors There's nothing like cooking in the great outdoors. Whether you're planning a day trip or a longer excursion, pack a few aluminium pie dishes. Put a small hole in the middle of each dish, then push them up on to sticks that you use for roasting sausages or potatoes. The pie dishes deflect the heat of the fire, protecting your hands and your children's hands.

Apples

Roast a juicy chicken If your roast chicken tends to emerge from the oven tough and dried out, try this trick. The next time you roast a chicken, stuff an apple inside the bird before placing it in the roasting dish. When it has finished cooking, remove the apple and enjoy a delicious and juicy main course.

Keep cakes fresh Extend the shelf life of a cake by storing it alongside half an apple. It will help the cake to maintain its moisture considerably longer than popping it in the fridge or in a cake tin.

Ripen green tomatoes Quickly ripen tomatoes by placing them, along with an already-ripe apple, in a paper bag for a couple of days. For best results, try to maintain a ratio of about five or six tomatoes to every apple.

Soften up hardened brown sugar Brown sugar has an irritating habit of becoming hard and clogged when exposed to humidity. Place an apple wedge in a self-sealing plastic bag with the chunk of hardened brown sugar. Tightly seal the bag and put it in a dry place for a day or two. Your sugar will once again be soft enough to use.

Absorb salt in soups and stews It is too easy to overdose on salt. If you've been heavy-handed with the salt shaker when cooking, simply drop a few apple (or potato) wedges into the pan. After cooking for another 10 minutes or so, remove the wedges which will have absorbed the excess salt.

Make decorative candleholders Add a country feel to a table setting by creating a natural candleholder. Use an apple corer to carve a hole three-quarters of the way down into a pair of large apples, insert a tall decorative candle into each hole and surround the apples with a few leaves, branches or flowers.

DID YOU KNOW?

The old saying 'One bad apple spoils the barrel' is actually pretty close to the truth. Apples are among a diverse group of fruits – others include apricots, avocados, bananas, blueberries, cantaloupes and peaches – that produce ethylene gas, a natural ripening agent. So the increased level of ethylene produced by a single rotten apple in a bag can significantly accelerate the ageing process of the other apples around it.

Ethylene-producing fruits can help to speed the ripening of something (like a green tomato, see above). But they can also have unwanted effects. Placing a bowl of ripe apples or bananas too close to freshly cut flowers, for instance, can cause them to wilt. And if potatoes are sprouting buds too soon, they may be too close to the apples.

Ashes

Clean glas stove doors You probably wouldn't think of using dirty wood ashes to clean the glass doors of a woodburning stove, but it does work. Mix some ashes with a bit of water, and apply them with a damp cloth, sponge or paper towel or simply dip a wet sponge into the ashes. Rub the mixture over the surfaces of the doors. Rinse with a wet paper towel or sponge, then dry with a clean cloth.

Reduce sun glare Sportsmen often smear black stripes under their eyes to cut down glare from the sun or bright stadium lights. If you're troubled by sun glare while driving or hiking, you may want to try it too. Just put a drop or two of baby oil on your finger, dip it in some wood ashes and apply under your eyes.

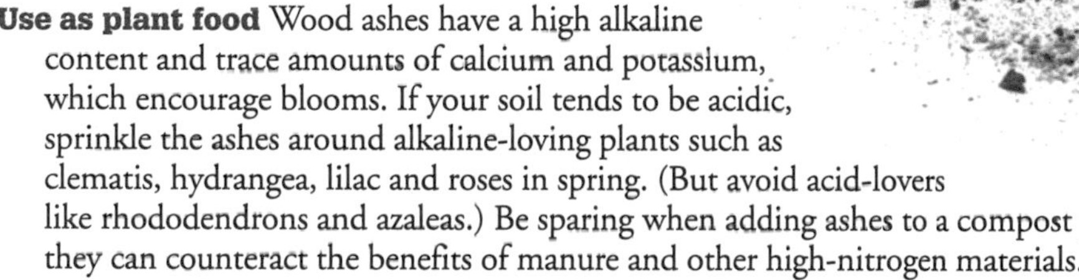

Use as plant food Wood ashes have a high alkaline content and trace amounts of calcium and potassium, which encourage blooms. If your soil tends to be acidic, sprinkle the ashes around alkaline-loving plants such as clematis, hydrangea, lilac and roses in spring. (But avoid acid-lovers like rhododendrons and azaleas.) Be sparing when adding ashes to a compost pile; they can counteract the benefits of manure and other high-nitrogen materials.

Repel insects Scatter a border of ashes around the garden to deter worms, slugs and snails. It sticks to their bodies and draws moisture from them. Sprinkling small amounts of ashes over garden plants will also deter soft-bodied insects. Wear eye protection and gloves as getting ashes in your eyes can be quite painful.

TIP* SELECTING FIREWOOD

For a hot-burning and long-lasting fire, ash, beech, hornbeam, hawthorn, crab apple and wild cherry are among the best woods. Green or wet woods burn poorly and build up heaps of creosote (the leading cause of chimney fires) in the chimney; pine is another major producer of creosote. You should never burn scraps of pressure-treated wood (used for decking) as it contains chemicals that can be extremely harmful when burned.

Don't be fanatical about cleaning ashes from the fireplace. Leave a 2.5 to 5cm layer of ash under the andiron to reflect heat back up to the burning wood and protect your fireplace floor against hot embers. Just be sure not to let the ashes clog up the space under the grate and block the airflow a good fire needs.

Clean pewter Restore a soft shine to pewter by cleaning it with cigarette ashes. Dip a dampened piece of cheesecloth into the ashes and rub it well over the item. It will turn darker at first, but the shine will return after a thorough rinse.

Remove water spots and heat marks from wood furniture Use cigar and or cigarette ashes to remove the white rings left on wooden furniture by wet glasses or hot cups. Mix the ashes with a few drops of water to make a paste and rub lightly over the mark to remove it. Then add a shine with furniture polish.

* Aspirin

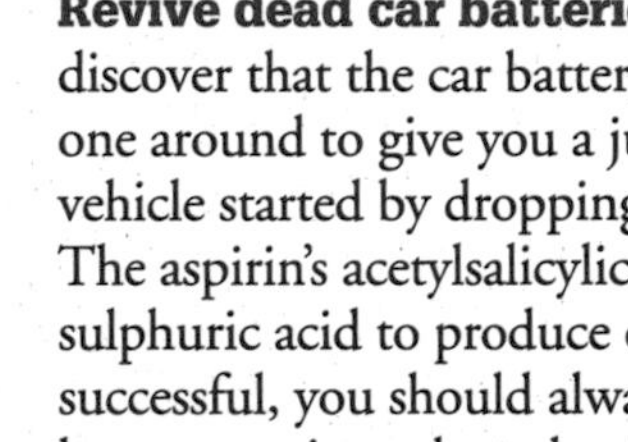

Revive dead car batteries If you get behind the wheel only to discover that the car battery has given up the ghost – and there's no one around to give you a jump start – you may be able to get the vehicle started by dropping two aspirin tablets into the battery itself. The aspirin's acetylsalicylic acid will combine with the battery's sulphuric acid to produce one last charge. Even if this method is successful, you should always have the battery checked immediately by an experienced mechanic.

Remove perspiration stains Before giving up hope of removing a stubborn perspiration stain from a smart white shirt, try this. Crush two aspirins and mix the powder in 100ml warm water. Soak the stained part of the garment in the solution for 2-3 hours.

Restore hair colour Swimming in a chlorinated pool can have a noticeable and often detrimental, effect on your hair colouring if you have light-coloured hair. You can usually return your hair to its former shade by dissolving six to eight aspirins in a glass of warm water. Rub the solution thoroughly into your hair and let it set for 10-15 minutes. Rinse off and the greenish tinge should be gone.

Treat hard skin on feet Soften hard callouses on your feet by grinding five or six aspirins into a powder. Make a paste by adding ½ teaspoon each of lemon juice and water. Apply the mixture to the affected areas, then wrap your foot in a warm towel and cover it with a plastic bag. Put your feet up for at least 10 minutes, remove the bag and towel and file down the softened callous with a pumice stone.

Control dandruff Keep a flaky scalp in check by crushing two aspirins to a fine powder and adding it to the normal amount of shampoo you use each time you wash your hair. Leave the mixture on your hair for 1-2 minutes, then rinse well and wash again with plain shampoo.

Help cut flowers last longer Put a crushed aspirin in water before adding flowers to a vase. Other household items that you can add to water to extend the life of flower arrangements include a multivitamin tablet, a teaspoon of sugar, a pinch of salt and baking soda and even a copper coin. Also, don't forget to change the water in the vase every day if possible.

Give the garden first aid Aspirin is not only a first-aid essential for you, but for the garden as well. Some gardeners grind it up for use as a rooting agent or mix it with water to treat fungus conditions in the soil. But be careful when using aspirin

DID YOU KNOW?

The bark of the willow tree is rich in salicin, a natural painkiller and fever reducer. In the 3rd century BC, Hippocrates used it to relieve headaches and pain. Later many traditional healers, including Native Americans, used salicin-containing herbs to treat cold and flu symptoms. But it wasn't until 1899 that Felix Hoffmann, a chemist at the German company Bayer, developed a modified derivative, acetylsalicylic acid, better known as aspirin.

around plants; too much of it can cause burns or other damage to the greenery. When treating soil, the typical dosage should be a half or a full aspirin tablet in a litre of water.

Dry up pimples Even those of us who are well past adolescence can still get the occasional spot. Crush an aspirin and moisten it with a little water. Apply the paste to the pimple and let it sit for a couple of minutes before washing off with soap and water. It will reduce the redness and soothe the sting. If the pimple persists, repeat the procedure as needed until it has gone.

Remove egg stains from clothes Scrape off as much of the egg as you can and then try to sponge out the rest with lukewarm water. Never use hot water – it will cook and set the egg. If that doesn't completely remove the stain, mix water and cream of tartar into a paste and add a crushed aspirin. Spread the paste on the stain and leave it for 30 minutes. Rinse well in warm water and the egg should be gone.

Soothe insect bites and stings Control the inflammation caused by mosquito bites or bee stings by wetting your skin and rubbing an aspirin over the spot.
WARNING If you are allergic to bee stings – and have difficulty breathing, develop abdominal pains, or feel nauseated following a bee sting – you must seek medical attention at once.

{ TAKE CARE }

About 10 per cent of people with severe asthma are also allergic to aspirin – and, in fact, to all products containing salicylic acid, aspirin's key ingredient, including some cold medicines, fruits, food seasonings and additives. That jumps to 30 to 40 per cent for older asthmatics who also suffer from sinusitis or nasal polyps. Acute sensitivity to aspirin is also seen in a small percentage of the general population without asthma – particularly people with ulcers and other bleeding conditions. Always consult a doctor before using any medication and do not apply aspirin externally if you are allergic to taking it internally.

Baby oil

Remove a plaster You can eliminate – or at least, significantly lessen – the 'ouch' factor and subsequent tears, when removing a child's plaster by first rubbing some baby oil into the adhesive parts on top and around the edges. If you see the plaster working loose, let the child finish the job to help him overcome his fear. Adults who have sensitive or fragile skin may also want to try this.

Make your own bath oil If you have a favourite perfume or cologne, you can literally bathe in it by making your own scented bath oil. Add a few drops of the scent to 50ml baby oil in a small plastic bottle. Shake well and add it to the bath.

Buff up golf clubs Don't waste money on special cleaning kits for chrome-plated carbon steel golf club heads. Just keep a small bottle filled with baby oil in your golf bag along with a chamois cloth or towel. Dab a few drops of oil on the cloth and polish the head of the club after each round of golf.

Slip off a stuck ring Do you find that rings frequently get jammed on your fingers? Try this. First lubricate the ring area with a generous amount of baby oil. Then swivel the ring around to spread the oil underneath it. You should be able to slide the ring off with ease.

Clean a bath or shower Remove dirt and built-up soap scum around a bath or shower enclosure by wiping surfaces with a teaspoon of baby oil on a moist cloth. Use another cloth to wipe away any leftover oil. Finally, spray the area with a disinfectant cleaner to kill any remaining germs. This technique is also great for cleaning soap film and watermarks off glass shower doors.

Shine stainless-steel sinks and chrome trim Buff up a dull-looking stainless-steel sink by rubbing it down with a few drops of baby oil on a clean, soft cloth. Rub dry with a towel and repeat if necessary. This is also a terrific way to remove stains on the chrome trim of kitchen appliances and bathroom fixtures.

Polish leather bags and shoes Just a few drops of baby oil applied with a soft cloth can add new life to an old leather bag or pair of patent-leather shoes. Don't forget to wipe away any oil remaining on the leather when you've finished.

Get scratches off dashboard plastic Disguise scratches on the plastic lenses covering the indicators on the car dashboard by rubbing over them with a little baby oil.

Remove emulsion paint from skin Do you get almost as much paint on your face and hands as you do on the walls when decorating? Quickly remove emulsion paint from your skin by first rubbing it with some baby oil, followed by a thorough wash with soap and hot water.

Treat cradle cap Cradle cap is a common, somewhat unsightly, but usually harmless, phase in many babies' development. To combat it, gently rub in a little baby oil and lightly comb it through your baby's hair. If your child gets upset, comb it a bit at a time, but do not leave the oil on for more than 24 hours. Then, thoroughly wash the hair to remove all of the oil. Repeat the process in persistent cases. Note: if you notice a lot of yellow crusting or if the cradle cap has spread behind the ears or onto the neck, you should speak to a doctor before trying any other treatment yourself.

Baby powder

Give sand the brush-off How many times have you come back from a day at the seaside only to discover that you've brought most of the beach back into the living room? Minimise the mess by sprinkling some baby powder over sweaty, sand-covered children (and adults) before they enter the house. In addition to soaking up excess moisture, the powder makes sand incredibly easy to brush off.

Cool sheets in summer Sprinkle a little baby powder between the sheets before getting into bed on warm summer nights – it will keep them – and you – beautifully cool and smooth.

Dry-shampoo your pet Is the dog in need of a bath but you just don't have time to do it? In between proper shampoos, vigorously rub a handful or two of baby powder into your pet's fur. Let it settle in for a couple of minutes and follow up with a thorough brushing. Your dog should both look and smell much fresher. You can even occasionally 'dry shampoo' your own hair using the same technique.

DID YOU KNOW?

Most ordinary baby powder is talc-based and not good for infants to breathe. In addition, the base material for talc is often extracted from environmentally sensitive regions and should be avoided for this reason.

Paediatricians often recommend using a cornflour-based powder – if one is needed at all – when changing nappies. Cornflour powder is coarser than talcum powder but does not have the health risks. But it may promote fungal infection and should not be applied in skin folds or to broken skin. An alternative 'natural' powder is available, based on powdered tapioca.

Medicated baby powder includes zinc oxide added to either talcum powder or cornflour-based powder. It is generally used to soothe skin afflicted with nappy rash and to prevent chafing.

Absorb grease stains on clothing Frying foods can be a dangerous business – especially for clothes. If you get a splash of grease on your clothing, try dabbing the stain with some baby powder on a powder puff. Make sure you rub it in well and then brush off any excess powder. Repeat until the mark has gone.

Clean grimy playing cards Here is a simple way to keep your playing cards from sticking together and getting grimy. Loosely place the cards in a plastic bag along with a bit of baby powder. Seal the bag and give it a few good shakes. When you remove the cards from the bag, they should feel fresh and smooth to the touch.

Slip on rubber gloves Don't jam or squeeze your fingers into rubber gloves when the inner layer inside the gloves wears out. Instead, lightly dust your fingers with baby powder. The rubber gloves should slide on as good as new.

Remove mould from books If some of your books have been stored in a less than ideal environment and have become mouldy or mildewed, this should help. First, let them thoroughly air-dry. Then, sprinkle some baby powder between the pages and stand the books upright for several hours. Afterwards, gently brush out the remaining powder from each book. They may not be as good as new, but they should be in a lot better shape than they were.

Dust off flower bulbs Many gardeners use medicated baby powder to dust flower bulbs before planting them. Simply place 5-6 bulbs and about 3 tablespoons of medicated baby powder in a sealed plastic bag and give it a few gentle shakes. The medicated-powder coating helps both to reduce the chance of rot and keep away moles, voles, grubs and other bulb-munching pests.

* Baby wipes

Use for quick, on-the-move cleanups Baby wipes can be used for far more than just cleaning babies' bottoms. They're great for wiping your hands after filling the car with petrol, mopping up small spills in the car and cooling a sweaty brow after exercise. In fact, they make ideal travel companions. So the next time you set off on a journey, pack a small stack of wipes in a tightly closed self-sealing sandwich bag and keep it in the glove compartment of the car or in your handbag or rucksack.

Shine your shoes Just wipe over and buff to put the shine back into leather shoes.

Recycle as dust cloths Believe it or not, some brands of baby wipes – Huggies, for instance – can be laundered and reused as dusters and cleaning rags. Only 'mildly' soiled wipes should be considered candidates for laundering and you should always wash them at 60°C or above.

Buff up the bathroom When you have company coming over and not much time to tidy up the house, try this double-handed trick. Take a baby wipe in one hand and start polishing the bathroom surfaces. Keep a dry facecloth or hand towel in your other hand to buff things up as you make your rounds.

Remove stains from carpet, clothing and upholstery Use a baby wipe to blot up coffee spills from a rug or carpet; it absorbs both the liquid and the stain. Wipes can also be effectively deployed when attacking various spills and drips on clothing and upholstered furniture.

Clean a PC keyboard Periodically shaking out a computer keyboard is a good way to get rid of the dust and debris that gathers underneath and in between the keys. But that's just half the job. Use a baby wipe to remove the dirt, dried spills and unspecified gunk and grime that builds up on the keys themselves. Always turn off the computer or unplug the keyboard before you wipe the keys.

Soothe sunburn You can temporarily cool sunburn by gently patting the area with a baby wipe. Baby wipes can also be used to treat cuts and scrapes. Although most wipes don't have any antiseptic properties, there's nothing wrong with using one for an initial cleansing before applying the proper medical treatment.

Remove makeup It is one of the fashion industry's worst-kept secrets: many models consider a baby wipe to be their best friend when it is time to remove stubborn make-up from their faces, particularly black eyeliner. Try it and see for yourself.

Baby wipes containers

Organise your stuff Don't throw away empty wipes containers. The sturdy plastic boxes are incredibly useful for storing all sorts of items. And rectangular ones are stackable as well. Wash and dry the containers thoroughly and remove the labels, then use them to store everything from sewing supplies, recipe cards, coupons and craft and office supplies to old floppy disks, small tools, photos, receipts and bills. Label the contents of each with a marker on masking tape.

Make a first-aid kit Gather up your own choice of essential first-aid items (such as plasters, sterile gauze rolls and pads, adhesive tape, scissors and antibiotic cream) and use a rectangular baby wipes container to hold it all. Before you add your supplies, wash the container well – and rub the inside with surgical spirit after it dries.

Use as a decorative wool or string dispenser A clean cylindrical wipes container makes a perfect dispenser for a roll of wool or string. Simply remove the container's cover, insert the roll and thread it through the slot in the lid, then reattach the cover. You can paint or paper over the container to give it a more decorative look.

TIP* REMOVING LABELS

Use a blow-drier on a high setting to heat up the labels on baby wipes containers and make them easier to pull off. You can get rid of any leftover adhesive by applying a little WD-40 oil or orange citrus cleaner.

Store plastic shopping bags Do you save plastic shopping bags for lining small wastebaskets or to reuse when shopping? If so, bring order to the puffed-up chaos they create by storing the bags in cleaned, rectangular wipes containers. Each container can hold 40 to 50 bags – once you squeeze the air out of them. You can also use an empty large rectangular tissue box – the kind with a perforated cutout dispenser – in a similar manner.

Make a piggy bank Well maybe not a 'piggy' bank per se but a money bank nonetheless and one that gives you a convenient place to put excess change. Take a clean rectangular container and use a knife to cut a slot – make it wide enough to easily accommodate a £2 coin – on the lid. If you're making the bank for a child, you can either decorate it or let her put her own personal 'stamp' on it.

Hold towels or rags in the workshop A used baby wipes container can be a welcome addition in the workshop for storing rags and paper towels – and to keep a steady supply on hand as needed. You can easily keep a full roll of detached paper towels or six or seven good-sized rags in each container.

*Balloons

Protect a bandaged finger Bandaging an injury on your finger is easy; keeping the dressing dry as you go about your day can be a different story. But slip a small balloon over your finger when doing dishes, bathing, or even washing your hands and you'll find that the bandage stays secure, clean and dry.

Keep track of your child The inexpensive floating helium-filled balloons sold in many shopping centres can be more than just a treat for a youngster; they could be invaluable in locating a child who wanders off into a crowd. Even if you keep close tabs on your kids, buy a little peace of mind by loosely tying a balloon to your child's wrist on a weekend shopping trip.

Make a party invitation Inflate a balloon (using a pump if possible – it's more hygienic). Pinch off the end, but don't tie a knot in it. Write the invitation details on the balloon with a bright permanent marker, making sure the ink is dry before you deflate it. Place the balloon in an envelope and send one out to each guest. When your guests receive it, they'll have to blow it up to see what it says.

Transport cut flowers Don't use awkward, water-filled plastic bags when travelling with freshly cut flowers. Fill up a balloon with about 100ml water and slip it over the cut ends of your flowers. Wrap a rubber band several times around the mouth of the balloon to keep it from slipping off.

Use as a hat mould To keep the shape in a freshly washed knitted cap or cloth hat, fit it over a balloon, inflated to the size of the owner's head while it dries. Use a piece of masking tape to keep the balloon attached to a worktop or railing.

Mark a campsite Take a number of helium-filled balloons to attach to your tent or a post on your next camping holiday. They'll make it easier for the members of your party to locate your tent among a host of others or to spot it from a distance.

Make an ice pack Here is how to make a flexible ice pack you can use for everything from icing a sore back to keeping food cold in a cooler. Fill a large, durable balloon with as much water as you need and put it in the freezer. You can even mould it into specific shapes – for example, put it under something flat if you want a flat ice pack for your back. Smaller latex balloons can be used to make mini ice packs to put into lunch boxes.

{ SCIENCE FAIR }

INFLATE A BALLOON THE FUN WAY

Use the gas produced by mixing bicarbonate of soda and vinegar to blow up a balloon. First, pour 100ml vinegar into the bottom of a narrow-neck bottle (such as an empty water bottle) or jar. Then insert a funnel into the mouth of an average-sized balloon, and fill it with 5 tablespoons bicarbonate of soda. Carefully stretch the mouth of the balloon over the opening of the bottle, then gently lift it up so that the bicarbonate of soda empties into the vinegar at the bottom of the bottle. The fizzing and foaming you see is actually a chemical reaction between the two ingredients. This reaction results in the release of carbon dioxide gas – which will soon inflate the balloon.

Keep a punch bowl cool To keep a party punch bowl cold and well filled, pour juice into several balloons using a funnel and place them in the freezer. When you are ready, peel the latex off the ice and periodically drop a couple of the ice spheres into the punch bowl.

Repel unwanted garden visitors Old deflated shiny metallic balloons from past birthday parties can be put to work in the garden. Cut them into vertical strips and hang them from poles around the vegetables and on fruit trees to scare off invading birds, rabbits and squirrels.

* Bananas

Make a face mask You can use a banana as a natural moisturising face mask to leave your skin looking and feeling softer. Mash up a medium-sized ripe banana into a smooth paste, then gently apply it to your face and neck. Let it set for 10-20 minutes, then rinse it off with cold water. Another popular mask recipe calls for 50g plain yogurt, 2 tablespoons honey and a medium banana.

Make a frozen banana lolly As a summer treat for friends and family, peel and cut four ripe bananas in half (across the middle). Stick a wooden ice-lolly stick into the flat end of each piece. Place them all on a piece of greaseproof paper and then put it in the freezer. A few hours later, serve them up as delicious frozen banana lollies. For an even more indulgent treat, quickly dip the frozen bananas in 200g melted butterscotch or chocolate (you could also add chopped nuts or shredded coconut), then re-freeze.

Tenderise a roast Banana leaves are commonly used in many Asian countries to wrap meat as it is cooking to make it more tender. Some people also believe that the banana itself has this ability. So the next time you fear a roast may turn out too tough, try softening it up by adding a ripe, peeled banana to the roasting pan.

Polish silverware and leather shoes It may sound ridiculous, but using a banana skin is actually an excellent way to put the shine back into both silverware and leather shoes. First, remove any of the leftover stringy material from the inside of the skin, then just start rubbing the inside of the peel on the shoes or silver. When you've finished, buff up the object with a paper towel or soft cloth. You could even use this technique to restore leather furniture – but test it on a small section first before you take on the whole item.

Brighten up houseplants It's easy to restore the shine and lustre to the leaves of dusty and dingy houseplants. Wipe down each leaf with the inside of a banana skin. It will quickly remove all the grime on the leaves' surface.

Deter aphids If aphids are attacking rosebushes or other garden plants, try burying dried or cut-up banana skins a few centimetres deep around the base of the aphid-prone plants and they will quickly be deterred. Don't use whole skins or the bananas themselves, though; they tend to be viewed as tasty treats by squirrels, rats, mice and other animals, who will just dig them up.

Use as fertiliser or mulch Banana skins, like the fruit itself, are rich in potassium – an important nutrient for both people and plants. Dry out banana skins during the winter. In early spring, grind them up in a food processor or blender to make a mulch. It can be spread around near new plants and seedlings to give them a healthy start. Many cultivars of roses and other plants, like staghorn ferns, also benefit from the nutrients found in banana skins; simply cut up some skins and use them as plant food around established plants.

Add to compost pile With their high content of potassium and phosphorus, whole bananas and their skins are useful additions to any compost pile. The fruit will break down especially fast in hot temperatures. But don't forget to remove any glued-on tags from the skins and be sure to bury the bananas deep within the compost – otherwise they may simply turn out to be a welcome meal for a foraging four-legged visitor.

Attract butterflies and birds Bring more butterflies and various bird species to the garden by putting out overripe bananas (as well as other fruits such as mangoes, oranges and papayas) on a raised platform. Punch a few holes in the bananas to make the fruit more accessible to the butterflies. The fruit is also likely to attract more bees and wasps as well, so make sure that the platform is well above head level and not centrally located. You may want to remove the remaining food before sunset, to discourage visits from nocturnal scavengers.

Basters

Pour perfect batter To make perfect pancakes, biscuits and muffins, fill a baster with batter so that you can pour just the right amount onto a griddle or baking sheet or into a muffin tin.

Remove excess water from a coffeemaker The perfect cup of coffee in an automatic coffeemaker requires a perfect balance of water and ground coffee. If you pour in too much water, you may have to add more coffee or suffer through a weak pot. But there's another, often overlooked option: just use a baster to remove the excess water to bring it in at just the right level.

Water hard-to-reach plants Do you often get drips all over yourself, the floor or the furniture when trying to water hanging plants or other out-of-reach houseplants? Instead, fill a baster with water and squeeze it directly into the pot. You can also use a baster to water a Christmas tree and to add small, precise amounts of water to trays containing seedlings or germinating seeds.

Refresh water in a flower arrangement Cut flowers last longer when their water is changed regularly. But pouring out the old water and adding the new is not a particularly easy or pleasant task. Unless, that is, you use a baster to suck out the old water and then to squirt in fresh water.

{TAKE CARE}

Never use your kitchen baster for tasks such as cleaning out a fish tank or spreading or transferring chemicals. Get a number of basters to keep around the house specifically for non-cooking chores. Label with a piece of masking tape to make sure you always use the same baster for the same task.

Place water in a pet's bowl Are you getting tired of chasing an escaped rabbit, hamster, or other caged pet around the house whenever you try to change its water? Use a baster to fill the water dish. You can usually fit the baster between the slats without having to open the cage.

Clean the aquarium A baster makes it easy to change the water in a fish tank or to freshen it up. Simply use it to suck up the dirt that collects in the corners and in the gravel at the bottom of the tank.

Blow away cockroaches and ants Sprinkle boric acid along any cracks or crevices where you have spotted insect intruders such as ants or cockroaches. Use a baster to blow small amounts of the powder into hard-to-reach corners and any deep voids you come across. **WARNING** Keep in mind that boric acid can be toxic if ingested by young children or pets.

Transfer paints and solvents The toughest part of any quick paint job is invariably pouring the paint from a large can into a small cup or container. To avoid the inevitable spills, use a baster to take the paint out of the can. In fact, it is a good idea to make a baster a permanent addition to a workshop to use for transferring any solvents, varnishes and other liquid chemicals.

Cure a musty-smelling air conditioner If you detect a musty odour blowing out of the vents of an air-conditioner, it is probably caused by a clogged drain hole. First, unscrew the front of the unit and locate the drain hole. It will usually be located under the barrier between the evaporator and compressor, or underneath the evaporator. Use a bent wire hanger to clear away any obstacles in the hole or use a baster to flush it clean. You may also need to use the baster to remove any water that may be pooling up at the bottom of the unit to gain access to the drain.

Fix a leaky refrigerator Is water leaking inside the fridge? The most likely cause is a blocked drain tube. This plastic tube runs from a drain hole in the back of the freezer compartment along the back of the fridge and drains into an evaporation pan underneath. Try forcing hot water through the drain hole in the freezer compartment with a baster. If you can't get to the drain hole, try disconnecting the tube on the back to blow water through it. After clearing the tube, pour a teaspoon of bleach into the drain hole to prevent a reoccurrence of algae spores, the probable cause of the blockage.

Bath oil

Remove glue from labels or plasters Get rid of sticky leftover adhesive marks from plasters, price tags and labels by rubbing them away with a bit of bath oil applied to a cotton-wool ball. It works brilliantly on glass, metal and most plastics.

Use as a hot-oil treatment Heat 100ml bath oil mixed with 100ml water on the High setting in the microwave for 30 seconds. Place the solution in a deep bowl and soak your fingers or toes in it for 10-15 minutes to soften cuticles or hard skin on your feet. After drying, use a pumice stone to smooth over callouses or a file to push down cuticles. Follow up by rubbing in hand cream until fully absorbed.

Pry apart stuck drinking glasses When moisture seeps in between stacked glasses, separating them can be very difficult – not to mention dangerous. But you can break the bond by applying a few drops of bath oil along the sides of the glasses. Give the oil a few minutes to work its way down, then simply slide them apart.

Loosen chewing gum from hair and carpeting If your child comes home with chewing gum in his or her hair – or tracks a lump onto the rug or carpet – don't reach for the scissors. Instead, rub a liberal amount of bath oil into the gum. It should loosen it up enough to comb out. On a carpet, test the oil on an inconspicuous area before applying to the spot.

Remove scuff marks It is easy to remove scuff marks from patent-leather shoes or handbags. Apply a bit of bath oil to a clean, soft cloth or towel. Gently rub in the oil, then polish with another dry towel.

Clean grease or oil from skin It doesn't take much tinkering around the inside of a car or mower engine to get your hands coated in grease or oil. But before you use a heavy-duty grease remover, try this. Rub a few squirts of bath oil onto your hands, then wash them in warm, soapy water. It works and it's a lot easier on the skin than harsh chemicals.

Revitalise vinyl upholstery Give a car's dreary-looking vinyl upholstery a makeover by using a small amount of bath oil on a soft cloth to wipe down the seats, dashboard, armrests and other surfaces. Polish with a clean cloth to remove any excess oil. As a bonus, a scented bath oil will make the interior smell better, too.

Slide together pipe joints If you can't find any all-purpose lubricating oil or WD-40 when you're trying to join pipes together, try this instead: a few drops of bath oil should provide sufficient lubrication to fit pipe joints together with ease.

Beans (dried)

Treat sore muscles If a bad back or tennis elbow is acting up again, a hot beanbag may be just the cure. Place a couple of handfuls of dried beans in a cloth shoe bag, an old sock, or a folded towel (tie the ends tightly) and microwave it on High for between 30 seconds and 1 minute. Let it cool for a minute or two, then apply it to your aching muscles.

Make a beanbag Pour 200-300g dried beans into an old sock, shaking them down to the toe section. Tie a loose knot and tighten it up as you work it down against the beans. Then cut off the remaining material about 2.5cm above the knot. You now have a beanbag for tossing around or juggling. Or you can use it as a squeeze bag for exercising the muscles in your hands.

Practise your percussion Make a homemade percussion shaker or maraca for yourself or a child. Add 100g dried beans to a small plastic jar, or a drink or juice can – even an empty coconut shell. Cover any openings with adhesive or gaffer tape. You can use the rattle at sporting events or as a dog-training tool (try giving it a couple of shakes when the dog misbehaves).

Decorate a jack-o'-lantern Embellish the fright potential of a Halloween jack-o'-lantern by gluing on various dried beans for the eyes and teeth.

Recycle a stuffed animal Make your own beanie creation by removing the stuffing from one of your child's old, unused stuffed animals. Replace the fluff with dried beans and sew it closed. It should rekindle your child's interest.

Use as playing pieces The racing car, Scottie dog and all their companions on the Monopoly board go missing all too frequently. But dried beans work well as replacement pieces for everything from Cluedo to Snakes and Ladders to Bingo.

Beer

Use as setting lotion Put life back into flat hair with some flat beer. Before you get into the shower, mix 3 tablespoons beer in 100ml warm water. After you shampoo your hair, rub in the solution, let it set for a couple of minutes, then rinse it off. You may be so pleased by the results that you'll want to keep a six-pack in the bathroom.

Soften up tough meat Beer makes a great tenderiser for tough, inexpensive cuts of stewing meat. Pour a can over the meat and let it soak for about an hour before cooking. Even better, marinate it overnight in the fridge or put the beer in the slow cooker with the meat.

Polish gold jewellery Get the shine back in solid gold (that is, without any gemstones) rings and other jewellery by pouring a little lager on to a soft cloth and rubbing it gently over the piece. Use a clean second cloth or towel to dry.

Clean wood furniture Use old or flat beer to clean wooden furniture. Just wipe it on with a soft cloth and then off with another dry cloth.

Make a trap for slugs and snails Like some people, certain garden pests find beer irresistible – especially slugs and snails. If you're having problems with slimy invaders, bury a container, such as a clean, empty juice container cut lengthways in half, in the area where you've seen the pests, pour in about half a can of warm, leftover beer and leave it overnight to make your own irresistible 'slug pub'.

Remove coffee or tea stains from rugs Getting a coffee or tea stain out of a rug may seem impossible, but you can literally lift it out by pouring a little beer right on top. Rub the beer lightly into the material and the stain should disappear. You may have to repeat the process a couple of times to remove all traces of the stain.

DID YOU KNOW?

The art of beer brewing is almost as old as civilisation itself and, along with bread making, is probably the most ancient form of manufacturing known to man. The Chinese were known to have brewed beer some 5000 years ago and the ancient Babylonians perfected the art – a tablet in New York's Metropolitan Museum records the production of several different types of beer. Beer brewing in Australia began around 1794, encouraged by a government anxious to prevent the excessive consumption of rum.

Super item

88 USES!

BICARBONATE OF SODA...

...in the kitchen

Tenderise meat To soften a tough cut of meat, try rubbing it down with bicarbonate of soda. Let it sit in the refrigerator for 3-5 hours and rinse thoroughly before cooking.

Soak out fish smells Get rid of a strong fishy smell by soaking the raw fish for about an hour in the fridge in 2 tablespoons bicarbonate of soda in a litre of water. Rinse the fish well and pat dry before cooking.

Rid your hands of food odours Chopping garlic or cleaning fish can leave their 'essence' on your fingers long after the chore is done. Remove unpleasant food smells from your hands by simply wetting them and vigorously rubbing with about 2 teaspoons bicarbonate of soda instead of soap. The smell should wash off with the powder.

Reduce acids in recipes If you or someone in your family is sensitive to the high-acid content of tomato-based sauces or coffee, you can lower the overall acidity by sprinkling in a pinch of bicarbonate of soda while cooking (or, in the case of coffee, before brewing). A bit of bicarbonate of soda can also counteract the taste of vinegar if you happen to pour in a bit too much. Be careful not to overdo it with bicarb – if you add too much, the combination will start foaming.

Bake better beans Do you love baked beans but not their after effects? Adding a pinch of bicarbonate of soda to baked beans as they are cooking will significantly reduce their gas-producing properties.

Fluff up an omelette To make lighter, fluffier omelettes, add ½ teaspoon bicarbonate of soda for every three eggs used.

Use as yeast substitute If you have run out of yeast when making dough, you can use powdered vitamin C (or citric acid) and bicarbonate of soda instead. Just mix in equal parts to in the same quantity as the yeast required. As a bonus, the dough does not need to rise before baking.

Cleaning fresh produce You can't be too careful when it comes to food handling and preparation. Wash fruits and vegetables in a bowl of cold water along with 2-3 tablespoons bicarbonate of soda: the bicarbonate of soda will remove some of the impurities tap water leaves behind. Or put a small amount of bicarbonate of soda onto a wet sponge or vegetable brush and scrub your produce. Rinse before cooking or serving.

Clean baby bottles and accessories Keep baby bottles, teats, caps and brushes sterile and ready to use by soaking them overnight in a container filled with hot water and 200g bicarbonate of soda. Be sure to give everything a good rinse afterwards and dry thoroughly before using. Baby bottles can also be boiled in a full pan of water and 3 tablespoons bicarbonate of soda for 3 minutes.

Clean a chopping board Keep a wooden or plastic cutting board clean by occasionally scrubbing it with a paste made from 1 tablespoon each of bicarbonate of soda, salt and water. Rinse thoroughly with hot water.

Clear a clogged drain Most kitchen drains can be unclogged by pouring in 200g bicarbonate of soda followed by 200ml hot vinegar (simply heat it up in the microwave for 1 minute). Give it several minutes to work, then add 1 litre boiling water. Repeat if necessary. If you know the drain is clogged with grease, use 100g each of bicarbonate of soda and salt followed by 200ml boiling water. Let the mixture work overnight; then rinse with hot tap water in the morning.

Boost the potency of washing-up liquid Add 2 tablespoons bicarbonate of soda to your usual amount of washing-up liquid and watch it cut through grease.

Make your own dishwasher detergent If you discover that you have run out of powdered dishwashing detergent or tablets, you can make your own by combining 2 tablespoons bicarbonate of soda with 2 tablespoons borax. You may be so pleased with the results that you will switch for good.

Deodorise the dishwasher Eliminate odours inside the dishwasher by sprinkling 100g bicarbonate of soda on the bottom of the machine between wash loads. To freshen it fully, pour in 200g bicarbonate of soda and run the empty machine through a complete rinse cycle.

BICARBONATE OF SODA...

..in the kitchen

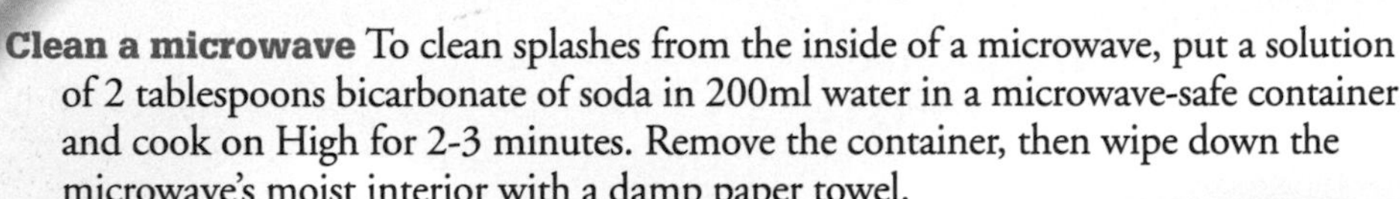

Remove coffee and tea stains from china Don't let murky coffee and/or tea stains on best china spoil a special occasion. Remove the stains by dipping a moist cloth in bicarbonate of soda to form a stiff paste and gently rubbing the cups and saucers. Rinse clean, dry well and set the table with pride.

Clean a microwave To clean splashes from the inside of a microwave, put a solution of 2 tablespoons bicarbonate of soda in 200ml water in a microwave-safe container and cook on High for 2-3 minutes. Remove the container, then wipe down the microwave's moist interior with a damp paper towel.

TIP* NO BAKING POWDER ON HAND?

If you have run out of baking powder, you can usually substitute 2 parts bicarbonate of soda mixed with 1 part each cream of tartar and cornflour. To make the equivalent of 1 teaspoon baking powder, for instance, mix ½ teaspoon bicarbonate of soda with ¼ teaspoon cream of tartar and ¼ teaspoon cornflour. The cornflour slows the reaction between the acidic cream of tartar and the alkaline bicarbonate of soda so that, like commercial baking powder, it maintains its leavening power for longer.

To remove residue on the inside of a Thermos, mix 50g bicarbonate of soda in 1 litre water. Fill the Thermos with the solution – if necessary, scrub with a bottle brush to loosen things up – and let it soak overnight. Rinse clean before using.

Clean the fridge To get rid of smells and dried-up spills inside the fridge, remove the contents, then sprinkle some bicarbonate of soda on a damp sponge and scrub the sides, shelves and compartments. Rinse with a clean, wet sponge. To keep the fridge smelling fresh, place an opened box of powder inside when you have finished cleaning.

Clean burned or scorched pots and pans It usually takes a lot of heavy-duty scrubbing to remove scorched-on food from the bottom of a pot or pan. But you can make life much easier for yourself by simply boiling a few cups of water (enough to get the pan about a quarter full) and adding 5 tablespoons bicarbonate of soda. Turn off the heat and let the powder settle in for a few hours or overnight. The burned-on mess will virtually slide off.

DID YOU KNOW?

Bicarbonate of soda is the main ingredient in many commercial fire extinguishers. And you can use it straight out of the box to extinguish small fires throughout your home.

Keep bicarbonate of soda near the cooker and barbecue so you can throw on a few handfuls to quell a flare-up. In the case of a grease fire, first turn off the heat, if possible and try to cover the fire with a pan lid. Be careful not to let the hot grease splatter you.

Keep a box in the garage and inside your car to quickly extinguish mechanical or car-interior fires. Bicarbonate of soda will also snuff out electrical fires and flames on clothing, wood, upholstery and carpeting.

Freshen a sponge or towel When a kitchen sponge or dishcloth starts to smell sour, soak it overnight in 2 tablespoons bicarbonate of soda and a couple of drops of antibacterial washing-up liquid dissolved in 450ml warm water. The following morning, squeeze out the remaining solution and rinse with cold water. It should smell completely fresh.

Remove stains and scratches on worktops If a kitchen worktop has become covered with stains or small knife cuts, use a paste of 2 parts bicarbonate of soda to 1 part water to 'rub out' most of them. For stubborn stains, add a drop of chlorine bleach to the paste. Immediately wash the area with hot, soapy water to prevent the bleach from causing fading.

Shine up stainless steel and chrome trim To restore the shine to a stainless-steel sink, sprinkle it with bicarbonate of soda, then rub it down with a moist cloth, moving in the direction of the grain. To polish dull chrome trim on the kettle and toaster, pour a little bicarbonate of soda onto a damp sponge and rub over the chrome. Let it dry for an hour or so, then wipe down with warm water and dry with a clean cloth.

Get rid of grease stains on the hob Get rid of cooked-on grease stains on a hob or splashback. First wet the stains with a little water and cover with a bit of bicarbonate of soda. Then rub off with a damp sponge or towel.

Clean an automatic coffeemaker If you care for a coffeemaker properly you will never have to worry about bitter or weak coffee. Every two weeks or so, brew a pot of 1 litre water mixed with 50g bicarbonate of soda, followed by a pan of clean water. Freshen the coffeemaker's plastic basket by using an old toothbrush to scrub it with a paste of 2 tablespoons bicarbonate of soda and 1 tablespoon water. Rinse thoroughly with cold water when you have finished.

BICARBONATE OF SODA...

...in the kitchen

Care for coffeepots and teapots Remove mineral deposits in metal coffeepots and teapots by filling them with a solution of 200ml vinegar and 4 tablespoons bicarbonate of soda. Bring the mixture to a boil, then let simmer for 5 minutes. Or try boiling 1 litre water with 2 tablespoons powder and the juice of half a lemon. Rinse with cold water when finished. To remove exterior stains, wash pans with a plastic scouring pad in a solution of 50g bicarbonate of soda in 1 litre warm water. Follow with a cold-water rinse.

Remove stains from non-stick cookware It may be called non-stick cookware, but sometimes food does cook onto the surface and can be hard to remove. Blast stains away by boiling 200ml water mixed with 2 tablespoons bicarbonate of soda and 100ml vinegar for 10 minutes. Then wash in hot, soapy water. Rinse well and let dry, then season with a bit of vegetable oil.

Clean cast-iron cookware Although it is more prone to stains and rust than the non-stick variety, many cooks swear by their iron cookware. Remove even the toughest burned-on food remnants from iron pots by boiling 1 litre water with 2 tablespoons bicarbonate of soda for 5 minutes. Pour off most of the liquid, then lightly scrub with a plastic scrubbing pad. Rinse well, dry and season with a few drops of olive oil.

Deodorise your rubbish bin If something smells 'off' in the kitchen, it is most likely to be coming from the bin. But some smells linger even after you dispose of the offending rubbish bag. Give a kitchen bin an occasional cleaning with a wet paper towel dipped in bicarbonate of soda (wear rubber gloves to do this). Rinse it out with a damp sponge and let it dry before inserting a new bag. You can also ward off future bad smells by sprinkling a little bicarbonate of soda into the bottom of the bin before inserting the bag.

...around the house

Wash wallpaper Is the wallpaper looking a little dingy? Brighten it up by wiping with a rag or sponge moistened in a solution of 2 tablespoons bicarbonate of soda in 1 litre water. To remove grease stains from wallpaper, make a paste of 1 tablespoon bicarbonate of soda and 1 teaspoon water. Rub it on the stain, let it set for 5-10 minutes, then rub off with a damp sponge.

Clean up baby accidents Infants do tend to throw up – and usually not at opportune moments. Never leave home without a small bottle of bicarbonate of soda in your nappy bag. If a child vomits on his or her (or your) shirt after feeding, simply brush off any solid matter, moisten a washcloth, dip it in a bit of bicarbonate of soda and dab the spot. The odour (and the potential stain) will soon be gone.

Deodorise rugs and carpets Freshen up carpets or rugs by lightly sprinkling them with bicarbonate of soda, let it settle in for 15 minutes or so, then vacuum up.

Remove wine and grease stains from carpet If someone drops a knob of butter or a glass of red wine on a light coloured carpet, don't panic. Get a paper towel and blot up as much of the stain as possible. Then sprinkle a liberal amount of bicarbonate of soda over the spot. Give the powder at least an hour to absorb the stain, then vacuum up the remaining powder.

Freshen musty drawers and cupboards Put bicarbonate of soda sachets to work on persistent musty odours in drawers, cupboards or wardrobes. Fill the toe of a clean sock or stocking with 3-4 tablespoons powder, put a knot about 2cm above the bulge and either hang it up or place it away in an unobtrusive corner. Use a few sachets in large spaces like wardrobes and attic storage areas. Replace them every other month if needed. This treatment can also be used to get rid of the strong smell of mothballs.

Remove crayon marks from walls Has a junior artist redecorated the walls or wallpaper with some original artworks in crayon? Take a damp rag, dip it in some bicarbonate of soda and lightly scrub the marks. They should come off with a minimal amount of effort.

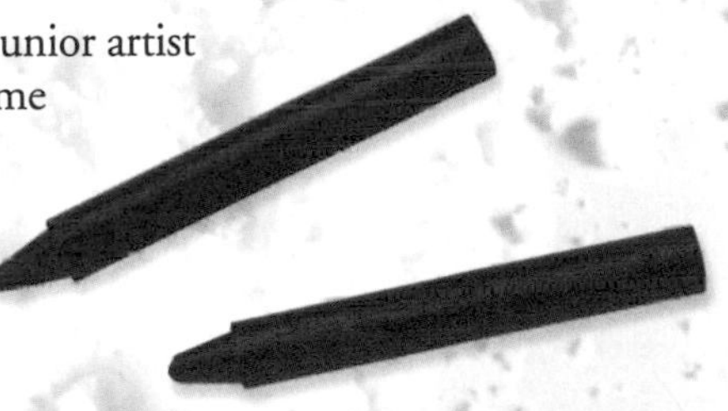

{ KIDS' STUFF }

MAKING WATERCOLOUR PAINTS

Make watercolour paints for your children using ingredients from the kitchen. (1) In a small bowl, combine 3 tablespoons each of bicarbonate of soda, cornflour and vinegar with 1 ½ teaspoons liquid glucose (available from a pharmacist). (2) Wait for the fizzing to subside, then separate the mixture into several small containers or jar lids. (3) Add eight drops of food colouring to each batch and mix well. Put a different colour in each batch or combine colours to make new shades. Children can either use the paints right away, or wait for them to harden, in which case, they'll need to use a wet brush before painting.

BICARBONATE OF SODA...

...around the house

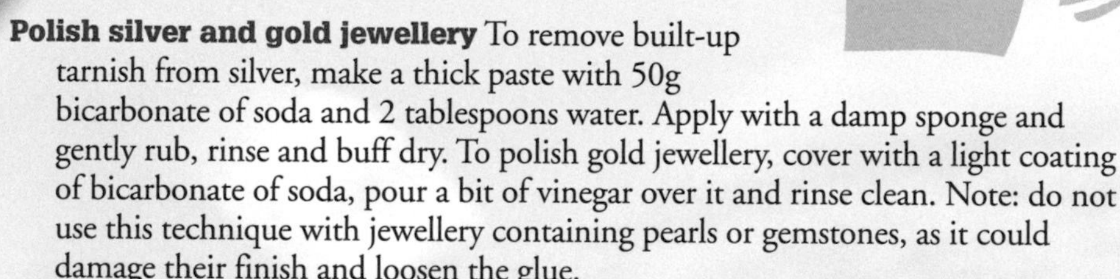

Remove the musty odour from books If books that you have taken out of storage emerge with a musty smell, place each one in a brown paper bag with 2 tablespoons bicarbonate of soda. Don't shake the bag, just tie it up and let it sit in a dry environment for about a week. When you open the bag, shake any remaining powder off the books and the smell should be gone.

Polish silver and gold jewellery To remove built-up tarnish from silver, make a thick paste with 50g bicarbonate of soda and 2 tablespoons water. Apply with a damp sponge and gently rub, rinse and buff dry. To polish gold jewellery, cover with a light coating of bicarbonate of soda, pour a bit of vinegar over it and rinse clean. Note: do not use this technique with jewellery containing pearls or gemstones, as it could damage their finish and loosen the glue.

Remove yellow stains from piano keys Although your old piano still plays beautifully, its yellowed keys may be showing their age. Remove stains by mixing a solution of 50g bicarbonate of soda in 1 litre warm water. Apply to each key with a dampened cloth (you can place a thin piece of cardboard between the keys to avoid seepage). Wipe again with a cloth dampened with plain water and then buff dry with a clean cloth. (You can also clean piano keys using lemon juice and salt.)

Remove stains from a brick fireplace surround You may need to use a bit of elbow grease, but you can clean smoke stains from fireplace bricks by washing them with a solution of 100g bicarbonate of soda in 1 litre warm water.

Remove white marks on wood surfaces White marks – caused by hot cups or sweating glasses – can wreck the appearance of a coffee table or other wooden furniture. Remove them by making a paste of 1 tablespoon bicarbonate of soda with 1 teaspoon water. Gently rub the spot using a circular motion until it disappears. Remember to use the minimum amount of water.

TIP* HOW LONG DOES BICARB LAST?

How can you tell if the bicarbonate of soda you have had stored away in the back of a cupboard is still good? Just pour out a small amount – a little less than a teaspoon – and add a few drops of vinegar or fresh lemon juice. If it doesn't fizz, it is time to replace it. A sealed box of baking powder has an average shelf life of 18 months, while an opened box lasts six months

Remove cigarette odour from furniture To eliminate the lingering smell of cigarette or cigar smoke from upholstered furniture, lightly sprinkle chairs or sofas with some bicarbonate of soda. Let it sit for a few hours, then vacuum off.

Give a shine to marble-topped furniture Revitalise a marble top on a coffee table or worktop by washing it with a soft cloth dipped in a solution of 3 tablespoons bicarbonate of soda and 1 litre warm water. Let it stand for 15 minutes to half an hour, then rinse with plain water and wipe dry.

Clean enamel baths and sinks Remove ugly tidemarks and soap stains from old enamelled bath tubs and sinks by applying a paste of 2 parts bicarbonate of soda and 1 part hydrogen peroxide. Let the paste set for about half an hour. Scrub and rinse well; the paste will also remove lingering odours from your drain as it washes down.

Absorb bathroom odours Keep the bathroom smelling fresh by placing a dish filled with 100g bicarbonate of soda either on top of the toilet cistern or on the floor behind the toilet. You can make your own bathroom freshener by filling small dishes with equal parts of bicarbonate of soda and bath salts.

Make the toilet bowl sparkle You don't need a host of chemicals to clean the toilet. Pour 250g bicarbonate of soda into the cistern once a month. Let it stand overnight, then give it a few flushes in the morning. This will actually clean both the cistern and the bowl. You can also pour several tablespoons of bicarbonate of soda directly onto stains into the toilet bowl and scrub well. Wait a few minutes then flush away

Remove mineral deposits from a showerhead Cover the head with a heavy-duty sandwich-size bag filled with 50g bicarbonate of soda and 200ml vinegar. Loosely fasten the bag with adhesive tape or a large twist tie (it needs to be loose so some of the resultant gas can escape). Leave for about an hour. Then remove the bag and turn on your shower to wash off any remaining debris. Not only will the deposits disappear, but the showerhead will be bright and shiny again.

...in the medicine cabinet

Treat minor burns The next time you grab the wrong end of a frying pan or forget to use a pot holder or oven glove, quickly pour some bicarbonate of soda into a container of ice water, soak a cloth or gauze pad in it and apply it to the burn. Keep applying the solution until the burn no longer feels hot. This treatment will also prevent many burns from blistering.

BICARBONATE OF SODA...

...in the medicine cabinet

Soothe heat rash Prickly heat – itchy red bumps – particularly on your neck, chest, armpits and groin is caused by sweat that can't evaporate. The pores become blocked and skin erupts into a stinging rash. To soothe it add a few tablespoons of bicarbonate of soda to a bath and have a long soak. You can also apply it directly to the rash to absorb sweat and additional moisture.

Make a salve for bee stings Take the pain from a bee sting – fast. Make a paste of 1 teaspoon bicarbonate of soda mixed with several drops of cool water and let it dry on the affected area.
WARNING Many people have severe allergic reactions to bee stings. If you have difficulty breathing or notice a dramatic swelling, you should get medical attention at once.

Fight nappy rash Soothe a baby's painful nappy rash by adding a couple of tablespoons bicarbonate of soda to a lukewarm – not hot – bath. If the rash persists or worsens after several treatments, however, consult a doctor.

Combat cradle cap Cradle cap is a common and typically harmless condition in many infants. An old but often effective way to treat it is to make a paste of about 3 teaspoons bicarbonate of soda and 1 teaspoon water. Apply it to your baby's scalp about an hour before bedtime and rinse it off the following morning. Do not use with shampoo. You may need to apply it on several consecutive nights before the cradle cap recedes. (You can also treat cradle cap using baby oil. See page 55.)

Control your dandruff To get dandruff under control, wet your hair and then rub a handful of bicarbonate of soda vigorously into your scalp. Rinse thoroughly and dry. Do this every time you normally wash your hair, but only use bicarbonate of soda, not shampoo. Your hair may feel somewhat dried out at first. But after a few weeks your scalp will start producing natural oils, leaving your hair softer and free of flakes.

Cool off sunburn and other skin irritations

- To get quick relief from the pain of sunburn, soak a couple of gauze pads or large cotton balls in a solution made up of 4 tablespoons bicarbonate of soda mixed in 200ml water and apply it to the affected areas.
- To ease a bad burn on your legs or torso – or to relieve the itching of chicken pox – take a lukewarm bath with 250-500g bicarbonate of soda added to the running water.
- To ease the sting of razor burns, dab your skin with a cotton wool ball soaked in a solution of 1 tablespoon bicarbonate of soda in 200ml water.

...in the bathroom

Use as a gargle or mouthwash Are you suffering from an overdose of onions or too much garlic? Try gargling with 1 teaspoon bicarbonate of soda in half a glass of water. The bicarbonate of soda will neutralise the odours on contact. When used as a mouthwash, bicarbonate of soda will also relieve pain from mouth ulcers.

Scrub teeth and clean dentures If you run out of toothpaste or if you are looking for a natural alternative to commercial toothpaste, just dip your wet toothbrush in some bicarbonate of soda and brush and rinse as usual. You can also use bicarbonate of soda to clean retainers, gum shields and dentures. Use a solution of 1 tablespoon bicarbonate of soda dissolved in 200ml warm water. Let the object soak for a half hour and rinse well before using.

Remove built-up gel, hair spray, or conditioner from hair When it comes to personal grooming, overuse of hair products can be bad news for your hair. But a thorough cleansing with bicarbonate of soda at least once a week will wash all of the residue out of your hair. Simply add 1 tablespoon powder to your hair while shampooing. In addition to removing all the chemicals you put in your hair, it will wash away water impurities and may actually lighten the colour of your hair.

Clean combs and brushes Freshen up combs and hairbrushes by soaking them in a solution of 600ml warm water and 2 teaspoons bicarbonate of soda. Swirl them around in the water to loosen up all the debris caught between the teeth, then let them soak for about half an hour. Rinse well and dry before using.

Clean and freshen toothbrushes Keep your family's toothbrushes squeaky clean by immersing them in a solution of 50g bicarbonate of soda and 50ml water. Let the brushes soak overnight about once every week or two. Be sure to give them a very thorough rinse before using again.

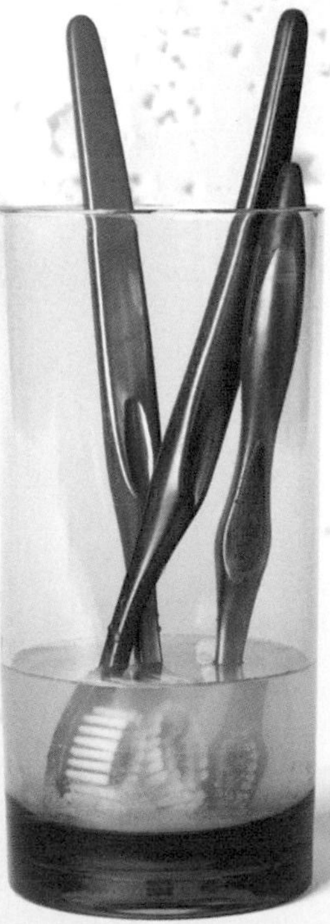

Use as an antiperspirant If you are looking for an effective, all-natural deodorant, try applying a small amount – about a teaspoon – of bicarbonate of soda with a powder puff under each arm. It should keep you fresh and dry all day.

Soothe tired, smelly feet When your feet are sore and not at their most fragrant, treat them to a soothing bath of 4 tablespoons bicarbonate of soda in 1 litre warm water. Besides relaxing your aching feet, the bicarbonate of soda will remove the sweat and lint that gathers between your toes. Regular bicarb footbaths can also be an effective treatment for persistent foot odour.

BICARBONATE OF SODA...

...in the bathroom

Deodorise shoes and trainers Even the smelliest shoe or trainer is no match for the power of bicarbonate of soda. Liberally sprinkle powder in the offending loafer or lace-up and let it sit overnight. Discard the powder in the morning. (Be careful when using bicarbonate of soda with leather shoes, as repeated applications can dry them out.) You can also make your own reusable 'odour eaters' by filling the toes of old socks with 2 tablespoons bicarbonate of soda and tying them up in a knot. Stuff the socks into each shoe at night before going to bed. Remove the socks in the morning and you should be able to breathe more easily around your trainers.

Relieve itching inside a cast Wearing a plaster cast on your arm or leg is a misery at any time of year, but wearing one in the summer can be torture. The sweating and itchiness you feel underneath your 'shell' can be intolerable. Find temporary relief by using a hair drier – on the coolest setting – to blow a little bicarbonate of soda down the edges of the cast. Note: get someone to help you, to avoid getting the powder in your eyes.

Alleviate athlete's foot You can deploy wet or dry bicarbonate of soda to combat a case of athlete's foot. First, try dusting your feet (along with your socks and shoes) with dry bicarbonate of soda to dry out the infection. If that doesn't work, try making a paste of 1 teaspoon bicarbonate of soda and ½ teaspoon water and rubbing it between your toes. Let it dry and wash off after 15 minutes. Dry your feet thoroughly before putting on your shoes.

... in the laundry

Remove mothball smell from clothes If your clothes have come out of storage reeking of mothballs, add 100g bicarbonate of soda during the washing machine's rinse cycle to get rid of the smell.

Boost the strength of liquid detergent and bleach It may sound like a cliché, but adding 100g bicarbonate of soda to your usual amount of liquid laundry detergent really will give you 'whiter whites' and brighter colours. The bicarbonate of soda also softens the water, so you can actually use less detergent. Adding 50g bicarbonate of soda to a white cotton wash also increases the potency of bleach, so you need only half the usual amount.

{ SCIENCE FAIR }

BLOW UP A BALLOON

Use the gas produced by mixing bicarbonate of soda and vinegar to blow up a balloon. Pour 100ml vinegar into the bottom of a narrow-neck bottle (such as an empty water bottle) or jar. Insert a funnel into the mouth of an average-sized balloon, and fill it with 5 tablespoons bicarbonate of soda. Carefully stretch the mouth of the balloon over the opening of the bottle, then gently lift it up so that the bicarbonate of soda empties into the vinegar at the bottom of the bottle. The fizzing and foaming you see is actually a chemical reaction between the two ingredients. This reaction results in the release of carbon dioxide gas – which will soon inflate the balloon!

Wash new baby clothes Get all of the chemicals out of your newborn baby's clothing – without using any harsh detergents. Wash your baby's new clothes with some mild soap and 100g bicarbonate of soda.

Rub out perspiration and other stains Pre-treating clothes with a paste made from 4 tablespoons bicarbonate of soda and 50ml warm water can help to vanquish a variety of stains. For example, rub it into shirts to remove perspiration stains; for really bad stains, let the paste dry for about 2 hours before washing. Rub out tar stains by applying the paste and washing in plain bicarbonate of soda. For grimy collar stains, rub in the paste and add a bit of vinegar as you are putting the shirt in the wash.

Wash mildewed shower curtains Just because a plastic shower curtain or liner gets dirty or mildewed doesn't mean you have to throw it away. Try cleaning it in the washing machine with two bath towels on a low temperature setting. Add 100g bicarbonate of soda to the detergent during the wash cycle and 100ml vinegar during the rinse cycle. Let it drip-dry; never put it in a tumble drier.

...for the DIY-er

Use as a de-icer Salt and commercial de-icer formulations can stain and actually eat away at concrete paths and patios. For an equally effective, but completely harmless, way to melt the ice on steps and paths during cold winter months, try sprinkling them with generous amounts of bicarbonate of soda. Add a bit of sand for better traction.

BICARBONATE OF SODA...

...for the DIY-er

Tighten cane chair seats The bottoms of cane and wicker chairs can start to sag with age, but you can tighten them up again easily. Just soak two cloths in a solution of 100g bicarbonate of soda in 1 litre hot water. Saturate the top surface of the caning with one cloth, while pushing the second up against the bottom of the caning to saturate the underside. Use a clean, dry cloth to soak up the excess moisture, then put the chair in the sun to dry.

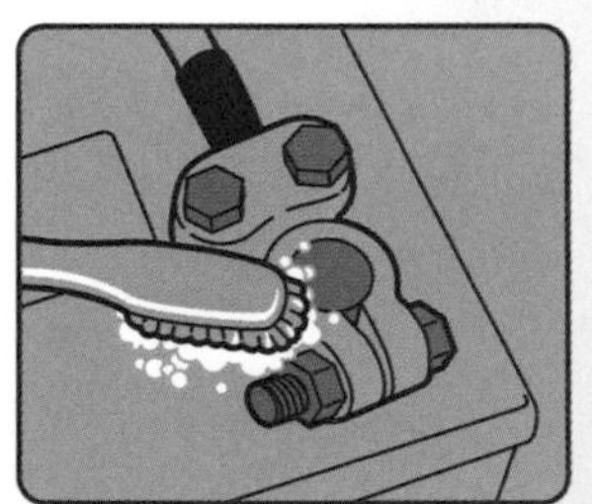

Clean car battery terminals Eliminate the corrosive buildup on a car's battery terminals. Scrub them clean using an old toothbrush and a mixture of 3 tablespoons bicarbonate of soda and 1 tablespoon warm water. Wipe off with a wet towel and dry with another towel. Once the terminals have fully dried, apply a little petroleum jelly around each terminal to deter future corrosive buildup.

Remove tar from a car It may look an impossible job, but it is not that hard to get tar off a car without damaging the paint. Make a soft paste of 3 parts bicarbonate of soda to 1 part water and apply to the tar spots with a damp cloth. Let it dry for 5 minutes, then rinse clean.

Give decking the weathered look You can instantly give a wooden deck a weather-beaten look by washing it in a solution of 400g bicarbonate of soda in 4 litres water. Use a stiff brush to work the solution into the wood, then rinse with cool water.

Keep a humidifier odour-free Eliminate the musty smell from a humidifier by adding 2 tablespoons bicarbonate of soda to the water each time you change it. Note: check first with the owner's manual or consult the unit's manufacturer before trying this.

...for your pet

Make a deodorising dog shampoo The next time your dog rolls around in your compost heap, use some bicarbonate of soda to freshen him up. Just rub a few handfuls of the powder into his coat and give it a thorough brushing. In addition to removing the smell, it will leave his coat shiny and clean.

Wash inside your pet's ears If your pet is constantly scratching at its ears, it could indicate the presence of an irritation or ear mites. Ease the itch (and wipe out any mites) by using a cotton wool ball dipped in a solution of 1 teaspoon bicarbonate of soda in 1 cup warm water to gently wash the inside of the ears.

Deodorise a cat litter tray Don't waste money on expensive deodorised cat litter (which your cat may in fact hate). Just put a thin layer of bicarbonate of soda under ordinary litter to absorb the odour. Or mix bicarbonate of soda with the litter as you are changing it.

{ KIDS' STUFF }

INVISIBLE INK

Here's how to send a message or draw a picture with invisible ink. Mix 1 tablespoon each of bicarbonate of soda and water. Dip a toothpick or paintbrush in the mixture and write your message or draw a picture or design on a piece of plain white paper. Let the paper and the 'ink' dry completely. To reveal your message or see your picture, mix 6 drops food colouring with 1 tablespoon water. Dip a clean paintbrush in the solution and lightly paint over the paper.

Keep insects away from pets' dishes Placing a border of bicarbonate of soda around your pet's food bowls will keep away insects and other intruders. And it won't harm your pet if it happens to lap up a little (though most pets aren't likely to savour the powder's bitter taste).

...in the great outdoors

Clean plastic garden furniture Most commercial cleaners are too abrasive to be used on plastic garden furniture. But you won't have to worry about scratching or dulling the surface if you clean the furniture with a wet sponge dipped in bicarbonate of soda. Wipe using a circular motion, then rinse well.

Keep weeds out of paving cracks Are you keen to find a safe way to keep weeds and grasses from growing in the cracks of paved patios, driveways and garden paths? Sprinkle handfuls of bicarbonate of soda onto the concrete and simply sweep it into the cracks. The added sodium will make it much less hospitable to dandelions and their friends.

Use as plant food Give flowering, alkaline-loving plants, such as clematis, delphiniums and dianthus, an occasional shower in a mild solution of 1 tablespoon bicarbonate of soda in 2 litres water. They'll show their appreciation with fuller, healthier blooms.

Scour barbecue grills Keep a barbecue grill in top condition by making a soft paste of 50g bicarbonate of soda and 50ml water. Apply the paste with a wire brush and let dry for 15 minutes. Then wipe it down thoroughly with a dry cloth and place the grill over hot coals for at least 15 minutes to burn off any residue before placing food on top.

Bleach

Remove mould and mildew Bleach and ammonia are both useful for removing mould and mildew both inside and outside the home. However, the two should never be used together. Bleach is especially suited for the following chores:

- Wash mildew out of washable fabrics. Wet the mildewed area and rub in some powdered detergent. Then wash the garment in the hottest water setting permitted by the manufacturer, using 100ml chlorine bleach. If the garment can't be washed in hot water and bleach, soak it in a solution of 50ml oxygen bleach (labelled 'all fabric') in 4 litres warm water for 30 minutes before washing in the machine.
- Remove mould and mildew from the grout between bathroom tiles. Mix equal parts of chlorine bleach and water in a spray bottle and spray it over the grout. Let it sit for 15 minutes, then scrub with a stiff brush and rinse off. You can also do this just to make your grout look whiter.
- Get mould and mildew off a shower curtain. Wash them – along with a couple of bath towels (to prevent the plastic curtains from getting crumpled) – in warm water with 100ml chlorine bleach and 50ml laundry detergent. Let the machine run for a couple of minutes before loading. If you have one, put the shower curtain and towels in a tumble-drier on the lowest temperature setting for 10 minutes, then hang up to dry.
- Rid a rubber shower mat of mildew. Soak in a solution of 25ml chlorine bleach in 4 litres of water for 3-4 hours. Rinse well.
- Get mildew and other stains off unpainted cement, patio stones or stucco. Mix a solution of 200ml chlorine bleach in 8 litres water. Scrub vigorously with a stiff brush and rinse. If any stains still remain, scrub again using 100g washing soda (this is sodium carbonate, not bicarbonate of soda) dissolved in 8 litres warm water.
- Remove mildew from painted surfaces. Make a solution of 50ml chlorine bleach in 400ml water and apply with a brush to mildewed areas. Let the solution set for 15 minutes, then rinse. Repeat as necessary.

{TAKE CARE}

Never mix bleach with ammonia, lye, rust removers, oven or toilet-bowl cleaners or vinegar. Any combination can produce toxic chlorine gas fumes, which can be deadly. Some people are even sensitive to the fumes of undiluted bleach itself. Always make sure you have adequate ventilation in your work area before you starting pouring.

Sterilise secondhand items Remember your mother saying, 'Put that down. You don't know where it's been'? She had a point – especially when it comes to toys or kitchen utensils picked up at charity shops and car boot sales. Just to be on the safe side, take used, waterproof items and soak them for 5-10 minutes in a solution of 150ml bleach, a few drops of antibacterial washing-up liquid and 4 litres warm water. Rinse well, then air-dry, preferably in sunlight.

Clean butchers' blocks, cutting boards and wooden worktops Never use furniture polish or any other household cleaner to clean a butcher's block, cutting board or worktop. Instead, scrub the surface with a brush dipped in a solution of 1 teaspoon bleach diluted in 2 litres water. Scrub in small circles and be careful not to saturate the wood. Wipe with a slightly damp paper towel, then immediately buff dry with a clean cloth.

Brighten up glass dishware Put the sparkle back into glasses and dishes by adding a teaspoon of bleach to your soapy dishwater as you're washing the glassware. Be sure to rinse well and dry with a soft towel.

Shine white porcelain If you want to get a white porcelain sink, candleholder or pottery item looking as good as new, place several paper towels over the item (or across the bottom of the sink) and carefully saturate them with undiluted bleach. Make sure you do this in a well-ventilated area on a work surface protected by heavy plastic. Let it soak for 15 minutes to half an hour, then rinse and wipe dry with a clean towel. Note: do not try this with antiques; you can diminish their value or cause damage. And never use bleach on coloured porcelain, because the colour will fade.

{TAKE CARE}

Some people prefer not to use bleach when cleaning their toilets, fearing that lingering ammonia from urine – especially in households with young children – could result in toxic fumes. Unless you are sure there is no such problem, you may want to stick with ammonia for this job.

Make a household disinfectant spray Here is a good, all-purpose disinfectant to use around the house. Mix 1 tablespoon bleach in 4 litres hot water. Then fill a clean, empty spray bottle and use it (sprayed onto a paper towel) to clean worktops, tablecloths, garden furniture – basically, wherever it's needed. Just be sure not to use it in the presence of ammonia or other household cleaners.

Disinfect rubbish bins Even the best housekeepers must confront a dirty kitchen bin every now and again. On such occasions, take the bin outside and flush out any loose debris with water. Then add 100ml to 200ml bleach and several drops of washing-up liquid to 4 litres warm water. Use a long-handled scrubbing brush to splash and scour the solution on the bottom and sides of the container. Empty, then rinse, empty it again and let it air-dry.

Increase cut flowers' longevity Freshly cut flowers will stay fresh longer if you add ¼ teaspoon bleach per litre of water to the vase. Another popular recipe calls for 3 drops bleach and 1 teaspoon sugar in a litre of water. This will also keep the water from getting cloudy and inhibit the growth of bacteria.

Clean plastic garden furniture Is your white plastic garden furniture looking dingy? Before you get rid of it, try washing each item with mild detergent mixed with 100ml bleach in 4 litres water. Rinse it clean, then air-dry.

Kill weeds in paths and patios Do weeds seem to thrive in the cracks and crevices of your paths? Try pouring a bit of undiluted bleach over them. After a day or two, you can simply pull them out and the bleach will stop them from coming back. Just be careful not to get bleach on the grass or plantings bordering the paths.

Get rid of moss and algae To remove slippery moss and algae from brick, concrete or stone paths, scrub them with a solution of 150ml bleach in 4 litres water. Be careful not to get bleach on the grass or any border plants.

Sterilise garden tools If you have used a pair of secateurs to cut a diseased stalk off a rosebush, avoid spreading the disease the next time you use them. Washing with 100ml bleach in a litre of water will sterilise a tool for its next use. Let the tool air-dry in the sun, then rub on a few drops of oil to prevent rust.

* Blow-driers

Remove wax from wood furniture It may have been a romantic evening, but hardened candle wax on a wooden dining table is not the sort of lingering memory you want to keep. Melt it using a blow-drier on its slowest, hottest setting. Remove the softened wax with a paper towel, then wipe the area with a cloth dipped in equal parts vinegar and water. Repeat if necessary. You can also remove wax from silver candlestick holders with a blow-drier: use the blow-drier to soften the wax, then just peel it off.

Clean behind radiators Is half-hidden dust and grime making your radiators something of an eyesore? To clean them, hang a large, damp cloth behind each radiator. Then use a blow-drier on its highest, coolest setting to blow dust and hidden dirt onto the cloth.

Remove bumper stickers Do you need to remove old stickers from a car bumper? Use a blow-drier on its hottest setting to soften the adhesive. Move the drier slowly back and forth for several minutes, then use a fingernail or credit card to lift up a corner and slowly peel off.

Dust off silk flowers and artificial houseplants They may require less care than their living counterparts, but silk flowers and artificial houseplants can be magnets for dust and dirt. Use a blow-drier on its highest, coolest setting for a quick, efficient way to clean them. As this will blow the dust onto the furniture surfaces and floor around the plant, do this just before you vacuum those areas.

Borax

Clear a clogged drain Before you use a caustic drain cleaner to unclog a blocked kitchen or bathroom drain, try this much gentler approach. Use a funnel to insert 100g borax into the drain, then slowly pour in 400ml boiling water. Let the mixture set for 15 minutes, then flush with hot water. Repeat for stubborn clogs.

Rub out heavy sink stains Get rid of stubborn stains – even rust – on a stainless steel or porcelain sink. Make a paste with 200g borax and 50ml lemon juice. Put some of the paste on a cloth or sponge and rub it into the stain, then rinse with running warm water. The stain should wash away with the paste.

Clean windows and mirrors When you want to get windows and mirrors spotless and streak-free, wash them with a clean sponge dipped in 2 tablespoons borax dissolved in 600ml water.

Remove mildew from fabric To remove mildew from upholstery and other fabrics, soak a sponge in a solution of 100g borax dissolved in 400ml hot water and rub it into the affected areas. Let it soak for several hours until the stain disappears, then rinse well. To remove mildew from clothing, soak it in a solution of 400ml borax in 2 litres water.

Get out rug stains Remove stubborn stains from rugs and carpets. Thoroughly dampen the area, then rub in some borax. Let the area dry, then vacuum or blot it with a solution of equal parts vinegar and soapy water and let dry. Repeat if necessary. Don't forget to first test the procedure on an inconspicuous corner of the rug or on a carpet offcut before applying it to the stain.

Sterilise a waste disposal unit A waste disposal is a great convenience but can also be a breeding ground for mould and bacteria. To maintain a more hygienic unit, pour 3 tablespoons borax down the drain every couple of weeks and let it sit for an hour. Then turn on the disposal unit and flush it with hot water from the tap.

{ KIDS' STUFF }

MAKING SLIME

Help children brew up some gooey, stretchy 'slime', Mix 200ml water, 200ml white glue and 10 drops food colouring in a medium bowl. In a larger bowl, dissolve 4 teaspoons borax in 250ml water. Slowly pour the contents of the first bowl into the second. Use a wooden spoon to roll the glue-based solution around in the borax solution 4 or 5 times. Lift out the glue mixture and knead for 2-3 minutes. Store in an airtight container or a self-sealing plastic storage bag. **WARNING** The mixture is not edible and children should avoid touch their eyes after handling it.

{ TAKE CARE }

Borax, like its close relative, boric acid, has relatively low toxicity levels and is considered safe for general household use, but the powder can be harmful if ingested in sufficient quantities by young children or pets. Store it safely out of their reach.

Borox is toxic to plants, however. In the garden, be very careful when applying borax onto or near soil. It doesn't take much to leach into the ground to kill off nearby plants and prevent future growth.

Clean your toilet Here is a good way to disinfect a toilet bowl and leave it glistening without having to worry about dangerous or unpleasant fumes. Use a stiff brush to scrub it using a solution of 100g borax in 4 litres water.

Eliminate urine odour on mattresses Toilet training can be a difficult experience for everybody involved. If your child has an accident in bed, here's how to get rid of any lingering smell. Dampen the area, then rub in some borax. Let it dry, then vacuum up the powder.

Make your own dried flowers Give homemade dried flowers a professional look. Mix 200g borax with 400g cornmeal. Place a 2cm coating of the mixture in the bottom of an airtight container, such as a large flat plastic food storage container. Cut the stems off the flowers you want to dry, then lay them on top of the powder and lightly sprinkle more of the mixture on top of the flowers (be careful not to bend or crush the petals or other flower parts). Cover the container and leave it alone for 7-10 days. Then remove the flowers and brush off any excess powder with a soft brush.

Keep away weeds and ants Get rid of weeds that grow in the cracks of the concrete outside your house by sprinkling borax into all the crevices where you've seen weeds growing in the past. It will kill them off before they have a chance to take root. When applied around the foundations of your home, it will also keep ants and other insect intruders from entering your house. But be very careful when applying borax – it is toxic to plants (see Take Care warning).

Control smothering creepers Is your garden being overrun by an invasive perennial weed such as bindweed? You may be able to conquer it with an application of borax. First, dissolve 230-280g borax in 120ml warm water. Then pour the solution into 10 litres warm water – this is enough to cover 90 square metres. Apply this treatment only once every two years. If you still have problems, consider switching to a standard herbicide. (See Take Care warning about using borax in the garden.)

* Bottle openers

Remove chestnut shells An easy way to remove the shells from chestnuts is to use the pointed end of a bottle opener to pierce the tops and bottoms of the shells and then boil the chestnuts for 10 minutes.

Cut packing tape on cartons It's hard to resist opening a long-awaited package on the doorstep. If you don't have a penknife handy, just run the sharp end of a bottle opener along the tape. It should do the job quite nicely.

Deploy as a prawn de-veiner If you don't have a small paring knife on hand when you're de-veining a batch of prawns, don't worry. Just use the sharp end of a bottle opener. It just happens to be the perfect shape to complete this messy chore with ease.

Scrape a barbecue grill An easy way to clean off the burned remnants of last weekend's meal from a barbecue grill is to use a bottle opener and a metal file. File a notch 3mm wide into the flat end of the opener and it will be ready to use.

Loosen plaster or remove grout The sharp end of the opener is useful for removing old grout between bathroom tiles before regrouting. It may not be the builder's best friend, but the sharp end of a bottle opener can be handy for removing loose plaster from a wall before patching it. It's great for running along cracks and you can use it to undercut a hole – that is, make it wider at the bottom than at the surface – so that the new plaster will 'key' into the old.

* Bread

Remove the scorched taste from rice When you have left rice cooking too long and it has burned, place a slice of white bread on top of the rice while it is still hot to get rid of the scorched taste. Replace the pot lid and wait several minutes. When you remove the bread, the burned taste should be gone.

DID YOU KNOW?

The old-fashioned bottle opener with one flat end and one pointed end is often referred to as a 'church key'. Although no one is exactly sure how or when this association came into being, it originated years ago in the brewery industry and was used to describe a flat opener with a hooked cutout used to lever off bottle caps – it is widely believed that the term derived from the early openers' resemblance to the heavy, ornate keys used to unlock big, old doors, such as those found on churches. Ironically, the term is now applied only to openers with both flat and pointed ends.

Soften up hard marshmallows If a bag of marshmallows has gone stale, try placing a couple of slices of fresh bread in the bag and seal it shut (you may want to transfer the marshmallows to a self-sealing plastic bag). Leave it for a couple of days. When you reopen the bag, your marshmallows should taste as good as new.

Absorb vegetable odours Do you love cabbage or broccoli, but hate the smell while it's cooking? Try putting a piece of white bread on top of the pot when cooking 'smelly' vegetables. It will absorb most of the odour.

Soak up grease and stop flare-ups One of the best ways to prevent a grease flare-up when grilling meat is to place a couple of slices of white bread in the drip pan to absorb the grease. It will also cut down on the amount of smoke that is produced.

Clean walls and wallpaper Dirty fingerprints on walls are an inevitable sign of children in the house. But you can remove most dirty or greasy fingerprints from painted walls by rubbing the area with a slice of white bread. Bread does a good job cleaning non-washable wallpaper as well. First cut off the crusts to minimise the chance of scratching the paper.

Pick up glass fragments Picking up the large pieces of a broken glass or dish is usually easy enough, but gathering tiny slivers can be difficult and dangerous. The easiest way to make sure you don't miss any is to press a slice of bread over the area. Just be careful not to prick yourself when you throw the bread into the bin.

Dust oil paintings You shouldn't try this with an original Renoir, or with any museum-quality painting, but you can clean off the everyday dust and grime that collects on the surface of an oil painting by gently rubbing the surface with a piece of white bread.

Bubble wrap

Prevent condensation in the toilet cistern If a toilet cistern 'sweats' in warm, humid weather, bubble wrap can help to prevent it. Lining the inside of the cistern with bubble wrap will keep the outside from getting cold and causing condensation when it comes in contact with warm, moist air. To line the cistern, shut off the water supply and flush to drain the cistern. Then wipe the inside walls clean and dry. Use silicone sealant to glue appropriate-sized pieces of bubble wrap to the major flat surfaces.

Protect patio plants Keep outdoor container plants warm and protected from winter frost damage. Wrap each container with bubble wrap and use gaffer tape or string to hold the wrap in place. Make sure the wrap extends a couple of inches above the lip of the container. The added insulation will keep the soil warm all winter.

DID YOU KNOW?

Inventors Alfred Fielding and Marc Chavannes initially came up with the idea of making a 'bubble wallpaper' when they began developing their product in the late 1950s. They soon realised that their invention had far greater potential as packaging material and in 1960 they raised $85,000 (£50,000) and founded the Sealed Air Corporation.

Today Sealed Air is a top US company with $3.5 billion (£2 billion) in annual revenues. The company produces bubble wrap cushioning in a multitude of sizes, colours and properties, along with other protective packaging materials such as padded Jiffy bags

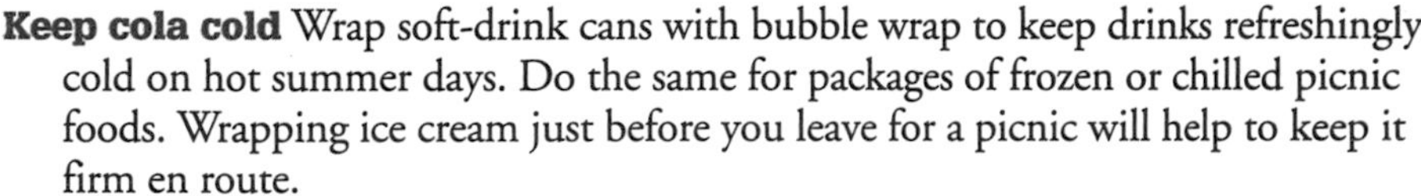

Keep cola cold Wrap soft-drink cans with bubble wrap to keep drinks refreshingly cold on hot summer days. Do the same for packages of frozen or chilled picnic foods. Wrapping ice cream just before you leave for a picnic will help to keep it firm en route.

Protect produce in the fridge Line the crisper drawer with bubble wrap to prevent bruises to fruit and other produce. Cleaning the fridge will be easier, too – when the lining gets dirty, just throw it away and replace it with fresh bubble wrap.

Add insulation to windows Cut window-sized pieces of wide bubble wrap and gaffer tape them to the inside of the windows for added warmth and savings on fuel bills in winter. Lower the blinds or draw curtains to make it less noticeable.

Make a bedtime buffer in winter Keep cold air from creeping into your bed on a chilly night by placing a large sheet of bubble wrap between the bedspread or duvet and the top sheet. You'll be surprised at how effective it is in keeping warm air in and cold air out.

Cushion a work surface When repairing delicate glass or china, cover the work surface with bubble wrap to help to prevent breakages.

Cushion a toolbox Reduce wear and tear on good-quality tools and extend their lives by lining your toolbox with bubble wrap. Use gaffer tape to hold it in place.

Sleep on air while camping Get a better night's sleep on a camping trip. Take a 2m roll of wide bubble wrap to use as a mat under a sleeping bag. If you don't have a sleeping bag, just fold a 3.6-metre-long piece of wide bubble wrap in half, bubble side out and gaffer-tape the edges. Then slip in and enjoy a restful night in your makeshift padded sleeping bag.

Buckets

Make a lobster pot If you don't have a large stock pot you can cook lobsters in an old metal bucket. Make sure to use pot holders and tongs when cooking and removing the lobster. Let the bucket cool before handling it again.

Create a food-storage bin A large, tightly sealed bucket is an ideal waterproof (and animal-proof) food-storage bin to bring along on a riverboat, canoeing or sailing holiday.

Build a camp washing machine Here's a clever way to wash clothes when camping. Make a hole in the lid of a large plastic bucket and insert a new toilet plunger. Put in clothes and laundry detergent. Snap on the lid and move the plunger up and down as an agitator. You can safely clean even delicate garments using this method.

Camp shower A bucket perforated with holes on the bottom makes an excellent campsite shower. Hang it securely from a sturdy branch, fill it using another bucket or jug and then take a quick shower as the water comes out. If you want to shower in warm water, paint the outside of another bucket matt black. Fill it with water and leave it out in the sun all day.

Paint high Avoid messy paint spills when painting on a scaffold tower or ladder. Put your paint can and brush into a large bucket and use hooks to hang the bucket and the brush. If the bucket is large enough, you'll even have room for your paint scraper, putty knife, rags, or other painting tools you may need.

Paint low Use the lids from big plastic buckets as trays for 4 litre cans of paint. The lids act as platforms for the paint cans and are also large enough to hold a paintbrush as well.

Make stilts Make working on a ceiling less of a stretch. Use two heavy-duty buckets (minus their handles) and a pair of old shoes to make your own mini-stilts. Drive screws through the shoe soles and into wood blocks inside the buckets to keep them rigid. Or punch holes in the bucket bottoms and tie or strap down the shoes.

TIP* FINDING BIG BUCKETS

Ten to twenty litre plastic buckets are versatile, virtually indestructible and offer a host of handy uses. And you can usually get them for free. Ask nicely and your local fast-food restaurant or supermarket deli counter may be willing to give you the buckets that beans or coleslaw came in. Or check with neighbours doing home improvements. Don't forget to get the lids as well. Wash a bucket with water and household bleach, then let it dry in the sun for a day or two. Put some scented cat litter, charcoal, or a couple of drops of vanilla inside and it should remove any lingering odours.

{ KIDS' STUFF }

MAKING TOM TOMS

Add the beat of bucket tom-toms to make improvised music at a children's party. Cut plastic buckets to different lengths to create a distinct tone for each drum or use a mix of various-sized plastic and galvanised buckets. For more musical accompaniment, make a broom-handle string bass using a bucket as the sound box.

Keep extension cords tangle-free A bucket can help you keep a long extension cord free of tangles. Cut or drill a hole near the bottom of the bucket, making sure it is large enough for the cord's plug end to pass through. Then coil the rest of the cord into the bucket. The cord will come out when pulled and is easy to coil back in. Plug the ends of the cord together when it's not in use. You can use the centre space to carry tools to the site where you're working.

Garden in a bucket Use a large plastic bucket as a mini garden or planter. Use another as a composter for scraps and cuttings. Bucket gardens are just the right size for balconies and roof gardens.

Make a Christmas tree stand Partly fill a bucket with sand or gravel and insert the base of the tree in it. Then fill it the rest of the way and pour water on the sand or gravel to help to keep the tree from drying out.

Butter

Keep mould off cheese Why waste good cheese by letting the cut edges get hard or mouldy? Give semi-hard cheeses a light coat of butter to keep them fresh and free from mould. Each time you use the cheese, coat the cut edge with butter before you rewrap it and put it back in the fridge.

Make cat feel at home Is the family feline freaked out by your move to a new home? Moving is often traumatic for pets as well as family members. Here's a good way to help an adult cat adjust to its new home. Spread a little butter on the top of one of its front paws. Most cats love the taste of butter so much they'll keep coming back for more.

Get rid of a fishy smell Do you have fishy smelling hands following a fishing trip or fish preparation? Rub some butter on your hands, wash with warm water and soap and your hands will smell clean and fresh again.

Swallow pills with ease If you have difficulty getting pills to go down, try rolling them in a small amount of butter or margarine first. The pills should slide down your throat far more easily.

Soothe aching feet To soothe tired feet, massage them with butter, wrap in a damp, hot towel and sit for 10 minutes. Your feet will feel revitalised.

Remove sap from skin If you've just come home from a pleasant walk in the woods, but your hands are still covered with sticky tree sap that feels like it will never come off, don't worry. Just rub butter onto your hands and the black sap will wash straight off with soap and water.

Keep a left-over onion fresh If recipe calls for half an onion and you want to keep the remaining half fresh as long as possible, rub butter on the cut surface and wrap the leftover onion in aluminum foil before putting it in the fridge. The butter will keep it fresh for longer.

Remove an ink stain on a doll's face Many a favourite doll has been given an ink-pen makeover by an over-zealous, under-aged beautician. You can undo their handy work by rubbing butter on the pen stains and leaving the doll face-up in the sun for a few days. Then wash it off with soap and water.

Cut sticky foods with ease Rub butter on knife or scissor blades before cutting sticky foods like dates, figs or marshmallows. The butter will act as a lubricant and keep the food from sticking to the blades.

Emergency shaving cream If you run out of shaving cream, try slathering some butter onto wet skin for a smooth, close shave.

Prevent pots from boiling over You take your eye off the pasta for two seconds and the next thing you know, the pot is boiling over onto the hob. Keep the boiling water within the pot next time by adding a tablespoon or two of butter.

Treat dry hair Has your hair become dry and brittle? Try buttering it up for a luxuriant shine. Massage a small chunk of butter into your dry hair, cover it with a shower cap for 30 minutes, then shampoo and rinse thoroughly.

{ KIDS' STUFF }

MAKING BUTTER

Making butter is fun and easy, especially when there are several children around to take turns churning. All you need is a jar, a marble and 200-400ml of thick whipping cream or double cream. Use the freshest cream possible and leave it out of the fridge until it reaches a temperature of about 15°C. Pour the cream into the jar, add the marble, close the lid and let the children take turns shaking (churning), about one shake per second. It may take anywhere from 5 to 30 minutes, but they will see the cream go through various stages from sloshy to coarse whipped cream. When the whipped cream suddenly seizes and collapses, fine-grained bits of butter will be visible in the liquid buttermilk. Before long a glob of yellowish butter will appear. Drain off the buttermilk and enjoy the delightful taste of freshly made butter.

DID YOU KNOW?

Butter is the semi-solid material that results from churning cream – a process that is depicted on a Sumerian tablet from 2500 BC. A butter-filled churn was found in a 2,000-year-old Egyptian grave and butter was plentiful in King Tutankamun's day, when it was made from the milk of water buffaloes and camels. The Bible also contains many references to butter – as the product of cow's milk. Later, the Vikings are believed to have introduced butter to Normandy, a region now world-renowned for its butter.
Pure butter should contain at least 80 per cent milk fat. The remaining 20 per cent is composed of water and milk solids. It may be salted or unsalted. Salt adds flavour and also acts as a preservative. It takes 10kg of fresh cow's milk to make 500g of butter.

Buttons

Decorate a doll's house Use buttons to make sconces, plates and wall hangings in a child's doll's house. The more variety, the better.

Beanbag filler Use small unmatched buttons the next time you make little beanbags. They will work just as well as dried beans.

Decorate a Christmas tree Give a Christmas tree an old-fashioned look. Make a garland by knotting large buttons on a sturdy length of string or dental floss.

Use as game pieces or poker chips Don't let lost pieces stop you from playing games like backgammon or Monopoly. Substitute buttons for the lost pieces and keep playing to your heart's content. For an impromptu game of poker, use buttons as chips, with each colour representing a different value.

Keep tape unstuck If you're trying to wrap a present and you can't find the end of the tape roll, stick a button on the end of the tape and as you use the tape, keep moving the button.

Make a necklace or bracelet To make a necklace, string attractive buttons on two strands of heavy-duty thread or dental floss. Make an attractive design by alternating large and small buttons of various colours. Use 3mm wide leather thonging (available from craft shops) to make a bracelet. Or make a 'cuff' bracelet, simply by sewing buttons onto wide elastic.

Candles

Unstick a drawer If a drawer is sticking, remove it and rub a candle on the runners. The drawer should open more smoothly when you slip it back into place.

Make a pincushion A short wide candle makes an ideal pincushion. The wax will help pins and needles glide more easily through fabric too.

Weatherproof address labels After addressing a package with a felt-tip pen, weatherproof the label by rubbing a white candle over the writing. Neither rain, sleet or snow will smear the label.

Make a squeaky door silent If a squeaky door is driving you to distraction, take it off its hinges and rub a candle over the hinge surfaces that touch each other. The offending door should stop squeaking instantly.

Mend the ends of shoelaces If the plastic or metal tips come off the ends of shoelaces, don't allow the laces to fray. Dip the end into melted candle wax and the lace will hold until you can buy a new pair.

Use a trick candle to ignite fires Don't let a draught blow out the flame when you're trying to light a fire or barbecue. Start the fire with a trick puff-proof birthday candle, designed to be a practical joke aid that prevents birthday celebrants from blowing out the candles on their cakes. Once the fire is up and roaring, smother the candle flame and save the trick candle for future use.

Make a secret drawing Get a child to make an 'invisible' drawing with a white candle. Then let him or her cover it with a wash of watercolour paint to reveal the picture. The image will show up because the wax laid down by the candle will keep the paper in the areas it covers from absorbing the paint. If you have a few children to entertain, they can all make secret drawings and messages to swap and reveal.

DID YOU KNOW?

Beeswax, the substance secreted by honeybees to make honeycombs, wasn't used for candles until the Middle Ages. Until then, candles were made from a rendered animal fat known as tallow that produced a smoky flame and gave off acrid odours. Beeswax candles, by contrast, burned pure and clean, with no unpleasant smell. But they were not widely used at the time, being too expensive for most ordinary people.

The growth of whaling in the late 1700s brought a major change to candlemaking as spermaceti – a wax-like substance derived from sperm-whale oil – became available in bulk. The 19th century saw the advent of mass-produced candles and low-cost paraffin wax. Made from oil and coal shale, paraffin burned cleanly with no unpleasant odour.

Cans

Keep tables together If you need more seating space for a large dinner party, you can lock card tables together by setting adjacent pairs of legs into empty cans. You won't have to clean up any spills caused by the tables moving around.

Make light reflectors It's easy to make reflectors for camping or garden lights. Just remove the bottom of a large empty can with a can opener and take off the label. Then use tin snips to cut the can in half lengthways to make two reflectors.

Make a quick floor patch Nail can lids under wooden floorboards to plug knotty holes and keep rodents out.

Tuna can egg poacher A shallow tuna can is the perfect size to use as an egg poacher. Remove the top and bottom of the can as well as the paper label. Then place the metal ring in a frying pan of simmering water and crack an egg into it.

Feed the birds A bird doesn't care if the feeder is plain or fancy as long as it is filled with seeds. For a basic bird feeder, wedge a small can filled with seeds between a couple of tree branches or posts.

TIP* GLUING METALS

When gluing cans and other metal pieces together, use a glue that adheres well to metal, such as polyvinyl chloride (PVC), liquid solder or epoxy. If the joint won't be subject to stress, you can use a hot-glue gun. Make sure to wash and dry the cans and to remove any labels first. Also let any paint dry thoroughly before gluing.

Make a tool carrier Are you fed up with fumbling around in your tool belt to find the tool you need? Use small empty fruit juice cans to transform the deep, wide pockets of a nail pouch into a convenient holder for wrenches, pliers and screwdrivers. Make sure to remove the bottom of each can as well as the top. Glue or tape the cylinders together to keep them from shifting around and slip them into the pouches to create dividers.

Make a pedestal Fill several wide identically-sized cans with rocks or sand and glue them together, one on top of the other. Screw a piece of wood into the bottom of the top can before attaching it, upside down, to the others. Paint the pedestal and place a potted plant, lamp, or statue on top. See the Tip above for suggestions on the type of glue to use for this project.

Make pigeonholes Assemble half a dozen or more empty cans and paint them with brightly coloured enamel. After they are dry, glue the cans together and place them on their sides on a shelf. They can be used to store silverware, nails, office supplies or other odds and ends.

Store scissors safely Use a punch-type can opener to pierce evenly spaced holes around the bottom of a large, clean can. Place the inverted can on a workbench or work table and slip the points of the scissors into the holes. This is also a good way to store screwdrivers.

DID YOU KNOW?

Cans are often described as 'hermetically sealed'. The word hermetic comes from Hermes Trismegistus, a legendary alchemist who is reputed to have lived in the first three centuries AD and to have invented a magic seal to keeps vessels airtight.

The hermetically sealed can was invented in 1810 by British merchant Peter Durand. His first cans were so thick they had to be hammered open! Two years later, Englishman Thomas Kensett set up America's first cannery on the New York waterfront to can oysters, meats, fruits and vegetables. He patented the process in 1825. In 1957, the first all-aluminium can appeared.

Make a pair of child's stilts Pierce a hole in opposite sides of the bottom of two identical large, sturdy cans. Knot thin rope or nylon cord through the holes to form handles – the length of the handles will depend on the height of the child, but they need to reach up as far as their hands. The child has only to step up onto the cans and pull up the handles and he or she is ready to walk tall.

Make a miniature golf course Remove both ends from a number of cans. Then arrange them so that the ball can pass through them, go up a ramp into them or ricochet off a board through them.

Create decorative tea-light holders Fill clean, empty cans of different sizes with water and freeze. Use a hammer and a large nail or an electric drill to pierce a pattern of holes in the sides of the cans, defrost the ice and insert small candles or tea lights.

Organise your desk If your desk is a mess, a few empty cans can be the start of a neat solution. Attach several tin cans of assorted sizes together in a group to make an office-supplies holder for your desk. Start by cleaning and drying the cans and removing any labels. Then spray paint them (or wrap them in felt). When the paint is dry, glue them together using a hot-glue gun. Your desk organiser is now ready to hold pens, pencils, paper clips, scissors and anything else you may need.

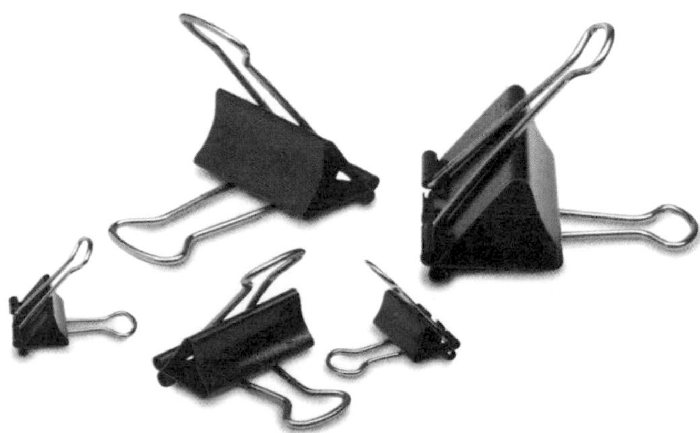

Make a fairground game Arrange a series (four or five) of same-sized cans in a row and tape them together using gaffer tape. Then add another two or three rows and tape them all together. You can either place the 'rack' vertically against the wall or on the floor. Gather some ping pong balls or other small balls, or some tiny bean bags. Each 'player' has three balls or bags per go. A point is scored for each ball or bag that stays in the can.

Make a home ten-pin bowling set Tape two clean, empty 400g cans together to make a skittle. You'll need ten skittles to make up a full set. Set up the skittles at the end of a hallway or a long straight path or on the lawn. Use a tennis ball or, if you are using the lawn, a more traditional bowling ball and see how many skittles you can hit at one go.

Super item
22 USES!

CARDBOARD BOXES...

...around the house

Make a bed tray Have breakfast in bed on a tray made from a cardboard box. Just remove the top flaps and cut arches from the two long sides to fit over your lap. Decorate the bottom of the box – which is now the top of your tray – with a wipeable adhesive plastic or some oilcloth.

Create gift-wrap suspense Take a cue from the Russian tradition of nesting matryoshka dolls. Next time you are giving a small special gift to a friend, or better still a child, place the gift-wrapped little box inside a series of increasingly larger brightly wrapped boxes.

Shield doors and furniture Use cardboard shields to protect doors and furniture from stains when you polish doorknobs and furniture handles. Cut out an appropriately-sized shield and slide it over the items you are going to polish. This works best when you make shields that slip over the neck of knobs or knoblike handles. But you can also make shields for hinges and U-shaped handles.

DID YOU KNOW?

Cardboard was first invented by the Chinese in the early 1500s. In 1871 a New Yorker named Albert Jones patented the idea of gluing a piece of corrugated paper between two pieces of flat cardboard to create a material rigid enough to use for shipping. But it wasn't until 1890 that another American, Robert Gair, invented the corrugated cardboard box. His boxes were pre-cut flat pieces manufactured in bulk that could be folded into cartons, exactly like the cardboard boxes that we use today.

Make dustcovers Keep dust and dirt out of a small electrical appliance, power tool or keyboard by cutting the flaps off a cardboard box that fits over the item. Then decorate it or cover it with self-adhesive decorative paper and use it as a dustcover.

Make an office in-box Make an in-box or out-box for your desk. Simply cut the top and one large panel off a cereal box, then slice the narrow sides at an angle. Cover with self-adhesive decorative paper.

Make place mats Cut several 30 x 45cm pieces of cardboard – or they can be round or oval if you like – and cover them with colourful adhesive shelf paper. Or use another decorative paper and seal it with clear plastic.

...for storing things

Protect glassware or lightbulbs A good way to safely store crystal glassware is to put it in an empty wine or spirits carton with partitions. You can also use it for storing lightbulbs, but make sure you sort the bulbs by wattage so that it is easy to find the right one when you need a replacement.

Make a magazine holder Store a collection of magazines in holders made from empty detergent boxes. Remove the top, then cut the box at an angle, from the top of one side to the bottom third of the other. Cover the holders with self-adhesive decorative paper, colourful wrapping paper or wallpaper.

Poster and artwork holder A clean wine carton with its dividers intact is a great place to store rolled-up posters, drawings on paper and unmounted canvases. Just insert the items upright between the partitions.

Store Christmas ornaments When you take down a Christmas tree, wrap each ornament in newspaper or tissue paper and store it in an empty wine box with partitions. Each of the carton's segments will be able to hold several of the wrapped Christmas tree ornaments.

CARDBOARD BOXES...

...for the kids

Create an impromptu sled Use a large, flat cardboard box to pull a small child over the snow or let them slide down grassy embankments.

Organise children's sporting gear Keep a decorated empty wine or spirits carton with partitions, and with the top cut off, in your child's room and use it for easy storage of tennis rackets, cricket bats, fishing rods and other similar items.

Make a play castle Turn a large cardboard box from a new washing machine or similar appliance into a medieval castle. Cut off the top flaps and make battlements by cutting notches along the top. To make a notch, use a craft knife to make a cut on either side of the section you want to remove, then fold the cut section forward and cut along the fold. To make a drawbridge, cut a large fold-down opening on one side that is attached at the bottom. Connect the top of the drawbridge to the side walls with ropes on either side, punching holes for the rope and knotting the rope on the other side. Use gaffer tape or electrical tape to reinforce the holes. Finally, cut out narrow window slits in the walls. Let the children draw or paint stones and bricks on the sides to make castle 'walls'.

Garage for toy vehicles Turn an empty large appliance box on its side and let the children use it as a 'garage' for their larger wheeled vehicles. They can also use a smaller box as a garage for miniature cars, trucks and buses.

{ SCIENCE FAIR }

FOLLOW THE SUN

Making a simple cardboard sundial is a great way for children to observe how the sun's path changes every day. Take a 25 x 25cm piece of cardboard and push a stick through the middle. If necessary, screw or nail a small board to the bottom of the stick to hold it upright. Place the sundial in a sunny spot. Every hour, get the children to mark where the shadow from the stick falls on the cardboard. Check again the next day and the sundial will still seem quite accurate. Check a week later, though and the shadows won't align to the marks at the right times. When curious children start wondering what has happened, give them a hint – the Earth is tilted on its axis.

...for the DIY-er

Protect your fingers Ouch! You've just hammered your finger instead of the tiny nail you were trying to drive into a piece of wood. To stop this from happening again, stick the little nail through a small piece of thin cardboard before you do your hammering. Hold the cardboard by an edge, position the nail, and hammer it home. When you have finished, you can use your bruise-free fingers to tear away the cardboard.

Repair a roof To make temporary repair to a leaky roof, put a piece of cardboard into a plastic bag and slide it under the tiles.

Organise your workshop A sectioned wine or spirits carton is a good place to store dowels, mouldings, battens and metal rods.

Store tall garden tools Turn three empty wine cartons into a sectioned storage bin for long-handled garden tools. Put a topless box on the floor with the dividers left in. Then cut the tops and bottoms off two similar boxes and stack them on top of each other so that the dividers match up. Use gaffer tape to attach the boxes to each other. Use the bin to store hoes, rakes and other long-handled garden tools.

Protect work surfaces Keep work surfaces from being damaged when you are doing DIY or craft projects. Flatten a large box or cut a large flat piece from a box and use it to protect a kitchen worktop, workbench, table or desk from ink, paint, glue or nicks from knives and scissors. Replace it when it becomes too roughened or damaged to use.

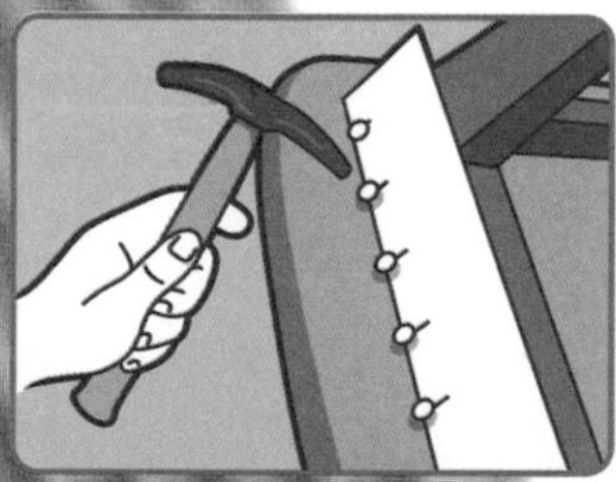

Keep upholstery tacks straight If you are upholstering a chair or sofa, this is a clever way to get a row of upholstery tacks perfectly straight and evenly spaced. Mark the spacing along the edge of a lightweight cardboard strip and press the tacks into it. After tapping all of the tacks most of the way in, tug on the strip to pull the edge free before driving them in the rest of the way.

Make a drip pan Prevent an oil leak from soiling the garage floor or driveway. Make a drip pan by placing a few sheets of corrugated cardboard on a baking sheet and placing the pan under the spot which is dripping. For better absorption, sprinkle some cat litter, sawdust or oatmeal into the pan on top of the cardboard. Replace with fresh cardboard as needed.

Help your mechanic If something is dripping from your car's engine, but you don't know what it is, place a large piece of cardboard under the engine overnight and bring it with you when you take the car in for service. The colour and location of the leaked fluid will help the mechanic to identify the problem.

 Cardboard tubes

Extend the reach of a vacuum cleaner If you can't reach a cobweb on the ceiling with an ordinary vacuum cleaner attachment, try using a long, empty wrapping paper tube to extend the reach. You can even crush the end of the paper tube to create a crevice tool. Use gaffer tape to make the connection airtight.

Make a sheath Flatten a paper towel tube and gaffer tape one end shut to make a perfect sheath for a picnic/camping knife. Use toilet paper rolls for smaller cutlery.

Keep electrical cords tangle-free Keep computer and appliance cords tangle-free. Neatly fold the cord and pass it through a toilet paper tube before plugging in. You can also use the tubes to store extension cords when they're not in use. Paper towel tubes will also work. Just cut them in half before using them to hold the cords.

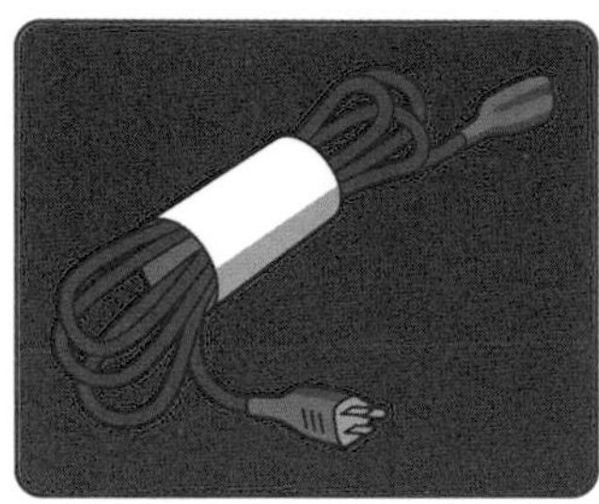

Make a fly and pest strip Get rid of flies and mosquitoes with a homemade pest strip. Just cover an empty paper towel or toilet paper roll with transparent tape, sticky side out and hang up where it's needed.

Use as kindling and logs Turn toilet paper tubes and paper towel tubes into kindling and logs for the fireplace. To make a fire starter, use scissors to cut the cardboard into 3mm strips. Keep the strips in a bin near the fireplace so they'll be close to hand next time you want to start a fire. To make logs, tape over one end of the tube with paper packing tape and pack shredded newspaper inside. Then tape the other end. The tighter you pack the newspaper, the longer your log will burn.

Make boot trees To keep the tops of long, flexible boots from flopping over and developing creases when they are stored at the bottom of the wardrobe, insert cardboard poster tubes into them to help them to hold their shape.

DID YOU KNOW?

It took nearly 500 years for toilet paper to make the transition from sheets to rolls. Toilet paper was first produced in China in 1391 for the exclusive use of the emperor, in sheets that measured a massive 60 x 90cm each. Toilet paper in rolls was first made in the USA in 1890 by the Scott Paper Company. Scott began making paper towels in 1907, thanks to a failed attempt to develop a new crepe toilet tissue. This paper was so thick it couldn't be cut and rolled into toilet paper, so Scott made larger rolls, perforated into 33 x 45cm sheets and sold them under the brand name, Sani-Towels.

Make a plant guard It's easy to accidentally scar the trunk of a young tree when you are chopping weeds around it. To avoid doing this, cut a large cardboard posting tube in half lengthways using a sharp craft knife and tie the two halves around the trunk while you work near the tree. Then slip it off and use it on another tree.

Protect important documents Before storing diplomas, marriage certificates and other important documents, roll them tightly and insert them in paper towel tubes. This prevents creases and keeps the documents clean and dry. With precious or ancient documents you may want to wrap them in a layer of acid-free tissue before placing them in the tube.

Start seedlings Don't go to a garden centre to buy biodegradable starting pots for seedlings. Just use the cardboard tubes from paper towels and toilet paper. Use scissors to cut each toilet paper tube into two pots, or each paper towel tube into four. Fill a tray with the cut cylinders packed against each other so they won't tip when you water the seedlings. This will also prevent them from drying out too quickly. Now fill each pot with seed compost, gently pack it down and sow your seeds. When you plant the seedlings, make sure to break down the side of the roll and make sure all the cardboard is completely buried.

Keep Christmas lights tidy Do you spend more time untangling Christmas lights than it takes to put them up? Make life easier by wrapping the lights around a cardboard tube. Secure them with masking tape. Put small strands of lights or garlands inside cardboard tubes, and seal the ends of the tubes with masking tape.

Store knitting needles To keep knitting needles from bending and breaking, use a long cardboard tube from a pack of kitchen foil or cling film. Cover one end with sticky tape. Pinch the other end closed and secure it tightly with tape. Slide the needles in through the tape on the taped end. The tape will hold them in place for secure, organised storage.

Store fabric scraps Roll up leftover fabric scraps tightly and insert them inside a toilet or kitchen paper tube. For easy identification, tape or staple a sample of the fabric to the outside of the tube.

Store string Nothing is more useless and frustrating than tangled string. To keep string ready to use, cut a notch into each end of a toilet paper tube. Secure one end of the string in one notch, wrap the string tightly around the tube, and then secure the other end in the other notch.

Keep linens crease-free Wrap tablecloths and napkins around cardboard tubes after laundering to avoid the creases that would occur if they were folded. Use long tubes for tablecloths and paper towel or toilet paper tubes for napkins. To prevent any staining on the fabric, cover the tubes with cling film first.

TIP* FINDING BIG CARDBOARD TUBES

Many carpet shops discard long, thick cardboard tubes. If you ask, they will probably be happy to provide you for free. Because the tubes are very solid and can be as much as 3.6m long, you may want to ask for them to cut one to the size you want before you take it away.

Keep trousers crease-free You go to the wardrobe for a pair of trousers that you haven't worn for a while, only to find a deep crease at the fold site from the hanger rack. To stop this happening again, cut a paper towel tube lengthways, fold it in half horizontally and place it over the rack before you hang up your trousers. Before hanging the trousers, tape the sides of the cardboard together at the bottom to keep it from slipping.

Make a hamster toy Place a couple of paper towel or toilet paper tubes in the hamster (or gerbil or mouse) cage. Your little friends will love running and walking through them and they enjoy chewing on the cardboard too. When the tubes start looking ragged, just replace them with fresh ones.

Protect fluorescent lights Keep fluorescent light tubes from breaking before they are used. They will fit neatly into long, slim cardboard tubes that have been sealed with tape at one end.

Make a kazoo Cut three small holes in the middle of a paper towel tube. Then cover one end of the tube with greaseproof paper secured with a strong rubber band. Hum into the other end, while using your fingers to plug one, two or all three holes to vary the pitch.

Instant megaphone Don't shout yourself hoarse when you're calling outside for a child or pet to come in. Give your vocal chords a rest by using a wide cardboard tube as a megaphone to amplify your voice.

Preserve childrens' artwork If you want to save some of your children's precious artwork for posterity (or you don't want it to clutter up the house), simply roll up the artwork and place it inside a paper towel tube. Label the outside with the child's name and date. The tubes are easy to store, and you can safely preserve the work of budding young artists. Use this method to hold and store documents, such as certificates and licences, too.

Build a toy log cabin Notch the ends of several long tubes with a craft knife and then help your children to build log cabins, fences or huts with them. Use different-sized tubes for added versatility. For a bit of realism, have the kids paint or colour the tubes before construction begins.

Make 'exploding' crackers Use toilet paper tubes to make crackers, which 'explode' into tiny gifts. For each cracker, tie a string about 20cm long around a small gift such as a sweet, balloon or a tiny toy or figurine. After tying, there should be about 15cm of string to spare. Place the gift into the tube so the string dangles out one end. Cover the tube with bright-coloured crepe paper or tissue and twist the ends. When you pull the string, the gift will pop out.

Carpet remnants

Muffle noisy appliances Does the washing machine or spin dryer shake and rattle when you're doing a load? Put a carpet offcut underneath it and with any luck it will be all you need to stop the machine from rattling.

Catch a falling sock You may never be able to stop socks and other articles of clothing from falling to the floor en route from the washing machine to the drier. But if the appliances are side by side, you can make retrieval a lot easier by placing a narrow piece of carpet on the floor between them. If something falls, pull out the carpet strip and the article will come with it.

Keep garden paths weed-free Place a series of carpet offcuts upside down and cover them with bark mulch or straw for a weed-free garden path. Use smaller scraps as mulch around your vegetable garden.

Exercise in comfort To make an instant exercise mat, cut a length of old carpet about a metre wide and as long as your height. When you're not using it for yoga or sit-ups, roll it up and store it under the bed.

Make your own car mats Why buy expensive car mats when you can make your own? Just cut carpet remnants to fit the floor of your car.

Protect your knees To protect knees when you're washing the floor, weeding or doing other work on all fours, make some kneepads. Cut two pieces of carpeting 25cm square and then cut two parallel slits or holes in each. Run an old tie, scarf or strip of fabric through the slits and use them to tie the pads to your knees.

Keep floors dry Don't let the floor get soaked when you water indoor plants. Place 30cm circles of carpet under houseplants to absorb any excess water.

Prevent scratched floors Stop chairs and tables from scratching or making black marks on wood or vinyl floors. Glue small circles of carpet remnants to the bottom of all chair and table legs.

Make a buffer Use epoxy resin to glue an old piece of carpet to a block of wood to make a buffer. Make several and use one to buff shoes, another to wipe blackboards and one to clean window screens.

Cushion kitchen shelves Reduce noisy clattering when putting away pots and pans by cushioning kitchen shelves and cabinets with small, clean pieces of carpet.

Add traction Keep a few good-sized carpet remnants in the boot of the car to add traction if you're stuck in snow or ice. Keep one piece with your spare tyre so that you won't have to kneel or lie on the dirty ground when you have to look under the car or change a flat tyre.

Protect workshop tools Is there a concrete or hard stone floor in your workshop or garage? If so, put down a few carpet remnants in the area closest to the workbench so that tools or containers that fall to the floor will be far less likely to break.

Keep Fido's home dry Don't let the raindrops keep falling on your dog's head. Weatherproof a kennel or doghouse by making a rain flap by nailing a carpet remnant over the entrance to your dog's shelter. In colder areas, you can also use small pieces of carpet to line interior walls and the floor to add insulation.

Make a scratching post If the cat is clawing the living room sofa, this may help to distract it. Make a scratching post by stapling carpet scraps to a post or board and place it near the cat's favourite target. If you want it to be freestanding, nail a board to the bottom of the post to serve as a base.

Car wax

Stop CDs from skipping tracks Don't throw away a scratched compact disc. Try fixing it first with a small dab of car wax. Spread a cloth on a flat surface and place the CD on top of it, damaged side up. Then, holding the disc with one hand, use the other to wipe the polish into the affected area with a soft cloth. Wait for it to dry and buff using short, brisk strokes along the scratch, not across it. A cloth sold to wipe spectacles or camera lenses will work well. When you can no longer see the scratch, wash the disc with water and let it dry before playing again.

Keep bathroom mirrors fog-free Prevent a bathroom mirror from steaming up after taking a hot shower or bath. Apply a small amount of car wax to the mirror, let it dry and buff with a soft cloth. Next time you step out of the shower, you should be able to see your face in the mirror immediately. Rub the wax on other bathroom fixtures to prevent water spots.

Eliminate bathroom mildew To get rid of grime and mildew in a shower, first clean the soap and water residue off the tiles or shower wall. Then rub on a layer of car wax and buff with a clean, dry cloth. You'll only need to reapply the wax about once a year. Don't wax the bathtub as it will become dangerously slippery.

Eradicate furniture stains If an ugly white ring is disfiguring a wooden table and ordinary furniture polish doesn't work, try using a dab of car wax. Trace the ring with your finger to apply the wax. Let it dry and buff with a soft cloth.

Keep snow from sticking When it's time to clear a driveway after heavy snow, apply two thick coats of car wax to the work surface of the shovel before you begin shovelling. The snow won't stick to the shovel and the job will be far easier.

Castor oil

Soften cuticles If you were ever forced to swallow castor oil as a child, it may come as a pleasant surprise that the high vitamin-E content of that awful-tasting thick oil can work wonders on brittle nails and ragged cuticles. And you don't have to swallow the stuff to get the benefits. Just massage a small amount on your cuticles and nails each day and within three months you will have supple cuticles and healthy nails

DID YOU KNOW?

Castor oil is more than an old-fashioned medicine cabinet staple. It has hundreds of industrial uses. Large quantities are used in paints, varnishes, lipstick, hair tonic and shampoo. Castor oil is also converted into plastics, soap, waxes, hydraulic fluids and ink. And it is made into lubricants for jet engines and racing cars because it does not become stiff with cold or unduly thin with heat.

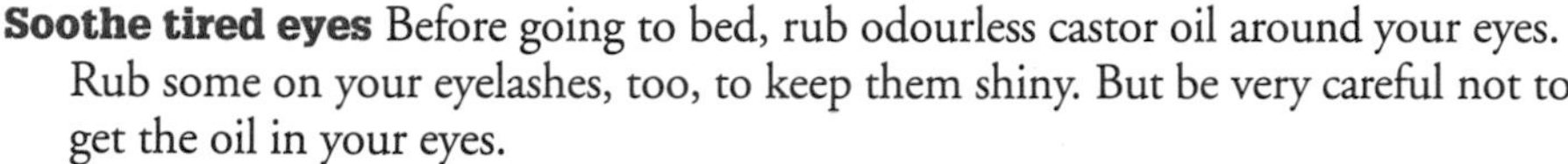

Soothe tired eyes Before going to bed, rub odourless castor oil around your eyes. Rub some on your eyelashes, too, to keep them shiny. But be very careful not to get the oil in your eyes.

Lubricate kitchen scissors Use castor oil to lubricate kitchen scissors and other utensils that touch food.

Repel moles If moles are destroying your lawn, try using castor oil to deter them. Mix 100ml castor oil and 8 litres water and drench the molehill with it. It won't kill or hurt them, but they may start looking for another garden to dig up.

Enjoy a massage Castor oil is just the right consistency to use as a soothing massage oil. For a real treat, warm the oil on the hob or on half-power in the microwave.

Perk up ailing ferns Give sickly indoor ferns a tonic made by mixing 1 tablespoon castor oil and 1 tablespoon baby shampoo with a litre of lukewarm water. Give the fern about 3 tablespoons of the tonic, then follow with plain water. Your plants should be perky by the time your supply of tonic is finished.

Condition your hair For a natural conditioning treatment, mix 2 teaspoons castor oil with 1 teaspoon glycerine and one egg white. Massage it into wet hair, leave for several minutes and wash out.

Cat litter

Make a mud mask Mix two handfuls of fresh cat litter with enough warm water to make a thick paste. Smear the paste over your face, let it set for 20 minutes, and rinse clean with water. The clay in cat litter detoxifies your skin by absorbing dirt and oil from the pores. When your friends compliment you on your complexion and ask how you did it, just tell them it's your little secret.

Trainer deodoriser If your trainers reek, fill a couple of old cotton or wool socks with scented cat litter, tie them shut and place them in the shoes overnight.

Add traction on ice Keep a bag of cat litter in the boot of the car. You can use it to add traction if you're stuck in ice or snow.

Prevent grease fires Don't let a fire spoil a barbecue: pour a layer of cat litter into the bottom of the grill for trouble-free outdoor cooking.

DID YOU KNOW?

American salesman, Ed Lowe might not have had the idea for cat litter if a neighbour hadn't asked him for some sand for her cat litter tray one day in 1947. Ed, who worked for his father's company selling industrial absorbents, suggested clay instead because it was more absorbent and would not leave tracks around the house. When she returned for more, he knew he had a winning idea. Soon he was crisscrossing the US, selling bags of his new Kitty Litter from the back of his Chevy Coupe. By 1990 Edward Lowe Industries, Inc., was the nation's largest producer of cat litter with annual retail sales of more than $210 million (£125 million).

Stop musty odours Get rid of musty smells in a wardrobe or little-used room by placing a shallow box filled with cat litter in each musty cupboard or room. Cat litter works well as a deodorant because it's so effective at absorbing odours.

Preserve flowers The fragrance and beauty of freshly cut flowers is so fleeting. You can't save the smell, but you can preserve their beauty by drying your flowers on a bed of cat litter in an airtight container for 7-10 days.

Remove a foul stench from bins Rubbish bins don't have to smell disgusting. Sprinkle some cat litter into the bottom of each bin to keep it smelling fresh. Change the litter after a week or so or if it becomes damp. If you have a baby in the house, use cat litter the same way to freshen nappy buckets.

Keep tents must-free Keep tents and sleeping bags fresh smelling and free of must when the are not in use. Pour some cat litter into an old sock, tie the end and store inside the bag or tent.

Repel moles Moles may hate the smell of soiled cat litter even more than you do. Pour some down their tunnels and it will send them scurrying to find new homes.

Make grease spots disappear Get rid of dirty grease and oil spots on a driveway or garage floor. Simply cover them with cat litter. If the spots are fresh, the litter will soak up most of the oil right away. To remove old stains, pour a little paint thinner on the stain before putting the cat litter on top. Wait for 12 hours and then sweep the floor or drive clean.

Freshen old books Rejuvenate musty old books by sealing them overnight in a container filled with clean cat litter.

Chalk

Repel ants The easiest way to keep ants at bay is by drawing a chalk line around their home entry points. The ants will be repelled by the calcium carbonate in the chalk, which is actually made up of the ground-up and compressed shells of marine animals. You can also scatter powdered chalk in the garden to repel snails and slugs.

Polish metal and marble To make metal shine like new, put some chalk dust on a damp cloth and wipe. (Make chalk dust by using a pestle and mortar to pulverise pieces of chalk.) Buff with a soft cloth for an even shinier finish. Wipe clean marble with a damp soft cloth dipped in powdered chalk. Rinse with clear water and dry thoroughly.

Keep silver from tarnishing If you enjoy setting a dinner party table using silver tableware, but hate polishing it before each use, put one or two pieces of chalk in the drawer. It will absorb moisture and slow tarnishing. Put some in your jewellery box to delay tarnishing there too.

Remove grease spots Rub a piece of chalk on a grease spot on clothing or table linens and let it absorb the oil before you brush it off. If the stain lingers, rub chalk into it again before laundering. Get rid of dirty collar stains too. Mark the stains heavily with chalk before laundering. The chalk will absorb the oils that are holding the stain in.

Reduce dampness in the wardrobe Tie a dozen pieces of chalk together and hang them up in the damp wardrobe. The chalk will absorb moisture and help to prevent mildew. Replace with a fresh bundle every few months.

Stop a slipping screwdriver Rub some chalk on the tip of the screwdriver blade before using and it won't slip nearly as much.

DID YOU KNOW?

In 16th-century Italy, artists began using chalk to make temporary drawings on the pavement. They often made paintings of the Virgin Mary (or Madonna in Italian) and thus they became known as madonnari. The madonnari of old were itinerant artists known for a life of freedom and travel. But they always managed to attend the many regional holidays and festivals that took place in each Italian province. The madonnari and their street paintings continue to be a colourful part of the street scene in modern Italy.

Hide ceiling marks Temporarily cover up water or stain marks on the ceiling until you have time to paint or make a permanent repair. Rub a stick of white chalk over the mark until it lightens or disappears.

Keep tools rust-free Eliminate moisture and prevent rust from invading a toolbox by placing a few pieces of chalk in the box. The tools and box will stay rust-free.

Charcoal briquettes

Keep books mould-free Professional librarians use charcoal to get rid of musty odours on old books. You can do the same. If the bookcase has glass doors, it may provide a damp environment that can harbour must and mould. A piece of charcoal or two placed inside will help to keep the books dry and mould-free.

Make a dehumidifier A humid wardrobe, attic or cellar can wreak havoc on your health as well as your clothes. Get rid of the humidity with several homemade dehumidifiers. Put some charcoal briquettes in a coffee can, punch a few holes in the lid and place in the humid areas. Replace the charcoal every few months.

Keep plant rooting water fresh Put a piece of charcoal in the water when you're rooting plant cuttings. The charcoal will keep the water fresh.

Banish bathroom moisture and odours Hiding a few pieces of charcoal in the nooks and crannies of your bathroom is a great way to soak up moisture and cut down on unpleasant odours. Replace them every couple of months.

DID YOU KNOW?

Strangely enough, the first mass-produced charcoal briquettes were manufactured by the Ford Motor Company. They were made from waste wood that came from a Ford-owned sawmill in Kingsford, Michigan, USA which had been built to provide wood for the bodies of Ford's popular 'Woody' station wagons. The charcoal was manufactured into briquettes and sold as Ford Charcoal Briquettes. Henry Ford II closed the sawmill in 1951 and sold the plant to a group of local businessmen, who formed the Kingsford Chemical Company. The company continues to make the charcoal briquettes that are now a household name, despite relocating to Louisville, Kentucky, in 1961.

Cheesecloth

Make a homemade fishing net Sew cheesecloth into a bag and glue or staple it to a hoop formed from a wire coat hanger and let your children use it as a little net for when they are exploring the river edge, ponds and rockpools.

Make a mini-mummy For an inexpensive Halloween costume, wrap a child in cheesecloth from head to toe and send him out with the ghosts and witches.

Convert a colander into a strainer If you can't find a strainer when you need one, a colander lined with cheesecloth will work just as well.

Cut vacuuming time Here is a simple, time-saving way to vacuum the contents of a drawer filled with small objects without having to remove the contents. Cover the nozzle of the vacuum cleaner with cheesecloth, secured with a strong rubber band, and the vacuum will pick up only the dust.

Reduce waste when drying herbs When drying fresh herbs, wrap them in cheesecloth to prevent seeds and smaller crumbly pieces from falling through.

Picnic food tent Keep insects and dirt away from picnic food by wrapping a piece of cheesecloth around an old wire umbrella frame and placing it over the plates. Use a hacksaw to remove the umbrella handle and tack the cheesecloth to the umbrella ribs with a needle and thread.

Make instant festive curtains Brighten a room for a celebration with inexpensive, colourful cheesecloth curtains. Dye cheesecloth (available in bulk from fabric shops) in bright colours and cut it to the lengths and widths you need. Fold over the top, sides and bottom and hem. Attach clip-on curtain hooks and your new curtains will be ready to hang.

Remove turkey stuffing with ease To keep turkey stuffing from sticking to the bird's insides, pack the dressing in cheesecloth before you stuff it into the internal cavity. When the turkey is ready to serve, pull out the cheesecloth and the stuffing will slide out with it.

Chest rub

Repel ticks and other insects If you're going for a walk in the woods, smear some chest rub on your legs and trousers before you leave the house. It will keep ticks from biting and may stop you from getting Lyme disease which is spread by ticks. Annoying biting insects like gnats and mosquitoes will look elsewhere for victims if you apply chest rub to your skin before venturing into the countryside as they hate the smell.

Get rid of tough skin on your feet Coat the hard skin with chest rub and then cover your feet with an adhesive bandage overnight. Repeat the procedure as needed. Most callouses will disappear after several days.

Soothe aching feet Try applying a thick coat of chest rub and covering your feet with a pair of socks before going to bed at night. When you wake up, your sore, tired feet should be both moisturised and rejuvenated.

Stop insect-bite itch Apply a generous coat of chest rub for immediate relief from itchy insect bites. Eucalyptus and menthol in the ointment soothe the itch.

Treat toenail fungus Try applying a thick coat of chest rub to the affected nail several times a day. Many users and even some doctors swear that it works. If you don't see results after a few weeks, consult a doctor.

DID YOU KNOW?

Lunsford Richardson, the pharmacist who created Vick's VapoRub in 1905, also originated America's first 'junk mail'. Richardson was working in his brother-in-law's pharmacy when he blended menthol and other ingredients into an ointment to clear sinuses and ease congestion. He called it Richardson's Croup and Pneumonia Cure Salve, but soon realised that he needed a more catchy name to sell it successfully. He changed the name to Vick's after his brother-in-law, Joshua Vick and convinced the US Post Office to institute a new policy allowing him to send advertisements addressed only to 'Boxholder'. Sales of Vick's first surpassed a million dollars during the Spanish flu epidemic of 1918.

Chewing gum

Retrieve valuables If you've just lost an earring or other small valuable down a drain, try retrieving it with a just-chewed piece of gum stuck to the bottom of a fishing weight. Dangle the gum from a string tied to the weight, let the object stick to it and reel it in.

Fill cracks Fill a crack in a clay flowerpot or a dog bowl with piece of chewed gum.

Use as makeshift window putty Hold a loose pane of glass in place temporarily with a pad or two of freshly chewed gum.

Repair glasses If one of the lenses on a pair of glasses suddenly becomes loose, put a small piece of chewed gum in the corner of the lens to hold it in place until you can get the glasses properly repaired.

Treat flatulence and heartburn Settle stomach gases and relieve heartburn by chewing a stick of spearmint gum. The oils in the spearmint act as an anti-flatulent. Chewing stimulates the production of saliva, which neutralises stomach acid and corrects the flow of digestive juices. Spearmint also acts as a digestive aid.

Lure a crab Briefly chew a stick of gum so that it is soft but still hasn't lost its flavour, then attach it to a crab line. The crabs will be attracted to the gum.

Chicken wire

Make a childproof enclosure If your garage or shed is full of dangerous tools and toxic substances, keep children away by enclosing them in a childproof enclosure. Make it by first attaching standard-width chicken wire to the walls in a corner. Then staple blocks of wood to the cut ends of the wire and install screw eyes in the wood to accommodate two padlocks.

DID YOU KNOW?

Humans have been chewing gum for a long time. Ancient Greeks chewed mastiche, a chewing gum made from the resin of the mastic tree. Ancient Mayans chewed chicle, the sap from the sapodilla tree. North American Indians chewed the sap from spruce trees, and passed the habit on to the Pilgrims. John B Curtis produced the first commercial chewing gum in 1848 and called it State of Maine Pure Spruce Gum. Wrigley's gum was first launched in the UK in 1911.

Repel deer and sheep If you live in a country area, your garden may be subject to invasions by sheep and deer. Make an almost invisible deterrent by staking chicken wire flat around the perimeter of your garden. The animals don't like to walk on it and it is not an eyesore like a chicken-wire fence.

Protect catnip plants If you are growing catnip for your cat, put a crown of chicken wire over the plant, close to the ground to protect it from being rolled on by enthusiastic felines. As the catnip grows through the wire and gets eaten, the roots will remain intact, growing new catnip. Make sure the edges of the wire are tucked in securely. Catnip is a hardy plant, even in harsh temperatures, so if the roots remain, it will keep coming back year after year.

Protect bulbs from rodents Keep creatures such as rats, squirrels and rabbits from damaging flower bulbs by lining the bottom of a prepared bed with chicken wire. Then plant the bulbs, and cover with soil.

Flower holder Keep cut flowers aligned in a vase by crumpling chicken wire into a ball and placing it in the bottom of the vase before inserting the flowers.

Firmer fence posts Before setting a fence post in concrete, wrap the base with chicken wire. This will make the anchoring firmer and the post more secure.

Secure insulation After you place glass fibre batting between roof rafters or floor joists, staple chicken wire across the joists to secure it and, in the case of the rafters, to keep it from sagging.

Cling film

Treat a hangnail You can get rid of a hangnail while you sleep. Before going to bed, apply hand cream to the affected area, wrap the fingertip with cling film and secure it in place with clear tape. The cling film will confine the moisture and soften the cuticle.

Treat psoriasis Here is a method often recommended by dermatologists to treat individual psoriasis lesions. After applying a prescribed steroid cream, cover the area with a small piece of cling film and use adhesive tape to fix the cling film to the skin. The cling film will enhance the effect of the steroid, seal in moisture and inhibit proliferation of the rash.

{TAKE CARE}

When microwaving foods covered with cling film, always turn back a corner of the film or cut a slit in it to let steam escape. Never use cling film when microwaving foods with a high sugar content; they can become extremely hot and melt it. You can buy special kinds of cling film developed specially for use in the microwave.

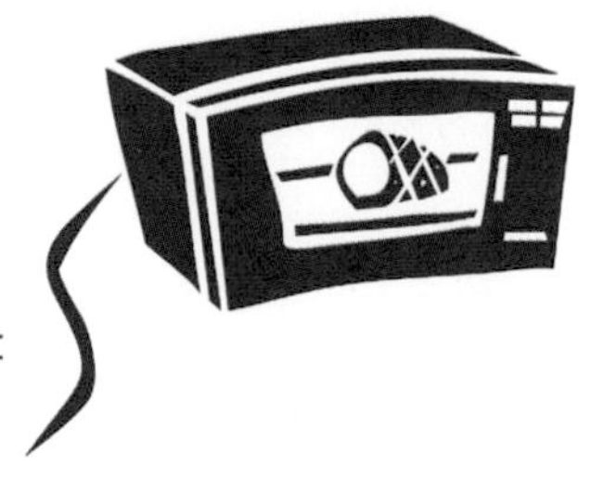

DID YOU KNOW?

Polyvinylidene chloride, the substance that is the basis of cling film, was accidentally discovered in 1933 by Ralph Wiley, a lab worker at the Dow Chemical Company. One day he came across a vial coated with a smelly, clear green film he couldn't scrub off. He called it eonite, after an indestructible material featured in the 'Little Orphan Annie' comic strip. Soon the material was being used by the US armed forces as a protective spray for fighter planes, while car makers used it to protect interior upholstery. Dow later found a way to dispense with the green colour and unpleasant smell and transformed it into a solid material, which was approved for food packaging after World War II and as a contact food wrap in 1956.

Protect computer keyboard If you're are off on holiday and won't be tapping a computer keyboard for a couple of weeks, cover the keyboard with cling film to keep out dust and grime during long periods of inactivity.

Enhance the effectiveness of a vapour rub For pain in a knee and other sore spots, massage in some vapour rub and wrap the area with cling film. The cling film will increase the heating effect of the vapour rub. Make sure to test on a small area first to make sure your skin does not burn.

Keep ice cream smooth Have you ever noticed how ice crystals form on ice cream in the freezer once the container has been opened? The ice cream will stay smooth and free of the crystals if you completely re-wrap the container in cling film before you return it to the freezer.

Keep the top of the fridge Make the next time you clean the top of your fridge the last time. After you've made it all clean and shiny, cover the top with overlapping sheets of cling film. Next time it's due for a clean, remove the old sheets, throw them away and replace with new layers of cling film.

Repair a kite Flying kites with children is a lot of fun, but it can be frustrating if the kite gets torn by a tree branch or fence. For a temporary fix that will keep the kite airborne for a while, cover the tear with cling film and fix it to the kite with clear tape.

Keep stored paint fresh Leftover paint will stay fresh longer if you stretch a sheet of high-quality cling film over the top of the can before tightly replacing the lid.

Clipboards

Makeshift trouser hanger If you can't find a hanger for a pair of trousers, use a clipboard instead. Just suspend the clipboard from a hook inside the wardrobe or on the bedroom door. Hang the trousers and keep them crease-free overnight by clipping the hems to the board.

Keep recipes at eye level When you are following a recipe clipped from a magazine or newspaper, it is hard to read and keep clean when the clipping is lying on the worktop. Solve the problem by securing a clipboard to a wall cabinet at eye level. Attach the recipe of the day onto the clipboard and it will be more convenient to read and stay free of food splatters.

Hold place mats Hang a clipboard inside a kitchen cabinet or pantry door and use the clamp as a convenient, space-saving way to store a set of place mats.

Keep sheet music in place Flimsy pages of sheet music are susceptible to draughts and can sometimes spend more time on the floor than on the music stand. To eliminate the problem, attach the music sheets to a clipboard before placing it in the stand. The pages will remain upright and in place.

Aid road-trip navigation Before starting out on a long drive, fold the map to the area you will be travelling in. Attach it to a clipboard and keep it close to hand so you can check your progress during rest stops.

Organise grades of sandpaper Most of the time, sandpaper is still good after the first or second time you use it. The trick is to find it again. Hang a clipboard on a hook on the workshop wall. Just clip still-usable sandpaper to the board when you are finished and the sandpaper will be handy next time you need it.

Clothes pegs

Fasten Christmas lights Keep outdoor Christmas lights in place and ready to withstand the elements by fastening them securely with clip-on clothes pegs as you fix the lights to gutters, trees and bushes.

Keep snacks fresh Use clip-on clothes pegs to reseal half-eaten bags of crisps and other snacks, cereal, biscuits and seeds. The foods will stay fresh longer and you won't have as many spills in the pantry or cupboard either. Use a clothes peg for an extra seal when you store food in a freezer bag too.

Make a clothes peg clipboard Organise a workshop, kitchen or bathroom with a homemade rack made with traditional straight 'dolly' clothes pegs. Space several clothes pegs evenly apart on a piece of wood and screw them on with screws coming through from the back of the board (pre-drill the holes so you don't split the clothes peg). Hang the finished rack on a door or wall.

DID YOU KNOW?

Between 1852 and 1857, the Patent Office in the USA granted patents for 146 different kinds of clothes pegs. Today wooden clothes pegs are much less common – both traditional 'dolly' pegs and the spring-loaded kind. They have been largely overtaken by moulded plastic pegs. The most recent innovation in clothes peg design is a peg that can sense whether rain is coming. It will then lock itself to prevent washing being hung on the line and drenched.

Organise the bottom of your wardrobe Use clip-on clothes pegs to hold together pairs of shoes, boots or trainers, and put an end to unscheduled hunting expeditions in the cupboard. This idea works for gloves as well.

Keep gloves in shape After washing wool gloves, insert a straight wooden 'dolly' clothes peg into each finger. The clothes pegs will help to keep the gloves in their proper shape.

Prevent the vacuum cord snapping back If your vacuum cleaner suddenly stops, you've probably accidentally pulled out the plug and the cord may automatically retract and snap back into the machine. To avoid a similar annoyance in the future, simply clip a clothes peg to the cord at the length you want.

Make an instant bib Make bibs for a child by using a clip-on clothes peg to hold a tea towel around the child's neck. Use bigger towels to make bibs for adults when needed with messy food. It's much faster than tying on a bib.

Make clothes peg puppets Traditional straight clothes pegs without metal springs are ideal for making little dolls or puppets. Using the knob as a head, get children to stick on bits of wool for hair and scraps of cloth or coloured paper for clothes to give each its own personality.

Hold a leaf bag open If you've ever tried to fill a large bag with leaves all by yourself, only to see half the leaves fall to the ground because the bag won't stay open, here is a solution. Next time use a couple of clip-on clothes pegs to help. After you shake open the bag and spread it wide, use the clothes pegs to clip one side of the bag to a chain-link fence or other convenient site. The bag will stay fully open for easy filling.

Mark a bulb spot When a flower that is supposed to bloom in the spring doesn't, push a straight clothes peg into the soil at the empty spot. In the autumn you will know exactly where to plant new bulbs to avoid gaps.

Grip a nail Hammer the nail and not your fingers. Just remember to use a clip-on clothes peg to hold nails when hammering in hard-to-reach places.

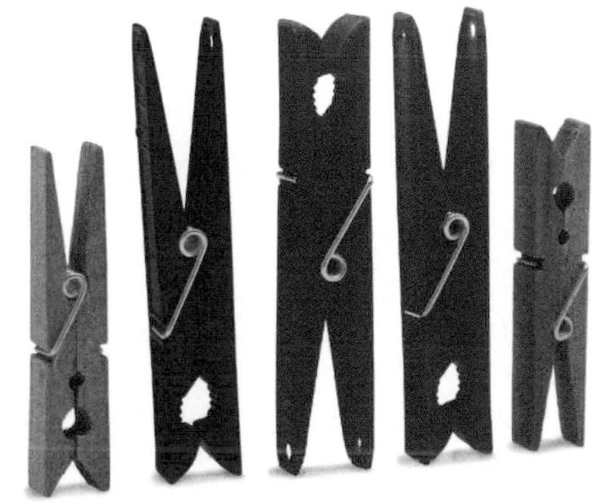

Clamp thin objects Use clip-on clothes pegs as clamps when you're gluing two thin objects together. Let the clothes peg hold them in place until the glue sets.

Keep paintbrush afloat Keep a paintbrush from sinking into the solvent residue when you are soaking it. Clamp the brush to the container with a clothes peg.

Coat hangers

Stop caulk-tube ooze To prevent caulk from oozing from a tube once the job is done, cut an 8cm piece of coat hanger wire; shape one end into a hook and insert the other, straight end into the tube. You should now be able to easily pull out the stopper as needed.

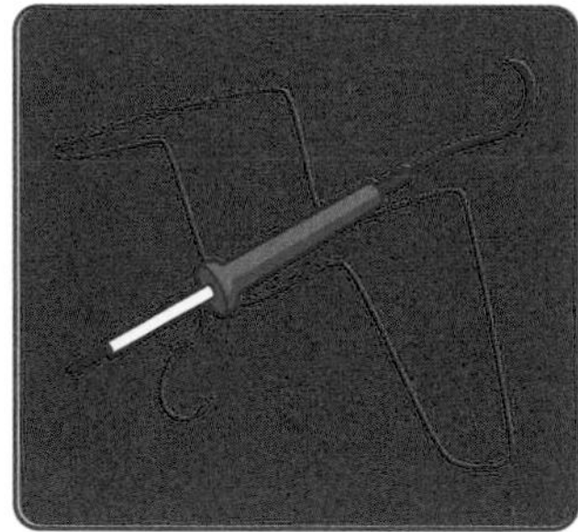

Secure a soldering iron Keeping a hot soldering iron from rolling away and burning something on the workbench can be a real problem. Twist a wire coat hanger into a holder for the iron to rest in. To make the holder, simply bend an ordinary coat hanger in half to form a large V. Then bend each half in half so that the entire piece is shaped like a W.

Extend your reach If you can't reach a utensil that has fallen behind the refrigerator or oven, try straightening a wire coat hanger (except for the hook at the end), and use it to fish for the object.

Make a giant bubble wand Children will love to make giant bubbles with a homemade bubble wand fashioned from a wire coat hanger. Shape the hanger into a hoop with a handle and dip it into a bucket filled with 1 part liquid dishwashing detergent in 2 parts water. Add a few drops of food colouring to make the bubbles even more visible.

Create arts and crafts Make a mobile for a child's room using wire coat hangers, paint in bright colours and attach a series of small toys or cut-outs.

{ SCIENCE FAIR }

NEWTON'S LAW

Here is a fun way to demonstrate Newton's first law of motion. Bend a wire coat hanger into a large loopy M-shape, as shown. Holding the wire in the middle, attach a ball made of modelling-clay to each of the hooks. Then place the low centre point of the M on top of your head. If you turn your head to the left or right, the inertia of the balls will be enough to keep them in place, demonstrating Newton's law that 'objects at rest tend to stay at rest'. With practice, you can actually turn all the way around and the balls will remain still.

DID YOU KNOW?

All Albert J Parkhouse wanted to do when he arrived at work was to hang up his coat and get on with doing his job. It was 1903, and Albert worked at Timberlake Wire and Novelty Company in Jackson, Michigan, USA. But when he went to hang his clothes on the hooks the company provided for workers, all were in use. Frustrated, Albert picked up a piece of wire, bent it into two large rectangular hoops opposite each other, and twisted both ends at the centre into a hook. He hung his coat on it and went to work. The company thought his idea was so good that they patented it and made a fortune. But poor Albert never got a penny for inventing the wire coat hanger.

Make fairy wings Use the wire from two or three wire coat hangers to make wings and similar accessories for fancy dress costumes.

Unclog a toilet If the toilet is clogged by a foreign object, you can fish it out with a straightened wire coat hanger.

Blocked vacuum cleaners Use a straightened hanger to unclog a blockage in a vacuum cleaner hose.

Make a mini-greenhouse To convert a window box into a mini-greenhouse, bend three or four lengths of coat hanger wire into U-shapes and place the ends into the soil. Punch small holes in a clear polythene dry-cleaning bag and wrap it around the box before putting it back in the window.

Hang a plant Wrap a straightened wire coat hanger around a 15-20cm flowerpot, just below the lip; twist it back on itself to secure it, then hang.

Make plant markers Here's how to make waterproof markers for outdoor plants. Cut up little signs from a plastic milk bottle or similar rigid but easy-to-cut plastic item. Write on the name of the plant with an indelible marker. Cut short stakes from wire hangers. Make two small slits in each marker and pass the wire stakes through the slits. The signs will remain clear whatever the elements throw at them.

Light a hard-to-reach pilot light If a pilot light goes out right inside your cooker or boiler and you'd rather not risk a burn by lighting a match and sticking your hand all the way inside. Instead, open up a wire hanger and tape the match to one end. Strike the match and use the hanger to reach the pilot.

Make a paint can holder When you are up on a ladder painting the house, one hand is holding on while the other is painting. How do you hold the paint can? Using a pair of wire snips, cut the hook plus 2.5cm of wire from a wire hanger. Use a pair of pliers to twist the section firmly around the handle of your paint can to make a useful hanger.

Coffee beans

Freshen your breath If you've run out of peppermints and want to freshen your breath, just suck on a coffee bean for a while and your mouth should smell clean and fresh again.

Remove odour from hands If your hands smell of garlic, fish or other strong-smelling foods that you've been handling, a few coffee beans may be all you need to get rid of the odour. Put the beans in your hands and rub them together. The oil released from the coffee beans will absorb the smell. When the odour is gone, wash your hands in warm, soapy water.

Fill a beanbag They don't call them beanbags for nothing. Dried coffee beans are ideal as a beanbag filler, but it is a good idea to wait for a sale and then buy the cheapest beans available.

Coffee cans

Bake a round loaf Use small coffee cans to bake perfectly cylindrical loaves of bread. Use your favourite recipe but put the dough into a well-greased coffee can instead of a loaf tin. For yeast breads use two cans and fill each only half full. Grease the inside of the lids and place them on the cans. For yeast breads, you will know when it is time to bake when the rising dough pushes the lids off. Place the cans, without their lids, upright in the oven to bake.

Separate hamburgers If you like to make hamburgers in bulk, before you put them in the freezer, stack them with a coffee-can lid between each and put them in a plastic bag. When they're are frozen you'll be able to peel off as many as you need.

Hold kitchen scraps Line a coffee tin with a small plastic bag and keep it near the sink to hold kitchen scraps and peelings. Instead of walking back and forth to the bin, you'll only have to make one trip to the bin to dump all the scraps.

Make a bank To make a bank for the children or a collection can for a favourite charity, use a utility knife to cut a 3mm slit in the centre of the plastic lid of a coffee can. Tape decorative paper or adhesive plastic to the sides of the childrens' bank; for a collection can, use the sides of the can to highlight the name of the charity you are helping.

Create a toy holder Make a decorative container for children's miniature books and small toys. Wash and dry a coffee can and file off any sharp edges. Paint on two coats of white acrylic paint, letting it dry between coats. Cut out a design from an old sheet or pillowcase to wrap around the can. Mix 4 tablespoons white glue with enough water to the consistency of paint. Paint on the glue mixture and gently press the fabric onto the can. Trim the bottom and tuck the top edges inside the can. Apply two coats of glue mixture over the fabric overlay to seal it, letting it dry between coats.

Store belts If you have more belts than you have places to hang them up, just roll them up and store them in a large, clean coffee can with a clear lid. Large coffee cans are just the right size to keep belts from creasing and a clear lid will let you find each belt easily.

Make a coffee-can bird feeder To fashion a coffee can into a sturdy bird feeder, begin with a full can and open the top only halfway. (Pour the coffee into an airtight container.) Then open the bottom of the can halfway the same way. Carefully bend the cut ends down inside the can so the edges are not exposed to cut you. Punch a hole in the side of the can at both ends, where it will be the 'top' of the feeder and put some wire through each end to make a hanger.

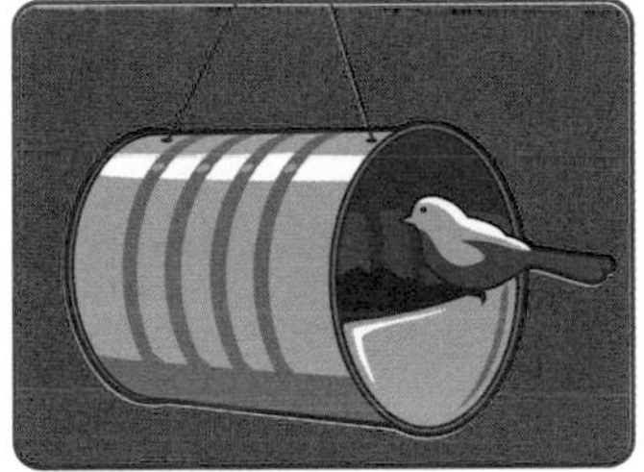

Keep bits and pieces from getting washed by accident Keep an empty coffee can nearby as you're going through children's pockets before putting in a load of washing. Use it to deposit gum and sweet wrappers, paper scraps and other assorted items that children like to stuff into their pockets. Keep another can handy for coins and notes.

Make a dehumidifier If your home suffers from damp, try this easy-to-make dehumidifier. Fill an empty coffee can with salt and leave it in a corner where it will be undisturbed. Replace the salt at monthly intervals or as needed.

Soak a paintbrush An empty coffee can is perfect for briefly soaking a paintbrush in thinner before continuing a job the next day. Cut an X into the lid with a craft knife and insert the brush handles so the bristles clear the bottom of the can by about 12mm. If the tin has no lid, attach a stick to the brush handle with a rubber band to keep the bristles off the bottom of the can.

Keep carpets dry Place plastic coffee-can lids under houseplants as saucers. They will protect carpets or floors and catch excess water.

Keep toilet paper dry when camping Bring a few empty coffee cans with you when camping. Use them to keep toilet paper dry in rainy weather or when you're carrying supplies in a boat.

Gauge rainfall or sprinkler coverage Find out if your garden is getting enough water from the rain. Next time it starts to rain, place empty coffee cans in several places around the garden. When the rain stops, measure the depth of the water in the cans. If they measure at least 2cm, there's no need for additional watering. This is also a good way to test if a sprinkler is getting sufficient water to the areas it is supposed to cover.

Make a spot lawn seeder When it's time to re-seed bare spots on the lawn, make a spot seeder from an empty coffee can and a pair of plastic lids for precise seeding. Drill small holes in the bottom of the tin, just large enough to let grass seeds pass through. Put one lid over the bottom of the can, fill it with seeds, and cap it with the other lid. When you're ready to spread the seeds, take off the bottom lid. When you have finished, replace it to seal in any unused seed for safe storage.

Eliminate workshop clutter If you want small items like screws, nuts and nails to be close to hand, but don't want them to take up workbench space, drill a hole near the top of a number of empty coffee cans so you can hang them on nails on the wall. Label the cans with masking tape so you will know what's inside.

Catch paint drips Turn the plastic lids from old coffee cans into drip catchers under paint cans and under furniture legs when you're painting. Stop cupboard shelves from getting sticky by putting them under jars of cooking oil and syrup too.

* Coffee filters

Cover food in the microwave Coffee filters are microwave-safe. Use them to cover bowls or dishes to prevent splatters when cooking or baking in a microwave oven.

Filter cork crumbs from wine Don't let bits of cork ruin your enjoyment of a good glass of wine. If your attempt at opening the bottle results in floating cork crumbs, just decant the wine through a coffee filter.

Line a frying basket If you save cooking oil for re-use after deep-fat frying, line the basket with a basket-style coffee filter to remove smaller food remnants and other kinds of impurities.

Stop messy food from dripping Serve wraps, deep-filled sandwiches, burgers, hot dogs, popcorn and other messy foods in cone or basket-style coffee filters. The filter is a perfect sleeve, helping to keep fingers clean and reducing drips.

Catch ice-cream drips Next time you give children a choc-ice bar or ice lolly, serve it with a drip catcher made from basket-style coffee filters. Just poke the stick through the centre of two filters and the drips will fall into the paper, not on the child or your carpet.

DID YOU KNOW?

The coffee filter was invented in 1908 by a housewife from Dresden, Germany. Melitta Bentz was looking for a way to brew a perfect cup of coffee without the bitterness often caused by overbrewing. She decided to make a filtered coffee, pouring boiling water over ground coffee and filtering out the grounds. She experimented with different materials, until she found that the blotter paper that her son used at school worked best. She cut a round piece of blotting paper, put it in a metal cup, and the first Melitta coffee filter was born. Shortly after, Melitta and her husband, Hugo, launched the company that still bears her name.

Make an instant funnel Cut the end off a cone-style coffee filter to make an instant funnel. Keep a few in your car and use them to avoid spillage when you top up oil in the engine

Clean your specs Next time you clean a pair of glasses, try using a coffee filter instead of a tissue. Good-quality coffee filters are made from 100 per cent virgin paper, so you can use them to clean your glasses without leaving any lint. You can also use them to safely polish mirrors and TV and computer-monitor screens.

Keep cast iron rust-free Prolong the life of good cast-iron cookware by putting a coffee filter in a frying pan, grill pan or casserole when it's not in use. The filter will absorb moisture and prevent rusting.

Prevent soil leakage When you're repotting a plant, line the pot with a coffee filter to keep the soil from leaking out through the drain hole.

Make an air freshener Fill a coffee filter with bicarbonate of soda and tie it closed with a twist-tie to make an air freshener. Make several and tuck them into shoes, wardrobes, drawers, the fridge and wherever else they may be needed.

Coffee grounds

Don't raise any dust Before you clean the ashes out of a fireplace, sprinkle them with wet coffee grounds. They'll be easier to remove and the ash and dust won't pollute the atmosphere of the room.

Deodorise a freezer Get rid of the smell of spoiled food if a freezer breaks down or you have a power cut. Fill a couple of bowls with used or fresh coffee grounds and place them in the freezer overnight. For a flavoured-coffee scent, add a couple of drops of vanilla to the grounds.

Keep bait worms alive A cup of used coffee grounds will keep bait worms alive and wiggling all day long. Just mix the grounds into the soil in the bait box before you put in the worms. They like coffee almost as much as we do and the nutrients in the grounds will help them to live longer.

DID YOU KNOW?

Ground coffee loses its flavour immediately unless it is specially packaged or brewed. While freshly roasted and ground coffee is often sealed in combination plastic-and-paper bags, vacuum-sealed cans keep coffee fresh for up to three years. The US is the world's largest consumer of coffee, importing over a million kilograms each year. The typical coffee drinker has three cups of coffee per day. That translates into 170 million cups of coffee swallowed daily in the UK.

DID YOU KNOW?

Coffee grows on trees that can reach a height of up to 6m, but growers keep them pruned to about 2m to simplify picking and encourage heavy berry production. The first visible sign of a coffee tree's maturity is the appearance of small white blossoms, which fill the air with a heady aroma reminiscent of jasmine and orange. The mature tree bears cherry-size oval berries, each containing two coffee beans with their flat sides set together. A mature coffee tree will produce 450g of coffee per growing season. It takes 2000 hand-picked Arabica coffee berries or 4000 beans to make 450g of roasted coffee.

Fertilise plants Don't throw out old coffee grounds. They're full of nutrients that acid-loving plants crave. Save them to fertilise rose bushes, azaleas, rhododendrons, evergreens and camellias. It's better to use grounds from a drip coffeemaker than the boiled grounds from a percolator as the drip grounds are richer in nitrogen.

Keep cats out of the garden Your neighbours' cats won't use your garden as a latrine again if you spread a pungent mixture of orange peel and used coffee grounds around your plants. The mix acts as a superb fertiliser too.

Boost carrot harvest To increase a carrot harvest, mix the seeds with freshly-ground coffee before sowing. Not only does the extra bulk make the tiny seeds easier to sow, but the coffee aroma may repel cutworms and other pests. As an added bonus, the grounds will help add nutrients to the soil as they decompose around the plants. You might also like to add a few radish seeds to the mix before sowing. The radishes will sprout in a few days to mark the rows and when you cultivate the radishes, you will be thinning the carrot seedlings and cultivating the soil at the same time.

Coins

Give carpet a lift When you move a chair, sofa, table or bed, you will notice deep indentations in the carpet made by the legs. To fluff it up again, simply hold a coin on its edge and scrape it against the flattened pile. If it still doesn't pop back up, hold a steam iron 5cm above the affected spot. When the area is damp, try fluffing it again with the coin.

{ SCIENCE FAIR }

OPTICAL ILLUSION

Scientists use optical illusions to show how the brain can be tricked. This simple experiment uses two coins, but you'll think you are seeing three. Hold two coins on top of each other between your thumb and index finger. Quickly slide the coins back and forth and you will see a third coin!

How does it work? Scientists say that everything we see is actually light reflected from objects. Our eyes use the light to create images on our retinas, the light-sensitive linings in our eyeballs. Because images don't disappear instantly, when something moves quickly you may see both an object and an after-image of it at the same time.

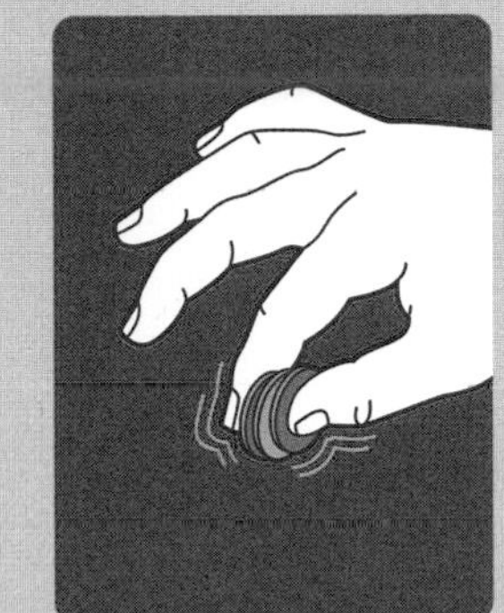

Keep cut flowers fresh Wild flower posies, bouquets and other cut flowers will stay fresh longer if you add a copper coin and a cube of sugar to the vase water.

Instant measure If you need to measure something but you don't have a ruler, just reach into your pocket and pull out a 2p piece. It measures exactly 2.5cm in diameter. Just line up a series of coins to measure the length of a small object.

Make a rattle Drop a few coins into an empty aluminium drink can, seal the top with gaffer tape and head for the stadium to support your favourite team. Take the rattle with you when you walk the dog and use it as a training aid. When the dog is naughty, just shake the rattle.

Test tyre tread Let the Queen's head tell you if it's time to replace the tyres on your car. Insert a one penny piece into the tread. If you can't cover the top of the head inside the tread, it's time to replace the tyres. Check tyres regularly and you will avoid breaking the law by having the correct depth of tyre tread.

Decorate a hair slide Use shiny 1p pieces to decorate a hair slide for a little girl. Gather enough pennies to complete the project and arrange them as you like on the hair slide and use a hot-glue gun to attach them. Allow 24 hours to dry.

Hang doors perfectly Next time you hang a door, use coins to ensure proper clearance between the outside of the door and the inside of the frame. When the door is closed, the gap at the top should be the thickness of a 50p, and the gap at the sides should be that of a 5p. If you do it right, you will keep the door from binding and it won't let in draughts.

Make a paperweight When you holiday abroad, you probably come home with plenty of foreign coins. Instead of leaving them lying around in a desk drawer, use them to make an interesting paperweight. Place the coins into a small glass jar with a sealable lid and cover the lid with decorative cloth or paper.

DID YOU KNOW?

Coins were first produced around 700 BC by the Lydians, a people who lived in what is now Turkey. From there, their use spread to ancient Greece and Rome. The minting of coins in Britain began in the 1st century BC and the earliest coins were crude imitations cast in moulds.

Next, coins were struck using hand-held tools, a technique that would be used for the next 1500 years. Following the Roman Conquest, the coinage of Iron Age Britain was discontinued and Roman coins circulated in large numbers.

In AD 650, a London mint began operating, at first a little precariously but from the time of Alfred the Great (871–899) it became a continous and important source of British coinage. At the end of 2004 there were 26,359 million coins in circulation in the UK.

Colanders

Prevent grease splashes Stop grease spitting all over the top of the cooker when you are frying by inverting a large metal colander over the frying pan. The holes will let heat escape but the colander will trap the splashes. But be careful: the metal colander will be hot so use an oven mitt to remove it.

Heat a pasta bowl Does your pasta get cold too quickly? To keep it warm for longer, heat the bowl first. Place a colander in the bowl, pour the pasta and water into the colander, and let the hot water stand in the bowl for a few seconds to heat it. Pour out the water, add the pasta and sauce and it will be ready to serve.

Keep berries and grapes fresh Do you find that berries and grapes often go mouldy before you have had a chance to enjoy them? To keep them fresh for longer, store them in a colander, not a closed plastic container, in the fridge. The cold air will circulate through the holes in the colander, keeping them fresh for days.

Keep bath toys tidy Don't let the bathroom that your children use look like another messy toy box. After each bath, collect your child's small playthings into a large colander and store it in the bath. The water will drain from the toys, keeping them ready for next time and the bathroom will stay tidy.

Use as a beach toy Don't spend money on expensive beach toys for budding diggers and archaeologists. A simple inexpensive plastic colander is perfect for digging on the beach or in a sandpit.

Cold cream

Erase temporary tattoos Children love temporary tattoos, but removing them can be a painful chore. To make removal easier, loosen the tattoo by rubbing cold cream on it and then gently rub it off with a facecloth.

Remove bumper stickers Is your bumper covered with tatty, partly peeling stickers? Rub cold cream on the stickers and let it soak in. Once it does, you should be able to peel them off with ease.

Make face paint This is a safe, easy recipe for party face paint. Mix 1 teaspoon cornflour, ½ teaspoon water, ½ teaspoon cold cream, and 2 drops food colouring (depending on the character) together. Use a small paintbrush to paint designs on your child's face. It can be removed with soap and water.

DID YOU KNOW?

Cold cream is cold because it is made with a lot of water that evaporates and cools your warm face. Cold cream is one of the oldest of all facial ointments. It was invented by the Greek physician Galen in AD 157. It's not known exactly why Galen created his mixture, but experts suggest that ancient medicine was based on treating with opposites. And Galen might have been seeking a cure for a hot and dry skin condition like eczema or psoriasis. But the women of ancient Greece soon discovered the soothing white cream was superb for removing make-up, which remains the primary use for cold cream to this day.

Compact discs

Use as holiday ornaments Decorate a Christmas tree in style by hanging CDs shiny-side out to create a flickering array of lights, or paint and decorate the label side to create inexpensive personalised ornaments. For variety, cut some of the CDs into stars and other shapes with sharp scissors. Drill a 6mm hole through each CD shape and thread a ribbon through to hang.

Make artwork in a teenager's room Old CDs make inexpensive and quirky wall decorations for a teenager's room. Attach the CDs with thumbtacks and use them to create a border at the ceiling or halfway up the wall. Or let your child use them to frame his or her favourite posters.

Use as garden/driveway reflectors Drill small holes into a CD and screw it onto a gate post or wooden stake and push it into the ground. Install several of them to light a night-time path to your front door.

TIP* CD REPAIR

Before throwing away or recycling a scratched CD, try to repair it. First, clean it thoroughly with a lint-free cloth or mild soap and a little water. Hold the CD by the edge to keep from getting fingerprints on it. Polish it from the middle to the edge, but not in a circular motion. If your CD still skips, try fixing it with a little non-gel toothpaste. Dab some toothpaste on the end of your finger and rub it lightly onto the entire CD. Use a damp paper towel to remove the toothpaste and dry it with a fresh paper towel. The fine abrasive in the toothpaste may smooth out the scratch. You might also want to try car wax on a scratch (see page 104).

Catch candle drips You should always use a candleholder specifically designed to catch melting wax. However, if one is not available, a CD will work almost as well. Make sure to use a short candle that can stand on its own and has a flat bottom. It should also be slightly larger than the CD hole. Place the candleholder on a stable, heat-resistant surface and keep a watchful eye on it.

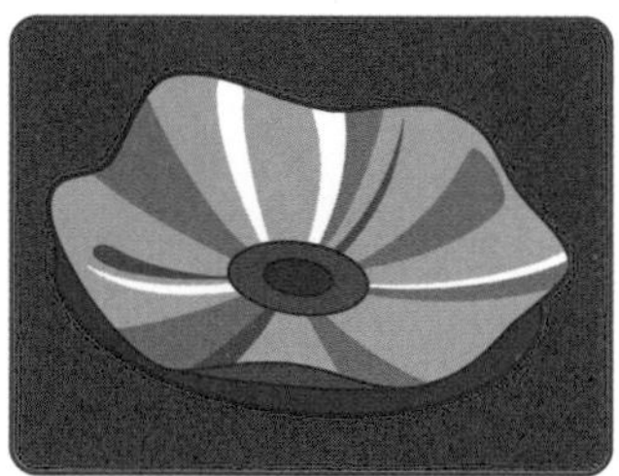

Make artistic bowls Create a decorative bowl by placing a CD in the oven on low heat over a metal bowl until the CD softens. Wearing protective gloves, gently bend the CD into the shape you want. Seal the hole by gluing the bottom edge to another surface such as a flat dish using epoxy or PVC glue. But don't use the bowl to hold food – even dry snacks like crisps and nuts or sweets.

Use as a template for a perfect circle If you need to draw a perfect circle, don't trace around a cup or use a cumbersome compass. Every CD provides two circle sizes – you can trace around the inner hole or the outer circumference.

Make a decorative sun catcher Sun catchers are attractive to watch and all you need to make one is a couple of CDs. Glue two CDs together, shiny side out, wrap wool or coloured string through the hole and hang them in a window. The prism will make a beautiful light show.

Create a spinning top Turn an old CD into a fun toy. With a knife, make two slits across from each other in the CD hole. Force a 1p piece halfway through the hole, and then spin the CD on its edge.

Make a CD clock Turn a disc into a funky clock. Paint and design one side of the CD and let it dry. Write (using a permanent marker) or use stickers to create the numbers around its edge. Attach a digital clock mechanism – available from craft shops – onto the back of the CD.

Cover with felt and use as coasters CDs can help to prevent unsightly stains from cups left on a table. Cut a round piece of felt to fit over the CD and glue it onto the label side of the CD so that the shiny side is facing upwards when you use the coaster.

 Cooking spray

Prevent rice and pasta from sticking Most cooks know that a little cooking oil in boiling water will keep rice or pasta from sticking together when you drain it. If you run out of cooking oil, however, a quick squirt of cooking oil spray will also do the job.

Cure door squeak Have you heard a door squeak just once too often? Put some non-stick cooking spray on the hinge. Make sure you have some paper towels handy to wipe up the drips.

Grating cheese Put less elbow grease into grating cheese by using a little non-stick cooking spray on the cheese grater for smoother grating. The spray also makes it easier and quick to clean the grater.

Prevent tomato sauce stains Are you few up with indelible tomato sauce stains on plastic containers? To prevent them, apply a light coating of non-stick cooking spray to the inside of the container before you pour in the tomato sauce.

Keep car wheels clean The fine black coating that collects on the wheels of the car and is so hard to clean is brake dust – produced every time you apply the brakes and the pads wear against the brake disks or cylinders. The next time you invest the elbow grease to get your wheels shiny, give them a light coating of cooking spray first. The brake dust should wipe right off.

De-bug your car When insects crash into your car at speed they can really stick. Give the grille a squirt of non-stick cooking spray so you can just wipe away any insect debris.

Lubricate a bicycle chain Do you have a creaky bike chain but no lubricating oil to hand? Give it a shot of non-stick cooking spray instead. Don't use too much – the chain shouldn't look wet. Wipe off the excess with a clean rag.

Remove paint and grease Use cooking spray to remove paint and grease from your hands. Work it in well and rinse. Wash again with soap and water.

DID YOU KNOW?

The first patent for a non-stick cooking spray was issued in 1957 to Arthur Meyerhoff and his partner, Leon Rubin, who began marketing PAM (Product of Arthur Meyerhoff) All Natural Cooking Spray in 1959. After appearing on local Chicago TV cooking shows in the early '60s, the product developed a loyal following and it quickly became a household name – and was copied all over the world.

DID YOU KNOW?

Cork, the bark of the cork oak, has been used to seal wine bottles and other vessels for more than 400 years. The bark has a unique honeycomb cell structure. Each cell is sealed, filled with air and not connected to any other cell. This makes it waterproof and a poor conductor of heat and vibration. Plus cork contains suberin, a natural waxy substance that makes it impermeable to liquids and gases and prevents the cork from rotting. It is still used for most sparkling wine and champagne but synthetic corks are frequently used in other wines.

Dry nail polish If you need nail polish to dry in a hurry, spray it with a coat of cooking spray and let it dry. The spray is also an excellent moisturiser for the dry skin on your hands.

Quick casting Take some cooking spray when you go fishing. Spray it on the fishing line and the line will cast more easily and go further.

Prevent grass from sticking Mowing the lawn should be easy, but cleaning stuck grass from the mower is tedious. Prevent grass from sticking on mower blades and the underside of the housing by spraying them with cooking oil before mowing.

Prevent snow sticking Shovelling snow is hard enough, but it can be more difficult when the snow sticks to the shovel. Spray the shovel with non-stick cooking spray before shovelling and the snow will slide right off.

Corks

Create a fishing bob It is by no means high-tech, but it is worth remembering that a cork makes an excellent substitute fishing float. Push a staple into the top of the cork, then pull the staple out just a little way so you can slide the fishing line through it to attach it.

Make an impromptu pincushion Do you need somewhere to keep pins while you sew? Save corks from wine bottles – they make brilliant mini-pincushions.

Prevent pottery scratches Beautiful, rustic pottery often has a rough base that can make ugly scratches on furniture. To protect table tops, cut thin slices of cork and lightly glue them to the bottom of ceramic objects.

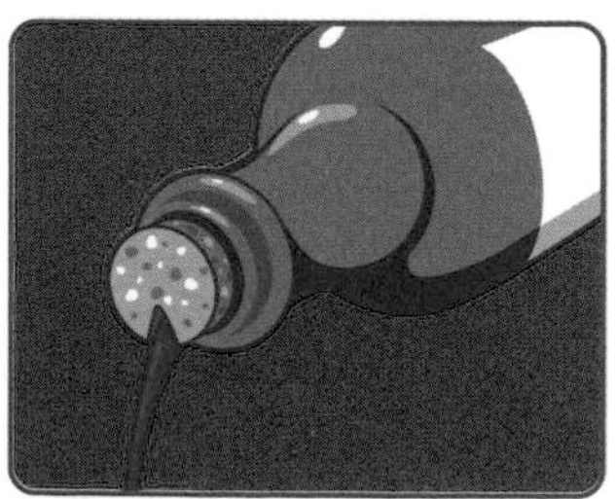

Make a pour spout If you don't have a fancy metal pouring spout to control the flow from your oil or vinegar bottle, don't buy one. Make your own spout by cutting out a wedge of the cork along its length. Use a utility or craft knife. Stick the cork in the bottle and pour away. When you've finished, cover the hole with a tab of masking tape.

Replace soft-drink bottle caps If you've lost the cap to a soft-drink bottle and need a replacement, cork it. Most wine corks fit most drinks bottles perfectly.

Use to make face paint Children love to dress up as tramps for fancy dress or Halloween parties. To create an authentic scruffy look, char the end of a piece of cork by holding it over a candle. Let it cool a little, then rub it on the child's face.

Block sun glare In the past, cricketers and American baseball players would burn cork and rub it under their eyes to reduce glare from the sun and stadium lights. These days, players use commercial products to do the same, but you can still use a cork to do the same job.

Prevent chair scratches The sound of a chair scraping across a beautiful floor can make your skin crawl. Solve the problem by cutting cork into thin slices and attaching them to the bottom of the chair legs with a spot of wood glue.

Create craft stamps You can use a cork to create a personalised stamp. Carve the end of a cork into any shape or design you want. Use it with ink from a stamp pad to decorate note cards. Or let the children dip carved corks in paint to make stamps and artwork.

Create a cool bead curtain Here is how to make a beaded curtain for a child's or teenager's room. Drill a hole through a number of corks and string them onto a cord along with some beads and other decorations. Make as many strings as you need and tie them onto a curtain rod.

Fasten earrings The backs of earrings always get lost and you can't always find a perfect-sized replacement when you need it. Instead, use a snippet of cork as a temporary substitute. Slice a small piece about the size of the earring backing and push it on. An eraser cut off the end of a pencil will also work.

Picture-perfect frames If you're always straightening picture frames, cut some small flat pieces of cork, all of the same thickness and glue them to the back of the frame. The cork will grip the wall and stop the sliding. It will also prevent the frame from marking the wall.

Mass-produce sowing holes Quickly sow seeds in straight rows of evenly spaced holes. Mark out the spacing you need on a board. Drill screws through the holes, using screws that will protrude about 2cm through the board. Now twist wine corks onto the screws. Just press the board, corks down, into the garden bed and you have made instant seed holes.

{TAKE CARE}

To open a bottle of wine, use a traditional corkscrew that twists into the stopper. Peel the top of the plastic to expose the cork. Insert the corkscrew into the centre. Twist the corkscrew straight down and then pull the cork straight out using an even pressure.

Never use a corkscrew to open a bottle of champagne or sparkling wine. Pushing down into a bottle of champagne against the pressure of the carbonation can actually make it explode. If possible, wait a day before opening and let the carbonation settle a little. Wrap the cork in a towel and twist the bottle, not the cork, slowly.

Cornflour

Dry shampoo If the dog needs a bath, but you just don't have time, rub cornflour into his coat and brush it out. The dry bath will fluff up and freshen his coat.

Soak up furniture polish residue If you've finished polishing the furniture, but there's still polish left on the surface, sprinkle some cornflour lightly onto the furniture after polishing. Wipe up the oil and cornflour, then buff the surface.

Remove ink stains from carpet Ink on the carpet doesn't have to be a disaster. In this case a little spilt milk might save you from crying. Mix the milk with cornflour to make a paste. Apply the paste to the ink stain. Allow the mixture to dry on the carpet for a few hours, then brush off the dried residue and vacuum it up.

Give carpets a fresh scent Before vacuuming a room, sprinkle a little cornflour onto the carpet. Wait about half an hour and then vacuum as usual.

Make your own paste The next time the children want to get creative with paper and paste, save money by making the paste yourself. Mix 3 teaspoons cornflour for every 4 teaspoons cold water. Stir until you reach a paste consistency. This is especially good for applying with fingers or a wooden ice lolly stick. If you add food colouring, the paste can be used for painting objects.

Make finger paints This simple recipe will keep the children happy for hours. Mix together 50g cornflour and 400ml cold water. Bring to a boil and continue boiling until the mixture becomes thick. Pour your product into several small containers and add food colouring to each container to make a collection of homemade finger paints.

Clean stuffed animals To clean a dingy stuffed animal toy, rub a little cornflour onto the toy, wait about 5 minutes, and then brush it clean. Or place the stuffed animal (or a few small ones) into a bag. Sprinkle cornflour into the bag, close it tightly and shake. Now brush their fur to remove grime and remaining cornflour.

Separate marshmallows Prise apart stuck marshmallows by adding at least a teaspoon of cornflour to the bag and shaking. The cornflour will absorb the extra moisture and force most of the marshmallows apart. Repackage the remaining marshmallows in a container and freeze them to avoid sticking in future.

Untangle knots Knots in string or shoelaces can be stubborn to undo, but the solution is easy. Sprinkle the knot with a little cornflour. It will then be easy to work the segments apart.

Lift a scorch mark from clothing Wet the scorched area and cover it with cornflour. Let the cornflour dry, then brush it away along with the scorch mark.

Remove grease splashes from walls Even the most careful cook cannot avoid an occasional splash. A busy kitchen will always be subject to wear and tear but this is a handy remedy for unsightly grease spots. Sprinkle cornflour onto a soft cloth. Rub the grease spot gently until it disappears.

DID YOU KNOW?

Correction fluid was invented in 1951 by Bette Nesmith Graham, mother of Michael Nesmith of The Monkees pop group. Working as a secretary in Texas, she began supplying small bottles of her invention to other secretaries, calling it Mistake Out. Five years later, she improved the formula and changed the name to Liquid Paper. Despite its proven use, Graham was turned down when she tried to sell it to IBM, so she marketed it on her own. In the 1960s her invention began to generate a tidy profit; by 1979, when she sold the product to the Gillette Corporation, she received $47.5 million (£28 million) plus a royalty on every bottle sold until 2000. Today, with the ease of correcting documents on a computer, correction fluid is no longer the office essential it once was.

Get rid of bloodstains With blood, the more quickly you act, the better the result. Whether it's on clothing or table linens, you can remove or reduce a bloodstain with this method. Make a paste of cornflour mixed with cold water. Cover the spot with the paste and rub it gently into the fabric. Now put the cloth in a sunny place to dry. Once dry, brush off the remaining residue. If the stain is not completely gone, repeat the process.

Polish silver Has the sparkle gone from your best silver? Make a simple paste by mixing cornflour with water. Use a damp cloth to apply this to your silverware. Let it dry, then rub it off with cheesecloth or another soft cloth to reveal the shine.

Make windows sparkle Create a streak-free window cleaning solution by mixing 2 tablespoons cornflour with 100ml ammonia and 100ml white vinegar in a bucket containing 3-4 litres warm water. Don't be put off by the milky concoction that results. Mix well and put the solution in a trigger spray bottle. Spray on the windows, then wipe with a warm-water rinse. Now rub with a dry paper towel or lint-free cloth for crystal clear, streakless windows.

Say good riddance to cockroaches Make a mixture of 50 per cent plaster of paris and 50 per cent cornflour. Spread this into crevices wherever cockroaches appear.

Correction fluid

Cover scratches on appliances Dab small nicks on household appliances with correction fluid. Once it dries, cover your repair with clear nail polish for protection. This works well on white china, too, but only for display. Now that correction fluid comes in a rainbow of colours, you may easily find a match for a coloured cooker, toaster or fridge.

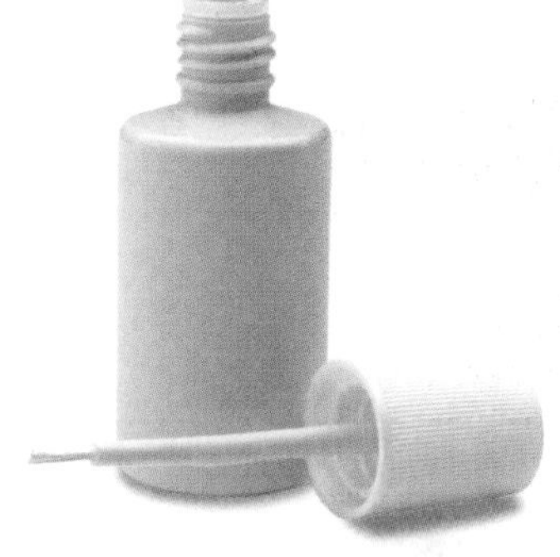

Touch up a ceiling Hide marks on white or beige ceilings with carefully applied strokes of correction fluid. You can tone down the brightness, if you need to, by buffing the repaired area with a paper towel once it has dried thoroughly.

Erase scuffs If you need a quick fix for scuffed white shoes, correction fluid will camouflage any marks. On leather, buff gently once the fluid dries. There is no need to buff on patent leather.

Paint the town Decorate a window for any occasion. Paint snowflakes, flowers or Welcome Home signs using correction fluid. Later you can remove your artwork using nail polish remover, vinegar and water or a commercial window cleaner. Or you can scrape it off with a single-edged razor blade set in a holder made for removing paint from glass.

Cotton wool balls

Scent the room Saturate a cotton wool ball with your favourite perfume or cologne and drop it into the vacuum cleaner bag. As you vacuum, the scent will be released and gently permeate the room.

Deodorise the refrigerator Sometimes the fridge just doesn't smell fresh. Dampen a cotton wool ball with vanilla extract and place it on a shelf. You'll find it acts as a natural deodoriser, suffusing the fridge with its own pleasant scent.

Fight mildew There are always hard-to-reach spots in the bathroom, usually around the taps, where mildew may breed in the grout between tiles. Soak a few cotton wool balls in bleach and place them in those difficult spots – tape them to the wall or tap where necessary. Leave them to sit for a few hours. When you remove them, you should find your job has been done. Finish by rinsing with warm water.

Protect little fingers Pad the ends of drawer runners with a cotton wool ball. This will prevent the drawer from closing completely and keep children from catching their fingers as the drawer slides shut.

Rescue your rubber gloves If you find that long, manicured nails sometimes puncture the fingertips of rubber gloves, push a cotton wool ball into each of the fingers of your gloves. The soft barrier should help to prolong their life.

Crayons

Use as a floor filler Crayons make an excellent filler for small gouges or holes in resilient flooring. Get out the crayon box and select a colour that most closely matches the floor. Melt the crayon in the microwave on medium power over a piece of greaseproof paper, a minute at a time until you have a pliant glob of colour. Now, with a plastic knife or putty knife, fill the hole. Smooth it over with a rolling pin, a book or another flat object. You'll find the crayon cools down quickly. Now wax the floor to provide a clear protective coating over the new filler.

Fill furniture scratches Do your pets sometimes use the furniture as if it were a scratching post? Don't despair. You can use a crayon to cover even quite deep scratches on wooden furniture. Choose the colour most similar to the wood finish, then soften the crayon with a hair drier or in the microwave on the defrost setting. Colour over the scratches, then buff the repair job with a clean rag to restore the lustre to the piece.

Carpet cover-up Even the most careful among us manage to stain the carpet. If you've tried to remove a stain and nothing works, here's a remedy you may be able to live with. Find a crayon that matches or will blend with the carpet. Soften the crayon a bit with a hair drier or in the microwave on the defrost setting. Now colour over the spot. Cover the repair with greaseproof paper and gently iron the colour in. Keep the iron on a low setting. Repeat as often as necessary.

Colourful decoration Here's a fun project to do with children. Make a multi-coloured sun catcher by shaving crayons onto a 10-12cm sheet of waxed paper using a potato peeler or grater. Place another sheet of waxed paper over the top and press with a hot iron until the shavings melt together. Poke a hole near the top through the layers of wax and crayon while they are still warm. Once the ornament cools, peel away the papers and thread a ribbon through it.

Cream of tartar

Make play clay for kids Here's a recipe for fun dough that's like the famous commercial stuff. Add together 2 tablespoons cream of tartar, 200ml salt, 800g plain flour, and 1-2 tablespoons cooking oil. Stir well with a wooden spoon to mix together, then slowly stir while adding 800ml water. Cook the mixture in a saucepan over a medium flame, stirring occasionally until it thickens. It is ready when it forms a ball that is not sticky. Work in food colouring, if you want. Let it cool, then let the children use their imaginations. It dries out more quickly than the commercial variety, so store it in an airtight container in the fridge.

Bath scrubber Let a simple solution of cream of tartar and hydrogen peroxide do the hard work of removing a stain in the bath for you. Fill a small, shallow cup or dish with cream of tartar and add hydrogen peroxide drop by drop until you have a thick paste. Apply to the stain and let it dry. When you remove the dried paste, you will find that the stain is gone too.

Brighten cookware Discoloured aluminum pots will sparkle again if you clean them with a mixture of 2 tablespoons cream of tartar dissolved into 1 litre water. Bring the mixture to a boil inside the pot and boil for 10 minutes.

Curtain rings

Hold your hammer Sometimes you need three hands when you're doing household repair jobs. Attach a sturdy metal shower curtain ring to your belt and slip your hammer through it. Now you can climb a ladder or otherwise work with both hands and just grab the hammer when needed.

Get hooked If you don't want to carry a backpack, lash a few items to your belt loop with the help of a curtain ring. Attach shoes or boots to your sleeping bag with a metal curtain ring; while gloves and cutlery can dangle from a metal shower curtain ring or a brass key ring.

Keep track of mini mittens Drive a nail into the hall wall or the back of a door. Hand your child a curtain ring and tell him or her to use it to clip his mittens together and hang them on the nail.

Dental floss

Remove a stuck ring Here is a simple way to slip off a ring that's stuck on a finger. Wrap the length of your finger from the ring to the nail tightly with dental floss. You should be able to slide the ring off over the floss 'corset'.

Lift biscuits off a baking tray It's frustrating when freshly baked biscuits get stuck on a baking tray. Broken biscuits may taste just as good as those in one piece, but they don't look as nice on a serving plate. Use dental floss to remove biscuits from a baking tray. Hold a length of dental floss taut and slide it neatly between the bottom of the biscuit and the tray.

Slice cake and cheese Use dental floss to cut cakes, especially delicate and sticky ones that tend to adhere to a knife. Just hold a length of the floss taut over the cake and then slice away, moving it slightly side to side as you cut through the cake. You can also use dental floss to cut small blocks of cheese cleanly – like an old-fashioned cheese wire.

Make hardwearing repairs to outdoor items Because dental floss is strong and resilient but fine, it is an ideal replacement for thread when you are repairing an umbrella, tent or rucksack. These items take a beating and sometimes get tiny nicks and splits. Sew up the small holes with floss. To fix larger rips, sew back and forth over the holes until you have covered the space with a floss 'darn'.

Extra-strong string for hanging things Considering how thin it is, dental floss is remarkably strong. Use it instead of string or wire to securely hang pictures, mobiles or wind chimes. Use it with a needle to thread together papers you want to hold together or as a mini clothesline for items you want to display.

Separate photos Sometimes photographs get stuck to each other and it seems the only way to separate them is to ruin them. Try working a length of dental floss between the pictures to gently prise them apart.

Secure a button permanently Has a button fallen off again? This time, sew it back on with dental floss – it's much stronger than thread, and is perfect for replacing buttons on coats, jackets, trousers and heavy shirts.

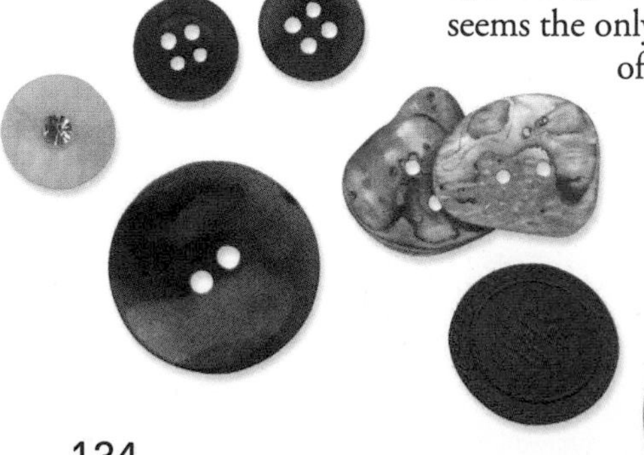

Denture tablets

Re-ignite a diamond's sparkle Has your diamond ring lost its sparkle? Drop a denture tablet into a glass of water. Follow with a ring or diamond earrings. Let them sit for a few minutes. Then remove your items of jewellery and rinse thoroughly to reveal their former sparkle and shine.

Banish mineral deposits on glass Fresh flowers often leave a ring on glass vases that seems impossible to remove no matter how hard you scrub. Here's the answer. Fill the vase with water and drop in a denture tablet. When the fizzing has stopped, all of the mineral deposits will be gone. Use the same method to clean Thermos flasks, cruets, glasses and coffee decanters.

Clean a coffeemaker Hard water leaves mineral deposits in the tank of an electric coffeemaker that not only slows its perking action but also affects the taste of your coffee. Denture tablets will fizz away the deposits and give the tank a bacterial clean-out as well. Drop two denture tablets in the tank and fill it with water. Run the coffeemaker. Discard the first pot of water and follow up with one or two rinse cycles with clean water.

Clean the toilet Here's how to get a sparkling toilet bowl. Porcelain fixtures respond to the cleaning agent in denture tablets. Drop a denture tablet in the bowl. Wait about 20 minutes and flush.

Clean enamel cookware Stains on enamel cookware are a natural for the denture tablet cleaning solution. Fill the pot or pan with warm water and drop in a tablet or two, depending on its size. Wait a bit – once the fizzing has stopped, your cookware will be clean.

Unblock a drain If a drain is slow and sluggish, try using denture tablets to sort the problem. Drop a couple of tablets into the drain and run water until the problem clears. For a more stubborn blockage, drop 3 tablets down the sink, follow that with 200ml white vinegar, and wait a few minutes. Now run hot water into the drain until the blockage has gone.

DID YOU KNOW?

Bleaching agents are a common component of denture cleaning tablets, providing the chemical action that helps the tablets to remove plaque and to whiten and bleach away stains. This is what makes them surprisingly useful for cleaning toilets, coffeemakers, jewellery and enamel cookware, among other things.

Disposable nappies

Keep a plant watered longer Before potting a plant, place a clean disposable nappy in the bottom of the flowerpot, absorbent side up. It will absorb water that would otherwise drain out the bottom and will keep the plant from drying out too fast. You'll also cut back on how often you have to water the plant.

Make a heating pad Soothe your aching neck. Or, for that matter, your aching back or shoulder. Use a disposable nappy's high level of absorbency to your advantage by creating a soft, pliable heating pad. Moisten a disposable nappy and place it in the microwave on medium-high setting for about 2 minutes. Check that it is not too hot for comfort and then apply to your sore joint.

Pad a package If want to post a fragile item to a friend, but don't have any protective wrapping, wrap the item in disposable nappies or insert them as padding before sealing the package. Nappies cost more than ordinary protective packaging wrap, but at least you will have sent the package out quickly and you can be assured your gift will arrive in one piece.

Make a crash pad for delicate items Line a large flat-bottomed shopping bag with a couple of disposable nappies and keep it in the back of your car. You can use it to transport glass jars and bottles or delicate fruit on a shopping trip.

DID YOU KNOW?

It took a mother to invent disposable nappies. Looking for an alternative to messy cloth nappies, Marion Donovan first created a plastic covering for nappies. She made her prototype from a shower curtain and later parachute fabric. Manufacturers weren't interested, but when she created her own company and released the product in 1949 at Saks Fifth Avenue in New York City, it was an instant success. Donovan soon added disposable absorbent material to create the first disposable nappy and, in 1951, sold her company for $1 million (£600,000).

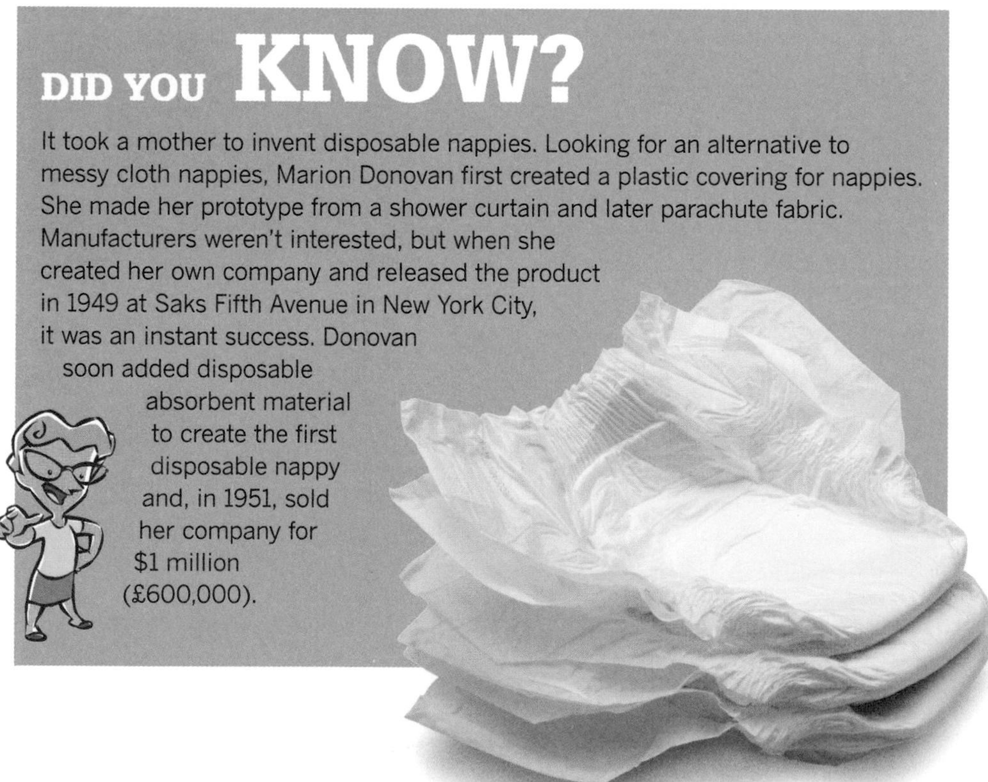

Dustpans

Decorate the front door with an autumnal wreath Gather dried autumn foliage, including brilliant red and yellow leaves, and evergreen branches with berries. Tie them together as a bouquet with a rubber band or tape. Spread them out in a fan shape and cover the binding with a ribbon. Now set this against a copper dustpan. Use super glue or a glue gun to attach your bouquet to the pan. If you don't have a copper duspan, you can spray a plastic one with copper-coloured metallic paint.

Enlist the smallest shoveller Most children love mimicking their elders. While you shovel snow, sweep up leaves or other garden debris, let a little one help using a spare dustpan as a shovel.

Use as a sand toy Pack a clean dustpan along with beach toys. It makes a great sand scoop and will really help the sand castle builders in their task.

Make toy pick-ups speedy Picking up lots of little toys can get really tiresome. Scoop them up with a dustpan and deposit them in the toy bin. It's a brilliant time-saver and will save your back as well.

Sweep up spiders and other insects If you prefer not to have spiders or other insects in the bath or elsewhere in the house but are too soft-hearted to flush them down the plug hole, use a dustpan to scoop up the unwanted visitors and transfer them out into the garden.

Get rid of dog mess in the garden If you have a dog or cat, keep an old dustpan by the back door and use it to clean up any messes that are lying around on the lawn. Every so often, scrub it out using a strong disinfectant.

Clear a rabbit or guinea pig hutch quickly Changing the straw and other bedding in a rabbit hutch is not anyone's favourite job. Use a dustpan to swiftly scoop soiled bedding into a rubbish bag.

Earrings

Use as a bulletin board tack Lend a little personal style to a bulletin board. Use cheap pierced earrings that have lost their other halves to tack up pictures, notes, souvenirs and clippings.

Create a brooch If you have a batch of single pierced earrings collecting dust, use wire cutters to snip off the stems and use your creativity. Arrange the earrings on a piece of coloured card and secure them with a glue gun. Add a pin backing to make a new brooch. Use the same method to jazz up a plain picture frame.

Decorate a Christmas tree Scatter clip-on earrings around the boughs of the Christmas tree as an eye-catching accent to larger tree decorations. Or use them as the main adornment on a small tree or wreath.

Make a magnet Give your fridge some glitz. Use wire cutters to cut the stem off an orphan earring and glue it to a magnet.

Clip your scarf If you've lost a favourite clip earring wear the survivor by using it to secure a scarf. Just tie the scarf as desired, then clip it with the earring.

Make an instant button. If you're dressed to go out and you discover a button missing, just dip into your collection of clip-on earrings. Clip the earring onto the button side of the garment to create a new 'button', then button as usual using the buttonhole. If you have time, move the top button to replace the lost one and then use the earring at the top of the garment.

DID YOU KNOW?

People have been wearing – and probably losing – earrings for nearly 5000 years. According to historians who have studied jewellery, the tiny baubles were probably introduced in western Asia in about 3000 BC The oldest earrings that have been discovered date from 2500 BC and were found in Iraq. The popularity of earrings over time has grown or receded, depending on hairstyles and clothing trends. The clip-on earring was introduced in the 1930s, and by the 1950s, fashionable women simply did not pierce their ears. But twenty years later, pierced ears were back in fashion.

* Egg cartons

Make ice If you are making lots of ice for a picnic or party, use the bottom halves of clean polystyrene egg cartons as auxiliary ice trays.

Use for storing and organising With six or a dozen handy compartments, egg cartons are brilliant for storing and organising small items. Here are some ideas to get you going. You're bound to come up with more of your own.

- Instead of emptying coins from your pocket into a jar for sorting later, cut off a four-section piece of an egg carton and leave it on the dressing table. Sort your coins by value as you pull them out of your pockets. (Put pennies and two pence pieces in a larger container, such as a jar, or put them in a piggy bank.)
- Organise buttons, safety pins, threads, bobbins and fasteners on a sewing table.
- Organise washers, tacks, small nuts and bolts and screws on a workbench. Or use to keep disassembled parts in sequence.
- Keep small, delicate Christmas ornaments from being crushed by packing them in handy, stackable egg cartons.

Start a fire Fill a cardboard egg carton with briquettes (and a bit of leftover candle wax if it's handy), place on the barbecue and light. Egg cartons can also be filled with tinder, such as small bits of wood and paper and used as a fire starter in a fireplace or a woodstove.

Start seedlings An egg carton can become the perfect nursery for seeds. Use a cardboard egg carton, not a polystyrene one. Fill each cell in the carton with soil and plant a few seeds in each one. Once the seeds have sprouted, divide the carton into individual cells and plant, cardboard cells and all.

Reinforce a bin bag If you have ever pulled a plastic rubbish bag out of the kitchen bin only to have something horrible drip on the floor, put an opened empty egg carton at the bottom of the bin bag to prevent tears and punctures.

Post homemade goodies to distant parts Here is a great way to brighten the day of a faraway friend or loved one. Cover an egg carton with bright wrapping paper. Line the individual cells with sweet wrappers or coloured tissue paper. Nestle homemade treats inside each. Include the carton in your next package or birthday gift and rest assured that the treats will arrive intact.

Golf ball caddy Keep an egg carton in a golf bag. It is a great way to keep golf balls clean, organised and ready for teeing off.

Eggs

Make a facial For a little pampering, head to the refrigerator for an egg. If you have dry skin that needs moisturising, separate the egg and beat the yolk. Those with oily skin should use the egg white, to which a bit of lemon or honey can be added. For normal skin, use the entire egg. Apply the beaten egg, relax and wait 30 minutes, then rinse. Your skin should be soft, fresh and clean.

Use as glue If you have run out of white glue, egg whites can act as a glue substitute for gluing paper or light cardboard together.

Add to compost Eggshells are a great addition to your compost because they are rich in calcium, a nutrient that is beneficial to plants. Crushing them thoroughly before you put them in your compost heap will help them to break down faster.

Water your plants After boiling eggs, don't pour the water down the drain. Instead, let it cool, then water plants with the nutrient-filled water.

Start seeds You can plant seeds in eggshells. Place the eggshell halves in the carton, fill each with soil, and press the seeds inside. The seeds will draw extra nutrients from the eggshells. Once the seedlings are about 7.5cm tall, they are ready to be transplanted into the garden. Remove them from the shell before you put them in the ground. Then crush the eggshells and put them on the compost heap or plant them in the garden.

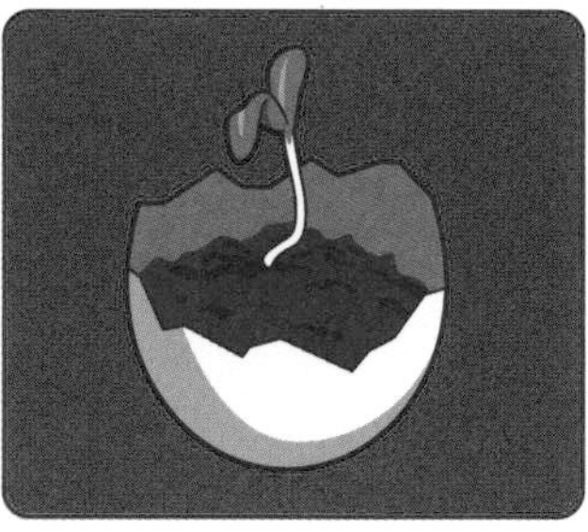

Electrical tape

Stop ants in their tracks Stop an army of ants marching towards the biscuit jar on a worktop or a tasty snack in the pantry. Create a 'moat' around the object by surrounding it with electrical tape placed sticky side up.

Make a lint-lifter To lift lint and pet hair off clothing and upholstery, you don't need a special lint remover. Simply wrap your hand with electrical tape, sticky side out and rub it against the surface of the material.

Cover casters Prevent wheeled furniture from leaving marks on a wood or vinyl floor by wrapping caster wheels with electrical tape.

Clean a comb Remove the dirt that builds up between the teeth of a comb, by pressing a strip of electrical tape along the comb's length. Lift it off, then dip the comb in a solution of alcohol and water or ammonia and water to sterilise it.

Organise tubes of glue and caulk If an untidy pile of glue and caulk tubes is cluttering a workbench, cut a strip of electrical or gaffer tape several centimetres long and fold it over the bottom of each tube, leaving a flap at the end. Punch a hole in the flap with a paper hole punch and hang the tube on a nail or hook. You'll free up space on the bench and be able to find the right tube quickly.

Safely remove glass from a broken window Removing a broken pane of glass can be dangerous as there is always the possibility that a sharp fragment will fall out and cut you. To prevent this, crisscross both sides of the broken pane with electrical tape before removing a sash or hinged window. Don't forget to wear heavy leather gloves when you pull the glass shards out of the frame.

Reinforce book binding Electrical tape is perfect for repairing broken book binding. Using coloured tape of a suitable colour (matching or contrasting the cover so that it looks appealing), run the tape down the length of the spine and cut shorter pieces to run perpendicular to that if you need extra reinforcement.

Cover a book Use electrical tape in any colour to create a durable book cover for a textbook or a paperback that you want to read on the beach. Make a pattern for the cover on a sheet of newspaper; fit the pattern to your book, then cover the pattern, one row at a time, with electrical tape, overlapping the rows. The resulting removable cover will be waterproof and sturdy.

Wrap Christmas presents For a novel way to wrap a special gift, don't bother with the paper; go straight for the tape. Press electrical tape directly onto the gift box. Make designs or cover in stripes and then add decorative touches by cutting shapes, letters and motifs from tape to attach to the 'wrapped' surface.

Repair a rear-light If someone has backed into your car and smashed the rear-light, this is a quick fix that will last until you have time to get it repaired. Depending on where the cracks lie, use yellow or red electrical tape to hold the remaining parts of the rear-light cover together.

Repair outdoor cushions Don't let a little rip in the cushions that go with your garden furniture get any worse. Repair the tear with closely matched electrical tape and it will hold up for several seasons.

Make bicycle streamers Add streamers to the handlebars of a child's bicycle. Make them using electrical tape in various colours. Cut the tape into strips about 1cm wide by 25cm long. Fold each strip in half, sticky sides together. Once you have about half a dozen for each side, stick them into the end of the handlebar and secure them with lengths of electrical tape. Make sure that the child will still be able to get a good grip on the handlebars.

 Emery boards

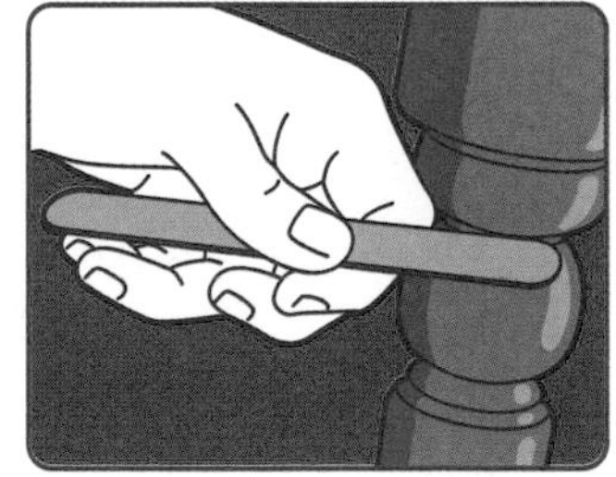

Sand deep crevices When refinishing an elaborate piece of wood such as turned table legs or chair spindles, you can use emery boards to gently smooth any hard-to-reach crevices before applying stain or finish. These file-like nail sanders are easy to handle and provide a choice of two sanding grades.

Remove dirt from an eraser To clean a dirty eraser on the end of a pencil, take an emery board and rub lightly over the eraser until the dirt is filed off.

Prepare seeds for planting Use an emery board to remove the hard coating on seeds before you plant them. This will speed sprouting and help them to absorb moisture more effectively.

DID YOU KNOW?

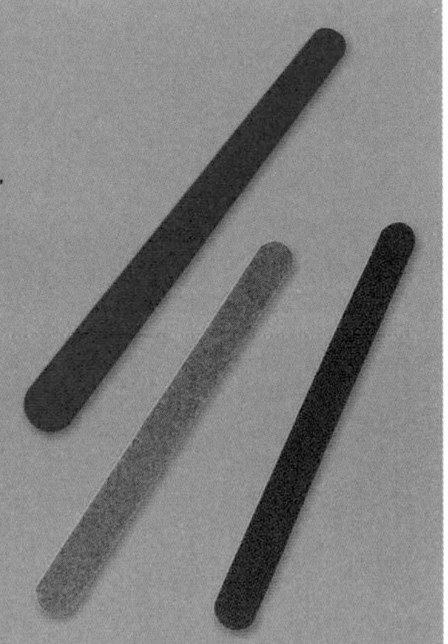

Emery boards were first introduced in around 1910. The emery coating is a natural mixture of corundum and magnetite – diamonds are the only minerals harder than corundum. Sapphires and rubies are also varieties of corundum. Not surprisingly perhaps, a manicurist's magazine urged women to 'treat their nails like jewels, not tools'. These days, emery boards come adorned with bright designs, give off scents, or may be shaped as hearts and stars.

Revitalise suede If a favourite pair of suede shoes have become stained and tired, an emery board can revive them. Rub the stain lightly with an emery board, and then hold the shoe over the steam from a kettle or pan of boiling water to remove the stain. This technique will work for suede clothing too.

* Envelopes

Shred old receipts faster The best way to get rid of receipts that may have your credit card number or other personal information in it is to shred them. But feeding tiny receipts into a shredder can be tedious. Instead, place all the old receipts into a few old envelopes and shred the envelopes.

Make a small funnel It is much cheaper to buy spices in bulk and transfer them to smaller, handier bottles for use in the kitchen. To make the job of transferring them much easier, make a couple of disposable funnels from an envelope. Seal the envelope, cut it in half diagonally and snip off one corner on each half to make two funnels for pouring spices into smaller jars.

Sort and store sandpaper Stop sheets of sandpaper from curling up into useless tubes and keep them organised by storing them in A5 card-backed envelopes. Use one envelope for each type of grit and write the grit grade on the envelopes.

Make file folders Don't let papers get disorganised just because you have run out of file folders. Cut the short ends off a light card-backed A4 envelope. Cut a 2cm wide strip lengthwise off the top of one side. The other edge will become the place where you label your file.

Make bookmarks Recycle envelopes by making them into useful bookmarks of different sizes. Cut off the gummed flap and one end of the envelope. Then slip the remainder over the corner of the page where you have stopped reading to make a quick placeholder that won't damage your book. Give a batch to the children to decorate to make their own set or to give as a homemade gift.

 Epsom salts

Get rid of foxes Are urban foxes raiding your rubbish bin, strewing mess around the front of the house? A few tablespoons of Epsom salts spread around bins should deter them as they won't like the taste. Reapply after it rains.

Deter slugs Are you tired of going out into the garden only to find the patio and lawn crawling with slimy slugs? Sprinkle Epsom salts where they glide and they will soon find another spot to gather in.

Fertilise tomatoes and other plants Every week, for each 30cm of the height of a tomato plant, add one tablespoon of Epsom salts and the tomatoes will flourish. Epsom salts are also a good fertiliser for houseplants, roses, gardenias and other flowers and trees.

Make the grass greener Use Epsom salts to add extra brightness to a lawn and add needed magnesium and iron to your soil. Add 2 tablespoons to 4 litres of water. Spread on the lawn and then water with plain water to make sure it has thoroughly soaked into the grass.

Clean bathroom tiles Clean grubby grout with some Epsom salts. Mix it in equal parts with washing-up liquid, then dab it onto the offending area and start scrubbing. The Epsom salts work with the detergent to dissolve the grime.

Regenerate a car battery If a car battery is starting to sound as if it won't turn over, and you are worried that you'll be stuck the next time you try to start your car, give the battery a little more life with this potion. Dissolve about 30g of Epsom salts in warm water and add it to each battery cell.

Get rid of blackheads Here is a sure-fire way to dislodge blackheads. Mix a teaspoon of Epsom salts and 3 drops iodine in 100ml boiling water. When the mixture cools enough to stick your finger in it, apply it to the blackhead with a cotton wool ball or bud. Repeat this three or four times, reheating the solution if necessary. Gently remove the blackhead and then dab the area with an alcohol-based astringent.

Frost your windows for Christmas If you are dreaming of a white Christmas, but the weather won't co-operate, you can make your windows look frosty. Mix Epsom salts with some stale beer until the salts stop dissolving. Apply the mixture to the windows with a sponge. For a realistic look, sweep the sponge in an arc at the bottom corners. When the mixture dries, the windows will look frosted.

{ KIDS' STUFF }

TWO FUN WINTER PROJECTS

Here are two fun winter-inspired projects to make using Epsom salts.

Make snowflakes by folding a piece of blue paper several times (1) and snipping shapes into the resulting square of paper (2). Unfold your snowflake. Brush one side with a thick mixture of water and Epsom salts (3). After it dries, turn it over and brush the other side. When it's finished, you'll have a frosty-looking snowflake that you can hang in the window.

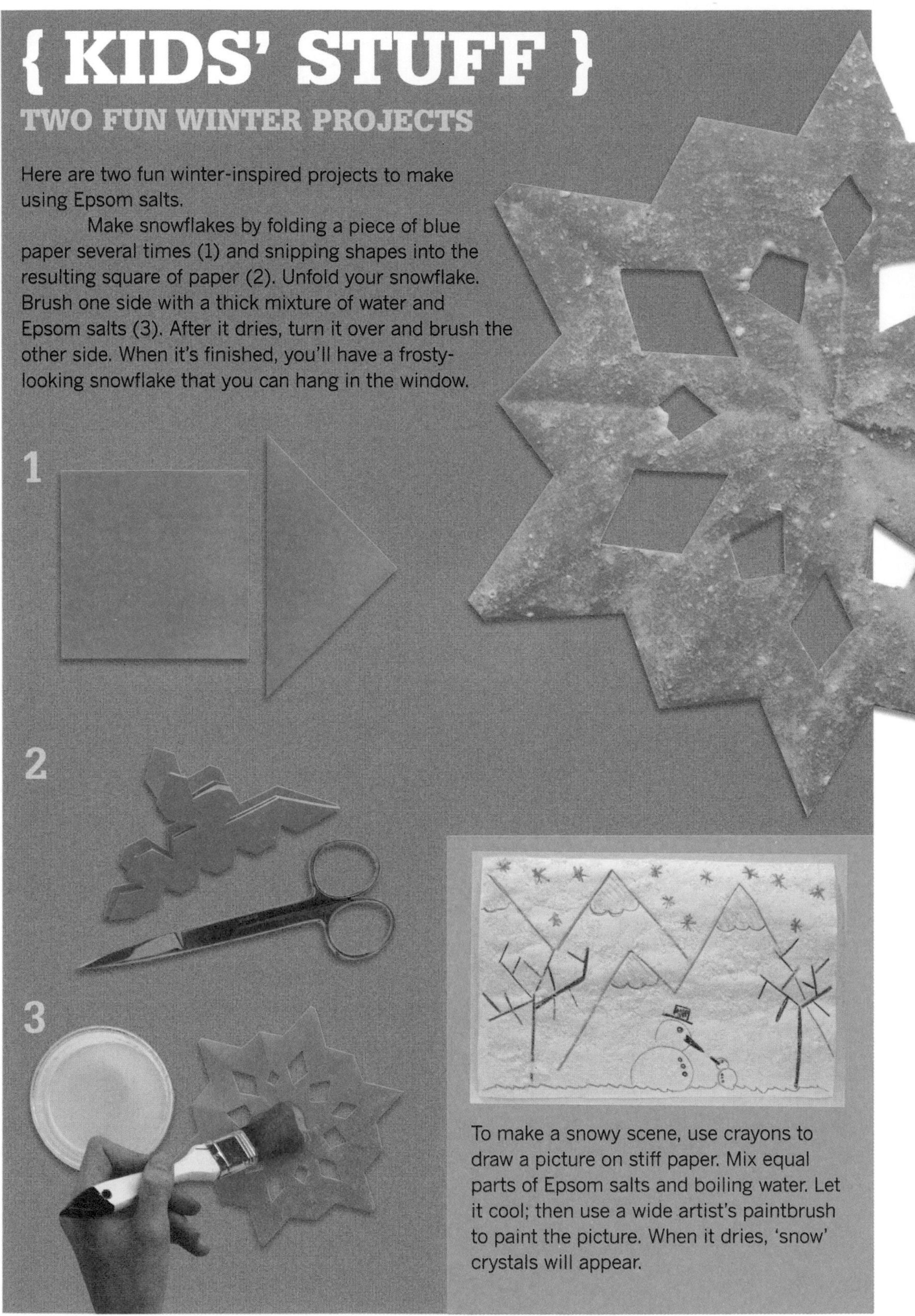

To make a snowy scene, use crayons to draw a picture on stiff paper. Mix equal parts of Epsom salts and boiling water. Let it cool; then use a wide artist's paintbrush to paint the picture. When it dries, 'snow' crystals will appear.

Fabric softener

End clinging dust on the TV Does dust fly back onto the television screen and other plastic surfaces, as soon as they have been cleaned? To eliminate the static that attracts dust, simply dampen a duster with a little fabric softener straight from the bottle and dust as usual.

Remove old wallpaper Removing old wallpaper is easy if you use fabric softener. Just stir 1 capful liquid softener into a litre of water and sponge the solution onto the wallpaper. Let it soak in for 20 minutes, then scrape the paper from the wall. If the wallpaper has a water-resistant coating, score it with a wire-bristle brush before treating with the fabric softener solution.

Abolish carpet shock To eliminate static shock when you walk across a carpet, spray the carpet with a fabric softener solution. Dilute 200ml softener with 2.5 litres water; fill a spray bottle and lightly squirt onto the carpet. Take care not to saturate it and damage the carpet backing. Spray in the evening and let the carpet dry overnight before walking on it. The effect should last for several weeks.

Remove hair-spray residue Dried-on hair spray can be tough to remove from walls and mirrors, but even a build-up of residue is no match for a solution of 1 part liquid fabric softener to 2 parts water. Stir to blend, pour into a spray bottle, squirt the surface and polish it with a dry cloth.

DID YOU KNOW?

How does fabric softener reduce cling as well as soften clothes? The secret is in the electrical charges. Positively charged chemical lubricants in the fabric softener are attracted to negative charges in the clothes, softening the fabric. The softened fabrics create less friction and less static, as they rub against each other in the drier and because fabric softener attracts moisture, the slightly damp surface of the fabrics makes them electrical conductors. As a result, the electrical charges travel through them instead of staying on the surface to cause static cling and sparks as you pull the clothing from the drier.

Clean now, not later Clean glass tables, shower doors, and other hard surfaces, and repel dust with liquid fabric softener. Mix 1 part softener into 4 parts water and store in a squirt bottle, such as an empty window-cleaning liquid bottle. Apply a little solution to a clean cloth, wipe the surface, and then polish with a dry cloth.

Float away baked-on grime Don't scrub. Instead, soak burned-on foods from casseroles with liquid fabric softener. Fill the casserole with water, add a squirt of liquid fabric softener and soak for an hour or until the residue wipes easily away.

Keep paintbrushes pliable After using a paintbrush, clean the bristles thoroughly and rinse them in an old can full of water with a drop of liquid fabric softener mixed in. After rinsing, wipe the bristles dry and store the brush as usual.

Untangle and condition hair Liquid fabric softener diluted in water and applied after shampooing can untangle and condition fine, flyaway hair, as well as curly, coarse hair. Experiment with the amount of conditioner to match it to the texture of your hair, using a weaker solution for fine hair and a stronger solution for coarse, curly hair. Comb through your hair and rinse.

Remove hard-water stains Hard-water stains on windows can be difficult to remove. To speed up the process, dab full-strength liquid fabric softener onto the stains and let it soak for 10 minutes. Then wipe the softener and stain off the glass with a damp cloth and rinse.

Make your own fabric softener sheets Fabric softener sheets are convenient to use, but they're much more expensive than liquid softeners. You can make your own drier sheets and save money. Just moisten an old facecloth with 1 teaspoon liquid softener and put it into the tumble drier with your next load.

* Fabric softener sheets

Pick up pet hair Pet hair can get a pretty tenacious grip on furniture and clothing. But a used fabric softener sheet will suck that fur right off the fabric with a couple of swipes. Just throw the dirty wipe into the bin.

Freshen up your car Has a pleasant new-car smell gradually turned into a stale old-car stench? Tuck a new fabric softener sheet under each car seat to counteract musty odours and cigarette smells.

Lift burned-on casserole residue The next time you get burned food on a casserole dish, fill the dish with hot water and place three or four used softener sheets in the dish. Soak overnight, remove the sheets, and you will have no trouble washing away the residue. Be sure to rinse it well afterwards.

Freshen drawers Don't buy scented drawer-liner paper; give drawers a fresh fragrance by tucking a new fabric softener sheet under existing drawer liners, or taping one to the back of each drawer.

Wipe soap scum from shower screens If you're tired of scrubbing crusty soap deposits from shower doors and screens, wipe the soap scum away with a used fabric softener sheet.

Repel dust from electrical appliances Because television and PC screens are electrically charged, they actually attract dust, making dusting them a never-ending chore. This isn't the case if you dust them with used fabric softener sheets. The sheets are designed to reduce static cling, so they remove the dust and keep it from resettling for several days or more.

Buff chrome to a brilliant shine After chrome is cleaned, it can still look streaky and dull, but whether it's a toaster or hubcaps, you can easily buff up the shine with a used fabric softener sheet.

Do away with dog odour If your best friend comes in from the rain bearing his own special wet-dog scent, wipe him down with a used fabric softener sheet and he should smell as fresh as a daisy.

People with allergies or chemical sensitivities may develop rashes or skin irritations when they come into contact with laundry treated with some commercial fabric softeners or fabric softener sheets. If you are sensitive to softeners, you can still soften your laundry by substituting 50ml white vinegar or adding the same amount of your favourite hair conditioner to the washing machine's last rinse cycle. It will give you noticeably softer, fresher-smelling laundry.

Freshen laundry hampers and wastebaskets There is still plenty of life left in a fabric softener sheet after it's been used. Place one in the bottom of the laundry basket and wastebaskets to counteract any stale odours.

Get trainers and gym bags smelling fresh Deodorising trainers and gym bags can call for strong stuff. Tuck a new fabric softener sheet into each trainer and leave overnight to neutralise odours (remember to pull them out before wearing). Drop a fabric softener sheet into the bottom of a gym bag and leave it there until your nose lets you know it's time to renew it.

Use as an inconspicuous air freshener Don't spend money on plug-in air fresheners. Just tuck a few sheets of tumble-drier fabric softener into wardrobes, chest of drawers, cupboards, behind curtains and under chairs.

Keep dust off blinds Cleaning venetian blinds is a tedious chore, so make the results last by wiping them down with a used fabric softener sheet to repel dust. Wipe them with another sheet whenever the effect wears off.

Use as a safe mosquito repellent For a safe mosquito repellent, look no futher than the laundry cupboard. Save used fabric softener sheets and pin or tie one to your clothing when you go outdoors to help to repel mosquitoes.

Do away with static cling You'll never be embarrassed by static cling again if you keep a used fabric softener sheet in your handbag or dresser drawer. When faced with static, dampen the sheet and rub it over tights to put an end to clinging skirts.

Renew grubby stuffed toys Wash fake-fur stuffed animals in the washing machine on a delicates programme, then put the stuffed animals into the tumble drier along with a pair of old tennis shoes and a fabric softener sheet and they will come out fluffy and with silky-soft fur.

Remove sawdust before painting Get rid of all traces of sawdust on a woodworking project before you paint or varnish it, by rubbing with an unused dryer fabric softener sheet; it will attract sawdust and hold it like a magnet.

Organise sheets and make them smell pretty Stop duvet covers, sheets and pillowcases from getting separated from one another by storing the set in one of the matching pillowcases.Then tuck a new fabric softener sheet into the packet for a fresh fragrance.

Prevent musty odours in suitcases Place a single, unused fabric softener sheet into an empty suitcase or other piece of luggage before storing and it will smell great the next time you use it.

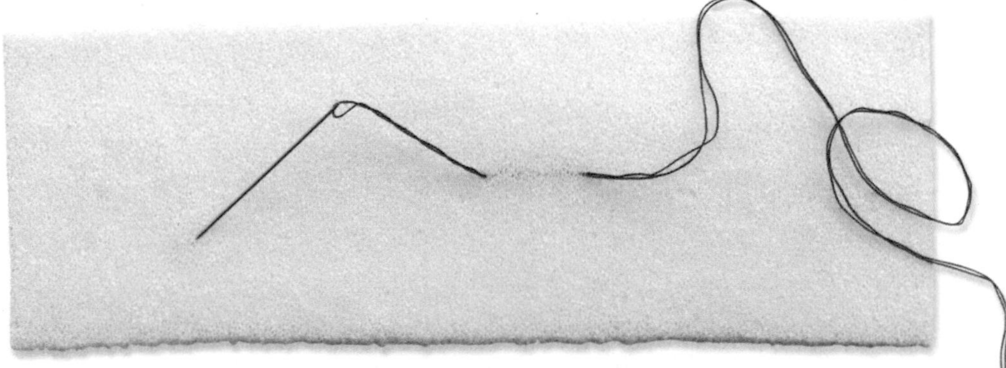

Abolish tangled sewing thread To put an end to tangled thread, keep an unused fabric softener sheet in your sewing kit. After threading the needle, insert it into the sheet and pull all of the thread through to give it a non-stick coating.

*Film canisters

Rattle toy for the cat Cats are amused by small objects that rattle and shake, and they really don't care what they look like. To provide endless entertainment for your cat, drop a few dried beans, a spoonful of dry rice or other small objects that won't be harmful if chewed or swallowed, into an empty film canister, snap on the lid and watch the fun begin.

Handy label dispenser To keep a roll of labels or stickers from being damaged, make a dispenser from an empty film canister. Hold the canister steady by taping it to a worktop with gaffer tape and use a craft knife to carefully cut a slit into the side of the canister. Drop the roll of labels in, feed it out through the slit, snap the cap on and it is ready to use.

Use as hair rollers You can collect all the hair rollers you'll ever need if you save empty plastic film canisters. To use, pop the top off, roll damp hair around the canister, and hold it in place by fastening a hair clip over the open end of the canister and your hair.

Emergency sewing kit You'll never be at a loss if you lose a button or a hem unravels if you fill an empty film canister with buttons, pins and a pre-threaded needle. Make several and tuck one into each travel bag, handbag or gym bag.

Store fishing flies You can save a lot of money and grief by storing fishing flies and hooks in labelled film canisters. They don't take up much room in a jacket pocket and if you do drop one in the water, the airtight lid will keep it floating long enough for you to rescue it.

On-the-road pill dispensers Use empty film canisters as travelling pill bottles to keep in a handbag or overnight bag. If you take more than one kind of medication, use a separate canister for each. Write the medication and dosage on a peel-and-stick label and attach to each canister. For at-a-glance identification, colour the labels with different-coloured highlighter pens.

TIP* THE VANISHING FILM CANISTER

Plastic film canisters have myriad uses, from emergency ashtrays to spice bottles. But with the rise of digital cameras, these small wonders are rapidly going the way of the rotary dial phone or the phonograph needle. A good source for free film canisters has always been the one-hour photo shop. But these days you may find that even they have a canister shortage. If so, check the phonebook or internet for a professional film developer, because most high-quality, professional photographers still use film – and film canisters.

Carry spices for cooking when camping Just because you are roughing it, doesn't mean that you have to eat bland food. You can store a multitude of seasonings in individual film canisters to take along when you go camping, and you will still have plenty of room for the food itself in your rucksack or car boot. It's a good idea for a caravan or holiday home as well.

Carry small change for laundry and tolls Film canisters are just the right size to hold smaller change. Tuck a canister of change into a laundry bag or the car's glove compartment and you'll never have to hunt for change when you're at a launderette or a toll booth.

Bring your own diet aids If you are on a special diet, you can easily and discreetly transport favourite salad dressings, artificial sweetener or other condiments to restaurants in plastic film canisters. Clean, empty canisters hold single-sized servings, have snap-on, leakproof lids and are small enough to tuck into a handbag with ease.

Keep jewellery close at hand An empty film canister doesn't take up much room in a gym bag, and it'll come in handy for keeping rings and earrings from being misplaced while you exercise.

Emergency nail polish remover Create a small, spill-proof carry case for nail polish remover by tucking a small piece of sponge into a plastic film canister. Saturate the sponge with polish remover and snap on the lid. For an emergency repair, simply insert a finger and rub the nail against the fluid-soaked sponge to remove the polish.

Flour

Repel ants with flour Sprinkle a line of flour along the backs of pantry and kitchen cabinet shelves and wherever you see ants entering the house. Repelled by the flour, the ants won't cross over the line.

Make modelling clay Keep children busy with some homemade modelling clay – they can even help you to make it. Knead together 600g flour, 50g salt, 200ml

DID YOU KNOW?

Have you ever wondered why the word 'flour' is pronounced exactly like the word 'flower'? Flour is actually derived from the French word for flower, which is fleur. The French use the word to describe the most desirable, or floury (flowery) and protein-rich, part of a grain after processing removes the hull. And, because much of our food terminology comes from the French, we still bake and make sauces with the flower of grains, such as wheat, which we call flour.

DID YOU KNOW?

For thousands of years people have been putting plants into pots to transport native plants to a new land or to bring exotic plants home. In 1495 BC, Egyptian queen Hatshepsut sent workers to Somalia to bring back incense trees in pots. And in 1787 Captain Bligh reportedly had more than 1,000 breadfruit plants in clay pots aboard the HMS Bounty. The plants were destined for the West Indies, where they were to be grown as food for the islands' slave population.

water, 1 tablespoon vegetable oil and 1 or 2 drops food colouring. If the mixture is sticky, add more flour; if it's too stiff, add more water. When the 'clay' is of a workable consistency, it can be stored until needed in a self-sealing plastic bag.

Freshen playing cards After a few games, cards may accumulate a greasy patina, but you can restore them with some flour in a paper bag. Drop the cards into the bag with enough flour to cover, shake vigorously and remove the cards. The flour will absorb the oils and it can be easily knocked off the cards by giving them a thorough shuffle.

Safe paste for children's crafts Look no farther than your kitchen for an inexpensive, non-toxic paste that is ideal for children's paper craft projects, such as papier-mâché and pasting items into a scrap book. To make the paste, add 600ml cold water to a saucepan and blend in 200g flour. Stirring constantly, bring the mixture to a boil. Reduce heat and simmer, stirring until smooth and thick. Cool and pour into a plastic squeeze bottle to use. This simple paste will keep for weeks in the refrigerator, and can be easily cleaned up with soap and water.

Polish brass and copper Don't buy special cleaners for brass and silver. You can make your own far cheaper. Combine equal parts of flour, salt and vinegar, and mix into a paste. Spread the paste onto the metal, let it dry and buff it off with a clean, dry cloth.

Bring back the lustre to a dull sink To buff a stainless steel sink back to a warm shine, sprinkle flour over it and rub lightly with a soft, dry cloth. Then rinse the sink and polish again to restore its shine.

* Flowerpots

Container for baking bread Take a new, clean medium-sized clay flowerpot, soak it in water for about 20 minutes and then lightly grease the inside with butter. Place bread dough, prepared in the usual way, in the pot and bake. The clay pot will give the bread a crusty exterior while keeping the inside moist.

Create a firewood container Spare yourself the expense of buying a special brass or metal holder for firewood and put an extra-large empty ceramic or clay flowerpot beside the hearth instead. It's a perfect – and cheap – place to keep kindling and small logs ready for when the temperature drops.

Unfurl wool without knots The sweater you're knitting will take forever if you're constantly stopping to pull out tangles in the wool. To prevent this, place your ball of wool under an upturned flowerpot and thread the end through the draining hole. Set it next to where you are sitting for relaxed, tangle-free knitting.

Create an aquarium fish cave Some fish love to lurk in shadowy corners of their tanks, keeping themselves safe from imagined predators. Place a mini flowerpot on its side on the aquarium floor to create a cave for shy fish.

Help container plants to root The plants that you want to put in a beautiful deep container on the patio have a shallow root system and you don't want to go to the bother – and expense – of filling a huge container completely with potting mix. Is there a solution? When planting shallow-rooted plants in a deep container, one easy solution is to find another smaller flowerpot that will fit upside down in the base of the deeper pot and occupy a lot of that space. After you insert it, fill around it with soil before putting in your plants.

Keep soil in a flowerpot Soil from a houseplant won't slip away when it's watered if you place broken clay flowerpot shards in the bottom of the pot when re-planting. When you are watering the plants, the water will drain out, but not the soil.

Foam food trays

Make knee pads for gardening If you find that all the kneeling that planting entails makes your knees ache, tape some foam food trays to your knees. Or attach them to your legs using the top halves of old tube-shaped socks (with the feet removed). The trays will give much-needed extra padding while you pull out weeds and fertilise your plants.

Release your innersoles If your tired feet need a little padding, take a couple of clean meat trays and cut them to fit inside a pair of shoes or boots. You should have happy feet and some extra cushioning for free.

Produce a disposable serving dish If you need a quick disposable serving platter while you're cooking outside or camping, you can make one from a large foam food tray. Wash it with soap and water, cover it with foil and load it up with food. You can also use these serving dishes to bring goodies to a school cake stall or a meal to a sick or housebound neighbour.

Provide an art palette Create a paint palette for a budding Picasso. A thoroughly cleaned and dried food tray is the perfect place for children to squirt their tempera or oil paints. If they are experimenting with watercolours, use two trays. Put watercolor paint in one and water in the other. At the end of the artwork session, you can just throw them away.

Protect pictures when posting Why buy expensive padded envelopes to send photographs to loved ones? Cut foam trays slightly smaller than the envelope. Insert the photographs between the trays, place in the envelope and post. The photos should arrive free of creases or bends.

Foldback clips

Strengthen your grip Does a weak grip or arthritis make it hard for you to open jars and do other tasks with your hands? A large foldback clip can help to boost your grip. Squeeze the folded-back wings of the clip, hold for a count of five and relax. Do this a dozen or so times with each hand a few times a day. It will strengthen your grip and release tension too.

Mount a picture Here is a stylish way to mount and hang a picture so that it has a clean frameless look. Sandwich the picture between a sheet of glass or clear plastic and piece of hardboard or stiff cardboard. Then use tiny binder clips along the edges to clamp the pieces together. Use two or three clips on each side. After the clips are in place, remove the clip handles at the front. Tie picture wire to the rear handles to hang the picture.

Keep your place A medium-sized foldback clip makes an ideal bookmark. If you don't want to leave impression marks on the pages, tape a soft material like felt or even just some adhesive tape, to the inside jaws of the clip before using.

Make a money clip To keep paper money in a neat bundle in your pocket or purse, stack the bills, fold them in half and put a small foldback clip over the fold.

Keep passport handy If you are at an airport and you know you will be asked to show your passport and tickets a number of times, instead of fishing in your bag, use a foldback clip to firmly and conveniently attach your passport and other travel documents to your belt. You can also use a small binder clip to secure your office ID to your belt or a breast pocket if you need to keep it to hand.

* Freezers

Eliminate unpopped popcorn Eliminate stale popcorn that won't pop by keeping the unpopped supply in the freezer.

Remove wax from candlesticks Grandma's heirloom silver candlesticks will get a new life if you place them in the freezer and then pick off any accumulated wax drippings. But don't do this if the candlesticks are made from more than one type of metal. The metals may expand and contract at different rates and damage the candlesticks.

TIP* FREEZER TACTICS

Here are some ways to get the most out of your freezer or your refrigerator's freezer compartment:

- To prevent food from spoiling, keep the freezer at –18°C. To check the temperature, place a freezer thermometer (sold at hardware stores) between two frozen food containers.
- A full freezer runs the compressor less often and stays colder longer which is worth remembering the next time there's a power cut.
- The shelves on a freezer door are a little warmer than the freezer interior, making them ideal for storing items such as bread and coffee.
- When defrosting the freezer, place a large towel or sheet on the bottom. Water will drip onto it, making cleaning up much easier.
- The next time you defrost the freezer, apply a thin coat of petroleum jelly to the walls to keep any frost from sticking.

Unstick photos If water has dripped onto a batch of photographs, causing them to stick together, place them in the freezer for about 20 minutes. Then use a butter knife to gingerly separate the photos. If they don't come free, place them back in the freezer. This method works for envelopes and stamps too.

Extend candle life Place candles in the freezer for at least 2 hours before burning. They will last longer.

Clean a pan If a pan has been left on the hob for too long and you have a burned-on mess to clean up, place the pan in the freezer for a couple of hours. When the burned food is frozen, it will be easier to remove.

Remove odours If you have a musty-smelling book or a plastic container with a fish odour, place them in the freezer overnight. By morning they'll be fresh again. This simple trick works with almost any other small item with a bad smell that you want to get rid of.

 Fruit baskets

Keep vegetable peelings out of the drain Don't clog up the kitchen plughole with peelings from potatoes or carrots. Use a fruit basket as a sink strainer to catch vegetable shavings as they fall.

Store soap pads and sponges If you're tired of throwing away prematurely rusted steel wool soap pads or smelly sponges, place a fruit basket near the corner of the kitchen sink and line the bottom with a layer of heavy-duty aluminium foil. Fashion a spout on a corner of the foil closest to the sink that can act as a drain to keep water from pooling up at the bottom of the basket. The wire soap pads and sponges should last significantly longer.

Use as a colander If you need a small colander to wash individual servings of fruits and vegetables or to drain off a child's portion of hot macaroni shells, use an empty fruit basket. It makes an excellent mini-colander.

Arrange flowers Droopy or lopsided flower arrangements are not elegant. That's why professionals use a substance known as oasis to keep cut flowers in place. For an alternative stabiliser, insert an inverted fruit basket into a vase (cut the basket to fit, if necessary). It should keep flower stalks standing tall.

{ KIDS' STUFF }

BASKETS FOR CRAFT PROJECTS

Fruit baskets can be useful for all sorts of children's crafts. For example, you can cut apart the panels and carve out geometric shapes for them to use as stencils. You can also turn one into an Easter basket by adding some fake grass and a (preferably pink) pipe cleaner for a handle. Or use one as a multiple bubble maker; simply dip it in some water mixed with washing-up liquid and wave it through the air to create swarms of bubbles. Lastly, let children decorate the baskets with ribbons, stiff paper or lightweight card and use them to store their own little trinkets and toys.

Fashion a string dispenser or screwdriver holder If you don't want to have to untangle knots every time you need a piece of string, twine or wool, make a dispenser with two fruit baskets. Place the ball inside one fruit basket. Feed the cord through the top of a second, inverted basket, then tie the two baskets together with twist ties. You can mount an inverted fruit basket on your workshop wall to hold and organise screwdrivers which will fit neatly between the slats.

Use as a dishwasher basket If the smaller items you place in the dishwasher (such as baby bottle caps, jar lids and food-processor accessories) won't stay put, try putting them in a fruit basket. Place the items inside one basket, then cover with a second basket. Fasten them together with a thick rubber band and place on the dishwasher's upper rack. Because the baskets are perforated, water will be sieved through them when the machine is running.

Organise pills and medicines A clean fruit basket is ideal for organising vitamins and medicine bottles. If you're taking several medicines, a fruit basket is a convenient way to place them all – or pre-packaged individual doses – in one, easy-to-remember location. You can also use baskets to organise medicines in your cupboard or medicine cabinet according to their expiry dates or uses.

Protect seedlings Help young plants to thrive in the garden by placing inverted fruit baskets over them. The baskets will let water, sunlight and air in, but keep rabbits, rats and squirrels out. Make sure the basket is buried below ground level and tightly secured (placing a few large stones around it may suffice).

Make a bulb cage Squirrels and other rodents view freshly planted flower bulbs as nothing more than tasty morsels and easy pickings. But you can put a damper on their meal by planting bulbs in fruit baskets. Be sure to place the basket at the correct depth, then insert the bulb and cover with soil.

Build mini hanging planters Making little hanging baskets for small-scale plants such as violas, or to highlight your favourite annuals. Fill a series of berry baskets with sphagnum moss mixed with a bit of potting soil, plant your desired combination of plants and suspend them from a balcony or outside a back door with a length of monofilament fishing line.

Funnels

Separate eggs To make an exceptional egg separater, use a funnel. Simply crack the egg into the funnel. The white will slide out of the spout into another container, while the yolk stays put. Just be careful not to break the yolk when you're cracking the egg.

Make a string dispenser Don't get tied up in knots over tangled string. Nail a large funnel to the wall, with the stem pointing down. Place a ball of string in the funnel and thread the end through the funnel's stem. You will have an instant knot-free string dispenser.

Make a kids' telephone Use two small plastic funnels to make a durable string telephone for your children. For each funnel, tie a button to one end of a length of kite string and thread it through the large end of the funnel. Tie another button at the bottom of the spout to keep the string in place and let the children start talking to each other on their free telephone.

Gaffer tape see page 160

Garden hose

Capture earwigs Stop earwigs from making a meal of prize dahlias by luring them into a bit of hose. Cut the hose into 30cm lengths, making sure the inside is completely dry. Place the hose segments where you have seen earwigs crawling around and leave them overnight. By the morning the hoses should be filled with the earwigs and they can be transferred far away from their favourite meal.

Unclog a drainpipe When leaves and debris clog up your drainpipe and guttering, use a garden hose to get things flowing again. Push the hose up the pipe and poke it through the blockage. You won't even have to turn the hose on, because the water in the gutters will flush out the blockage.

Stabilise a tree A short length of old garden hose is a good way to tie a young tree to its stake. You'll find that the hose is flexible enough to bend when the tree does, but at the same time, it's strong enough to keep the tree tied to its stake until it can stand on its own. Also, the hose will not damage the bark of the young tree as it grows.

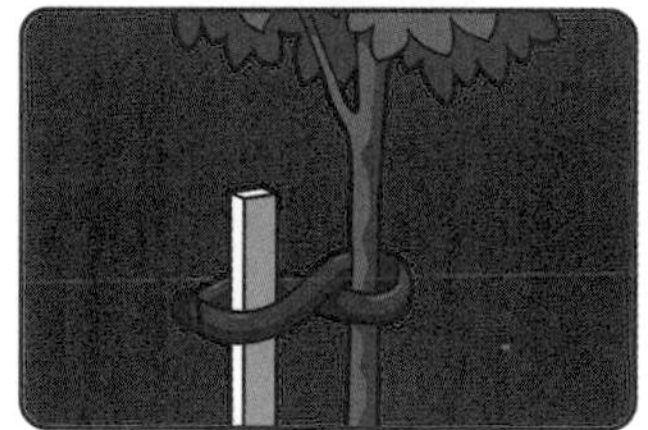

Cover the chains on a child's swing No parent wants to see a child hurt on a garden swing. Put a length of old hose over each chain to protect little hands from getting pinched or twisted. If you have access to one end of the chains, just slip the chain through the hose. Otherwise, slit the hose down the middle, and slip it over the chains of the swing. Close the slit hose with a few wraps of gaffer tape.

Protect handsaw and ice skate blades Keep a handsaw blade sharp and safe by protecting it with a length of garden hose. Cut a piece of hose to the length you need, slit it along its length and slip it over the teeth. This is a good way to protect the blades of ice skates on the way to the rink and cooking knives when you're packing for a camping trip.

Make a paint can grip To stop a heavy paint can from slipping and spilling and stop thin wire handles from cutting into your hand use a short length of hose. Slit it down the middle and encase the handle of the paint can to make it easier and more comfortable to carry.

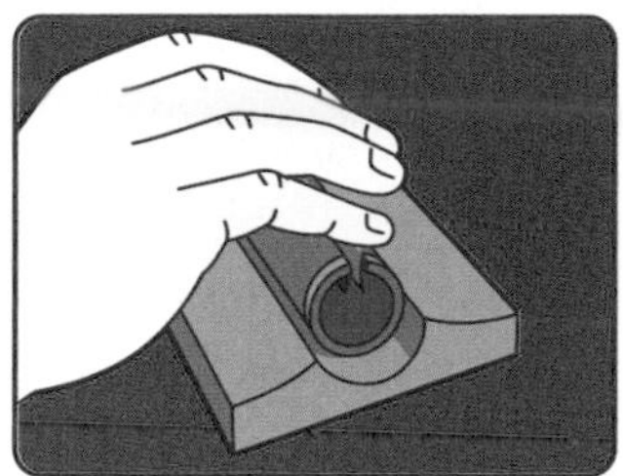

Make a sander for curves To sand a tight concave surface – for example a piece of cove moulding, take a 25cm length of garden hose, split it open lengthways and insert one edge of a piece of sandpaper. Wrap the sandpaper around the hose, cut it to fit and insert the other end in the slit. Firmly close the slit with a piece of gaffer tape and you should be able to get at the most awkward bend.

Create a template for a new garden design When planning a new garden design, use a garden hose to create a template for curves, circles and other free-form elements of the design. Using the line of the hose, you should be able to mark the edges of new curved beds, patios or pathway features and get a smooth, elegant line to follow.

Corral leaves and autumn fruit In autumn, curl an unused garden hose into a large circle to make a holding area for a pile of dead leaves, picked apples or pears (or windfalls) or any other garden debris that you want to keep neatly contained in one part of the garden.

Make a play phone Transform an old garden hose into a fun new telephone for the children. Cut any length of hose you desire. Stick a funnel at each end and attach it with glue or tape.

TIP* BUYING A HOSE

Bear these points in mind when going to buy a new hose – it's one of the most important outdoor tools:

- To determine how long a hose you need, measure the distance from the tap to the farthest point in the garden. Add a couple of metres to allow for watering around corners; this will help you to avoid the annoying kinks that cut water pressure.
- Vinyl and rubber hoses are generally sturdier and weather resistant than those made of cheaper forms of plastic. If a hose flattens when you step on it, it is not up to gardening duties.
- Buy a hose with a lifetime warranty; only good-quality hoses will have one.

GAFFER TAPE...

...around the house

Temporarily hem your jeans If you have found a well-fitting pair of jeans, but the length isn't right, you expect a little shrinkage anyway, so why spend time hemming; thick denim jeans can be difficult to sew through. Make a temporary hem with gaffer tape. The new hem will last through a few washes.

Remove lint on clothing To remove pet hairs, wrap one hand with a length of gaffer tape, sticky side out. Then roll the sticky tape against the article of clothing in a rocking motion until every last hair has been picked up. Don't wipe, since that may affect the nap of the fabric.

Make a DIY bandage Here's how to protect a bad scrape until you can get a proper dressing. Fold tissue paper or paper towel to cover the wound and cover it with a piece of gaffer tape. It will keep the wound clean until you can treat it properly.

Reseal bags of crisps To keep a half-finished bag of potato crisps or a similar snack from going stale, fold up the top and seal it tight with a small piece of gaffer tape.

Protect a wallet Old wallets may lose their resilience but are otherwise still useful. Cover an old wallet with gaffer tape; reinforce between each section and it will be as good as new.

Bumper sticker If you have got something you want to say to others, make your own bumper or windscreen sticker. Cut a length of gaffer tape, fix it to your bumper or windscreen and write your message with a permanent marker.

Keep a secret car key You will never get locked out of your car again if you fix an extra key to the undercarriage with gaffer tape.

Catch flies and other insects If you have just checked into a rustic cottage near a lake or stream and you are ready to start enjoying your holiday but are plagued by swarms of flies and midges, take a roll of gaffer tape and tear off a few 30cm strips. Hang them from the rafters to use as flypaper. You should soon get rid of the flies and you can roll up the tape and throw it away.

Replace a shower curtain eyelet How many times have you yanked a shower curtain aside only to rip through one of the eyelets? Make a simple repair with gaffer tape. Once the curtain is dry, cut a rectangular piece of tape in a matching colour and fold it from front to back over the torn hole. Slit the tape with a craft knife, razor blade or scissors, and push the shower curtain ring back in place.

Repair a vacuum cleaner hose If a vacuum cleaner hose has cracked and developed a leak, you don't need to buy a whole new machine. Repair the broken hose with gaffer tape and your vacuum cleaner will last until the motor wears out.

Reinforce book binding Gaffer tape is perfect for repairing a broken book binding. Run the tape down the length of the spine and cut shorter pieces to run perpendicular to that if you need extra reinforcement.

Repair a photo frame Many people enjoy displaying family photographs in easel-type frames on mantels and side tables throughout the house. But sometimes the foldout leg that holds a frame upright pulls away from the back of the frame and your photograph won't stand up properly. Use gaffer tape to firmly reattach the broken leg to the back of the frame.

Hang Christmas lights Festive holiday lights on the outside of the house are fun in season, but can be a real chore when it is time for them to come down. Use gaffer tape to hang the lights and the removal job will be much easier. Tear the gaffer tape into thin strips. At intervals, wrap strips around the wire and then tape the strand to the gutter or wherever you hang your lights.

DID YOU KNOW?

In the USA, gaffer tape is known as duct tape. But it really did start being known as duck tape. In the Second World War, the US military needed a flexible, durable, waterproof tape. Permacell, a division of Johnson & Johnson, devised a tape which used its own medical tape as a base but added a strong polycoat adhesive and a polyethylene coating laminated to a cloth backing. The resulting strong flexible tape, coloured army green and easy to rip into useful strips, was used for everything from sealing ammunition cases to repairing windscreens. GIs nicknamed it duck tape because it was waterproof, like a duck's back.

After the war, the tape, now available in a new silvery colour was used for joining heating and air-conditioning ductwork and became known as duct tape. In the UK it is known as gaffer tape after the electrician in charge of lighting on a film or television set.

GAFFER TAPE...

...for children

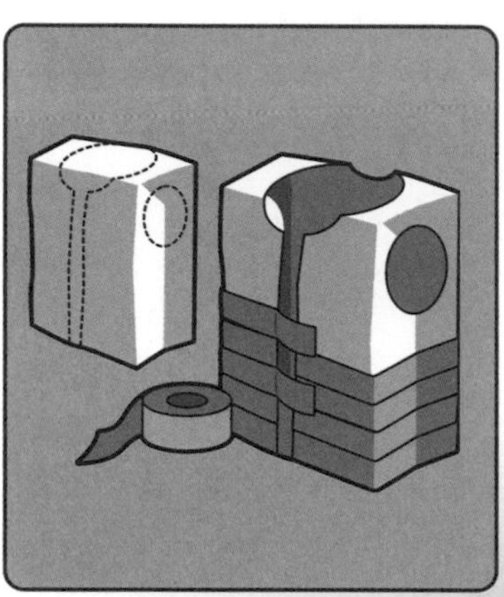

Make fancy dress costumes Use classic silver gaffer tape to make a costume for the Tin Man from *The Wizard of Oz* or a robot. Make a basic costume from flat-bottomed paper bags, with openings in the back so the child can easily put on and take off the costume. Cover this pattern with rows of gaffer tape. For the legs, cover over an old pair of trousers, again giving your little robot or Tin Man an easy way to remove the outfit for toilet breaks. Gaffer tape and electrical tape comes in a number of colours, so let your imagination lead your creativity by adding 'go faster' strips and other special robot markings.

Make a toy sword If you have a couple of would-be swashbucklers rushing around the house, make toy swords for the junior pirates and swordsmen by sketching a child-size sword onto a piece of cardboard. Use two pieces if you don't have one thick enough. Be sure to make a handle that the child's hand can fit around comfortably once it has been increased in thickness by several layers of gaffer tape. Wrap the entire blade shape in silver gaffer tape. Wrap the handle in black tape.

Make play rings and bracelets Make rings by tearing gaffer tape into strips about 1cm wide, then folding the strips in half lengthways, sticky sides together. Continue to put more strips over the first one until the ring is thick enough to stand on its own. You can adjust the size with scissors and tape the ends closed. To make a stone for the ring, cover a small item such as a pebble and attach it to the ring. Make a bracelet by winding gaffer tape around a stiff paper pattern.

Make hand puppets Gaffer tape is superb for puppet making. Use a small, strong paper bag as the base for the body of the puppet. Cover the bag with overlapping rows of gaffer tape. Make armholes through which fingers can poke out. Create a head from a tape-covered ball of crumpled paper and stick on buttons or beads to make the eyes and mouth.

...for the do-it-yourselfer

Make a temporary roof tile If you have lost a roof tile, make a temporary replacement by wrapping gaffer tape in strips across a piece of 6mm plywood cut to size. Wedge the makeshift tile in place to fill the space. It will close the gap and repel water until you can repair the roof properly.

Fix a wing mirror If you have just nudged the wing mirror trying to manoeuvre out of a tight space and the delicate mechanism is out of alignment, use a bit of gaffer tape to stick it back into position. Or if you like the wing mirror to stay firmly in the same place, use gaffer tape to stick it into your preferred position.

Short-term auto hose fix Until you can get to a mechanic, gaffer tape makes a strong and dependable temporary fix for broken water hoses on your car. But don't wait too long. Gaffer tape can only withstand temperatures up to 93°C. Also, don't use it to repair a leak in a car's fuel line – the petrol will dissolve the adhesive and the repair simply won't last.

Replace webbing on garden chairs When summer comes and you go to the shed to get the garden furniture out, don't be disappointed to find that the webbing on your favourite garden chair has worn out. And don't throw it out either. Gaffer tape makes a great, sturdy replacement webbing. Cut strips twice as long as you need. Double the tape, putting sticky sides together, so that you have backing facing out on both sides. Then screw it in place.

Tape a broken window Before removing broken window glass, crisscross the broken pane with gaffer tape to hold it all together. This will ensure a shard doesn't fall out and cut you.

Repair a dustbin Plastic dustbins often split or crack along the sides. But don't throw out the bin with the rubbish. Repair the tear with gaffer tape. It's strong enough to withstand the abuses a dusbin takes and is easy to manipulate on the curved or ridged surface of the bin. Put tape over the crack both outside and inside the bin.

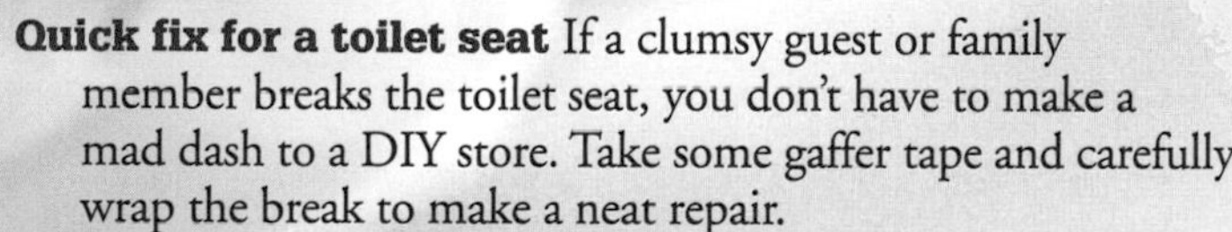

Quick fix for a toilet seat If a clumsy guest or family member breaks the toilet seat, you don't have to make a mad dash to a DIY store. Take some gaffer tape and carefully wrap the break to make a neat repair.

...for sports & outdoor gear

Tighten cricket pads Cricketers and ice hockey players need plenty of extra protection. Use gaffer tape to attach pads firmly in place. Put on all the necessary equipment, including socks. Now split the gaffer tape to the width appropriate for your size – children might need narrower strips than adults – and start wrapping around the pads to keep them tight to your legs.

Add life to a hockey stick Hockey sticks take a beating. If you have one that is showing its age, breathe a little more life into it by wrapping the bottom of the stick with gaffer tape. Replace the tape as often as needed.

GAFFER TAPE...

...for sports and outdoor gear

Extend the life of a skateboarder's shoes Children who perform fantastic feats on their skateboards find their shoes wear out very quickly because a lot of the jumps involve sliding the toe or side of the foot along the board. They wear holes in new shoes fast. Protect their feet and prolong the life of their new shoes by putting a layer or two of gaffer tape on the area that scrapes along the board.

Repair ski gloves Gaffer tape is the perfect solution for ripped ski gloves because it is waterproof, incredibly adhesive, strong and can easily be torn into strips of any width. Make the repair lengthways or around the fingers.

Repair a tent If you open your tent at a campsite only to discover a small tear, it is no problem as long as you have brought your gaffer tape along. Cover the hole with a patch; for double protection mirror the patch inside the tent. The tape patch will keep insects and weather outside where they belong.

DID YOU KNOW?

The people at 3M, the manufacturer of gaffer tape, take a lot of calls about their product.

Three of the most commonly asked questions are:

1. Can duct tape be used for removing warts?
2. Can it be used to secure the duct from a household tumble drier to the outside of the house?
3. Is it waterproof?

The official answers are:

1. Gaffer tape is not recommended for removing warts, because it hasn't been scientifically tested.
2. The company does not recommend using gaffer tape for the drier duct, because the temperatures may exceed 93°C, the maximum temperature the tape can withstand.
3. The backing of the duct tape is waterproof, but the adhesive is not. So gaffer tape will stand up to water for a while, but eventually the adhesive will wear off.

Stay afloat You can repair a small hole in a canoe with gaffer tape. Pull the canoe out of the water, dry the area around the hole, and apply a gaffer tape patch to the outside of the canoe to make a watertight repair.

Waterproof footwear Make a waterproof pair of shoes for fishing, gardening or launching a boat by covering an old pair of canvas shoes or trainers with gaffer tape, overlapping the edges of each row. As you round corners, cut little V's in the edges of the tape so that you can lap the tape smoothly around the corner.

Pool patch Gaffer tape can repair a hole in a swimming pool liner well enough to stand up to water for at least a season. Be sure to cover the area thoroughly.

Protect yourself from ticks When you are out on a hike, on your way to your favourite fishing spot or just weeding in the garden, protect your ankles from ticks by wrapping gaffer tape around your trouser cuffs to keep them out. This is a good way to keep your trouser legs out of a bicycle chain, too.

Create a clothesline Whether you are on a camping holiday or in your garden, when you need a clothesline and you don't have any rope, use gaffer tape instead. Twist a long piece of gaffer tape into a rope and bind it between trees for a clothesline. It makes a skipping rope as well or a basic rope sturdy enough to lash two items together. You can even use your 'rope' to drag a child's wagon.

Protect your gas barbecue hose Mice and squirrels love to chew on rubber and one of their favourite snacks is often the rubber hose that connects the gas bottle to an outdoor barbecue. Protect the hose by wrapping it in gaffer tape.

Make an emergency shoe lace To make a temporary shoe-lace with gaffer tape, cut off a piece of tape that's as long as you need and rip off twice the width you need. Fold the tape in half along its length, sticky side in, then thread the lace as normal.

Repair your ski gear Repair a ripped protective nylon layer on skiing gear by slipping a piece of tape inside the rip, sticky side out and carefully pressing both sides of the rip together. The repair should be barely detectable.

Extra insulation Make winter boots a little bit warmer by taping the insoles with gaffer tape, silver side up. The shiny tape will reflect the warmth of your feet back into the boots.

Gloves

Grip a stubborn jar lid If the lid on a jar of jam or pickle won't come loose, put on some rubber gloves and you'll instantly have a better grip to unscrew the top.

Make an ice pack If you need an ice pack in a hurry, fill a kitchen rubber glove with ice. Close the wrist with a rubber band to contain water from the melting ice. When you're finished, turn the glove inside out to dry.

Paper-sorting finger Cut off the index finger piece from an old rubber glove and you have an ideal sheath for your finger the next time you have to quickly sort through a thick pile of papers.

Make strong rubber bands To make some extra-strong rubber bands, cut up a pair of old rubber gloves. Make horizontal cuts in the finger sections for small rubber bands and in the body of the glove for large ones.

Latex surgical gloves for extra insulation If your hands get cold when you are doing work in the garden, cleaning the car or other outdoor activities, even when you are wearing gloves or mittens, try slipping on a pair of latex surgical gloves underneath your usual mittens or gloves. The rubber is a superb insulator, so your hands should stay toasty warm and dry too.

Dust delicate knick-knacks To dust a collection of glass animals or other delicate items, put on some fabric gloves, the softer the better, and rub each item carefully using your fingers.

Dust a chandelier If a chandelier has become a haven for spiders' webs and dust, try this infallible dusting tip. Soak some old fabric gloves in window cleaning fluid. Slip them on and wipe off the lighting fixture for sparkling crystals in no time.

Remove cat hair Here's a quick and easy way to remove cat hair from upholstery. Put on a rubber glove and dampen it. When you rub it against fabric, the cat hair will stick to the glove. If you are worried about getting the upholstery slightly damp, test the wet glove in an inconspicuous area first.

Glycerine

Make your own soap Homemade soap is a great gift and very easy to make with some glycerine and a microwave. Cut the glycerine, which is usually sold in blocks, into 5cm cubes. Using a microwave set at half-power, heat several cubes in a glass container for 30 seconds at a time, checking and stirring as needed, until the glycerine melts. Add a few drops of coloured dye or a chosen scent at this point, if you wish. Pour the melted glycerine into soap or sweet moulds. If you don't have any moulds, fill the bottom 2cm of a polystyrene cup. Let it harden for 30 minutes.

DID YOU KNOW?

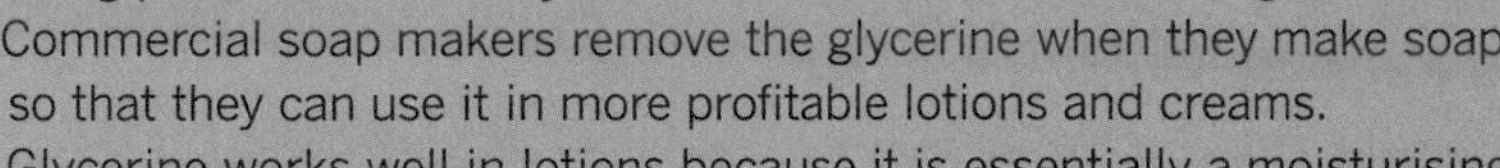

Glycerine is a clear, colourless thick paste that is a by-product of the soap-making process, in which lye is combined with animal or vegetable fat. Commercial soap makers remove the glycerine when they make soap so that they can use it in more profitable lotions and creams. Glycerine works well in lotions because it is essentially a moisturising material that dissolves in alcohol or water. Glycerine is also used to make nitroglycerine and sweets – such as jelly babies – and to preserve fruit and laboratory specimens. Look for glycerine alongside hand lotions in a pharmacy or a craft shop that carries soap-making equipment. You can also purchase it online at **www.aromantic.co.uk**

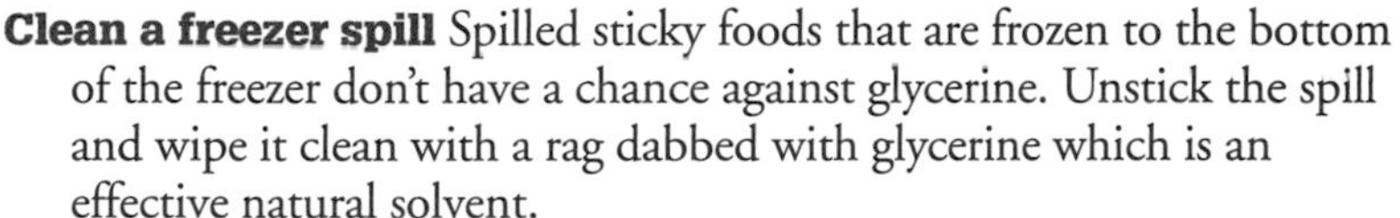

Clean a freezer spill Spilled sticky foods that are frozen to the bottom of the freezer don't have a chance against glycerine. Unstick the spill and wipe it clean with a rag dabbed with glycerine which is an effective natural solvent.

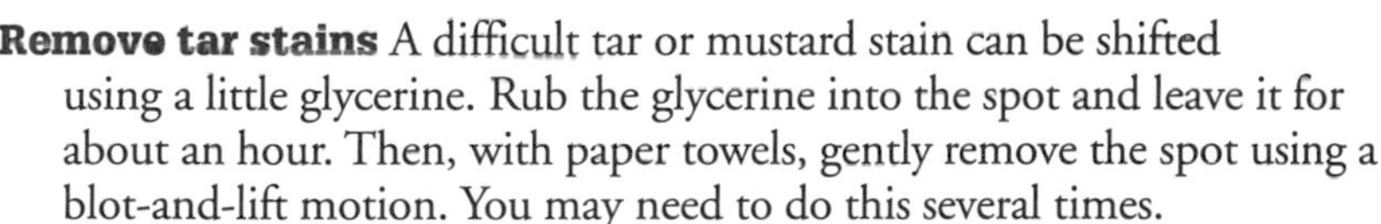

Remove tar stains A difficult tar or mustard stain can be shifted using a little glycerine. Rub the glycerine into the spot and leave it for about an hour. Then, with paper towels, gently remove the spot using a blot-and-lift motion. You may need to do this several times.

Make new liquid soap If you're wondering what to do with tiny leftover slivers of soap, add a bit of glycerine and crush them together with some warm water. Pour the mixture into a pump bottle to make liquid soap on the cheap.

Golfing equipment

Aerate a lawn Kill two birds with one stone by wearing golf shoes with metal spikes to aerate the lawn the next time you mow it. The grip that a golf shoe gives is also helpful if you have to push the mower up a hill.

Fill stripped screw holes If a screw won't grip because its hole has become too large, it's easy to fix. Dip the tip of a golf tee in wood glue and tap the tee into the hole. Cut the tee flush with the door frame surface with a craft knife. When the glue dries, you can drill a new pilot hole for the screw in the same spot.

Make a golf-tee tie rack If a collection of ties is scattered about the wardrobe or your bedroom, try using golf tees to get them organised. Sand and paint a length of pine board. Drill 3mm holes every 5cm. Dip the tip of each tee in wood glue and tap it into a hole. Hang the tie rack on the wardrobe door to make a perfect gift for a keen golfer.

Greaseproof paper

Fail-safe cake decorating Piping words or patterns onto a cake in sugar icing can be a tricky job. Here's a way to make it much easier and get impressive results. Cut a piece of greaseproof paper the same size as your cake, using the cake tin as a guide. Then pipe the name and the message (or pattern) onto the paper and freeze it. After just half an hour it should be easy to handle. Loosen the icing and slide it off onto the cake using a spatula. You'll be amazed at the professional results you can achieve using this simple technique.

Funnel spices into jars Filling narrow-mouthed spice jars can make a mess on a kitchen worktop. Roll a piece of greaseproof paper into a funnel shape and pour spices into the jars without spilling a single peppercorn. You can even funnel liquids into jars by using a couple of layers of greaseproof paper offset so the seams in the layers don't line up and let any drips of liquid through.

Make cleaning the kitchen quicker and easier Greaseproof paper can help to keep all kinds of kitchen surfaces clean.

- Line vegetable and meat containers with a layer of greaseproof paper. When it needs replacement, just throw it in the bin or, if it's not stained with meat juices, the compost heap.
- If your kitchen cabinets don't extend to the ceiling, a layer of greaseproof paper on top will catch dust and grease particles. Every month or two, just fold it up, discard it and put a fresh layer down.
- If you're worried about meat juices seeping into a cutting board, cover it with three layers of greaseproof paper before slicing raw meat and throw the paper out immediately as soon as you've finished.

Uncork bottles with ease If you keep a bottle of cooking wine in the kitchen, you may need to uncork it and recork it many times before using it up. Instead of struggling with the cork each time, wrap some greaseproof paper around the cork before re-inserting it. It'll be easier to remove the next time and the paper will help to keep crumbly little bits of cork from getting into the wine.

Keep cast iron rust-free Cast iron devotees agree that this superior cooking material is well worth a little extra effort to keep it at its best. To prevent rust from forming on cast iron between uses, rub a sheet of greasepaper over a grill pan or Dutch oven after washing and while it's still warm. Then place the sheet between the pot and the lid to store.

Store delicate fabrics Antique lace and other treasured fabric heirlooms may decay quickly if not stored with care. A sheet of greaseproof paper between each item will help to block extraneous light and prevent transfer of dyes without trapping moisture.

{ KIDS STUFF }

HOMEMADE STAINED GLASS

All children enjoy making homemade 'stained glass' artworks that take only minutes to make. First, make crayon shavings using a vegetable peeler. Keep each colour separate. Put a paper towel or bag on the worktop. Place a sheet of greaseproof paper on top, sprinkle it with crayon shavings and cover with another layer of greaseproof paper and a paper towel. Press it for a few minutes using a warm iron and remove the paper towel layers. Cut your new see-through artwork into sun-catching medallions or colourful bookmarks using craft scissors to create a decorative edge.

Keep candles from staining table linen Candles in colours that co-ordinate with a tablecloth and napkins make a lovely finishing touch to table settings – and it's convenient to store them all together – but if you store the candles with table linens, the candle colour may rub off on the linens. To avoid this, wrap brightly-coloured candles in plain greaseproof paper before storage. Avoid patterned paper that may also stain fabric.

Protect surfaces from glue Woodworkers know that there is enough glue in a wood joint if some squeezes out when they clamp the joint. They also know that excess glue will be difficult to remove if it drips on a workbench or, worse, bonds the clamping blocks to the project. To prevent this, cover the bench with strips of greaseproof paper and put pieces of greaseproof paper between the clamping blocks and the project. The glue won't adhere to, or soak through, the paper.

Hair conditioner

Take off make-up Why buy expensive make-up removers when there is a perfectly good substitute in the bathroom already? A dab of hair conditioner quickly and easily removes make-up for far less money than name-brand make-up removers.

Unstick a ring If Grandma's antique ring has just got stuck on your middle finger, slick the finger with a little hair conditioner. The ring should slide right off.

Protect your shoes in foul weather Keep salt and chemicals off your shoes during the winter by lathering heavy-duty shoes or boots with hair conditioner to protect them from winter's harsh elements. It's a good leather conditioner as well.

Lubricate a zipper When a zip on a jacket sticks, it is tempting to tug and pull until it finally zips up. A dab of hair conditioner rubbed along the teeth of the zip can help you to avoid this bother next time.

Smooth post-shave legs After you shave your legs, they may feel rough and irritated. Rub on hair conditioner; it acts like a lotion and will smooth and soften just-shaved legs.

Smooth-sliding shower curtain Are you tired of yanking on a shower curtain? Instead of closing smoothly, does it stutter along the curtain rod, letting the showerhead spray water onto the floor? Rub the rod with hair conditioner and the curtain should glide across it.

DID YOU KNOW?

Hair conditioner has been around for about 50 years. While researching ways to help burn victims during the Second World War, Swiss chemists developed a compound that improved the health of hair. In the 1950s, other scientists developing fabric softeners found that the same material was also good for softening hair.

Despite our efforts to keep hair healthy, we still lose on average between 50 and 100 strands a day. For most of us, thankfully, there are still many more strands left. Interestingly, people with blonde hair have an average of 140,000 strands of hair, brown-haired people, 100,000 and those with red hair, 90,000.

Prevent rust on tools Every good do-it-yourselfer knows how important it is to take care of the tools in a toolbox. One way to condition them and keep rust from invading is to rub them down with hair conditioner.

Oil skate wheels Do your child's skateboard wheels squeak? Or are well-used in-line and roller skates getting a bit sticky? Rub hair conditioner on the axles of the wheels and the wheels should be running smoothly in no time.

Shine stainless steel Don't buy expensive polishes specifically designed for stainless steel: apply hair conditioner to taps, golf clubs, chrome fixtures or anything else that needs a shine. Rub it off thoroughly with a soft cloth and you will be impressed with the bright gleam.

Clean silk garments Do you dare ignore the 'dry clean only' label in a silk shirt? Here's a low-cost alternative. Fill the sink with water (warm water for whites and cold water for colours). Add a tablespoon of hair conditioner. Immerse the shirt in the water and let it sit for a few minutes. Then pull it out, rinse and hang it up to dry. The conditioner will keep the shirt feeling silky smooth.

Clean and shine your houseplants If your houseplants need a good dusting, put a bit of hair conditioner onto a soft cloth and rub the plant leaves to remove dust and shine the leaves.

Hair spray

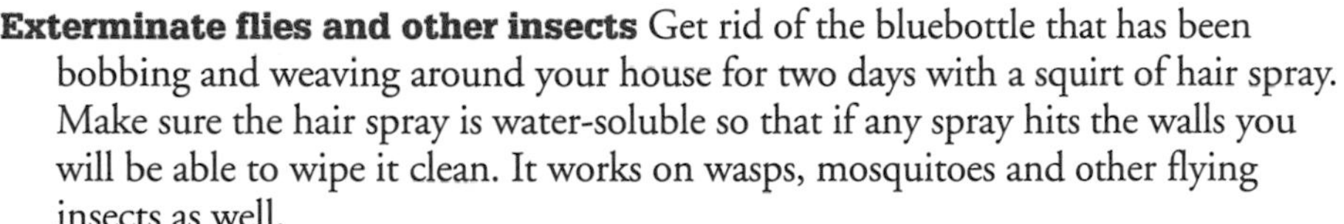

Exterminate flies and other insects Get rid of the bluebottle that has been bobbing and weaving around your house for two days with a squirt of hair spray. Make sure the hair spray is water-soluble so that if any spray hits the walls you will be able to wipe it clean. It works on wasps, mosquitoes and other flying insects as well.

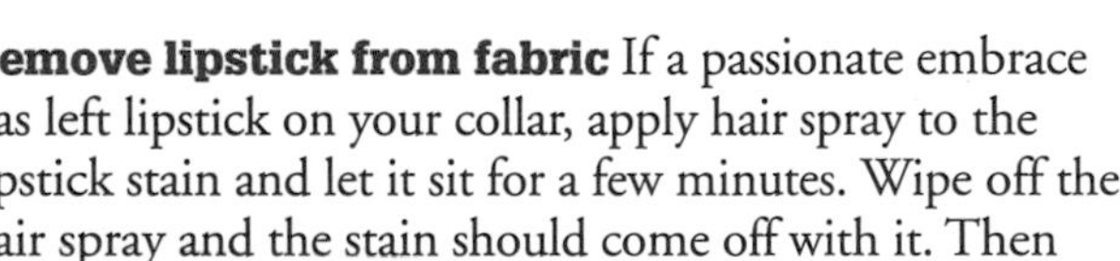

Remove lipstick from fabric If a passionate embrace has left lipstick on your collar, apply hair spray to the lipstick stain and let it sit for a few minutes. Wipe off the hair spray and the stain should come off with it. Then wash the shirt in the usual way.

Reduce runs in tights and stockings Runs in tights or stockings often start at the toes. Head off a running disaster by spraying hair spray on the toes of a new pair of tights. The spray strengthens the threads and makes them last longer.

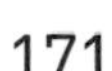

Preserve a Christmas wreath When you buy a festive wreath it is fresh, green and lush. A week later, it is starting to shed needles and look a little dry. To make the wreath last longer, take a can of hair spray and squirt it all over as soon as you get the fresh wreath home. The hair spray traps the moisture in the needles.

Protect children's artwork To keep a child's priceless work of art at its very best before you put it on the pinboard or fridge door, preserve it with hair spray to help it to last longer. This works especially well on unstable chalk or pastel pictures as it stops them from getting smudged so easily.

Preserve your shoes' shine After you've lovingly polished your shoes to give them a fresh-from-the-box look, lightly spray them with hair spray. The shoe polish won't rub off so easily with this added protection.

Keep curtains dirt-free Have you just bought new curtains or had the old ones cleaned and want to keep the as-new look for a while? The trick is to apply several coats of hair spray, letting each coat dry thoroughly before the next one.

Remove ink marks on garments If a toddler has just gone mad with a ballpoint pen on white upholstery or a new shirt, squirt the stain with hair spray and the pen marks should come straight off.

Extend the life of cut flowers Postpone the wilting of a beautiful bouquet of cut flowers with a squirt of hair spray. Stand 30cm away from the bouquet and give the flowers a quick spray on the undersides of the leaves and petals.

Keep recipe cards splatter-free Don't let spaghetti sauce bubbling on the hob splatter a favourite recipe card. A coating of hair spray will prevent the card from being ruined by kitchen eruptions. With the added protection, spills will wipe off easily.

Here are some great moments in hair spray history:

- A Norwegian inventor developed the technology that became the aerosol can in the early 1900s.
- L'Oréal introduced its hair spray, called Elnett, in 1960. The next year Alberto VO5 introduced its version.
- In 1964 hair spray surpassed lipstick as women's most popular cosmetic aid – possibly due to the fashion for enormous beehive hairstyles.
- In 1984 the hair spray on singer Michael Jackson's hair ignited while he was rehearsing a commercial for Pepsi.

DID YOU KNOW?

Hydrogen peroxide, (H_2O_2) was discovered in 1818. The most common household use for it is as an antiseptic and bleaching agent. (It's the key ingredient in most teeth-whitening kits and all-fabric oxygen bleaches, for example). Textile manufacturers use higher concentrations of hydrogen peroxide to bleach fabric. During the Second World War, hydrogen peroxide solutions also fuelled torpedoes and rockets.

Hydrogen peroxide

Remove stains of unknown origin If you don't know what has caused a stain but still want to remove it, mix a teaspoon of 3 per cent hydrogen peroxide with a little cream of tartar or a dab of non-gel toothpaste. Rub the paste on the stain with a soft cloth. Rinse. The stain, whatever it was, should be gone. **WARNING** Be sure that your fabric is colourfast before you try this.

Remove wine stains Hydrogen peroxide works well to remove wine stains so don't worry if you spill it on a white cloth – it will come off easily.

Remove grass stains If grass stains are ruining your children's clothes, hydrogen peroxide may be a solution. Mix a few drops of ammonia with just 1 teaspoon 3 per cent hydrogen peroxide. Rub on the stain. As soon as it disappears, rinse and launder.

Remove mildew The sight and smell of mildew can make any bathroom seem unloved. Bring out some tough ammunition: a bottle of 3 per cent hydrogen peroxide. Don't water it down, pour the peroxide directly on to the offending area. Wipe it clean and the mildew should be gone for good.

Remove bloodstains This works only on fresh bloodstains. Apply 3 per cent hydrogen peroxide directly to the stain, rinse with fresh water and launder as usual.

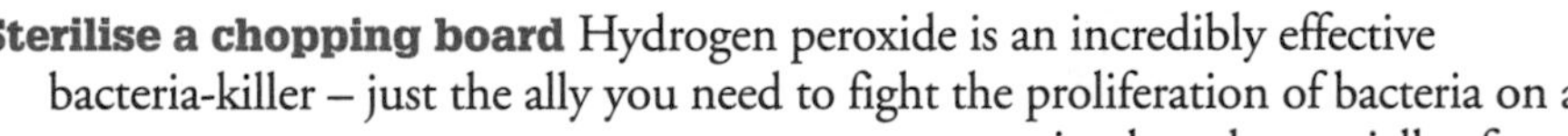

Sterilise a chopping board Hydrogen peroxide is an incredibly effective bacteria-killer – just the ally you need to fight the proliferation of bacteria on a cutting board, especially after preparing chicken or other meat. To kill the germs on a chopping board, use a paper towel to wipe the board down with vinegar, then use another paper towel to wipe it with hydrogen peroxide. Ordinary 3 per cent peroxide is fine.

{TAKE CARE}

Hydrogen peroxide is considered corrosive – even in a relatively weak 3 per cent solution. Don't put it in your eyes or around your nose. Don't swallow it or try to set it on fire either.

 Ice-cream scoops

Scoop meatballs and biscuit dough To make meatballs that are the same size every time, use an ice-cream scoop to measure out perfect spheres. This method works well for biscuits too. Dip the scoop in the dough and place the ball on the baking sheet. You'll end up with biscuits all the same size.

Make butter balls For an attractive way to present butter at a dinner party, scoop out large globes of butter to serve to guests with their bread. A smaller scoop, or melon baller, will create individual-size balls of butter.

Create special sandcastles On your next visit to the seaside, take along an ice-cream scoop. The children will have a fun tool for making sandcastles; the scoop allows them to make interesting rounded shapes with the sand.

DID YOU KNOW?

Spade, dipper, spatula or spoon – the styles of ice-cream scoop you can buy are almost as varied as the flavours of ice cream you will use them for. One web site lists 168 choices of scoops. Did you know that:

- A scoop introduced during the Depression of the 1930s, called the slicer, helped US ice-cream parlour owners to scoop out the same amount every time and not give away any extra.
- Many ways have been developed to help the ice cream plop out of a scoop. Some scoops split apart; others have a wire scraper to nudge it out. Still others have anti-freeze in the handle or a button on the back to make it pop out.
- Some ice-cream scoops, also called moulds, can imprint symbols on the ice cream.

Plant seeds If you're out in the garden about to start putting seeds into a plot of earth, use an ice-cream scoop to make equal-sized planting holes for the seeds for a future harvest.

Repot a houseplant Does dirt scatter everywhere when you are re-potting houseplants? An ice-cream scoop is the perfect way to add soil to the new pot without making a mess.

Ice cubes

Water hanging plants and Christmas trees If you struggle to reach hanging plants when you're watering, ice cubes can help. Just place several cubes into the pots. The ice will melt and water the plants and it also does it without causing a sudden downpour. This is also a good way to water a Christmas tree, whose base may be hard to reach with a watering can.

Remove dents in carpeting If you've recently rearranged furniture in the living room, you know that heavy pieces can leave ugly dents in the carpet. Use ice cubes to remove them. Put an ice cube, for example, on the spot where a chair leg stood. Let it melt, then brush up the dent.

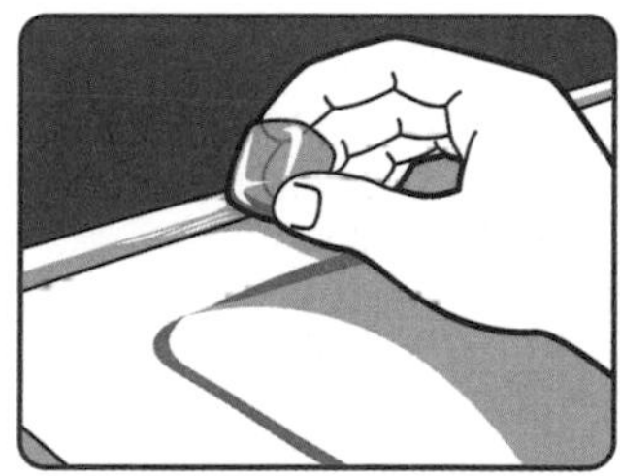

Smooth sealant seams If you're putting sealant around the bath, but the sticky compound keeps adhering to your finger as you try to smooth it and you know that if you don't do something about it, the finished job will look awful. You can solve the problem by running an ice cube along the sealant line. This forms the sealant into a nice even bead and it will never stick to the ice cube.

Help iron out creases If a shirt is full of creases and there's no time to wash it again, turn on the iron and wrap an ice cube in a soft cloth. Rub the cube over the crease just before you iron and the shirt will smooth out.

Mask the taste of medicine No matter what flavour is used in children's medicine, they may still turn up their noses at the taste. Get them to suck on an ice cube before taking the medicine. It will numb the taste buds and allow the medicine to go down, without any additional spoonful of sugar.

Pluck a splinter Removing a splinter from the hand of a screaming, squirming toddler is one of the most difficult jobs a parent can face. Before you start jabbing with a needle, grab an ice cube and numb the area. This should make splinter removal much quicker and more painless.

DID YOU KNOW?

Here are some cold, hard facts about ice cubes:

- To make clear ice cubes, use distilled water and boil it first. It's the air in the water that causes ice cubes to turn cloudy.
- A Canadian company sells fake ice cubes that glow and blink in your drink.
- They never use real ice cubes when photographing cool drinks for adverts, because they don't last under hot studio lights. They're actually made of plastic or glass.

Prevent a burn blistering Stop a burn from turning into a mass of blisters by applying an ice cube directly to surface of the burn.

Cool water for pets Imagine what it's like to wear a fur coat in the middle of summer. Rabbits, hamsters, mice, rats and gerbils will love your thoughtfulness if you place a few cubes in their water dish to cool down. This is also a good tip for the cat, who's spent the hot morning lounging on your bed or the dog, who's just come in thirsty after a long romp in the park.

Unstick a sluggish waste disposal If your waste disposal is not working at its best because of grease build-up (not a blockage), ice cubes may help. Throw some down the disposal and grind them up. The grease should cling to the ice, making the disposal residue-free.

Make creamy salad dressing Here's how to make homemade salad dressing as smooth and even as the bottled variety. Put all the dressing ingredients in a jar with a lid, then add a single ice cube. Close the lid and shake vigorously. Spoon out the ice cube and serve. Your guests will be impressed by how creamy your salad dressing is.

Stop sauces from curdling If you've made eggs Benedict for a posh Sunday brunch, but the butter and egg yolks mixed with lemon juice for hollandaise sauce have curdled, place an ice cube in the saucepan, stir and the sauce should turn back into a silky masterpiece.

De-fat soup and stews To quickly remove as much fat as possible from homemade soup or stew, fill a metal ladle with ice cubes and skim the bottom of the ladle over the top of the liquid in the soup pot. Fat will collect on the ladle.

Reheat rice Do you find that leftover rice dries out and becomes tough when it is reheated in the microwave? Try this solution: put an ice cube on top of the rice when you put it in the microwave. The ice cube will melt as the rice reheats, giving the rice much-needed moisture.

Remove gum from clothing Get rid of stuck-on chewing gum on a child's trousers with an ice cube. Rub the ice on the gum to harden it. You can then scrape it off with a spoon.

* Ice cube trays

Divide a drawer If a junk drawer is an unsightly mess, place a plastic ice cube tray inside to organise small items. One 'cube' can hold paper clips, the next, rubber bands, another, stamps.

Freeze extra eggs Did you know that you can freeze eggs for future baking projects? Medium eggs are just the right size to freeze in plastic ice cube trays with one egg in each cell, with no spillover. After they are frozen, put them into a self-sealing plastic bag. Defrost as many as you need when the time comes.

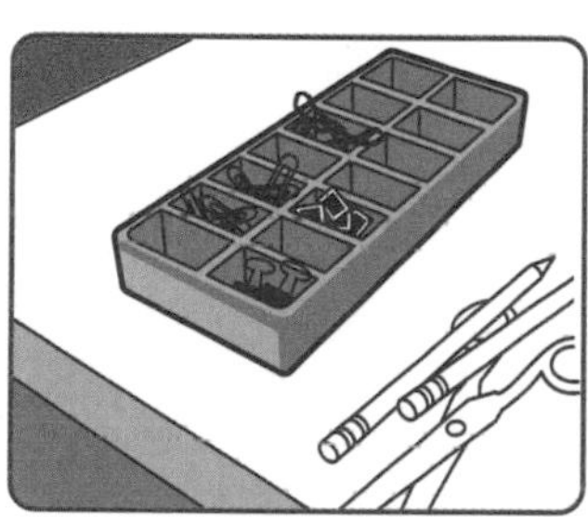

A painter's palette Your child, a budding Picasso or Rembrandt, needs a paint palette for mixing colours. A plastic ice cube tray provides the perfect sturdy container for holding and mixing small amounts of paints and watercolours.

Organise a workbench An ice cube tray can help you to organise and store small parts that you may need at one time or another, for example screws, nails, bolts and other diminutive hardware.

Freeze foods in handy cubes An ice cube tray is a great way to freeze small amounts of many different kinds of food for later use. The idea is to freeze the food in the tray's cells, pop out the frozen cubes and put them in a labelled self-sealing plastic bag for future use. Turn the page for some more ideas:

{ KIDS' STUFF }

ICE COOL JEWELLERY

This is a great summer project. Collect a bunch of small objects from around the house, including buttons, beads and tiny toys. Then get an ice cube tray and place one or more of the items in each tray cube. Fill the tray with water. Cut a length of wool (long enough to make a comfortable necklace, bracelet or anklet). Lay the wool in the ice cube tray, making sure it touches every cube and is fully submerged. Freeze. When frozen, pop out and tie on the 'jewellery'. The children will cool off while they see how long their creation takes to melt.

- If garden or windowsill pots are brimming with basil, but your family can't eat pesto as quickly as you make it, make a big batch of pesto (without the cheese) and freeze it in ice cube trays. Later, defrost as many cubes as you need, add cheese and mix with pasta.
- There's only so much mashed swede, carrot or squash that a growing baby will eat at one sitting. Freeze the rest in ice cube trays for future baby ready-meals.
- If a recipe calls for 100g chopped celery, but you have an entire head of celery and no plans to use it soon, chop it all, place in an ice cube tray, add a little water and freeze. The next time you need chopped celery, it's at your fingertips. This also works well for onions, carrots or any other vegetable that you use in soups and stews.
- Are you always throwing out leftover parsley? Just chop it up, put it in an ice cube tray with a little water and freeze for future use. This also works with other fresh herbs.
- If there's a bit of chicken soup left in the bottom of the pot – too little for another meal, but too much to throw it out. Freeze the leftovers and the next time you make soup or another dish that needs seasoning, use a cube or two.
- If you are cooking homemade broth, make an extra-large batch and freeze the excess in ice cube trays. You'll have broth cubes to add instant flavour to future quick-cook dishes. You can do the same with a leftover half-can of broth.
- Here's what to do with a half-drunk bottle of red or white wine. Freeze the wine into cubes that can be used later in pasta sauce, casseroles or stews.

*Ice lolly sticks

Emergency splint for a finger If a child appears to have a broken finger and you're on the way to casualty, use an ice lolly stick as a temporary splint for the finger. Tape it on with adhesive tape to help to stabilise the finger until it can be set.

Teach letters to future artists and writers Ice lolly sticks are just the thing for spreading finger paint. Or, for a fun way to help youngsters to practise writing letters, let them use lolly sticks to write letters into a pile of shaving cream, whipped cream or pudding.

Skewer kids' food It is often more fun to eat food if you get to play with it first, as the parents of many picky eaters know. Ice lolly sticks are useful to have in your bag of tricks at mealtimes. Skewer bites of sausage, chicken, pineapple, melon, cherry tomatoes and similar. Or give children a stick so that they can spread their own jam or Marmite.

{ KIDS' STUFF }

MAKE A BOOKMARK

Here's a great little gift to encourage young readers. All you need is an ice lolly stick, paint, coloured felt, glue and a marker pen. Paint the ice lolly stick in a bright colour, such as red. When it's dry, write on one side a reading slogan such as 'I love to read' or 'I'll hold the page'. Then cut a shape out of the felt, such as a heart, flower, a cat or a dog. Glue the shape to the top of the lolly stick, and you have a homemade bookmark.

Label your plantings If you've planted parsley, sage, rosemary or thyme in the garden, remember its location by using ice lolly sticks as plant labels. Just write the type of seeds on the stick using indelible marker.

Keep track of paint colours Don't get mixed up when storing paint colours. After you've painted a room, dip an ice lolly stick in the can. Let it dry. Write the name of the paint and the room where it was used on the stick. Now you'll know what colour to use when it's time to paint again. These guides can also help a home decorator pick out fabrics and decorative items to go with a newly painted room.

Ice scrapers

Remove splattered paint If you've just painted the bathroom and left paint splatters all over an acrylic bath, use an ice scraper to remove them without scratching the bath surface. Use ice scrapers to remove paint specks from other non-metallic surfaces too.

Smooth wood filler Do you have small gouges in a wooden floor that you want to get rid of? Once you've packed wood filler into a hole, an ice scraper is the perfect tool to smooth and level it.

Remove wax from skis Every experienced skier knows that old wax build-up on skis can slow you down. An ice scraper can swiftly and neatly take off the old wax and prepare the skis for the next coat.

Scrape out your freezer A windscreen isn't the only place where ice and frost build up. If the frost is building up in your freezer and you want to delay the defrosting chore for a while, head out to the car and borrow the scraper.

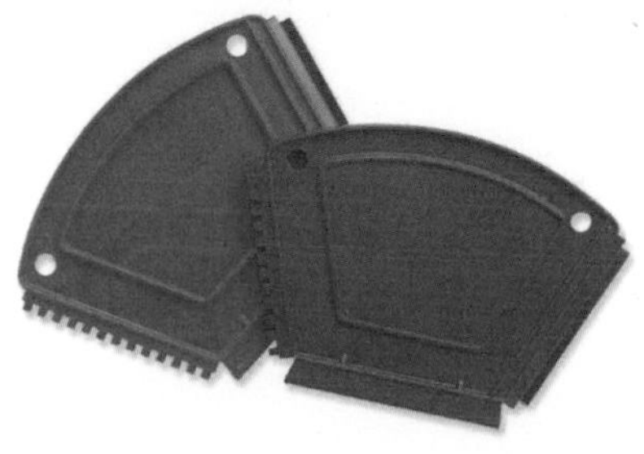

Clean up bread dough No matter how much flour you put on your work surface, some of the sticky bread dough always seems to stick to it. A clean ice scraper is just the tool for skimming sticky dough off the work surface. A plastic scraper can also substitute for a spatula for non-stick pans, but take care not to let it rest on the edge of a hot pan or it will melt.

Jar lids

Make safety reflectors Is is difficult to manoeuvre in your drive when it's dark? With some scrap wood and jar lids you can make inexpensive reflectors to guide drivers. Spray the lids with reflective paint, screw them to the sides of stakes cut from scrap wood and drive the stakes into the ground to make effective reflectors.

Cut biscuits Lids with deep rims or preserving jar bands (the part with the cut-out centre) can be used to make impromptu biscuit cutters. Use different-sized lids for adult and mini biscuits. Dip the bottom edge of the lid in flour to keep it from sticking when you press it into the dough. Avoid lids with rims that are rolled inwards; the dough can get stuck inside and be hard to extract.

Create a spoon rest Place a jar lid on the hob or the worktop next to the stove while cooking. After stirring a pot, rest the spoon on the lid and there won't be any drips and splashes to clean up later.

Drip catcher under honey jar Honey is delicious, but it can make a sticky mess. At the table, place the honey jar on a larger plastic lid to stop drips from getting everywhere. Store it that way, too and your cabinet shelf will stay cleaner.

Make coasters to protect furniture Drips from drinking glasses and hot coffee mugs can really ruin furniture finishes. The simple solution is to keep plenty of coasters on hand. Glue rounds of felt or cork to both sides of a jar lid (especially flat preserving jar lids, which shouldn't be re-used anyway), and keep a stack wherever cups and glasses accumulate in the house.

Saucers for potted plants Lids with a rim are perfect for catching excess water under small potted plants. Unlike ceramic saucers, if they get encrusted with minerals, you won't mind throwing them out.

Organise your desk Contain paper clips and other small office items that clutter up your desk, by putting them inside jar lids with deep rims. The lids are also good for holding loose change or earrings on a dressing table or desk too. A quick coat of matt spray paint and an acrylic sealant will make them more attractive and water-resistant.

{ KIDS' STUFF }

WHAT'S ON THE FRIDGE?

It is probably a collection of magnets and children's artwork. Combine the two to make something that is both useful and beautiful.

For a stimulating craft project, set out a variety of fun materials - paints, glue, fabrics, family photos, googly eyes, glitter, pompoms or even just paper and markers - and let your child decorate several jar lids.

Glue some strong magnets from a hardware shop on the backs using a glue gun and put them on the fridge.

Jars

Waterproof camping storage When you are boating or camping, keeping things like matches and paper money dry can be a challenge. Store items that you don't want to get wet in clear jars with screw tops that can't pop off. Even if you are backpacking, plastic jars with screw tops are light enough not to weigh you down, plus they provide more protection for crushable items than a resealable plastic bag.

Stamp out biscuits Just about any clean, empty wide-mouthed jar is just the right size for cutting biscuits out of any rolled dough.

Make baby-food portions Take advantage of the fact that baby-food jars are already the perfect size for baby's portions. Clean them thoroughly before re-using and fill them with anything from puréed carrots to vanilla pudding. Attach a spoon with a rubber band and you have a perfect portable meal for when you're on the move with a little one.

Use to quickly dry out gloves or mittens If you've taken a break from gardening or shovelling snow to come in for soup and a sandwich and want to get back to work, help your gloves or mittens dry out during lunch, by pulling each one over the bottom of an empty jar. Then stand the jar upside down on a radiator or hot-air vent. Warm air will fill the jar and radiate out to dry damp clothing in an instant.

Collect insects Help children to observe nature at close quarters by gently collecting insects in clear jars. Punch a few small airholes in the lids for ventilation. Don't make the holes too large, or your insects will escape. Don't forget to carefully let the creatures go after you've admired them.

Make a piggy bank Encourage a child to save by making a money bank out of a jar with a metal lid. Take the lid off the jar, place it on a flat work surface like a cutting board and tap a screwdriver with a hammer to carefully punch a slot hole in the centre. Then use the hammer or a rasp to smooth the rough edges on the underside of the slot to protect fingers from scratches. Personalising the mini-bank with paints or collage can be a fun rainy-day project.

Bring along baby's treats Dry cereal can be a nutritious snack for a baby. There's no need to bring the whole box when you leave the house; pack individual servings in clean, dry baby-food jars. If they get spilled, the mess is minimal.

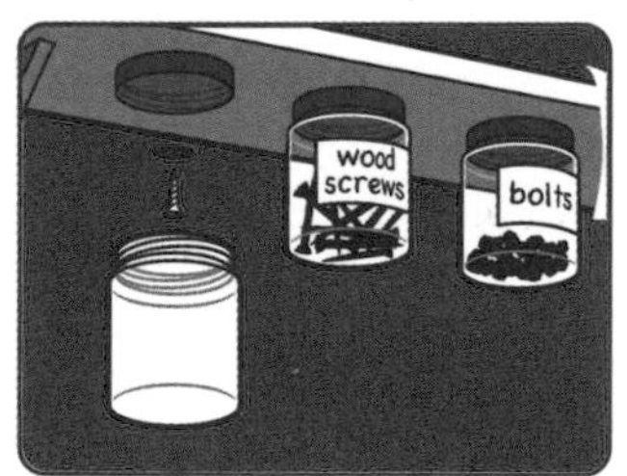

Create workshop storage Don't let various bits of hardware in your workshop get mixed up. Keep all your nails, screws, nuts and bolts organised by size and type by screwing jar lids to the underside of a wooden or melamine shelf. (Make sure the screw does not poke through the top of the shelf.) Then put each type of hardware in its own jar, and screw each jar onto its lid. By using clear jars, you can find what you need at a glance. This idea also works well for storing seeds in a potting shed.

{ SCIENCE FAIR }

MAKE A BIOSPHERE

Turn a large wide-mouthed jar into a miniature biosphere. Clean the jar and lid, then place a handful of pebbles and charcoal chips in the bottom. Add several trowelfuls of slightly damp, sterilised potting soil. Select a few plants that require similar conditions (such as ferns and mosses, which both like moderate light and moisture). Add a few colourful stones, seashells or a piece of driftwood. Add water to make the atmosphere humid. Tighten the lid and place the jar in dim light for two days. Then display in bright light but not direct sunlight. You shouldn't need to add water – it cycles from the plants to the soil and back again. It's important to use sterilised soil to avoid introducing any unwanted organisms. The charcoal chips will filter the water as it recycles.

Ketchup

Get rid of chlorine green If chlorine from swimming pools is turning your blonde hair green or just giving your hair an unwanted scent, eliminate the problem with a ketchup shampoo. To avoid a mess, do it in the shower. Massage ketchup generously into your hair and leave it for 15 minutes, then wash it out, using baby shampoo. The odour and colour should be gone.

Make copper pots gleam When copper pots and pans, or decorative moulds, become dull and tarnished, you can brighten them with ketchup. It's cheaper than commercial tarnish removers and completely safe to apply without gloves. Coat the copper surface with a thin layer of ketchup. Let it sit for 5 to 30 minutes. Acids in the ketchup will react with the tarnish and remove it. Rinse the pan and dry immediately.

Keep silver jewellery sparkling Let ketchup do the work of shining tarnished silver. If a ring, bracelet or earring has a smooth surface, soak it in a small bowl of ketchup for a few minutes. If it has a tooled or detailed surface, use an old toothbrush to work ketchup into the crevices. To avoid damaging the silver, don't leave the ketchup on any longer than necessary. Rinse the piece of jewellery clean, dry it and it will be ready to wear.

DID YOU KNOW?

Ketchup originated in the Far East as a salty fish sauce. The word ketchup (also spelled catsup) probably comes from Chinese or Malay. Brought to the West, it had been transformed by the 1700s into a huge variety of sauces with both vegetable and meat-based ingredients. To this day, you can still find banana ketchup, mushroom ketchup and other variants. Tomato ketchup is a relative newcomer, first sold in 1837, but it is now a favourite accompaniment for dishes ranging from fish and chips to a full English breakfast.

Keys

Weigh down curtains If you need to keep curtains hanging straight, just slip a few old keys in the hems. If you are worried about them falling out, tack them in place with a few stitches going through the holes in the keys. You can also keep cords for blinds from tangling by using keys as weights on their bottoms.

Create an instant plumb bob If you are getting ready to hang wallpaper and you need to draw a perfectly vertical line on the wall to get you started, take a length of cord or string and tie a key or two to one end. You've made a plumb bob that will give you a true vertical line. You can do the same using a pair of scissors too.

Make fishing sinkers Old unused keys make great weights for a fishing line. Since they already have a hole in them, attaching them to the line is easy. Whenever you come across an unidentified key, set it aside to use in your tackle box.

Ladders

Construct a rustic indoor trellis Give climbers and trailing plants something to climb on. Using rawlplugs, attach plastic-covered hooks to the wall and hang an attractive straight ladder (or a segment of one) from the hooks, positioning the ladder's legs on the floor a few centimetres from the wall. It's easy to train potted plants to grow up and around this rustic support. It will look good on a porch or terrace too.

Display quilts and other textiles It is a shame to let tapestries, quilts and decorative rugs languish in the attic or a cupboard. A ladder is a great way to display lacework, crochet, quilts and throws to give a country cottage effect. To stop rough surfaces from damaging delicate fabrics, smooth wooden ladder rungs with sandpaper or metal rungs with steel wool if necessary.

Set it down and plant it When a ladder is on its last legs, it can still be of service lying down. On the ground, a straight ladder or the front part of a stepladder makes a shallow planter with ready-made sections that look appealing filled with annuals, herbs or salad greens. After a couple of years of contact with soil, a wooden ladder will decompose, so once you've decided to use it like this, it can't be used again.

Create a garden focal point If you have some old straight wooden ladders that you no longer trust to bear your weight, use them to create a decorative garden archway. Cut two sections of old ladder to the desired height and position them opposite one another along a path. Screw the legs of each one to two strong posts sunk deeply into the soil. Cut a third ladder section to fit across the top of the two others and tie it to them using young willow twigs or heavy jute twine. Festoon the archway with fun and fanciful objects, such as old tools or let climbing plants clamber up and over it. It also works well as the entrance to an enclosed area.

Make a temporary table Create a makeshift table for a large picnic or buffet by placing a straight ladder across two trestles. Top it with plywood and cover it with a tablecloth. The ladder will provide sufficient strength to support your buffet, as well as any guests who might lean on it.

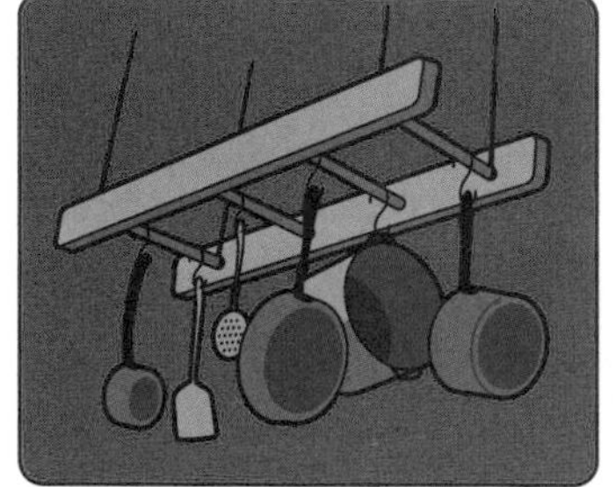

Make a pot rack Accessorise a country kitchen with a pot rack made from a sawed-off section of a wooden straight ladder with thin, round rungs. Sand the cut ends smooth; then tie two pieces of sturdy rope to the rungs at either end. To suspend a pot rack, screw four large metal eye hooks into the ceiling joists; then tie the other ends of the ropes to them. Hang some S-hooks from the rungs to hold other kitchenware. Leave the rack unfinished if you want a rustic look. Or paint or stain it if you want a more finished look.

Lemons see page 188

Lighter fluid

Wipe away rust Rust marks on stainless steel will come off in an instant. Just pour a little lighter fluid onto a clean rag and rub the rust spot away. Use another rag to wipe away any remaining fluid.

Get gum out of hair It happens to the best of us, particularly children. Gum in the hair is a pain to remove. Here is an easy solution that really works. Apply a few drops of lighter fluid directly to the sticky area, wait a few seconds and comb or wipe away the gum. The solvents in the fluid break down the gum, making it easy to remove from many surfaces besides hair.

Remove labels with ease Lighter fluid will remove labels and adhesives from almost any surface. Use it to quickly and easily remove the tape from new appliances or to take stickers off book covers.

Remove crayon marks Have children left their mark with crayon art on walls? Dab some lighter fluid on a clean rag and wipe till the marks vanish.

{TAKE CARE}

Lighter fluid is inexpensive, easy to find (look for a small bottle or can) and has many surprising uses. But it is highly flammable and can be hazardous to your health if inhaled or ingested. Always use it in a well-ventilated area. Do not smoke around it or use it near an open flame.

Remove heel marks from floors You don't have to scrub to remove black heel marks on the kitchen floor. Just pour a little lighter fluid on a paper towel and the marks will wipe straight off.

Rid cooking-oil stain from clothes If cooking-oil stains won't wash out of clothes, try pouring a little lighter fluid directly onto the stain before washing it the next time. The stain will come out in the wash.

*Lip balm

Remove a stuck ring There's no need to pull and tug on your poor finger to try to remove a stuck ring. Simply coat the finger with a little lip balm and gently wriggle the ring loose.

Groom wild eyebrows Use lip balm as a styling wax for grooming unruly moustaches, eyebrows and other wild hairs.

Stop shaving cuts from bleeding If you have cut yourself shaving and you've no time to spare, just dab a bit of lip balm directly onto the nick and the bleeding from most shaving cuts will quickly stop.

Lubricate a zip Rub a small amount of lip balm up and down the teeth of a sticky or stuck zip. Then zip and unzip it a few times. The lip balm will act as a lubricant to make the zip work smoothly.

Simplify carpentry Rub some lip balm over nails and screws that are being drilled or pounded into wood. The lip balm will help them slide in a little easier.

Keep a lightbulb from sticking Outdoor lightbulbs, which are exposed to the elements, often get stuck in place and become hard to remove. Before screwing a lightbulb into an outdoor socket, coat the threads on the bulb with lip balm. This will prevent sticking and make removal easier.

Lubricate tracks for sliding things Apply lip balm to the tracks of drawers and windows, or to the ridges on a medicine cabinet, to make opening and shutting easier.

Prevent windburn If you love skiing, but you hate wearing a ski mask, it can be hard on your skin. Next time you go skiing, try rubbing a lip balm, such as ChapStick, on your face before you hit the slopes. The lip balm will protect your skin from windburn.

TIP* THE BEST TIME TO USE LIP BALM

During the dry winter months you may be tempted to apply a layer of lip balm before you put on your lipstick. Beauty experts say this is not a good idea because the lip balm may interfere with the adherence of the lipstick. Instead of using lip balm during the day, experts recommend that you switch to a moisturising lipstick. Instead, save the lip balm for moisturising your lips before you go to bed.

Super item
36 USES!

LEMONS...

...around the house

Make a fire smell delightful There is nothing cosier on a cold winter's night than a warm fire burning in the fireplace, unless the fire happens to smell horrible. Next time you have a fire that's sending a foul smell into the room, try throwing a few lemon peels into the flames. Or simply burn some lemon peels along with the firewood as a preventative measure.

Polish chrome Get rid of mineral deposits and polish chrome taps and other tarnished chrome by rubbing lemon rind over the chrome. Rinse well and dry with a soft cloth.

DID YOU KNOW?

A lemon tree isn't very pretty and its flower isn't sweet either. The tree's straggly branches bear little resemblance to an orange tree's dense foliage and its purplish flowers lack the pleasant fragrance of orange blossoms. The fruit of the lemon is sour, thanks to its high citric acid content. But sailors have been sucking on vitamin C-rich lemons for hundreds of years to prevent scurvy. To this day, the British navy requires ships to carry enough lemons so that every sailor can have one ounce of juice daily.

Get rid of tough stains on marble You probably think of marble as stone, but it is really petrified calcium (or the remains of ancient seashells). That explains why it is so porous and easily stained and damaged. Stains on marble can be hard to remove, but here is a simple method that should do the trick. Cut a lemon in half, dip the exposed flesh into some table salt and rub it vigorously on the stain. You will be amazed how well it works.

Make a room scent/humidifier Freshen and moisturise the air in your home on dry winter days by making a room scent that also doubles as a humidifier. If you have a wood-burning stove, place an enamelled cast-iron pot or bowl on top, fill with water, and add lemon (and/or orange) peels, cinnamon sticks, cloves and apple skins. If you don't have a wood-burning stove, use the hob instead and just simmer the water periodically.

Neutralise cat-box odour You don't have to use an aerosol spray to neutralise foul-smelling cat-box odours or freshen the air in a bathroom. Just cut a couple of lemons in half. Then place them, cut side up, in a dish in the room, and the air will soon smell lemon-fresh.

Deodorise a humidifier When a humidifier starts to smell unpleasant, deodorise it by pouring 3 or 4 teaspoons lemon juice into the water. It will not only remove the 'off' odour but will replace it with a lemon-fresh fragrance. Repeat every couple of weeks to keep the smell from returning.

Clean tarnished brass Get rid of tarnish on brass, copper or stainless steel. Make a paste of lemon juice and salt (or substitute bicarbonate of soda or cream of tartar for the salt) and coat the affected area. Let it stay on for 5 minutes. Then wash in warm water, rinse and polish dry. Use the same mixture to clean metal kitchen sinks too. Apply the paste, scrub gently and rinse.

Make your own invisible ink Children love to send and receive secret messages and what better way to do it than by writing them in invisible ink? All they need is lemon juice (freshly squeezed or bottled) to use as ink, a cotton swab to write with and a sheet of white paper to write on. When the ink is dry and they are ready to read the invisible message, get them to hold the paper up to bright sunlight or a lightbulb. The heat will cause the writing to darken to a pale brown and the message can be read. Make sure they don't overdo the heating and ignite the paper.

...in the kitchen

Brighten dull aluminium Make dull pots and pans sparkle, inside and out. Just rub the cut side of half a lemon all over them and buff with a soft cloth.

Keep rice from sticking To keep rice from sticking together in a starchy mass, add a teaspoon of lemon juice to the boiling water when cooking. When the rice is done, let it cool for a few minutes, then fluff with a fork before serving.

LEMONS...

...in the kitchen

Prevent potatoes from turning brown Potatoes and cauliflower sometimes turn brown when boiling. Make sure white vegetables stay white by squeezing a teaspoon of fresh lemon juice into the cooking water.

Freshen the fridge Remove refrigerator odours by dabbing some lemon juice onto a cotton wool ball or sponge and leaving it in the fridge for several hours. Make sure to throw out any disintegrating items that might be causing the bad smell.

Refresh a chopping board You probably use your chopping board to chop onions, crush garlic, cut raw and cooked meat and poultry and prepare fish – it is no wonder it retains smells. To get rid of the smell and help to sterilise the cutting board, rub it all over with the cut side of half a lemon or wash it in undiluted juice straight from the bottle.

Keep guacamole green Stop guacamole from turning brown before you have time to serve it by sprinkling a liberal amount of fresh lemon juice over it. The dip will stay fresh and green. The flavour of the lemon juice is a natural complement to the avocados in guacamole. Make fruit salad hours in advance as well. Just squeeze some lemon juice onto apple slices and they will stay snowy white.

Make soggy lettuce crisp You don't have to throw soggy lettuce into the bin. With the help of a little lemon juice you can toss it in a salad instead. Add the juice of half a lemon to a bowl of cold water. Then put the limp lettuce in it and refrigerate for 1 hour. Make sure to dry the leaves completely before putting them into salads or sandwiches.

{ SCIENCE FAIR }

MAKE A BATTERY

You can turn a lemon into a battery. It won't start your car, but you will be able to feel the current with your tongue. Roll the lemon on a flat surface to 'activate' the juices. Then cut two small slices in the lemon about 1.25cm apart. Place a 1p piece into one slot and a 5p into the other. Now touch your tongue to the 1p and the 5p at the same time. You'll feel a slight electric tingle. Here's how it works: the acid in the lemon reacts differently with each of the two metals. One coin contains positive electric charges, while the other contains negative charges. The charges create current. Your tongue conducts the charges, causing a small amount of electricity to flow.

Keep insects out of the kitchen You don't need insecticides or ant traps to ant-proof your kitchen. Just give it the lemon treatment. First squirt some lemon juice on the thresholds of doors and windowsills. Then squeeze lemon juice into any holes or cracks where ants are getting in. Finally, scatter small slices of lemon peel around the outdoor entrance. The ants will get the message that they aren't welcome. Lemons are also effective against cockroaches and fleas. Simply mix the juice of four lemons (along with the rinds) with 2 litres water and wash the floor with it; then watch the fleas and roaches flee from a smell they hate.

Clean your microwave Is the inside of the microwave caked with bits of hardened food? You can give it a good cleaning without scratching the surface with harsh cleansers or using a lot of elbow grease. Just mix 3 tablespoons lemon juice into 300ml water in a microwave-safe bowl. Microwave on High for 5-10 minutes, allowing the steam to condense on the inside walls and the roof of the oven. Then just wipe away the softened food with a dishcloth.

Deodorise the waste disposal If a clogged waste disposal is beginning to make your sink smell unpleasant, here is an easy way to deodorise it. Save leftover lemon and orange peels and push them down the drain. To keep it smelling fresh, repeat once a month.

...in the laundry

Bleach delicate fabrics Ordinary household chlorine bleach can cause the iron in water to precipitate out into fabric, leaving additional stains. For a mild, stain-free bleach, soak delicates in a mixture of lemon juice and bicarbonate of soda for at least half an hour before washing.

Remove unsightly perspiration stains Avoid expensive dry-cleaning bills. You can remove unsightly stains from under the arms of light-coloured shirts and blouses simply by scrubbing them with a mixture of equal parts lemon juice (or white vinegar) and water.

Boost laundry detergent To remove rust and mineral discoloration from white cotton T-shirts and briefs, pour 200ml lemon juice into the washing machine during the wash cycle. The natural bleaching action of the juice will zap the stains and leave the clothes smelling fresh.

Rid clothes of mildew If you have unpacked clothes you have stored for the season only to discover that some of the garments are stained with mildew, get rid of it by making a paste of lemon juice and salt and rubbing it on the affected area, then dry the clothes in sunlight. Repeat the process until the stain is gone. This works well for rust stains on clothes too.

Whiten clothes Diluted or straight, lemon juice is a safe and effective fabric whitener when added to washing water. Clothes will also come out smelling lemon-fresh.

LEMONS...

...for health and beauty

Lighten age spots Before buying special creams to lighten liver spots and freckles, apply lemon juice directly to the area, let it sit for 15 minutes, and then rinse clean. Lemon juice is a safe and effective skin-lightening agent.

Create blonde highlights For blonde highlights worthy of the finest beauty salon, add 50ml lemon juice to 150ml water and rinse your hair with the mixture. Then sit in the sun until your hair dries. Lemon juice is a natural bleach. Don't forget to put on plenty of sunscreen before you sit out in the sun and to condition your hair thoroughly afterwads. To maximise the effect, repeat once daily for up to a week.

TIP* BEFORE YOU SQUEEZE

To get the most juice out of fresh lemons, bring them to room temperature and roll them under your palm against the kitchen worktop before squeezing. This will break down the connective tissue and juice-cell walls, allowing the lemon to release more liquid when you squeeze it.

Clean and whiten nails Pamper your fingernails without the help of a manicurist. Add the juice of ½ lemon to 200ml warm water and soak your fingertips in the mixture for 5 minutes. After pushing back the cuticles, rub some lemon peel back and forth against the nail.

Freshen your breath Make an impromptu mouthwash using lemon juice straight from the bottle. Rinse with the juice and then swallow it for longer-lasting fresh breath. The citric acid in the juice alters the pH level in your mouth, killing the bacteria that cause bad breath. Rinse thoroughly after a few minutes, because long-term exposure to the acid in the lemon can harm tooth enamel.

Remove berry stains It is great fun picking your own berries, but your fingers often get stained with juice that won't come off with soap and water. Try washing your hands with undiluted lemon juice. Wait a few minutes and wash with warm, soapy water. Repeat if necessary until the stain is completely gone.

Soften dry, scaly elbows It is bad enough that your elbows feel dry and itchy, but they look terrible too. Your elbows will look and feel better after a few special treatments. Mix baking soda and lemon juice to make an abrasive paste. Then rub the paste into your elbows for a soothing, smoothing and exfoliating treatment.

Cleanse your face Clean and exfoliate your face by washing it with lemon juice. You can also dab lemon juice on blackheads to draw them out during the day. Your skin should improve after several days of treatment.

Soothe nettle rash You won't need an ocean of calamine lotion the next time you or a child falls foul of a patch of stinging nettles. Just apply full-strength lemon juice directly to the affected area to soothe itching and alleviate the rash.

Treat flaky dandruff If itchy, scaly dandruff has you scratching your head, relief may be no farther away than the fridge. Just massage 2 tablespoons lemon juice into your scalp and rinse with water. Then stir 1 teaspoon lemon juice into 200ml water and rinse your hair with it. Repeat this daily until the dandruff disappears. Your scalp should stop itching and your hair will smell lemon-fresh.

Disinfect cuts and scrapes Stop bleeding and disinfect minor cuts and scrapes by pouring a few drops of lemon juice directly on the cut or apply the juice with a cotton wool ball and hold firmly in place for 1 minute.

Relieve rough hands and sore feet You don't have to take extreme measures to soothe your extremities. If you have rough hands or sore feet, rinse them in a mixture of equal parts of lemon juice and water, then massage with olive oil and dab dry with a soft cloth.

Remove warts If you have tried countless remedies to get rid of warts, and nothing seems to work, try this. Apply a dab of lemon juice directly to the wart, using a cotton bud. Repeat for several days until the acids in the lemon juice dissolve the wart completely.

M

Magazines

No-cost gift wrap Cut out pages with colourful advertisements and use them to make no-cost wrapping paper for small gifts.

Keep wet boots in shape Roll up a couple of old magazines and use them as boot trees inside a pair of damp knee-length boots. The magazines will help the boots maintain their shape as they dry.

Use in children's craft projects Save up old magazines for use in rainy-day craft projects. Let the children go through the magazines to find pictures and words to use in collages or decoupage. Suggest a number of themes to get them started.

Line drawers Pages from large magazines with heavy coated paper make excellent liners for small dresser and desk drawers. Look for advertisements with especially colourful designs or pictures. Tear out the page, place inside the drawer and press around the edges to define where to trim with scissors.

Magnets

Clean up a nail spill Keep a strong magnet on the workbench. Next time you spill a jar of small items like nails, screws, tacks or washers, save time and energy by letting the magnet help pick them up for you.

Prevent a frozen car lock Here is an unusual – and extremely useful – way to use fridge magnets during the winter. Place them over the outside door locks of the car overnight and they will keep the locks from freezing.

Keep a desk drawer neat Are your paper clips all over the place? Place a magnet in an office desk drawer to keep the paper clips together.

DID YOU KNOW?

The ancient Chinese and Greeks discovered that certain rare stones, called lodestones, seem to magically attract bits of iron and always pointed in the same direction when allowed to swing freely. Man-made magnets come in many shapes and sizes, but ever magnet has a north pole and a south pole. If you break a magnet into pieces, each piece, no matter h small, will have a north and south pole. The magnetic field, which every magnet creates, has long been used to harness energy, although scientists still don't know exactly what it is.

Store a broom in a handy place Why run to the hall cupboard every time you need to sweep the kitchen? Instead, just use a screw to attach a magnet about halfway down the broom handle. Then store the broom attached to the side of your refrigerator between the fridge and the wall, where it will remain hidden until you are ready to use it.

* Margarine tubs

Organise odds and ends Do you have loose drawing pins all over the house? Odd bolts and nails in a broken cup? Stray ping pong balls under the sofa? These are just some of the items waiting to be organised into spare plastic margarine tubs. Get a board game started more quickly by storing the loose pieces in a tub until the next time. If you've sorted out all the sky pieces for a puzzle, keep them separate and safe in their own tub. With or without their lids, a few clean margarine tubs can do wonders for a junk drawer in need of organising.

Make a baby footprint paperweight Make an enduring impression of a baby's foot, using quick-drying modelling clay. You should have a wide range of colours to choose from. Put enough clay in a margarine tub to hold a good impression. Put a thin layer of petroleum jelly on the baby's foot and press it firmly into the clay. Let the clay dry as directed, then flex the tub away from the edges until the clay comes free. Years from now you will be able to show Johnny that his size 13's were once smaller than the palm of your hand! You can also preserve a pet's paw print the same way.

Use as a paint container If you want to touch up little spots here and there in the living room, but don't want to lug around a large pot of paint, pour a little paint into a margarine tub to carry as you make your inspection. Hold it in a nest of paper towels to catch any possible drips. Tubs with lids are also perfect for storing a little bit of leftover paint for future touch-ups.

Make easy moulds for jelly desserts Use a large margarine tub as the mould for a jelly or mousse. For individual dessert moulds, use the smaller tubs and put a surprise gum or mini-marshmallow face on the top, which will show through from the bottom when the mould is inverted. The soft, flexible tubs are easy to squeeze when you want to release the dessert.

Make low-cost freezer storage Reuse clean, sturdy margarine and other plastic containers to freeze measured portions of soups and stocks and to break up leftovers into single servings. A 1kg container, for example, stores the perfect amount of sauce for 500g of pasta. Hint: before freezing, let the food cool just enough to reduce condensation.

Vary a child's lunch box As a break from the usual sandwich, put some fruit salad, rice or pasta salad or other interesting fare into one or two recycled margarine tubs for your child's lunch. The tubs are easy to open and will keep the food from getting crushed.

Bring fast food for baby If you need to take home-cooked baby food on a journey, use a disposable margarine tub to make a container that won't break in your baby bag. It's also a handy food bowl and you won't have to wrap it up and bring it home for cleaning.

Make a piggy bank Use a tall tub as a homemade money bank. Cut out a piece of paper to wrap around the side, tape it in place and encourage your child to decorate it with flair. Cut a slit in the top and start saving spare change.

Travel light with your pet Lightweight, disposable margarine tubs make perfect pet food containers and double as food and water bowls. And dog biscuits won't get crushed if you put them in a plastic tub. If your pet is staying at a friend's house while you're on holiday, make things a little easier for the petsitter by putting one serving into each container, to be used and discarded as needed.

Create seed starters Starting seeds indoors is supposed to save you money, so don't buy new large seed trays. Take a margarine tub, poke a few holes in the bottom, add moistened seed-compost, and sow the seeds following the packet instructions. Use permanent marker on the side of the tub to help you to remember what you've sown, and use the tub's lid as a drip saucer. Small tubs are space savers as well, especially if you want to start only one or two of each type of plant.

Make individual ice-cream portions Small margarine tubs are just the right size for a quick ice-cream snack. When it comes back from the supermarket, ice cream is the perfect consistency to portion out into the tubs. You won't have to spend ages getting out bowls, finding a scoop and waiting for the ice cream to soften up enough to dish out. Everyone can just go to the freezer and get themselves a tub.

Marshmallows

Separate toes when applying polish Get the comfort of a salon treatment when giving yourself a home pedicure. Just place marshmallows between your toes to separate them before you apply the nail polish. Make sure your feet are completely dry though or they may get sticky!

Keep brown sugar soft Sometimes brown sugar seems to harden overnight once you've opened the bag. Next time you open a bag of brown sugar, add a few marshmallows to the bag before closing it. The marshmallows will add enough moisture to keep the sugar soft for weeks.

Stop ice-cream drips Keep a leaky ice-cream cone from staining your clothes. Just place a large marshmallow in the bottom of the cone before you add the ice cream.

Keep wax off birthday cakes If one of your birthday wishes is to keep candle wax off the icing on the cake, try this trick. Push each candle into a marshmallow and put the marshmallow on top of the icing. The wax will melt onto the marshmallow, which you can then discard.

Impromptu cupcake icing Pop a marshmallow on top of each cake about a minute before they come out of the oven to make a delicious, instant, gooey topping.

DID YOU KNOW?

Ancient Egyptians made the first marshmallow sweets – honey-based concoctions flavoured and thickened with the sap of the root of the marshmallow plant (*Althaea officinalis*). Marshmallow grows in salt marshes and on banks near large bodies of water. Its sap was used to make marshmallow sweets and medicine until the mid 1800s. Today's commercial marshmallows are a mixture of corn syrup or sugar, gelatine, gum arabic and flavouring.

* Masking tape

Label foods and school supplies You don't need to buy labels or a special machine that makes them. Use inexpensive masking tape instead to mark food containers and freezer bags before putting them in the refrigerator or freezer and don't forget to include the date. You can also use masking tape to conveniently mark children's schoolbooks and supplies.

Fix a broken umbrella rib If a strong wind breaks a rib on your umbrella, it's easy to fix it. Use a piece of masking tape and a length of wire cut from a coat hanger to make a 'splint'.

Reuse a vacuum cleaner bag Save money by using a vacuum cleaner bag twice. After the bag is full the first time, don't empty it the usual way through the hole in front. Take out the bag and cut a slit down the middle of the back. After you have emptied the bag into a bin, hold the cut edges together, fold them closed and seal them securely with wide masking tape. Your bag is ready to be used again. Take care not to overfill during the second use.

Keep a paint can neat To prevent paint from filling the groove at the top of a paint tin, simply cover the rim of the tin with masking tape.

Make a road for toy cars Make a highway for tiny toy cars by taping two strips of masking tape to a floor or tabletop. Add a little handmade cardboard stop sign or two and the mini vehicles can go off to the races. Carefully guiding a toy car along the taped roadway is more than just fun for small children, it also helps them to gain motor control of their fingers for skills they will need later, such as writing.

DID YOU KNOW?

In 1923, when Richard Drew joined manufacturer 3M as an engineer, they made only sandpaper. Drew was testing one of the company's sandpapers at a local mechanic's when he noticed that workers found it difficult to make clean dividing lines on two-colour paint jobs. This inspired Drew to look for a solution, despite direct orders from 3M's president to devote his attention solely to sandpaper. Luckily for 3M, he didn't listen. In 1925 Drew invented the first masking tape, a 5-cm-wide tan-coloured paper with a pressure-sensitive adhesive backing. Five years later he invented Scotch cellophane tape.

Hang party streamers Use masking tape instead of transparent tape to put up streamers and balloons for your next party. The masking tape won't leave a residue on the wall like transparent tape does. But always remember to remove the masking tape within a day or two. If you wait too long, it may take paint off the wall when it comes off.

 Mayonnaise

Condition your hair Massage mayonnaise into your hair and scalp just as you would an ordinary hair conditioner. Cover your head with a shower cap, wait several minutes and shampoo. The mayonnaise will moisturise your hair and give it a lustrous sheen.

Give yourself a facial Why waste money on expensive creams when you can treat yourself to a soothing facial with whole-egg mayonnaise from your own refrigerator? Gently spread the mayonnaise over your face and leave it on for about 20 minutes. Then wipe it off and rinse with cool water. Your face will feel clean and smooth.

Strengthen your fingernails To condition your fingernails, just plunge them into a bowl of mayonnaise every so often. Keep them immersed for about 5 minutes and then wash with warm water.

Relieve sunburn pain If you've overdone the sunbathing, treat dry, sunburned skin by smoothing mayonnaise liberally over the affected area. The mayonnaise will relieve the pain and moisturise the skin.

Remove dead skin Soften and remove dead skin from elbows and feet. Rub mayonnaise over the dry, rough tissue, leave it on for 10 minutes and wipe it away with a damp cloth.

A safe way to kill head lice Many dermatologists now recommend using mayonnaise to kill and remove head lice from children instead of toxic prescription drugs and over-the-counter preparations. What's more, lice are becoming more resistant to such chemical treatments. To treat head lice with mayonnaise, massage a liberal amount of mayonnaise into the hair and scalp before bedtime. Cover with a shower cap and leave overnight to maximise the effect. Shampoo in the morning and then use a fine-tooth comb to remove any remaining lice and nits. To completely eradicate the infestation, repeat the treatment in 7 to 10 days.

Make plant leaves shiny Professional florists use this trick to keep houseplant leaves shiny and clean. You can do the same thing at home. Just rub a little mayonnaise on the leaves with a paper towel and they will stay bright and shiny for weeks and even months at a time.

Remove crayon marks Get rid of crayon marks from wooden furniture with the minimum of elbow grease. Rub some mayonnaise on the crayon marks and let it soak in for several minutes. Then wipe the surface clean with a damp cloth.

Clean piano keys If the keys on the piano are starting to yellow, apply a little mayonnaise with a soft cloth. Wait a few minutes, wipe with a damp cloth, and buff. The piano keys will look like new.

Remove bumper stickers When it's time to get rid of an out-of-date bumper sticker on your car, don't attack it with a razor and risk scratching the bumper. Instead, rub some mayonnaise over the entire sticker. Let it sit for several minutes and wipe it off. The mayonnaise will dissolve the glue.

Get tar off your car To remove tar or tree sap from your car with ease, rub some mayonnaise over the affected area, let it sit for several minutes, and wipe it away with a clean, soft rag.

Milk

Make frozen fish taste fresh If you want fish from the freezer to taste as if it's been freshly caught, try this trick. Place the frozen fish in a bath of milk until it thaws. The milk will make it taste fresher.

Boost the flavour of corn on the cob This is a simple way to make corn on the cob taste sweeter and fresher. Add 50g powdered milk to a pan of boiling water before you put in the corn.

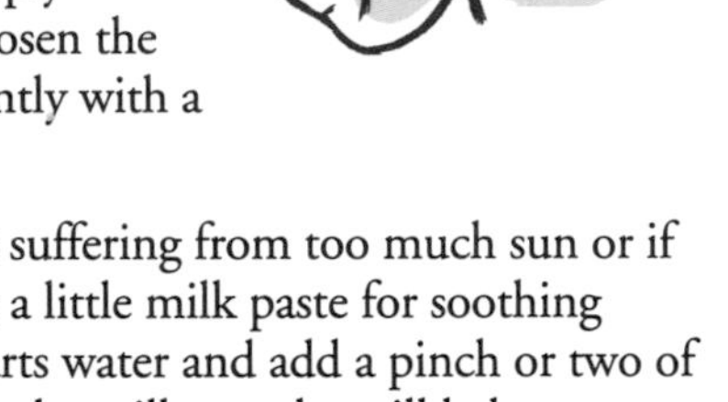

Polish silverware Tarnished silverware will look like new with a little help from some sour milk. If you don't have any sour milk available, you can make some by adding vinegar to fresh milk. Then simply soak the silver in the milk for half an hour to loosen the tarnish, wash in warm, soapy water and buff gently with a soft cloth.

Soothe sunburn and insect bites If your skin is suffering from too much sun or if itchy insect bites are driving you mad, try using a little milk paste for soothing relief. Mix one part powdered milk with two parts water and add a pinch or two of salt. Dab it on the burn or bite. The enzymes in the milk powder will help to neutralise the insect-bite venom and relieve the pain of sunburn.

Impromptu make-up remover If you run out of make-up remover, use powdered milk instead. Just mix 3 tablespoons powdered milk with 80ml warm water in a jar and shake well. Add more water or powder as necessary to achieve the consistency of heavy cream. Now you are ready to apply your makeshift make-up remover with a facecloth. When you have finished, wipe it off and rinse thoroughly with water.

Give yourself a facial Try another way to give yourself a luxurious facial at home. Make a mask by mixing 50g powdered milk with enough water to form a thick paste. Thoroughly coat your face with the mixture, let it dry completely, then rinse with warm water. Your face will feel fresh and rejuvenated.

Soften skin Treat yourself to a luxurious foamy milk bath. Toss 100g or so of powdered milk into the tub as it fills. Milk acts as a natural skin softener.

Clean and soften dirty hands If a heavy stint in the garden has left you with stained and gritty hands, that ordinary soap won't budge, make a paste of oatmeal and milk and rub it vigorously on your hands. The stains will be gone and the oatmeal-and-milk mixture will soften and soothe your skin.

Clean patent leather Make patent-leather bags or shoes look like new again. Just dab on a little milk, let it dry and buff with a soft cloth.

Remove ink stains from clothes To remove ink stains from coloured clothes, an overnight milk bath will often do the trick. Just soak the affected garment in milk overnight and launder as usual the next day.

Repair cracked china Before you throw out a cracked plate from your grandmother's old china set, try mending it with milk. Place the plate in a pan, cover it with milk (fresh or reconstituted powdered milk), and bring to the boil. As soon as it starts to boil, lower the heat and simmer for about 45 minutes. The protein in the milk will miraculously meld most fine cracks.

Milk cartons

Make ice blocks for parties Keep drinks cold at a barbecue or party with ice blocks made from empty milk cartons. Just rinse out the old cartons, fill them with water and put them in the freezer. Peel away the container when you're ready to put the blocks in the punch bowl; but if you intend to use them as cooler blocks, leave the container in place.

Make a lacy candle Use this easy method to make a delicate, lacy candle. Coat the inside of a milk carton with cooking spray, put a taper candle in the middle, anchoring it with a base of melted wax, then fill it with ice cubes. Pour in hot wax; when the wax cools, peel off the carton. The melting ice will leave beautiful, lacy voids in the wax.

Instant kids' bowling alley Make an indoor bowling alley with ninepins made from empty milk and juice cartons. Just rinse the cartons (use whatever sizes you like) and let them dry. Then take two same-sized cartons and slide one upside down into the other, squeezing it a little to make it fit. Once you've made ten, set the ninepins up at the end of the hall and let the children use a tennis ball to roll for strikes and spares.

Make seed starters Milk cartons are the perfect size to use for seed starters. Cut off the top half of a carton, punch holes in the bottom, fill with potting compost and sow the seeds according to instructions on the packet.

DID YOU KNOW?

John Van Wormer, a toy factory owner, didn't cry over spilt milk when he dropped a bottle on the floor one morning in 1915. Instead, he was inspired to patent a paper-based milk carton that he named Pure-Pak. It took him 10 years to perfect a machine that coated the paper with wax and sealed the carton with animal glues. The early waxy containers were slow to catch on with sceptical consumers and bore little resemblance to today's milk cartons, but now some 30 billion Pure-Pak cartons are sold annually.

Make vegetable garden collars Use empty milk cartons to discourage slugs and snails from attacking young tomato plants. Cut off the tops and bottoms of the containers and when the ground is soft, push them into the ground around the tomatoes when you are planting them out.

Collect food scraps for compost Keep an empty milk carton handy near the kitchen sink and use it to collect food scraps for the compost heap.

Disposable paint holder If you have a small painting job to complete and you don't want to lug a heavy can around, an empty milk carton can help. Cut off the top of the carton and pour in the amount of paint you need. When you have finished painting, throw the carton into the bin.

Feed birds in winter To make an attractive winter treat for feathered garden visitors, combine melted suet and birdseed in an empty milk carton. Suet is beef fat; you can get it from a butcher or buy it in blocks. To render it, chop or grind the fat and heat it over a low flame until it melts. Then strain it through cheesecloth into the carton. Insert a loop of string into the mixture while it is still soft. After it hardens, tear away the carton and tie your new mass of bird food to a branch. Only use this feed in cool or cold weather. Once the temperature gets above about 20°C, the suet will turn rancid and melt.

* Mothballs

Rinse woollens for storage It is a good idea to store woollens with mothballs to ward off moths. To give favourite sweaters even more protection, dissolve a few mothballs in the final rinse when you are washing them prior to seasonal storage.

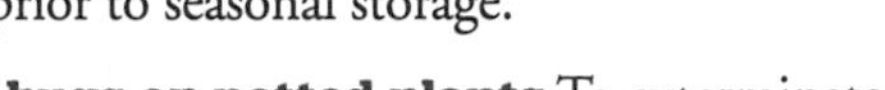

Kill bugs on potted plants To exterminate insects from a potted plant, put the plant in a clear plastic bag, such as a cleaning bag, add a few mothballs, and seal for a week. When you take the plant out of the bag, it will be insect-free. The treatment will also keep moths away for a while.

Repel mice from garage or shed Don't let mice spend their winter holidays with you. Place a few mothballs around the garage and the mice will seek alternative accommodation. To keep mice out of a potting shed, put the mothballs around the base of wrapped or covered plants.

Keep animals out of your garden Scatter old mothballs around the garden and lowerbeds to deter cats, dogs and rats, mice and squirrels. Most animals hate the smell.

Keep insects at bay Add mothballs to boxes stored in the attic and silverfish and other insects will stay away.

WARNING Take care to keep mothballs well out of the reach of pets and small children as they can be harmful if ingested.

{ SCIENCE FAIR }

MOTHBALL DANCE

Make mothballs dance and give children a basic science lesson too. Fill a glass jar about two-thirds full of water. Add about 50–75ml vinegar and 2 teaspoons bicarbonate of soda. Stir gently, then throw in a few mothballs and watch them bounce up and down. The vinegar and bicarbonate of soda create carbon dioxide bubbles, which cling to the irregular surfaces of the mothballs. When enough bubbles have accumulated to lift the weight of a mothball, it rises to the surface of the water. There, some of the bubbles escape into the air and the mothball sinks to the bottom of the jar to start the cycle again. The effect will last longer if the container is sealed.

Mouse mats

Pad under table legs When you get a new mouse mat for your computer, don't throw the old one away. Use it to make pads for table legs and chairs to prevent them from scratching wood and other hard floors. Just cut the foam and cloth pad into small pieces and superglue each piece to the bottom of a leg.

Make knee pads for the garden Old computer mouse mats are just the right size to cushion your knees when you're working in the garden. Either kneel on them as they are or attach them directly to your trouser legs with gaffer tape.

Pad under houseplants Keep potted plant containers from scratching or damaging hard floors. Set the pot on top of an old mouse mat and the floor will remain scratch-free. Use four mats for large pots.

Hot pad for the table Protect a dining table from hot casseroles, coffeepots and serving dishes. Use old mouse mats as hot pads. The fabric-topped foam mouse mat is the perfect size to hold most hot containers that you set on the table.

Mouthwash

Clean a computer monitor screen If you've run out of glass cleaner, a strong, alcohol-based mouthwash will work as well as, or better than, glass cleaner on a computer monitor or TV screen. Apply with a damp, soft cloth and buff dry. Remember to use only on glass screens, not liquid crystal displays as the alcohol can damage the material used in LCDs.

Cleanse your face An antiseptic mouthwash makes a wonderful astringent for cleansing your face. Check the ingredients to make sure it does not contain sugar, then use as follows. Wash your face with warm, soapy water and rinse. Dab a cotton wool ball with mouthwash and gently wipe your face as you would with

TIP* MAKE YOUR OWN MOUTHWASH

Freshen your breath with your own alcohol-free mouthwash. Place 30 whole cloves and/or 85g fresh rosemary in a 500ml jar and pour in 400ml boiling water. Cover the jar tightly and let it steep overnight before straining. If you need a mouthwash immediately, dissolve ½ teaspoon bicarbonate of soda in 100ml warm water.

any astringent. You should feel a pleasant, tingling sensation. Rinse with warm water followed by a splash of cold water. Your face will look and feel clean and refreshed.

Treat athlete's foot A sugarless antiseptic mouthwash may be all you need to treat mild cases of athlete's foot or a toenail fungus. Use a cotton wool ball soaked in mouthwash to apply to the affected area several times a day. It will sting a bit but athlete's foot should respond after a few days. Toenail fungus may take up to several months. If you do not see a response by then, make an appointment with a dermatologist or chiropodist.

Add to wash water Smelly sports socks are often full of bacteria and fungi that may not all come out in the wash, unless you add a cup of alcohol-based, sugarless mouthwash during the wash cycle.

Cure underarm odour Regular deodorants mask unpleasant underarm odours with a heavy perfume smell but may do little to attack the cause of the problem. To get rid of the bacteria that cause perspiration odour, dampen a cotton wool ball with a sugarless, alcohol-based mouthwash and swab your armpits. If you've just shaved your armpits, you should wait a day before trying this.

Disinfect a cut When you need to clean out a small cut or wound, use an alcohol-based mouthwash to disinfect the skin. Remember that before it was adopted as a mouthwash, the mixture was successfully used as an antiseptic to prevent infections after surgery.

Get rid of dandruff To treat a bad case of dandruff, wash your hair with your usual shampoo, then rinse with an alcohol-based mouthwash. You can follow with an ordinary conditioner.

Clean the toilet If you've run out of toilet cleaner, try pouring 50ml alcohol-based mouthwash into the bowl. Let it stand in the water for half an hour, then scrub with a toilet brush before flushing. The mouthwash will disinfect germs and leave the toilet bowl sparkling and clean.

Mustard

Soothe an aching back Take a bath in yellow mustard to relieve an aching back or arthritis pain. Simply pour a 200ml jar of powdered mustard into the hot water as the tub fills. Mix well and soak yourself for 15 minutes. If you don't have time for a bath, you can rub some mustard directly on the affected areas. Use only mild yellow mustard and make sure to apply it to a small test area first. Undiluted mustard may irritate your skin.

DID YOU KNOW?

Ancient Romans brought mustard back from Egypt and used the seeds to flavour unfermented grape juice, called must. This is believed to be how the mustard plant got its name. The Romans also made a paste from the ground seeds for medicinal purposes and may have used it as a condiment. The mustard we use today was first prepared in Dijon, France, in the 13th century. Dijon-style mustard is made from darker seeds than yellow or English mustard.

Relax stiff muscles Next time you take a bath in Epsom salts, throw in a few tablespoons of yellow mustard as well. The mustard will enhance the soothing effects of the Epsom salts and also help to relax stiff, sore muscles.

Relieve congestion Relieve congestion with a mustard plaster just like Grandma used to make. Rub your chest with prepared mustard, soak a facecloth in hot water, wring it out, and place it over the mustard.

Make a facial mask Pat your face with mild yellow mustard for a bracing facial that will soothe and stimulate your skin. Try it on a small test area first to make sure it will not be irritating.

Remove the odour from bottles If you've collected some attractive bottles, but after washing, they still smell like the substance they originally held, you can kill the smell with mustard. After washing, just put a little mustard in the bottle, fill with warm water and shake it up. Rinse well, and the smell will be gone.

 Nail varnish see page 212

 Nail varnish remover

Remove stains from china Rub the soiled areas with nail varnish remover and clean off the spots with a cotton bud.

Eliminate ink stains Use nail varnish remover to remove non-water soluble ink stains from skin. Take a cotton wool ball and wipe the affected areas with the solution. Once the ink stains are gone, wash skin with soap and water.

Rub the paint off windows Working in a well-ventilated area, dab nail varnish remover onto the painted areas of the window in small sections. Leave it for a few minutes before rubbing it off with a cloth. To finish, wipe again with a damp cloth.

Remove stickers from glass Wipe with acetone-based nail varnish remover to remove both the sticker and the gluey residue left behind.

Dissolve melted plastic

If you've ever come too close to a hot metal toaster with a plastic bag of bread or rolls you will know that the resulting mess can be a real cleaning challenge. Eliminate the sticky mess with nail varnisher remover. First unplug the toaster and wait for it to cool. Then pour a little nail varnish remover onto a soft cloth and gently rub over the damaged areas. Once the melted plastic has gone, wipe with a damp cloth and dry with a paper towel to finish. The same solution works for melted plastic on curling irons or hair straighteners.

{TAKE CARE}

Too-frequent use of nail varnish remover containing acetone (check the label) can cause dry skin and brittle nails. All nail varnish removers are flammable and potentially hazardous if inhaled for a long time; use them in a well-ventilated area away from flames. And work carefully; they can damage some synthetic fabrics, wood finishes and plastics.

Keep watches clean Get rid of scratches on the face of a watch with nail varnish remover. If the face is made from unbreakable plastic, rub the remover over the scratches until they diminish or disappear.

Unhinge superglue Superglue will stick tenaciously to just about anything, including your skin. Trying to peel it off your fingers can actually cause skin damage. Instead, soak a cotton wool ball with acetone-based nail varnish remover and hold it on the skin until the glue dissolves.

Clean patent shoes Scuff marks can show up badly on patent shoes, as they do on white or other light-coloured shoes. To remove the marks, rub them lightly but briskly with a soft cloth or paper towel dipped in nail varnish remover. Afterwards, remove any residue with a damp cloth.

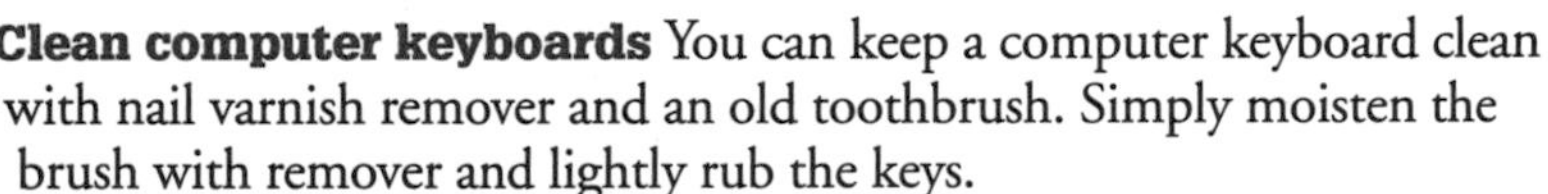

Clean computer keyboards You can keep a computer keyboard clean with nail varnish remover and an old toothbrush. Simply moisten the brush with remover and lightly rub the keys.

Dilute correction fluid To thin correction fluid or old nail varnish, dilute it with nail varnish remover. Pour just a few drops into the bottle and then shake. Add a little more varnish remover to the solution, if needed, to attain the desired consistency.

Prepare brass for relacquering Old or damaged lacquer coatings on brass can be safely removed with nail varnish remover. Take a soft cloth and pour a small amount of remover on it. Rub the brass object until the old lacquer has been lifted. Your brass item will be ready to be polished or professionally relacquered.

Newspaper

Protect glassware when moving If you are moving house or packing up items for long-term storage, use several sheets of soaking-wet newspaper to wrap up glass dishes, bowls, drinking glasses and other fragile items and then let them thoroughly dry before packing. The newspaper will harden and form a protective cast around the glass that will dramatically improve its chances of surviving the move without breaking.

Store sweaters and blankets Don't treat moths to a fine meal of woollen sweaters and blankets. When putting them into storage, wrap wool garments in a few sheets of newspaper (be sure to tape up the corners). It will keep away the moths and keep out dust and dirt.

Deodorise containers and luggage To freshen a plastic container or wooden box with a persistent, unpleasant odour, stuff it with a few sheets of crumpled newspaper and seal it closed for three or four days. You can also use this technique to deodorise trunks and suitcases.

DID YOU KNOW?

Newspapers were first published frequently and on a regular basis in the early 17th century. The German newspaper *Relation* was first published in 1605 while the UK's oldest surviving paper is the *London Gazette*, founded in 1665 and still published as a court journal. In 1785, John Walter founded the *Daily Universal Register* which became *The Times* on 1 January 1788 and is Britain's oldest surviving newspaper with continuous daily publication. The oldest Sunday newspaper is *The Observer*, founded in 1791.

Dry wet shoes If your shoes get soaked after walking through the rain or slogging through the snow, stuff them with dry, balled-up newspaper to prevent any long-term damage. Place the shoes on their sides at room temperature so the moisture can be thoroughly absorbed. If the shoes are extremely wet you may need to replace the stuffing a few times.

Create an emergency splint If someone you are with has a bad fall and you suspect there may be a bone injury to an arm or leg, it's important to immobilise the limb to prevent pain and additional damage. Fashion a makeshift splint by folding up several sheets of newspaper until they are stiff and attach beneath the limb using a few pieces of adhesive or gaffer tape. You may need to overlap a couple of folded sheets to make a splint long enough for a leg injury.

Remove oven residue They may call it a self-cleaning oven, but when it has finished, you always have to contend with mopping off the ashlike residue. Don't waste a roll of paper towels on the flakes; clean them up with a few sheets of moistened, crumpled newspaper.

Clean and polish windows Instead of using absorbent paper towels to dry off just-washed windows, try using crumpled-up newspaper instead. Many people reckon that it dries and polishes windows better than paper towels. And it's cheaper too.

Make an impromptu ironing board If you always pack a travel iron, it's easy to make your own travel ironing board. Fill a pillowcase with four or five newspapers, keeping the stack as level as possible. Place it on a flat surface or the floor before starting to iron.

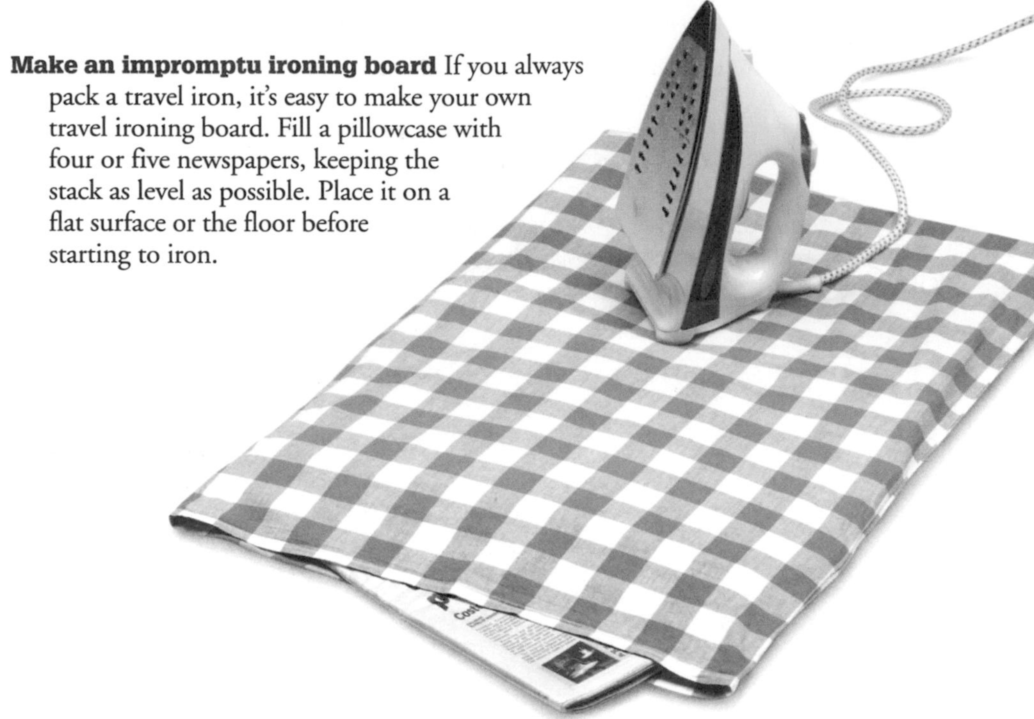

Unscrew a broken lightbulb To remove a broken lightbulb, make a pad of several sheets of newspaper, press the paper over the bulb, and turn it anticlockwise. (Make sure you're wearing protective gloves and that the power is off.) The bulb should loosen up enough to remove from the socket. Wrap it in the paper and throw it in the dustbin.

Slow-ripen tomatoes in autumn If frost is expected and you still have a bunch of tomatoes on the vine, pick the tomatoes and wrap each one in a couple of sheets of newspaper. Store them in airtight containers inside a dark cabinet or cupboard at room temperature. Check each one every three to four days; they will all eventually ripen to perfection.

Line a waste disposal unit Putting a few layers of newspapers at the bottom of a waste disposal unit will not only soak up the unpleasant odours caused by rotting foods, it will also protect the unit against damage caused by any sharp objects that manage to squeeze through.

DID YOU KNOW?

What we call newsprint – the type of paper used by newspapers around the world – was invented around 1838 by a Canadian teenager called Charles Fenerty. After hearing frequent complaints from local paper mills about maintaining adequate supplies of rags to make rag paper, Fenerty hit upon the idea of making paper from spruce pulp. Unfortunately, Fenerty didn't go public with his discovery until 1844. By then, a consortium of European investors had already patented a process for creating paper solely from wood fibre.

Use as mulch Newspaper makes excellent mulch for vegetables and flowers. It is superb at retaining moisture and does an equally fine job at fighting off and suffocating weeds. Just lay down several sheets of newspaper. Then cover the paper with about 8cm of wood mulch so it doesn't blow away. Don't use glossy paper and coloured newsprint for mulching (or composting); coloured inks may contain lead or harmful dyes that can leach into the ground. To check the content of your newsprint, contact the newspaper and ask about the inks they use; many papers now use only safe vegetable-based inks.

Add to compost Adding moderate amounts of wet, shredded newsprint, printed in black ink only, to the compost heap is a good and relatively safe way to reduce the smell and to give earthworms a tasty treat.

Farewell, earwigs If your garden is under siege from earwigs, get rid of them by making your own environmentally friendly traps. Tightly roll up a wet newspaper, and put a rubber band around it to keep it from unravelling. Place the 'trap' in the area you've seen the insects and leave it overnight. Repeat until your traps are free from earwigs.

Protect outdoor taps for winter To prevent damage from ice and cold temperatures, make sure you shut off the valve to each tap and drain off any excess water. Then insulate each tap by wrapping it with a few sheets of newspaper covered with a plastic bag (keep the bag in place by wrapping it with gaffer tape or a few rubber bands).

Protect windows when painting Don't bother buying thick masking tape when painting around windows. Simply dampen several long strips of newspaper and place them on the glass alongside the wood you're painting. The newspaper will easily adhere to the surface and keep the paint off the glass or frames and it is much easier to remove than tape.

Roll your own fireplace logs Bolster a supply of logs by making a few of your own out of old newspapers. Just lay out a number of sheets end to end, roll them up as tightly as you can, tie up the ends with string or wire and wet them in a solution of slightly soapy water. Although it will take a while, let them dry thoroughly, standing on end, before using. Note: do not use newspaper logs in a wood-burning stove unless the manufacturer specifies that it is safe.

Put traction under your wheels Unless you have a four-wheel drive vehicle, it's always a good idea to keep a small stack of newspapers in the boot of the car during the winter months to prevent getting stranded on a patch of ice or slush. Placing several sheets of newspaper under each rear wheel will often provide the traction you need to get your car back on the road.

Pick up broken glass shards If you break a large glass bowl or vase, a safe way to get up the small shards of glass that remain after you remove the large pieces is to blot the area with wet newspapers. The tiny fragments will stick to the paper, which makes for easy disposal. Then carefully drop the newspaper into the rubbish bin.

Super item
36 USES!

NAIL VARNISH...

...around the house

Make buttons glow in the dark In a dim light, it is too easy to grab the remote control to increase the TV volume, hit the wrong button and change the channel instead. Dab glow-in-the-dark nail varnish onto frequently used remote buttons so that they're easy to see in the gloom. You can also use phosphorescent polish to mark keys and keyholes and other hard-to-spot items.

Mark your thermostat setting When you wake up to a chilly house and don't have your glasses, it is easy to return to your comfort zone if you have marked a dial-type thermostat. Simply set it to the preferred temperature and then make a thin mark with coloured nail varnish from the dial into the outside ring.

Mark temperature settings on shower knobs Don't spend time in the shower fiddling with the water temperature. With the shower on, select your ideal settings, then turn off the flow to the shower and make a small mark with bright nail varnish onto the stationary lip of both the hot and cold knob indicating the handle position that you prefer.

Make kitchen measurements legible Find measuring jug markings more easily, especially if you like to measure roughly while cooking. Use a very visible colour of nail varnish to trace over the basic measurement levels. This also works well for dimly lit, late night bottle feedings, when you need to see how much your baby has drunk. And you won't have to squint to find the correct dosage on little plastic medicine cups if you first mark them with a thin line of dark polish.

Label your sports gear If you share a lot of interests with a golf partner, including the same brand of golf balls, make it clear who got to the green first, by putting a dot of bright nail varnish on your ball supply. This also works well with other items that don't have enough room for your name.

Label poison containers If everyone in the home has easy access to a medicine cupboard or other cupboard containing harmful substances, prevent someone from grabbing dangerous items in haste. Use dark red or other easily visible nail varnish to label anything that may be harmful. Draw an unmistakable X on the label as well as the lid or spout.

Seal an envelope If you don't trust of the security of self-sealing envelopes, brush a little nail varnish along the underside of the flap, seal it, and it won't open even if you steam it with a kettle. Add some flair to a special card by brushing your initial (or any design) in nail varnish over the sealed flap tip, as a modern type of sealing wax that doesn't need to be melted first.

Smudgeproof important medicine labels Preserve the important information on prescription medicines and other important medicine labels with a coat of clear varnish, and they won't get smudged as you grab for them after collecting your glass of water.

Mark levels inside a bucket When you are mixing in a big bucket, you can't usually lift the bucket to check the quantity. And it may not have the measurements clearly marked at all. Make sure you know you are using the right amounts by marking levels with lines of nail varnish. Use a colour that stands out against the bucket.

Waterproof address labels When you are sending a parcel on a rainy day, a little clear varnish brushed over the address label will ensure your package goes to the right place.

TIP* USING NAIL VARNISH

- To keep nail varnishes fresh and easy to use, store them in the fridge. Keep them together in a little square plastic container.
- Shaking a nail varnish bottle to mix the colour can cause bubbles. Roll the bottle between your palms instead.
- Wipe the inside threads of your nail varnish bottle and cap with a cotton wool ball dipped in nail varnish remover before closing them. It will open more easily.

NAIL VARNISH...

...around the house

DID YOU KNOW?

Nail varnish is certainly not a recent concept. As early as 3000 BC, ancient Chinese nobles are believed to have coloured their long nails with polishes, made from gum arabic, beeswax, gelatine and pigments. The nobility wore shades of gold, silver, red or black, while lower classes were restricted to pastel shades. Coloured nails were also popular with ancient Egyptians, who often dyed their nails with henna or stained them with berries. Polish wasn't just for women. In both Egypt and Rome, military commanders painted their nails red before going into battle.

Prevent rust rings from metal containers If guests are likely to peek into your medicine cabinet, you don't want them to see rust rings on the shelves. Brush nail lacquer around the bottom of shaving cream cans and other metal containers to avoid any unsightly stains.

Prevent rusty toilet seat screws If you have installed a new toilet seat, keep the screws from rusting by painting them with a coat or two of clear nail varnish; it will also help to prevent the seat wobbling by keeping the screws in place.

Paint shaker holes to restrict salt If your favourite salt shaker dispenses a little too generously, paint a few of the holes closed with nail varnish. It is a particularly good idea for those watching the salt intake in their diet.

Prevent tarnish on costume jewellery Inexpensive costume jewellery can add sparkle and colour to an everyday outfit, but not if it gets tarnished and the tarnish rubs off the jewellery and onto your skin. To keep fake jewels and your skin sparkling clean, brush clear nail varnish onto the back of each piece and allow it to dry before wearing.

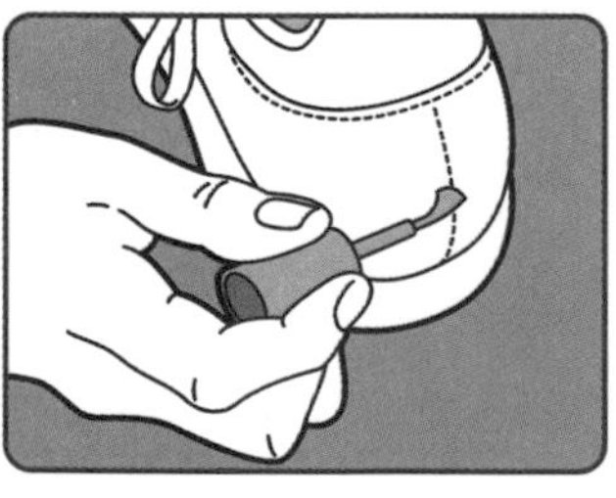

Seal out scuffs on shoes On leather shoes, it is the back and toes that really take the brunt of the surface wear and tear. Next time you buy a new pair of shoes, especially ones for a child or an active adult, give these areas the extra measure of protection they need. Paint a little clear nail varnish on the outside of the back seam and over the toes. Rub the polish in a little to feather out the shine of the polish. After it dries, you will be a step ahead of the perennial shoe problems 'driver's heel' and 'footballer's toe'.

Keep laces from unravelling Neaten the appearance of frayed shoelaces and extend their life. Dip the ends in clear nail varnish and twist the ravelled ends together. Repair the laces in the evening so that the polish will dry overnight.

Get rid of a wart Warts are unsightly and infectious. In order to get rid of them and prevent spreading the virus to others, cover them with nail varnish. The wart should be gone or greatly diminished in a week.

Protect a belt buckle's shine Cover new or just-polished belt buckles with a coat of clear varnish. You will prevent oxidation of the metal and guarantee a gleaming first impression.

Make a gleaming paperweight To create paperweights that look like gemstones, or interesting rocks for the base of potted cacti, find some palm-size, smooth clean rocks. Put about 1.25cm water into a pie tin, and put 1 drop clear nail varnish onto the water. The polish will spread out over the water surface. Holding a rock with your fingertips, slowly roll it in the water to coat it with the polish. Set the rock on newspaper to dry.

...in the sewing room

Prevent loss of buttons Keep a brand-new shirt in good shape by putting a drop of clear nail varnish on the thread in the buttons. It prevents the thread from fraying, so taking this precaution in advance could save you some embarrassment later. Put a dab on just-repaired buttons as well.

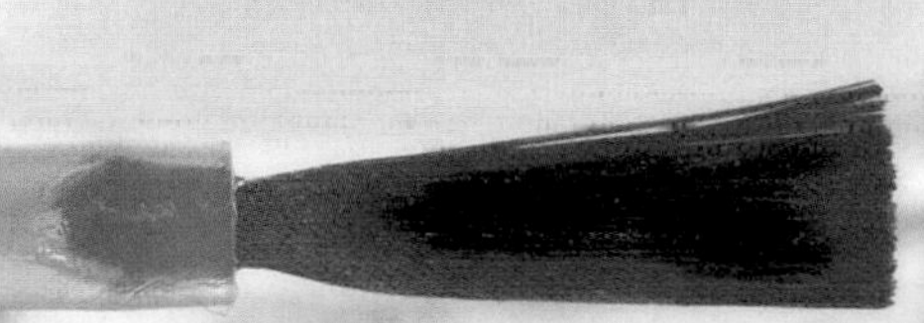

Make needle threading easier Do you fumble with your needle and thread, licking and re-licking the frayed thread end until it is too floppy to go through the eye? Try dragging the cut thread end through the application brush of a pot of nail varnish once or twice and then roll the thread end between your thumb and forefinger. It will dry in a second and the thread end will stay stiff enough to thread in a flash. Your sewing box can be a great retirement home for a nail colour you no longer use.

Keep ribbons from fraying Brush the cut ends of gift ribbon with a little clear nail varnish to stop them from unravelling. This is also the perfect solution for a little girl's hair ribbons on special occasions.

NAIL VARNISH...

...in the sewing room

Prevent frayed fabric from unravelling If frayed wisps are peeking out from the bottom of your skirt or the lining of your jacket is fraying at the cuffs, you can stop the fraying getting worse by brushing the frayed strands into place with some clear nail varnish.

Stop a run in your tights It can be a helpless feeling, realising that a small run in your tights is about to turn into a big embarrassment. Luckily you can stop runs permanently and prolong the life of fragile stockings with a dab of clear nail varnish. Simply apply polish to each end of a run (no need to remove the tights) and let it dry. This invisible fix stops runs and lasts through many hand washes.

Protect pearl buttons Delicate pearl buttons – both real and fake – will keep their brand-new sparkle with a protective coat of clear nail varnish.

...making repairs

Mend a fingernail If you have split a nail, cut open an unused teabag, empty out the tea, cut a piece of the bag into the shape of your nail and cover over it with clear nail varnish. Press it onto the nail, then apply coloured nail varnish. It will last until the break grows out.

Temporarily repair a pair of glasses If you have cracked a lens in your glasses, but can't get them repaired immediately, seal the crack on both sides with a thin coat of clear nail varnish. That will hold it together until you can get the lens replaced.

Stop a windscreen crack from spreading If a small crack has developed in the windscreen, working in the shade, brush the crack on both sides of the glass with nail varnish to fill it well. Move the car into the sun so the winscreen can dry. You will eventually need to replace it, but this repair will give you time to shop around for the best estimate.

Fill small nicks on floors and glass If children have been playing hockey or skating on wooden floors, you can fill the resultant chips and nicks by dabbing them with some clear nail varnish. It will be shiny when it dries, so sand the spot gently with some fine sandpaper. A thick coat of clear nail varnish also helps to soften the sharp edge on a nicked mirror or glass pane.

DID YOU KNOW?

Unless you work in a lab, you probably won't know that clear nail varnish is used for mounting microscopic slides. It is the preferred substance used around a cover glass to seal it onto a slide, protecting the specimen from air and moisture.

Reset loose stones in jewellery If a favourite ring or brooch has lost a stone or two, you don't have to put it in the dressing up box just yet. The stone can be reset using a little drop of clear nail varnish as the 'glue'. It will dry quickly and the repair will be invisible.

Repair lacquered items To fix a chip on a special lacquered vase or other lacquered item, try mixing a number of colours of nail varnish to match the piece. Paint over the chipped area to make it less noticeable. **WARNING** You may lower the value of an antique by doing this, so you should probably only attempt this kind of repair with inexpensive items.

Plug a hole in a cooler bag A small hole inside a cooler bag doesn't mean you have to throw it away just yet. Seal the hole with two coats of nail varnish to hold in ice and other melted substances.

Fill washtub nicks It's a mystery how they get there, but the washing machine may develop one or two nicks near the holes in the tub and they can cause snags in clothes or even rust spots. Seal the nicks with some nail varnish, feathering the edges so there is no 'lip'.

Keep chipped car paint from rusting If a car has a number of small dents and chips, you can keep them from rusting or getting larger by dabbing clear nail varnish onto the damaged areas.

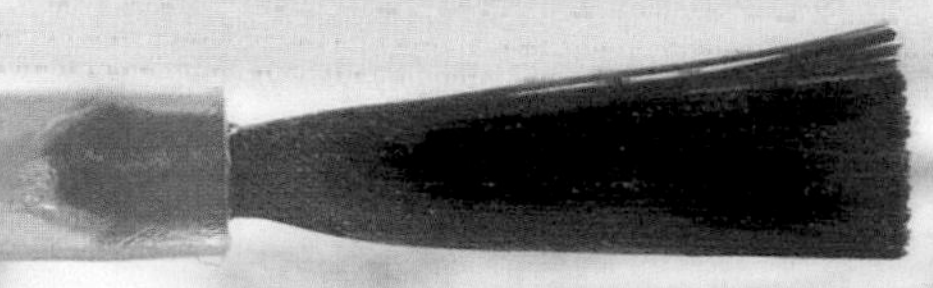

Smooth wooden hangers If you have noticed a few splinters or nicks in wooden coat hangers, brush some nail varnish over the rough edges to smooth the surface again and keep coat linings and delicate garments safe.

Fix torn window shades If you notice a small tear in a roller blind, you can usually seal it with a dab of clear nail varnish.

Tighten loose screws Keep knobs on drawers and cabinets in place by brushing a little clear polish on the screw threads. Then insert the screws, and let them dry before using again. This is also a great solution if you have been keeping a Phillips screwdriver in the kitchen for loose saucepan handles. You can also use clear nail varnish to keep nuts on machine screws or bolts from coming loose and if you need to take the nuts off, a twist with a wrench will break the seal. Clear nail varnish will also keep the tiny screws on a pair of spectacles in place.

Oatmeal

Treat chicken pox or an itchy rash Take the itch out of a case of chicken pox or a rash with a relaxing, warm oatmeal bath. Grind 200g oatmeal in a blender to make a fine powder, then pour it into a piece of cheesecloth, the foot section of a clean nylon stocking, or one leg of an old pair of tights. Knot the material and tie it around a bath tap so the bag is suspended under the running water. Fill the tub with lukewarm water and soak in it for 30 minutes. You may find additional relief by applying the oatmeal pouch directly to the rash or pox.

Add luxury to a regular bath You don't have to have itchy skin to make a luxurious bath mix with oatmeal. And it beats buying expensive bath oils. All you need is 200g oatmeal and your favourite scented oil, such as rose or lavender. Grind the oatmeal in a blender, put it in a cheesecloth bag, add a few drops of the scented oil, and suspend the bag under the running water as you fill your bathtub. You'll not only find it sweetly soothing, you can also use the oatmeal bag as a scrub cloth to exfoliate your skin.

Make a face mask If you're looking for a quick pick-me-up that will leave you feeling and looking better, give yourself an oatmeal facial. Combine 100ml hot – not boiling – water and 75g oatmeal. After the water and oatmeal have settled for 2 or 3 minutes, mix in 2 tablespoons plain yogurt, 2 tablespoons honey and 1 small egg white. Apply a thin layer of the mixture to your face, and let it sit for 10-15 minutes. Then rinse with warm water. (Be sure to place a metal or plastic strainer in the sink to avoid clogging the drain with the granules.)

DID YOU KNOW?

Thirty minutes. Five minutes. One minute? How long it takes to cook different kinds of oatmeal depends on how the oats were actually made into oatmeal. After the inedible hull is removed, the oat is called a groat. If the groats are just cut into about four pieces, the oatmeal takes up to 30 minutes to cook. If the groats are steamed and rolled but not cut, it takes about 5 minutes. If they are steamed, rolled and cut, the cooking time drops to a minute or so. Steaming, rolling and cooking breaks down the fibre, so if you want to maximise the fibre, use 30 minute oatmeal and cook it until it is chewy, not mushy.

Make a dry shampoo Do you occasionally skip washing your hair in order to get to work on time? Keep a batch of dry shampoo on hand in an airtight container specifically for those occasions when you're running late. Put 200g oatmeal in a blender and grind it into a fine powder. Add 200g baking soda, and mix well. Rub a bit of the mixture into your hair. Give it a minute or two to soak up the oils, then brush or shake it out of your hair (preferably over a towel or bag to avoid getting covered in it). This dry shampoo mixture is also ideal for cleaning the hair of bedridden people who are unable to get into a shower or bathtub. Plus, it's equally effective for freshening a bath-hating dog when you don't have the energy to wrestle with him.

 Olive oil

Remove paint from hair If you've got almost as much paint in your hair as on the walls when decorating, you can easily remove it by moistening a cotton wool ball with some olive oil and gently rubbing it into your hair. The same approach is also effective for removing mascara; just be sure to wipe your eyes with a tissue when you have finished.

Make your own furniture polish Restore lost lustre to wooden furniture by whipping up some homemade furniture polish that's just as good as anything you can buy commercially. Combine 2 parts olive oil and 1 part lemon juice or white vinegar in a clean recycled spray bottle, shake it up and squirt on. Leave on the mixture for a minute or two, then wipe off with a clean cloth or paper towel. If you're in a hurry, get fast results by applying olive oil straight from the bottle onto a paper towel. Wipe off any oil that remains with another paper towel or an absorbent cloth.

Use as a hair conditioner Put the moisture back into dry and brittle hair by heating 100ml olive oil (don't boil it) and then liberally applying it to the hair. Cover hair with a plastic bag, then wrap it in a towel. Let it set for 45 minutes, then shampoo and rinse thoroughly.

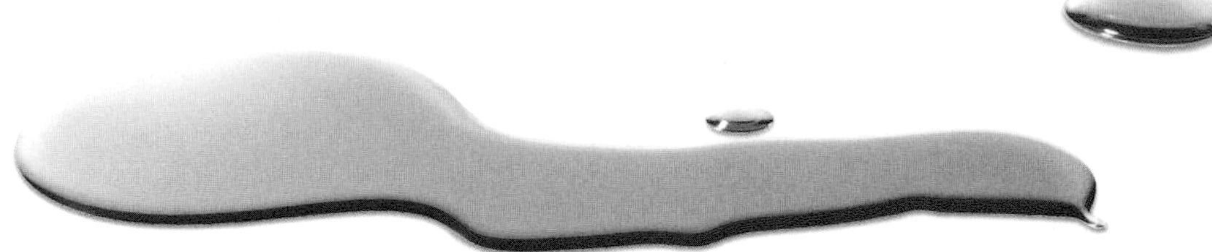

Clear up acne Although the notion of applying oil to your face to treat acne does sound a bit eccentric, it's a remedy that many people swear by. Make a paste by mixing 4 tablespoons salt with 3 tablespoons olive oil. Pour the mixture onto your hands and fingers and work it around your face. Leave it on for a minute or two, then rinse it off with warm, soapy water. Apply daily for one week, then cut back to two or three times weekly. You should see a noticeable improvement in the condition of the skin. (The principle is that the salt cleanses the pores by exfoliation, while the olive oil restores the skin's natural moisture.)

Substitute for shaving cream If you run out of shaving cream, don't waste time trying to make do with soap which can be rough on the skin. Olive oil, on the other hand, is a great substitute for shaving cream. It not only makes it easier for the blade to glide over your face or legs, but it will moisturise the skin as well. In fact, after trying this, you may not bother to use shaving cream again.

Clean greasy hands To remove motor oil or paint from your hands, pour 1 teaspoon olive oil and 1 teaspoon salt or sugar into your palms. Vigorously rub the mixture into your hands and between your fingers for several minutes; then wash it off with soap and warm water. Not only will your hands be cleaner, you will find they are softer as well.

TIP* LESS VIRGIN MORE VAMP

Expensive extra virgin olive oil is made from olives crushed soon after harvest and processed without excessive heat. It's ideal for culinary uses where the taste of the oil is important. But for everyday cooking and non-food applications, lower grades of olive oil work just as well and will save you money.

Onions

Eliminate the smell of new paint If your bedroom is freshly painted and looks great, but the smell is keeping you up all night, place several freshly cut slices of onion in a dish with a drop of water; it will absorb the smell within a few hours.

Stop pet destruction If Rover or Kitty is not respecting your property, whether it be by chewing, tearing or soiling, you may be able to get the message across by leaving several onion slices where the damage has been done. Neither cats nor dogs are particularly fond of the smell of onion and they should avoid returning to the scene of their crimes.

DID YOU KNOW?

How can you keep your eyes from watering painfully when cutting onions? Suggestions range from wearing protective goggles while chopping, to placing a fan behind you to blow away the onion's tear-producing vapours, to rubbing your hands with vinegar before you start slicing. Another trick from the experts is to chill onions in the freezer for 30 minutes prior to slicing them. Or cut off the top portion and peeling off the outer layers. The idea is to leave the root end intact, because it has the highest concentrations of the sulphur compounds that cause your eyes to water.

Remove rust from knives Forget about using steel wool or harsh chemicals – this is an easy way to get the rust off a kitchen or utility knife. Plunge the rusty knife into a large onion three or four times (if it's very rusty, it may require a few extra stabs). The only tears you shed will be ones of joy over the rust-free blade.

Soothe a bee sting If you have a nasty encounter with a bee at a barbecue, take one of the onion slices intended for your burger and place it over the sting. It will ease the soreness. (If you are severely allergic to bee or other insect stings, seek medical attention at once.)

Use as smelling salts If you are with someone at a party or in a restaurant who feels faint – and you don't normally carry smelling salts – use a freshly cut onion instead. The strong odour is likely to bring him round.

Use as a natural pesticide Create your own highly effective insect and animal repellent for the flowers and vegetables in your garden. In a blender, purée 4 onions, 2 cloves garlic, 2 tablespoons cayenne pepper and 1 litre water. Set the mixture aside. Now dilute 2 tablespoons soap flakes in 8 litres water. Pour in the contents of the blender, shake or stir well, and you have a potent, environmentally friendly solution to spray on your plants.

Make mosquito repellent Some people find that increasing their intake of onions or garlic in the summer, or rubbing a slice of onion over their exposed skin, is a good way to keep away mosquitoes and other biting insects.

Oranges

Use for kindling Dried orange and lemon peels are a far superior choice for use as kindling than newspaper. Not only do they smell better and produce less creosote than newspaper, but the flammable oils found inside the peels enable them to burn much longer than paper.

Cook up a potpourri Fill your home with a refreshing citrus scent by simmering several orange and/or lemon peels in 200-400ml water in a saucepan for a few hours. Add water as needed during the simmering. This process freshens up the pan as well as the air in your home.

Keep cats off the lawn Are the neighbours' cats still using your lawn as their litter tray? Gently point them elsewhere by making a mixture of orange peels and coffee grounds and distributing it around the cats' favourite haunts. If they don't take the hint, lay down a second batch and try moistening it with a bit of water to keep the smell strong and fresh.

Apply as a mosquito repellent If you're not convinced by the idea of rubbing onions all over yourself to keep away mosquitoes (see previous page), you may be happy to know that you can often get similar results by rubbing fresh orange or lemon peel over your exposed skin. Apparently mosquitoes and gnats are totally repulsed by either scent.

Show ants the door Get rid of the ants in the garden, on the patio and along the foundations of your home. In a blender, make a smooth puree with a few pieces of orange peel in 200ml warm water. Slowly pour the solution over and into the places where the ants tend to congregate.

Make a pomander Pomanders have been used for centuries to fill small spaces with a delightful fragrance as well as to combat moths. They are also incredibly easy to make. Stick cloves into an orange, packing them tightly until you have covered the whole surface. Suspend the pomander using a piece of ribbon, string or monofilament fishing line inside a wardrobe or cupboard and it will keep the space smelling fresh for years.

Oven cleaner

Put the style back in a curling iron or straightener Is your curling iron or hair straightener buried under a layer of caked-on styling gel or conditioner? Before you use it next time, spray on a light coating of oven cleaner. Let it sit for an hour, then wipe it off with a damp rag, and dry with a clean cloth.
WARNING Do not use the iron or straightener until it is completely dry.

Wipe away bathtub ring If there is a very stubborn stain or ring around a white enamel bath that refuses to come clean, call out the big guns by spraying it with oven cleaner. Let it sit for a few hours, then give it a thorough rinsing.
WARNING Do not apply oven cleaner to coloured baths; it can cause fading. And be careful not to get oven cleaner on a shower curtain; it can ruin both plastic and fabric.

Clean grimy tile grout lines Make a full-scale attack on grubby grout. First, make sure you have plenty of ventilation – it's a good idea to use an exhaust fan to suck air out of a small bathroom. Put on rubber gloves and spray oven cleaner into the grout lines. Wipe the cleaner off with a sponge within five seconds. Rinse thoroughly with water to reveal sparkling white grout lines.

{TAKE CARE}

Most oven cleaners contain highly caustic lye, which can burn the skin and damage the eyes. Always wear long rubber gloves and protective eyewear when using oven cleaner; even the mist from oven cleaner spray can irritate nasal membranes. Ingestion can cause corrosive burns to the mouth, throat and stomach that require immediate medical attention. Store oven cleaner well out of the reach of children.

Clean a cast-iron pot If you need to clean and re-season an encrusted cast-iron grill pan, start by spraying it with oven cleaner and placing it in a sealed plastic bag overnight. (This keeps the cleaner working by preventing it from drying.) The next day, remove the pot and scrub it with a stiff wire brush. Then, wash it thoroughly with soap and water, rinse well and immediately dry it with a couple of clean, dry cloths. Note: this technique will eliminate built-up dirt and grease, but not rust. For that, you'll need to use vinegar. Don't leave it on too long, though. Prolonged exposure to vinegar can damage your cast-iron utensil.

Remove stains from concrete Get rid of unsightly grease, oil and transmission fluid stains from a concrete driveway or garage floor by spraying them with oven cleaner. Let it settle for 5-10 minutes, then scrub with a stiff brush and rinse it off with a garden hose at high pressure. Severe stains may need a second application.

Strip paint or varnish For an easy way to remove paint or varnish from wooden or metal furniture, try using a can of oven cleaner; it costs less than commercial paint strippers and is easier to apply (that is, if you spray rather than brush it on). After applying, scrub off the old paint with a wire brush. Neutralise the stripped surface by coating it with vinegar, and then wash it off with clean water. Allow the wood or metal to thoroughly dry before repainting.
WARNING Never use oven cleaner to strip antiques or expensive furnishings; it may seriously darken the wood or discolour the metal.

Clean ovenproof glass cookware When you have tried everything to scrub baked-on stains off Pyrex cookware but they are still there, try this. Put on rubber gloves and cover the cookware with oven cleaner. Then place the cookware in a heavy-duty bin liner, close it tightly with twist ties and leave overnight. Open the bag outdoors, keeping your face away from the dangerous fumes. Use rubber gloves to remove and then thoroughly wash the cookware.

Oven mitts

Change a hot lightbulb If the lightbulb on a reading lamp has just blown, don't scorch your fingers when replacing it. Once you've removed the lampshade, put on an oven mitt, remove the dead bulb from the socket, and throw it into the bin. That way, you won't still be blowing on your fingertips when screwing in the new bulb.

Use as a tea cosy or egg warmer Keep a mug of tea from getting cold when you are called away by placing an oven mitt over it. The glove's insulation will keep it warm until you get back. You can also use an oven mitt to keep boiled eggs warm for up to half an hour. Conversely, an oven mitt will help to keep a cold drink colder longer.

Use for dusting and polishing Although oven mitts are typically confined to kitchen duty, they are actually great for dusting and polishing around your house. Use one side of the mitt to apply wax or polish to the furniture, and the other side to buff it up. It's a great way to use old mitts or any extra ones you've collected.

Remove hot engine parts Keeping an oven mitt in the car's glove compartment or boot can make life a lot easier when you need to handle hot radiator caps and the like during an on-the-road emergency.

When pruning thorny plants Although oven mitts may be a bit too awkward to use for weeding or planting seedlings in the garden, they can come in handy when it comes to pruning trees, hedges and bushes – particularly thorny plants such as holly and roses.

 Paintbrushes

Use for delicate dusting A feather or cloth duster is fine for cleaning shelves and larger surfaces, but neither is much good when you need to dust the tiny cracks and crevices of chandeliers, wicker furniture or baskets and knick-knacks. That's when a small natural-bristle paintbrush can be indispensable. The soft bristles are perfect for cleaning out areas that are impossible to reach. It is also excellent for dusting delicate items such as porcelain or carved-wood figurines.

Brush off beach chairs If your family are regular visitors to the seaside, keep a clean, dry paintbrush in the car for return trips. Use it to remove sand from beach chairs, towels, toys, the children and the dog before you open the car door or boot. You'll end up with a lot less sand to hoover up the next time you clean the car.

Brush on the sauce A small synthetic-bristle paintbrush can be invaluable in the kitchen. You can use it to brush on glazes, marinades and sauces while baking or roasting. You can also use it to paint on barbecue sauce when grilling burgers and steaks on a barbecue. A paintbrush is also easier to clean than most conventional pastry brushes.

Apply stain remover to clothes Pouring detergent or stain remover onto a soiled garment can be hit-and-miss. Use a small paintbrush to apply liquid stain remover to dirty shirt collars and cuffs and specific stains. It's neater and more accurate.

Cover up seeds when sowing Sow seeds with care. When planting seeds in rows, use a large paintbrush to gently brush them over with soil. This lets you distribute the exact amount of soil needed and prevents overpacking.

TIP* BRUSHES

Natural-bristle brushes work best with oil-based paints such as gloss. But use a synthetic-bristle brush with emulsion paint because the water in the paint can ruin natural bristles. Before cleaning a brush, wipe the excess paint onto newpaper. Clean a brush used with gloss paint in turpentine or white spirit until you get out all the paint, then shake out. To clean emulsion paint, wash the brush thoroughly with soapy water, rinse clean and shake out.

Super item

PAPER BAGS...

...around the house

Dust off a mop Dust mops make it easy to catch dust balls and pet hair, but how do you get the dust off a mop? Place a large paper bag over the mop head; use a piece of string or a rubber band to keep it from slipping off. Now give it several good shakes and gentle bumps. Lay the mop on its side for a few minutes to let the dust in the bag settle. Then carefully remove the bag for easy disposal of the dust.

Clean artificial flowers Authentic silk flowers are actually quite rare these days; most are now made of nylon or another synthetic. But regardless of whether they're silk or another fabric, you can easily freshen them up by placing them in a paper bag with 50g salt. Give the bag a few gentle shakes and your flowers will emerge as clean as the day you bought them.

Make your own wrapping paper Whem you need to wrap a present in a hurry, don't rush out to buy wrapping paper. Just cut a large glossy or colourful paper bag along the seams to make a flat rectangle. Position it so that any printing is facing up towards you, put your gift on top and fold, cut, and tape the paper around your gift. If you wish, personalise your homemade wrapping paper by decorating it with markers, paint, ribbons or stickers.

Cover school textbooks Few materials are as good as a paper bag when it comes to making a strong book cover. First, cut the bag along its seams to make it a flat, wide rectangle, then place the book in the centre. Fold in the top and bottom edges so the bag is only slightly wider than the book's height. Next, fold over the sides to form sleeves over the book covers. Cut off the excess, leaving 4-5cm on either side to slide over the front and back covers. Put a piece of masking tape on the top and bottom of each sleeve (over the paper, not the book) to keep it on tight. Lastly, let your child put his or her name and personal design on each cover.

Store bed linen sets Have you ever emptied the contents of your linen cupboard looking for pillowcases to match the duvet cover you have just pulled out? Use medium-sized paper bags to store complete sets of bed linen. Not only will your shelves be better organised, but you can also keep the bed linen smelling fresh by placing a used fabric softener sheet in each bag.

DID YOU KNOW?

Are paper shopping bags better for the environment than their plastic counterparts? Apparently not: paper bags generate 70 per cent more air pollutants and 50 times more water pollutants than plastic bags. What's more, it takes four times as much energy to make a paper bag as it does to manufacture a plastic bag, and 91 per cent more energy to recycle paper than plastic. On the other hand, paper bags come from a renewable resource (trees), while most plastic bags are made from non-renewable resources (polyethylene, a combination of crude oil and natural gas). And paper bags will degrade naturally, rather than clogging up landfill sites for years. So what's the answer? Using your own fabric or string bags is probably the most eco-friendly solution.

PAPER BAGS...

...around the house

Pack your bags When you are getting ready to leave on a family holiday, don't forget to pack a few large shopping bags – the kind with handles – in your luggage. They're guaranteed to come in handy to bring home the souvenirs you pick up or perhaps dirty laundry or beach towels.

Bag your recycled newspapers Double up on your recycling efforts by using large paper bags to hold newspapers for collection. It not only spares you the time and effort needed to tie up your bundles with string, but it also makes it easier to sort out magazines and newsprint.

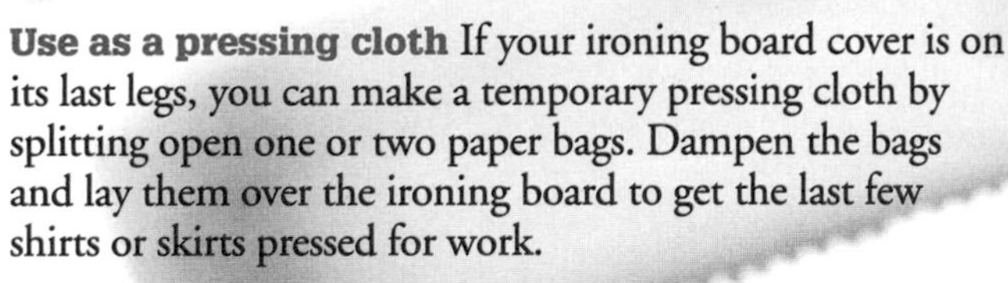

Use as a pressing cloth If your ironing board cover is on its last legs, you can make a temporary pressing cloth by splitting open one or two paper bags. Dampen the bags and lay them over the ironing board to get the last few shirts or skirts pressed for work.

Reuse as gift bags What can you do with the small gift bags with handles that you get from most boutiques? You could use them to package your own gifts. They're ideal for holding items such as bath supplies, jewellery, perfume and even most books. Simply add some shredded crêpe paper and a card.

Reshape woollens after washing Put the shape back into a woollen sweater or mittens by tracing the contours of the item on a paper bag before you wash it. Then use your outline to stretch the item back to its original shape.

...in the kitchen

Make tidying easier Cut open one or two paper bags and spread them out over the worktop when peeling potatoes or carrots, husking corn, shelling peas and beans or any other messy task. When you have finished, simply fold up the paper and throw it in the dustbin.

Use to ripen fruit Many fruits, including avocados, bananas, pears, peaches and tomatoes, will ripen more quickly when placed in a paper bag. To hasten the ripening process of any fruit, place an already ripe apple or a banana skin in the same bag and store it at room temperature. To ripen green bananas, wrap them in a damp tea towel before placing them in the bag. Once the fruit has started to ripen, you can halt the process by putting them in the fridge.

Keep bread fresh If your kitchen tends to be hot and steamy, your bread will stay fresher when stored inside a paper bag rather than a plastic one. The paper's ability to 'breathe' will keep the crust crisp while allowing the centre of the loaf to stay soft and moist.

{ KIDS' STUFF }

MAKE A BODY POSTER

Make a life-size body poster of your child using sturdy paper bags. Start by cutting up 4-6 paper bags so they lie completely flat (any print should be facing down). Arrange them into one big square on the floor and tape the undersides together. Then get the child to lie down in the middle and use a crayon to trace the outline of his or her entire body. Give him or her crayons or watercolour paints to fill in the face, clothing and other details. When it is finished, hang it up in your child's room as a wall decoration.

Store potatoes Stop potatoes from going green and sprouting by keeping them in a strong paper bag. Potatoes always keep better when stored in a dark place and the breathability of the paper will stop them from getting damp and rotting.

Carry lunch to work Keep a collection of small paper bags (preferably with handles) and use a bag to transport a sandwich or salad to work each day.

Store mushrooms Remove mushrooms from plastic packaging and place them in a paper bag in the fridge. This trick should keep them fresh for up to five days.

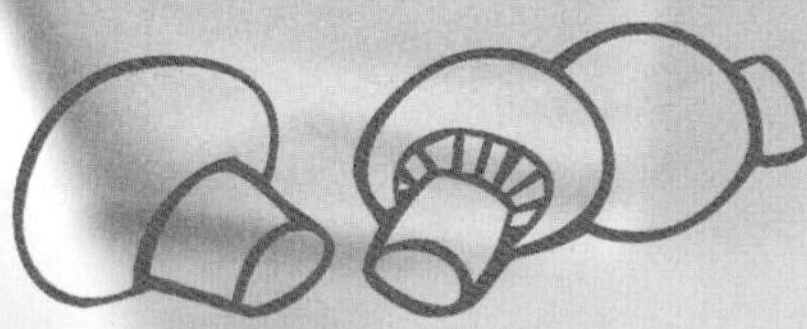

PAPER BAGS...

...for the DIY-er

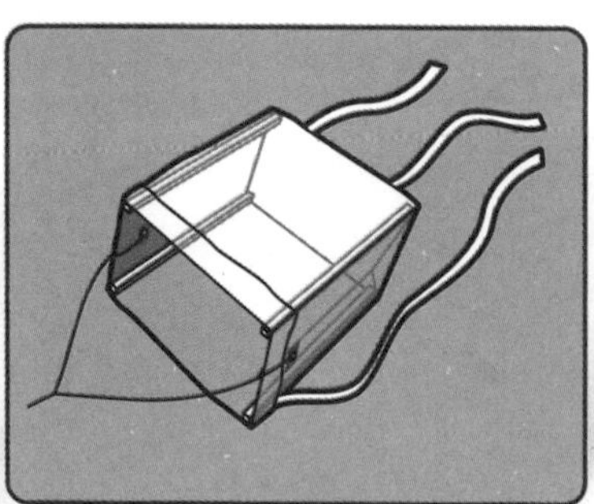

Build a bag kite Make a simple bag kite for your children to play with by folding over the top of a paper bag to keep it open. Glue on several pieces of party streamers under the fold. Reinforce the kite by gluing in some strips of balsa wood or a few thin twigs along the length of the bag. Poke a couple of holes above the opened end and attach two pieces of string or wool (put a piece of masking or transparent tape over the holes to prevent them from tearing) and tie the ends onto a roll of kite string. Take the kite out onto a beach, a heath or a windy hill and watch it fly.

Move ice and snow off your windscreen If you are tired of having to constantly scrape ice and snow off your car's windscreen during the winter months, keep some paper bags in the car. When snow or ice is forecast, go out to the car and turn on the wipers. Then, shut off the engine with the wipers positioned near the middle of your windscreen. Split open a couple of paper bags and use the car's wipers to hold them in place. After the last snowflake falls, pull off the paper to instantly clear your windscreen. Note: to prevent damaging your car's wipers, do not attempt to turn on the ignition until you have removed the snow and paper from the windscreen.

Make a fire starter For an easy way to get a fire going, fill a paper bag with some crumpled-up newspaper and perhaps some bits of candle wax. Place the bag under the logs, light it, then sit back and enjoy a roaring fire.

Spray-paint small items There is no need to make a mess when you need to spray-paint a small item. Place the object to be painted inside a large paper bag and spray away; the bag will contain the excess spray. Once the item has dried, remove it and throw away the bag.

...in the garden

Store geraniums in winter Although they are considered to be annuals, geraniums are easy to keep going over the winter. First, remove the plants from their pots or carefully dig them up from your garden bed, shake off as much soil as possible and place each plant in its own paper bag. Cover each bag with a second paper bag turned upside down and store them in a cool, dry place. In the spring, cut off all but 2.5cm of the stem and repot. Place them in a sunny spot, water regularly and watch the geraniums spring back to life.

Feed your plants Bonemeal is an excellent source of nutrients for all the plants in your garden. You can easily make your own by first drying leftover chicken bones in a microwave oven (depending on the quantity, cook them for 1-4 minutes on High). Then place the dried bones in a sturdy paper bag and grind them up using a mallet, hammer or rolling pin. Scatter the powder around the plants to help them to thrive.

Make dried herbs
To dry fresh herbs, first wash each plant under cold water and dry thoroughly with paper towels. Make sure the plants are completely dry before you proceed, to reduce the risk of mould. Take five or six plants, remove the lower leaves and place them upside down inside a large paper bag. Gather the end of the bag around the stems and tie it up. Punch a few holes in the bag for ventilation, then store it in a warm, dry area for at least two weeks. Once the plants have dried, inspect them carefully for any signs of mould. If you find any, throw away the entire bunch. Once you have removed the stems, you can grind them up with a rolling pin or a full soft drink bottle. Alternatively, keep them whole to retain the flavour longer. Store dried herbs in airtight containers and away from sunlight.

Add to compost Brown paper bags are a great addition to any garden compost heap. Not only do they contain less ink and pigment than newsprint, but they will also attract more earthworms to your pile (in fact, the only thing the worms like better than paper bags is cardboard). It is best to shred and wet the bags beforehand. Also, be sure to mix them in well to prevent them from blowing away after they have dried.

Paper clips

Open shrink-wrapped CDs Opening shrink-wrap, especially on CDs, can be a test of skill and patience. Save your fingernails and teeth from destruction; twist out the end of a paper clip and use it to slice the wrap. To prevent scratches, slip the clip under the folded section of wrap and lift up.

Use as hooks for hanging Paper clips make great impromptu hooks. If you are making a hanging ceramic plaque, insert a large, sturdy paper clip on the back before the clay hardens.

Use as a zip pull Don't stop using a jacket or handbag just because the zip pull is broken. Untwist a small paper clip enough to slip it through the hole. Twist it closed and zip it up. To make it look more decorative, you can thread beads over the paper clip or glue on sequins before closing.

{ SCIENCE FAIR }

THE ASTOUNDING FLOATING PAPER CLIP

Amaze your friends: challenge them to make a paper clip float on water. Give them a cup of water and a paper clip. When they fail, you show them how to do it. Tear off a piece of paper towel – larger than the clip – and place it on top of the water. Put the paper clip on top of the paper towel and wait a few seconds. The towel will sink, leaving the clip floating. It may look like magic, but it is actually the surface tension of the water that allows the clip to float. As the paper towel sinks, it lowers the paper clip onto the water without breaking the surface tension.

Make a bookmark Paper clips make excellent bookmarks because they don't fall out. A piece of ribbon or colourful string attached to the clip will make it even easier to use and find.

Stone cherries If you need seedless cherries for a recipe or don't like to stone cherries as you are eating them, use a paper clip. Over a bowl or sink, unfold a clean paper clip at the centre and, depending on the size of the cherry, insert either the clip's

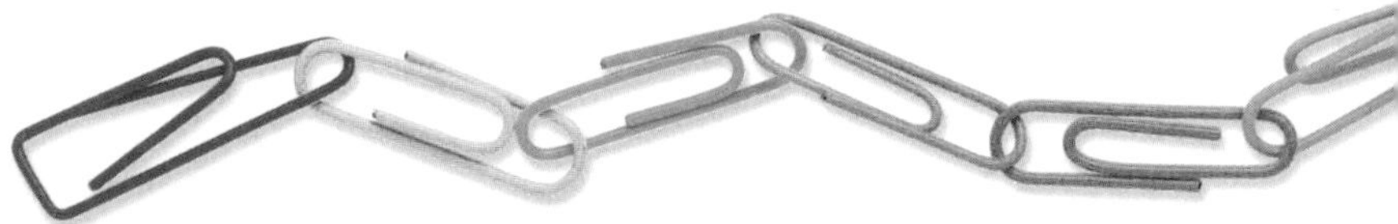

large or small end through the top. Loosen the stone and pull. To stone cherries but leave the stems intact, insert the clip at the bottom. Cherry juice stains badly, so watch your clothing.

Extend a ceiling fan chain Put an end to dancing on tiptoes while trying to reach a broken or too-short ceiling fan chain: to extend the chain, just fasten a chain of paper clips to the end.

Hold the end of clear tape If you have a roll of clear tape without a dispenser, don't drive yourself to distraction trying to locate and lift the end of the tape. Stick a paper clip under the end the next time you use the roll.

* Paper plates

Make index cards If you don't have any index cards, use paper plates and a ruler. Measure out a A7 (105 x 74mm) or A6 (148 x 105mm) card on the plate and cut. Use the first card as a template for the rest.

Protect stored dishes Prevent stored dishes from the risk of breakage, especially when you are moving house, by inserting a paper plate between each dish when packing.

Paint can drip catcher Most people scrape the paintbrush on the side of the can to remove excess paint. To prevent drips from falling on the floor, place a paper plate under the can.

Make Frisbee flash cards Drilling your children with flash cards can be a pain, but here is a way to make it fun. Write the numbers, letters, words or shapes you are teaching on paper plates and let the kids toss them like Frisbees across the room when they get a correct answer.

Make a snowman decoration When it is really cold and your children are getting bored and fidgety, paper plates can provide an inexpensive, creative outlet. They can use them to make masks, mobiles and seasonal decorations. To create a winter snowman, use two paper plates. Cut the rim off one plate to make it smaller. Staple the smaller plate to the larger plate, creating a head and body. Make boots and hat out of stiff black paper and mittens out of red paper and glue on. Decorate the face with googly eyes, buttons, pipe cleaners or draw on features with a crayon or marker.

Paper towels

Microwave bacon with no mess Here is a failsafe way to cook bacon in a microwave oven. Lay two paper towels on the bottom of the microwave. Lay the slices of bacon side by side, on the paper towels. Cover with two more paper towels. Run the microwave on High at 1 minute intervals, checking for crispness. It should take 3-4 minutes to cook. There is no grill pan to clean and the towels will absorb the grease – and can be thrown away when you have finished.

Clean silk from fresh corn If you find it hard to clean the silk off a freshly husked ear of corn, a paper towel can help. Dampen one and run it across the ear. The towel will pick up the silk and the corn will be ready for boiling or grilling.

Strain grease from broth Use a paper towel to absorb the fat from a homemade broth or stock. Place another pot in the sink. Put a colander (or a sieve) in the new pot and put a paper towel in the colander. Pour the hot broth through the towel into the waiting pot. You'll find that the fat stays in the towel, while the broth streams through. Wear cooking mitts or use potholders to avoid burning your hands with the boiling-hot liquid.

{ SCIENCE FAIR }

EXPLORE HOW COLOURS WORK

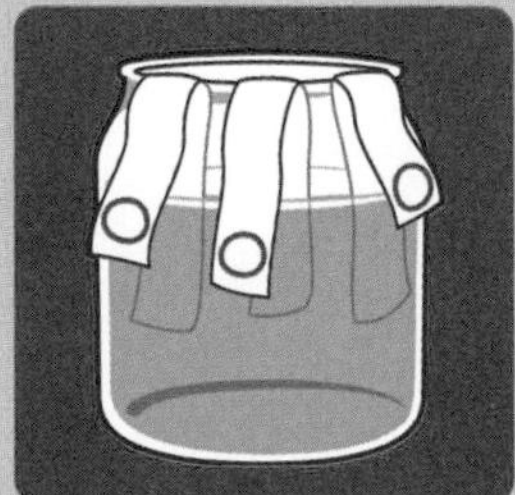

Learn how all other colours are actually mixes of the primary colours of red, blue and yellow. Cut a paper towel into strips. With a coloured marker, draw a rectangle or large circle on one end of each strip. Try interesting shades of orange, green, purple or brown. Black works well too. Place the other end of the strip into a glass jar filled with water, leaving the coloured end dry and draped over the side of the jar. As the water from the jar slowly (about 20 minutes) moves down the towel and into the colour blot, you will see the colours separate. This also demonstrates capillary attraction, the force that allows the porous paper to soak up the water and carry it over the side of the jar.

Keep produce fresh longer If you are always opening the crisper in your fridge to find last week's mouldy carrots mixed with yellowing lettuce or broccoli, line the crisper bins with paper towels. They absorb the moisture that causes fruit and vegetables to spoil and rot. The contents will last a lot longer and it will be easier to clean the bin as well.

Keep frozen bread from getting soggy If you like to buy bread in bulk, this tip will help you to freeze and thaw each loaf more easily. Place a paper towel in each bag of bread to be frozen. When you are ready to eat the frozen loaf, the paper towel will absorb the moisture as the bread thaws.

Clean a can opener Have you ever noticed the unpleasant debris that collects on the cutting wheel of a can opener? It is not something that you want to get into your food. Clean the can opener by 'opening' a paper towel. Close the wheel on the edge of a paper towel, close the handles and turn the crank. The paper towel will clean off the gunk as the wheel cuts through it.

Keep cast-iron pots rust-free Stop rust from invading a prized collection of cast-iron pots. After they're clean, place a paper towel in each to absorb any moisture. Store lids separately from the pots, separated by a lining of paper towels. There should be no rusty surprises the next time you use them.

Make a place mat for children If you are hosting your children's boisterous friends or your grandchildren are coming for an extended visit, paper towels can help you to weather the storm that they create at mealtimes. Use a paper towel as a place mat. It will catch spills and crumbs during the meal and makes cleaning up easy.

Test the viability of old seeds You've just found a packet of lettuce seeds with an expiry date of two years ago. Should you bother to plant them or has their shelf life expired so they're only fit to plant in the bin? To find out for sure, dampen two paper towels and lay down a few seeds. Cover with two more dampened paper towels. Over the next two weeks, keep the towels damp and keep checking on the seeds. If most of the seeds sprout, plant the rest of the batch in the garden.

Clean a sewing machine If your sewing machine is good as new after a recent service, but you are worried about getting grease from the machine on your fabric, thread the machine and stitch several lines up a paper towel first. It should take care of any residual grease so you will be able to resume your sewing projects.

Make a butterfly Use coloured markers to draw a bold design on a paper towel. Then lightly spray water on the towel. It should be damp enough so that the colours start to run, but do not soak in. When the towel is dry, fold it in half, open it up and then gather it together using the fold line as your guide. Loop a pipe cleaner around the centre to make the body of the 'butterfly' and twist it closed. To make antennae, fold another pipe cleaner into a V shape and slip it under the first pipe cleaner at the top of the butterfly.

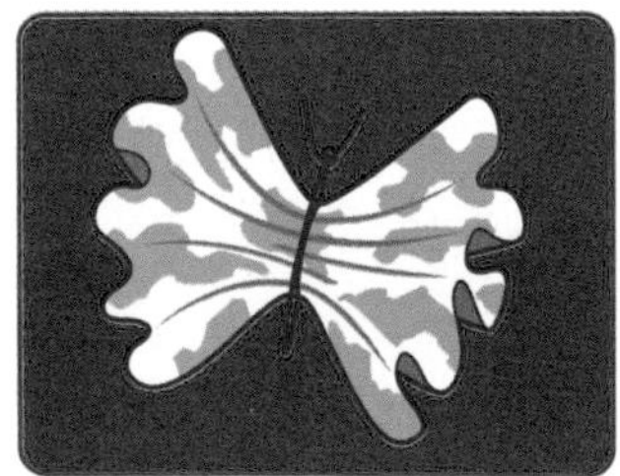

Peanut butter

Get chewing gum out of hair Apply some peanut butter to the matted gum and hair and rub the gum until it comes out. Your child's hair may smell like peanut butter until you wash it, but it is a better solution than having to cut the gum out.

Remove price-tag adhesives Even though you have removed the price tag from a new glass or ceramic item, you may still be left with a residue of gummy glue. Remove it easily by rubbing peanut butter on it.

Bait a mouse trap If you have a mouse problem, try laying traps baited with peanut butter. Mice love it and it is nearly impossible for them to get at the tasty bait without tripping the trap.

Eliminate fishy smells If you are trying to eat more fish for health reasons, but hate the smell that stays in the house after you have cooked it, try this trick. Put a good-sized dollop of peanut butter in the pan when frying fish. The peanut butter will absorb the odour instead of your carpet, curtains and furniture.

Plug an ice-cream cone Ice-cream cones are fun to eat but can be a bit messy. For a delectable solution, plug up the bottom of an ice-cream cone with a bit of peanut butter. Now, when munching through a scoop of double chocolate fudge, you will be protected from leaks. And there will be a delicious surprise at the end of the treat.

Pencils

Ease a new key into a lock If you have just had a new house key cut, but you can't seem to fit it into the lock on your front door, rub a pencil over the teeth of the key. The graphite powder should help the key to open the door.

Use as hair accessory If you don't have a wide-toothed hair pick, a pencil can help to give a lift to curly hair without making it frizz out. Two pencils crossed in an X-shape can also stabilise and decorate a bun.

Decorate a picture frame Make a frame for your children's class photograph with pencils. Glue two new brightly coloured sharpened pencils lengthways to the frame. Sharpen down two other pencils to fit the width of the frame.

Repel moths with pencil shavings If you are tired of finding winter sweaters filled with moth holes after they've been stored, this may help. Empty the shavings from an electric pencil sharpener into little cloth sacks and use as sachets in drawers and wardrobes. The cedar shavings are an effective moth repellent.

Stake a small plant If you have a small plant that needs some support or don't know when to water a houseplant, a pencil can help with both problems. It is the perfect-size stake for a small plant, tied on with a piece of old tights or a strip of cloth. Or stick a pencil in the pot to test if the soil needs watering.

Lubricate a sticky zip When a zip is refusing to budge, no matter how hard you tug and pull, run a pencil lead along the teeth of the zip. In no time you should be able to pull up the zip with ease.

{ SCIENCE FAIR }

MAKE YOUR OWN ANIMATION

Are your eyes deceiving you? Cut a small piece of paper, about 5cm square. Turn the square so it becomes a diamond. On one side, draw or stick on a picture of an animal or a person. On the other side, draw or stick a setting for the animal or a hat and hair for the person. Examples are a cheetah and grasslands or a boy with a hat. Next tape the bottom point of the diamond onto the point of a pencil. Then, holding the pencil so that the picture is upright, twirl the pencil rapidly between your hands. You should see both images from the two sides of the paper at the same time.

Pencil erasers

Shine up coins If you have just inherited a rather grimy coin collection, but you'd like to see it with more lustre, try using an eraser to shine up the coins. But don't do this to rare and valuable coins; you may erase their value along with their surface patina.

Store pins or drill bits A box is not the most handy place to keep sewing pins. Here is an alternative: stick pins in an eraser. They won't fall out and it is easy to grab the ones you need. This is also a good tip if you are storing several fine drill bits.

Clean off crayon marks Your toddler has gone wild with the crayons, but he has scribbled all over the walls instead of on paper. You have tried everything to get it off, but not this: an eraser. Gently rub at the crayon marks to get the wall back to a clean slate.

Remove scuff marks on vinyl floors If new shoes with dark soles have left black streak marks all over the kitchen floor, rub them with an eraser to get them off quickly and cleanly.

Clean piano keys Whether it is a baby grand piano that fills the corner of the living room, a more conventional upright or just a fold-away electronic keyboard, cleaning the keys can be a nightmare project of dust and finger marks. And when you clean it, it is hard to reach some spots to remove dirt. The sides of the black keys are especially difficult to clean. Find an eraser that fits between the ivories and the black keys and simply rub away the ingrained dirt. This works as well whether you have a piano with real ivory keys or the more common plastic ones.

Cushion picture frames Stop a heavy mirror or picture frame from getting crooked and stop the frame from making black marks and scrapes on the wall. Glue erasers to the bottom corners of the frame. The pictures will now hang straighter and not leave their mark.

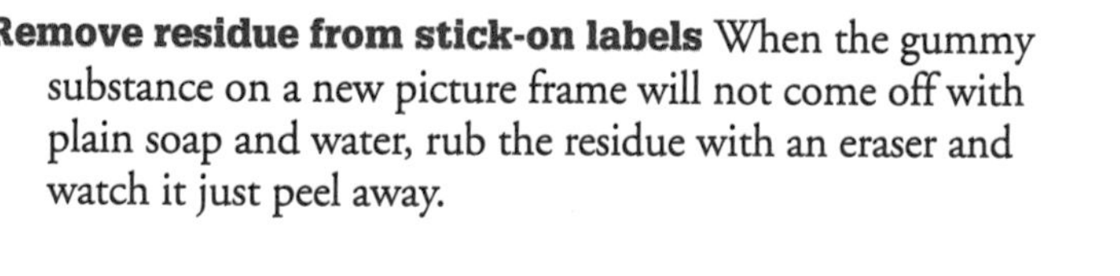

Remove residue from stick-on labels When the gummy substance on a new picture frame will not come off with plain soap and water, rub the residue with an eraser and watch it just peel away.

Pepper

Stop a car radiator leak A heat wave has hit and your ageing, leaking car radiator isn't too happy about it. If it is overheating because of a small leak, pepper may help. Before you take your car to a mechanic for a more thorough repair, pour a handful of pepper into the radiator. It will temporarily plug the leaks until you can get some professional help.

DID YOU KNOW?

Black pepper has been used to add flavour to food since ancient times and it is still the world's most commonly used spice. The black pepper in the grinder actually starts out as a red berry on a bush. When the pea-size berry is placed in boiling water for 10 minutes, it shrinks and turns black, becoming the familiar peppercorn that fill our pepper grinders.

Use as a decongestant Do you have a bunged-up nose or blocked ears? Is a cold stopping you from breathing properly? Ignore over-the-counter medicines. Nothing gets things flowing again faster than some cayenne pepper. Sprinkle some on your food and grab some tissues.

Keep colours bright The new cherry-red shirt you have just purchased is fantastic, but you are worried that it will fade after it has been washed a few times. Add a teaspoon of pepper to the wash load; pepper keeps bright colours bright and prevents them from running too.

Get insects off plants There is nothing more frustrating than a swarm of insects nibbling at a fledgling garden. Just when shoots are starting to emerge, the insects are there, having a feast. Mix black pepper with flour. Sprinkle around your plants and the ants, aphids and earwigs should find another source of food.

Deter deer from your garden If you live in the countryside and your freshly budding garden seems to be nothing but a café for the neighbourhood deer, they should find another place to dine out if you spray the bushes with a cayenne and water mixture.

Keep ants out of the kitchen Two or three (or 20) annual summer visitors have invaded the kitchen looking for sugar. Give them some pepper instead. Cayenne pepper sprinkled in spots where the ants are looking, such as along the backs of your worktops or on your kickboards, will tell them that no sugar is likely to be on offer.

PETROLEUM JELLY...

...for personal grooming

Moisturise your lips and much more If you don't want to pay a lot for expensive lip balm, make-up remover or even moisturiser, then your answer is a tube of petroleum jelly. It can soothe lips, take off foundation, eye shadow, mascara and more. It can even be used as a moisturiser on your face.

Make emergency make-up When you run out of your favourite shade of eye shadow, try making your own. Add a bit of food colouring to petroleum jelly and apply as usual. This is a quick way to make stopgap blusher, lipstick or eye shadow.

Remove a stuck ring Trying to remove a stuck ring can take a lot of painful tugging and pulling. Apply some petroleum jelly and it will glide right off.

Soften chapped hands If you are constantly applying hand lotion to tired, chapped hands, but then removing it so you can get on with your work, try this tip. Apply a liberal amount of petroleum jelly to your hands just before you go to bed. Wear a pair of cotton gloves if you don't want to get grease on the sheets. By morning, they will be soft and smooth.

Stop hair dye runs Have you ever finished dying your hair, only to find you have dyed your hairline and part of your forehead as well. Next time, run a bit of petroleum jelly across your hairline. If dye seeps off your hair, the petroleum jelly will catch it.

No more messy manicures During home manicures, it is hard to keep nail varnish from running over on your cuticles. Petroleum jelly can help a manicure to look more professional. Dab some along the base of your nails and the sides. If polish seeps off the nail during application, all you have to do is wipe off the petroleum jelly and the sloppy nail polish will completely vanish.

Smooth wild eyebrows If you have runaway eyebrows where the hairs won't lie flat but curl up instead, control the wildness with some petroleum jelly. Rub a dab into your brows. They should calm down immediately and stay smooth and well-behaved all day.

Heal windburned skin You've just had a glorious walk through the countryside in autumn, but the hike has left you with an unpleasant souvenir: windburn. Use petroleum jelly applied liberally to your face and hands. The jelly will help to relieve the soreness.

Help prevent nappy rash Painful nappy rash is one of the downsides of being a baby, but help is just a few moments away. A layer of petroleum jelly will set up a protective coat on the skin so the rash can heal.

Lengthen the life of perfume If you have chosen a gorgeous perfume to wear on your night out, how can you make it last? Dab a bit of petroleum jelly on your pulse points. Then spray on the perfume. You can now dance the night away and without worrying about your perfume fading away.

No more shampoo tears Don't buy special no-tears shampoo for your child. Petroleum jelly is a far cheaper solution. Rub a fair amount into your baby's eyebrows. It acts as a protective shield and will stop shampoo and suds running down into his eyes.

PETROLEUM JELLY...

...around the house

Get rid of lipstick stains You have used your favourite cloth napkins at a successful dinner party, but your friends have left their mark all over them. Now dotted with lipstick stains, the napkins may be heading for the dustbin. But try this first. Before you wash them, blot petroleum jelly on the stain. Launder as usual and hopefully the stains will be gone.

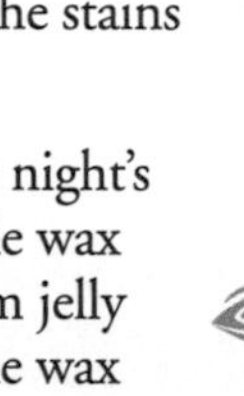

Eject wax from candlesticks The long red tapers used for last night's candlelit dinner were a beautiful sight until you saw the candle wax drippings left in the candleholders. Next time apply petroleum jelly to the insides of the holders before you put the candles in. The wax will pop out easily for cleaning.

Remove chewing gum from wood Have you ever discovered a mass of bubble or chewing gum stuck under the dining room table or behind the headboard of a child's bed? Squeeze some petroleum jelly on to the offending lump, rub it in until the gum starts to disintegrate, then remove.

Make vacuum cleaner parts fit together smoothly It is helpful that your vacuum cleaner comes with so many accessories and extensions. But it is frustrating when the parts get stuck together and you have to try to prise them apart. Apply a small amount of petroleum jelly to the rims of the tubes and the parts will easily slide together and apart.

Shine patent-leather shoes Keep a smart pair of patent-leather shoes and a shiny handbag lustrous for longer by polishing them with petroleum jelly.

Restore leather jackets You don't need fancy leather cream to take care of a favourite leather jacket. Petroleum jelly does the job just as well. Apply, rub it in, wipe off the excess and the jacket will stay smooth and supple.

Keep ants away from pet food bowls Poor Tiddles' food bowl has been invaded by ants. Since she prefers her food without them, help her out with this idea. Make a ring around her bowl with petroleum jelly. The ants will no longer be tempted by the food if they have to cross a mountain of petroleum jelly.

Keep a bottle lid from sticking If you are having a hard time unscrewing a bottle of glue or nail polish, remember this tip for when you finally do get it open. Rub a little petroleum jelly along the rim of the bottle. Next time, the top won't stick.

Soothe sore pet paws Sometimes your cat or dog's paw pads can get cracked and dry. Give a little tender loving care to your best friend. Squirt a little petroleum jelly on the pads to ease the dryness.

...for the DIY-er

Seal a plumber's plunger Before you reach for a plunger to unblock the bathroom toilet, find some petroleum jelly. Apply it along the rim of the plunger and it will help create a tighter seal. The blockage will disappear far more quickly.

Mask doorknobs when painting If you are about to start painting a door or window frame but don't want to fiddle with removing all the metal fixtures, including doorknobs, petroleum jelly rubbed on the metal will prevent paint from sticking. When you have finished painting, just wipe off the jelly and the unwanted paint will be gone.

Stop a battery terminal corroding It is no coincidence that a car battery always dies on the coldest winter day. Low temperatures increase electrical resistance and thicken engine oil, making the battery work harder. Corrosion on the battery terminals also increases resistance and might just be the last straw that makes the battery give up. Before winter starts, disconnect the terminals and clean them with a wire brush. Reconnect, then smear with petroleum jelly. The jelly will prevent corrosion and help to keep the battery working smoothly all winter long.

Protect stored chrome If you are getting ready to store children's bikes for the winter, or pack away a pushchair until the next baby comes along, take some petroleum jelly and apply it to the chrome parts of the equipment. When it is time to take the items out of storage, they will be free of rust. The same method works for other chrome-trimmed machinery stored in the garage.

Keep an outdoor lightbulb from sticking Have you ever unscrewed a lightbulb and found yourself holding the glass while the metal base remains in the socket? It won't happen again if you remember to apply petroleum jelly to the base of the bulb before screwing it into the fixture. This is an especially good idea for lightbulbs that are used outdoors.

Lubricate cabinets and windows If you can't stand the sound of a medicine cabinet door creaking along its runners or having to force a window every time you want a breeze through the house, then using a small paintbrush, apply petroleum jelly to window sash channels and cabinet door runners.

Stop squeaking door hinges It is so annoying when a squeaky door makes an ill-timed noise when you are trying to keep quiet. Put petroleum jelly on the hinge pins of the door for no more squeaks.

Remove watermarks on wood When a recent party has left lots of watermark rings on wooden furniture, make them disappear by applying petroleum jelly and let it sit overnight. In the morning, wipe the watermark away with the jelly.

Keep squirrels away from bird feeder Feed the birds, but not the squirrels. Keep them off the pole of a bird feeder by greasing it with petroleum jelly. The squirrels will slide straight off, leaving the birds to eat in peace.

Pillowcases

Dust ceiling fan blades Have you ever seen bundles of dust flying off a ceiling fan when you turn it on for the first time in weeks? Take an old pillowcase and place it over one of the ceiling fan blades. Slowly pull off the pillowcase. The blades will get dusted and the dust will stay in the pillowcase, instead of parachuting to the floor and spreading all around the house.

Clear out cobwebs Before you take a broom to a cobweb high up in the corner of a room, cover the broom with an old pillowcase. Now you can wipe away the cobweb without scratching the paint. It is also easier to remove the cobweb from the pillowcase than to pull it out of the broom bristles.

Cover a baby's changing table Use a cheap white pillowcase to cover the pad on a changing table. When it gets soiled, you can just slip it off and replace it with a clean one.

Make a set of linen napkins Who needs formal linen napkins that need to be pressed every time you use them? Pillowcases are available in a wide array of colours and designs. Pick a colour or design you like, cut it into eight matching squares and make a 1.25cm hem on each edge. You can make a new set of colourful napkins for a fraction of the cost of regular cloth napkins.

Use for wrapping difficult shapes If you are trying to wrap a football, a vase, a large cuddly toy or an awkwardly shaped piece of artwork and wrapping paper isn't up to the task, place the gift in a cheap, brightly coloured pillowcase and tie it closed with a ribbon.

Wash lettuce in washing machine If you are expecting lots of people for an outdoor lunch and have lots of lettuce to wash, place one pillowcase inside another. Pull apart the lettuce heads and fill the inside case with lettuce leaves. Close both pillowcases with string or a rubber band and throw the whole package in the washing machine with another large item, such as a towel, to balance it. Now run the rinse and spin cycle. Your leaves will come out rinsed and dried more effectively than in a salad spinner.

{ KIDS' STUFF }

CREATE A WALL HANGING

Children love to personalise their bedrooms. You can help kids as young as 4 or 5 do just that by making a pillowcase into a wall hanging. Let the child choose a pillowcase colour and then slit a hole about 2cm long in each side seam. Use fabric paints to create a design or scene or let your child rubber-stamp a picture on the pillowcase. Slot a dowel rod through the seam openings. Cut a length of wool about 75cm long. Tie one end of the wool to each end of the dowel. Hang on the wall and let the little one collect the compliments.

Store your sweaters Stored in plastic, winter sweaters may get musty. But stored just in a wardrobe or drawer, they're prey to moths. The solution can be found in the linen cupboard. Put the sweaters in a pillowcase for seasonal storage. They will stay free from dust but the cotton fabric will allow them to breathe.

Protect clothing hanging in a wardrobe You've just washed a favourite dress shirt or skirt but you know you won't be wearing it again for a while. To protect the garment, cut a hole in the top of an old pillowcase and slip it over the hanger and item of clothing.

Store leather accessories Stop leather handbags or suede shoes from getting dusty by storing items that you use only occasionally in a pillowcase. They'll be clean and ready to use when the occasion arises.

Keep matching sheets together Your recently arrived overnight guests want to go to bed, but it is not made. You go to the linen cupboard, but you can't find a matching set of sheets. To prevent this from happening next time, file away your bedlinens. Place newly laundered and folded sheets in a matching pillowcase before putting them in the cupboard.

Machine-wash your delicates Sweaters and tights can get pulled out of shape when they twist around in the washing machine. To protect these garments during washing, put them into a pillowcase and close it with string or a rubber band. Set the machine on the delicate setting and you won't have to worry about tangles.

Machine-wash stuffed animals Your child's soft toy collection is sweet but very dusty. When it is time for a bath, place washable toys (check the labels) in a pillowcase and put them in the washing machine. The pillowcase will ensure they get a gentle but thorough wash. If any parts fall off the stuffed animals, they'll be caught in the pillowcase so you can reattach them once they're clean again.

Use as a travelling laundry bag When you are travelling, it is natural to want to keep your dirty laundry separate from your clean clothes. Pack a pillowcase in your suitcase and use it to store the dirty laundry as it accumulates. When you get home, just empty the pillowcase into the washing machine.

 Pipe cleaners

Decorate a ponytail Pull hair into a ponytail then twist a coloured pipe cleaner around the hair band for an alternative hair decoration. Twist a couple of different coloured ones together for an even brighter effect.

Use as an emergency shoelace When you snap a shoelace just as you are about to go out onto the squash or tennis court, or out for a run, a pipe cleaner can be a good stopgap lace. Just thread it through your shoe as you would with a shoelace and twist it closed at the top.

Safety pin holder Safety pins come in so many sizes, it is hard to keep them together and organised. Thread safety pins – arranged according to size – onto a slim pipe cleaner, through the bottom loop of each pin, for easy access.

Clean gas burners Have you noticed that your hob burners are not firing on all jets? Can you see an interrupted circle of blue when you turn a burner on? Poke a pipe cleaner into the little vents. This will clean the burner and allow it to work more efficiently. This works for pressure cooker safety valves on pressure cookers too.

Make napkin rings Colourful pipe cleaners are an easy and fast way to make napkin rings. Just twist around the napkin and place on the table. If you want to get adventurous, use two, one for the napkin ring, attach the other pipe cleaner to it, shaped into a heart, shamrock, flower, curlicue or other inventive creation.

Use as a twist tie When you want to close a bag of kitchen rubbish but are out of twist ties, a pipe cleaner will work just as well instead.

Use as a travel toy If you are worried about having a bored, fidgeting child on your hands during your next long car or plane ride, take a bunch of pipe cleaners along. Whip them out when the 'Are we there yet?' questions start coming. Colourful pipe cleaners can be bent and shaped into fun figures, animals and flowers. They even make cool temporary bracelets and necklaces.

Use as a mini-scrubber Pipe cleaners are great for cleaning in tight spaces. Use one to remove dirt from the wheel of a can opener or to clean the bobbin area of a sewing machine.

DID YOU KNOW?

According to reliable sources, pipe cleaners were invented in the late 19th century in Rochester, New York, by J. Harry Stedman. Although pipe smoking has declined dramatically since then, pipe cleaners have flourished, having been co-opted by the arts-and-crafts community. Technically, craft pipe cleaners are called chenille stems. They come in various colours and widths and are much furrier than the simple pipe cleaners smokers use.

Decorate a gift To give a special touch to a birthday or holiday present, shape a coloured pipe cleaner into a bow or a heart. Poke one end through a hole in the card and secure it to the package with a spot of glue.

Plastic containers

Organise a sewing area You're sitting down at the sewing machine to start on a set of Christmas craft projects. But instead of sewing, you are hunting for an extra bobbin or the right-colour thread. Plastic containers can help you to bring order to your sewing area. Fill several with thread spools, others with implements such as seam rippers and measuring tapes. Yet another can be filled with pins.

Trap plant-eating slugs Sock it to the slugs that are eating your newly planted vegetable plants. Dig a hole the size of a plastic container near the plant. Place the container, flush with the ground, in the hole. Fill the container with beer or salted water and place cut potatoes around the rim to attract the slugs. Slugs will crawl in, but they can't crawl out.

Get rid of wasps If wasps have been getting a little too close for comfort, threatening to bring your outing to the park to an untimely end, take a plastic container and fill it with water sweetened with sugar. Cut a hole in the lid. Wasps will be attracted to the water and crawl inside.

Keep ants away from a picnic table You watch helplessly as the ants march up the picnic table leg, onto the tabletop, and into the picnic meal. Here is a foolproof way to stop them in their tracks. Place a plastic container on the bottom of each picnic table leg. Fill each with water. The ants will not be able to crawl past.

Use as a portable dog bowl The next time you go out for a long walk with your dog, pack a portion of his food in a plastic container so he won't go hungry en route. Of course, you can pack another container with a snack for yourself. An empty container also makes a great water bowl when you are travelling.

Super item

38 USES!

PLASTIC BAGS...

...around the house

Line a cracked flower vase Here is what to do if you have a magnificent vase that looks marvellous filled with blooms but leaks from a large crack that runs along its length. Line the vase with a strong plastic bag before you fill it with water and add the bouquet to give fresh life to a treasured heirloom.

Stuff crafts or cushions There are a number of ways to stuff a home made soft toy or special cushion: with beans, rice, fabric filler, plastic beads, tights and so on. But have you ever tried stuffing a craft item or cushion with plastic bags? There will always be plenty on hand, so you don't have to worry about running out and you are recycling too. Cut them into small pieces to get into tight spaces.

Make party decorations Create streamers for a party using coloured plastic bags. Cut each bag into strips starting from the open end and stopping short of the bottom. Then attach the bag bottom to the ceiling with tape.

Drain bath toys Don't let your child's bath toys go mouldy and create a potential hazard in the bathroom. After the bath is finished, gather them up in a plastic bag pierced with a few holes. Hang the bag on a tap to let the water drain out. The toys will be clean, dry and collected in one place, ready for the next bathtime.

Keep kids' mattresses dry There is no need to buy an expensive mattress guard if bed-wetting is a problem. Instead, line the mattress with plastic rubbish bags. Big bags are also useful to protect car seats or upholstery from toilet-training toddlers' or damp children coming home from a swimming lesson.

Treat chapped hands If your hands are cracked and scaly, rub a thick layer of petroleum jelly on your hands. Place them in a plastic bag. The jelly and your body's warmth will help to make your hands supple in about 15 minutes.

...for storing things

Store extra baby wipes Shopping at a discount warehouse, you can snap up a jumbo box of baby wipes at a bargain price – enough to last for several months, as long as they don't dry out before you can use them. To protect your investment, keep the opened carton of wipes in a plastic bag sealed with a twist tie.

Collect clothes for the charity shop If you are always setting aside clothes to give to charity, but then find them back in your wardrobe or drawers, try this solution. Hang a large rubbish bag in your wardrobe. The next time you find something you want to give away, you just put it in the bag. Once it is full, you can take it to the local charity shop. Don't forget to hang a new bag in the wardrobe.

Cover clothes for storage If you want to protect a suit or jacket to wear next season, take a large, unused rubbish bag. Slit a hole in the top and push the hanger through to make an instant garment cover.

Store your skirts If you find you have an over-flowing wardrobe but plenty of room to spare in a chest of drawers, do a clothes transfer. Roll up your skirts and place them each in a plastic bag. That will help them to stay crease-free until you are ready to wear one.

Keep handbags in shape Do you ever notice that if you change handbags and leave an empty one in the cupboard, it deflates and loses its shape? Fill your handbag with plastic bags to retain its original shape.

TIP* STORING PLASTIC BAGS

If a plethora of plastic shopping bags are spilling out of a drawer in the kitchen, here are some better ways to store them:

- Stuff them inside an empty tissue box for easy retrieval.
- Push a bunch into a cardboard tube, such as a paper towel or posting tube or even a section of a carpet tube.
- Fill a clean, 4 litre plastic milk carton. Cut a 10cm hole in the bottom. Stuff it with bags and hang by its handle on a hook. You can pull the bags out of the spout.
- Make a bag 'sock'. Fold a kitchen towel lengthways with the wrong side facing out. Stitch the long edges together. Sew 1.25cm casings around the top and bottom openings and thread elastic through them, securing the ends. Turn the sock right side out, sew a loop of ribbon or string onto the back to hang it up, stuff plastic bags into the top opening. Retrieve them by pulling them out from the bottom.

PLASTIC BAGS...

...for keeping things clean

Protect your hand when cleaning the toilet When cleaning a toilet, first wrap your hand in a used plastic bag. You will be able to do all the necessary scrubbing without your hand getting splashed in the process.

Prevent steel wool from rusting To prolong the life of a new steel wool pad, put it into a plastic bag after you have finished. It won't rust and you will be able to use it again and again.

Make bibs for kids If you get an impromptu tea time visit from hungry small children, but don't have any bibs to protect their clothes while they eat, make some by tying a plastic bag loosely around their necks. You can make quick aprons in this way as well.

Create a high-chair floor cloth Baby shops will happily sell you an expensive floor cloth to place under a child's high chair. Why spend the money on a sheet of plastic when you have lots of large bin bags to do the job? Split the seams of a bag and place it under the high chair to catch all the drips and dribbles. When it gets filthy, take it outside and shake or just throw it away.

Line the litter tray Nobody enjoys changing the cat's litter tray. Make the job quick and easy by lining the box with an open plastic bag before pouring in the litter. Use two bags if you think one is too flimsy. When it is time to change the litter, just remove the bags, tie them up and throw into the bin.

Needle-free Christmas tree removal Christmas trees are great until the needles start dropping – everywhere. When it is time to take down the tree, place a large bin bag over the top and pull down. If it doesn't fit in one bag, use another from the bottom and pull up. You can quickly remove the tree without needles trailing behind you. Then make sure you take it to be recycled.

Keep polish off your hand To polish a pair of scruffy white sandals without getting more polish on your hands than on your shoes, wrap your hand in a plastic bag before inserting it into the sandal. Then when polish runs off the sandal straps, your hand will be protected. Leave the bag in the sandal until the polish is completely dry.

...in the kitchen

Bag the phone It always happens. You are doing something exceptionally messy in the kitchen, such as preparing meat, chopping onions or kneading dough. And then the phone rings. Quickly wrap your hands in a plastic bag and answer it. You won't miss a call or have to clean the phone when you have finished.

Scrape dishes When it is time to clear the dishes after a large family meal, this is an easy way to get rid of scraps of food left on the plates. Line a bowl with a plastic bag and scrape the scraps into it. Once the bag is full, gather up the handles and throw it out. Place the bowl in a prominent place in the kitchen so everyone can scrape their own dishes when bringing them to the sink.

Cover a cookbook You're trying a new recipe from a borrowed cookbook that you don't want to get splattered during your creation. Cover the book with a clear plastic bag and you will be able to read the instructions, while the book stays clean.

Replace a mixing bowl If you are cooking for a crowd and are short of mixing bowls, try using a plastic bag instead. Place all the dry ingredients to be mixed in the bag, gather it up and gently shake. If the ingredients are wet, use your hands to mix.

Spin dry salad greens Children will enjoy helping you do this. Wash lettuce and other greens and shake out as much water as you can in the sink. Then place the greens in a plastic grocery bag that has been lined with a paper towel. Grab the handles and spin the bag in large circles in the air. After several vigorous whirls, the lettuce will be dry.

Ripen fruit To ripen rock-hard peaches and similar soft fruits, place the unripe fruits with a few already ripe pieces or some ripe bananas in a plastic bag. The ripe fruit will help to soften the others through the release of natural gas. But don't leave them for more than a day or two or they will turn purple and mouldy.

{ SCIENCE FAIR }

TEST THE STRENGTH OF A SHOPPING BAG

It is said that a plastic bag can carry about 9kg of groceries before you need to double-bag. Find out how much a bag can hold without its handles breaking. For this experiment, you will need bathroom scales, a plastic bag and a collection of rocks. Place the bag on the scales. Fill it with rocks until the scale reads 4kg. Lift the bag. Does it hold? Add more rocks in 1kg increments, testing the bag's strength after each addition. When the handles start to tear, you will know the bag's actual strength.

PLASTIC BAGS...

...in the garden

Protect plants from frost When frost is forecast, use plastic bags to protect small garden plants. Cut a hole in the bottom of each bag. Slip one over each plant and anchor it inside using small rocks. Then pull the bags over the plants, roll them closed, and secure them with clothespegs or paper clips. You can open the bags up again if the weather gets warmer.

Protect fruit on the tree To protect apples or plums that need a little more time to ripen, slip the fruit into clear plastic bags while it is still on the trees. You'll keep out insects and deter birds while the fruit continues to ripen.

Protect your shoes from mud If it has rained hard in the night, but you still need to get out in the garden to do the weeding, cover your shoes in plastic bags to avoid getting mud all over them. The mud gets on the bag, not on the shoes and your feet stay dry so you can stay out in the garden longer.

Clean a grill easily After a brilliant barbecue, your grill is probably a sorry mess. To clean it, take the racks off and place them in a bin bag. Spray oven cleaner on the grill and close up the bag. The next day, open the bag, making sure to keep your face well away from the fumes. All the burned-on food should wipe straight off.

Cover car boot sale signs If you have gone to the trouble of advertising an upcoming car boot sale with signposts but worry that rain may hurt your publicity campaign before even the early birds show up, protect the signs by covering them with pieces cut from clear plastic bags. Passers by can still see the lettering, which will be protected from the rain.

Store outdoor equipment manuals Your lawnmower has lost a cutting blade and you need to replace it. If you store all your outdoor equipment's warranties and owner's manuals in a plastic bag and hang it in the garage, you will know exactly where to look for advice on how to fix it.

Protect your car mirrors Be a step ahead of snow or ice by covering your car's wing mirrors with plastic bags before a storm starts. When you are cleaning off the car the next morning, just remove the bag.

DID YOU KNOW?

Worried about the growing number of plastic bags filling landfills, countries across the globe have started putting restrictions on the seemingly indispensable item. Bangladesh has banned plastic bags, blaming them for clogging drainage pipes and causing flooding. Some Australian towns also have banned plastic bags, and the country is pushing shops to halve their use of bags (estimated at 7 billion annually) in a few years. If you want to use a plastic bag in Ireland, you will be charged about 11p a bag. In Taiwan, it's 20p a bag.

...on the move

Store a wet umbrella When you are out in the rain and running to your next appointment, who wants to deal with a soggy umbrella dripping all over your clothes and car? One of the plastic bags that magazines are delivered in is the perfect size to cover your umbrella the next time it rains. Just fold the umbrella up and quickly slip it into the bag

Protect your hands when getting petrol You have stopped at the petrol station for a fill-up while on your way to meet friends for lunch. The last thing you want is to greet them with hands that smell of petrol. Take one of the plastic bags you keep in your car and cover your hands with it while you fill the tank.

Pack your shoes If a smart holiday means you have to take shoes for all occasions, but you are worried that packing them in the suitcase will get everything else dirty, wrap each pair in its own plastic bag. It will keep the dirt off all your clothes and you can rest assured that you have packed complete pairs of shoes.

Make an instant poncho Keep a large bin bag in the car. The next time it rains unexpectedly, cut some slits for arms and one for your head. Slip on your impromptu poncho and stay dry.

...for the DIY-er

Store paintbrushes If you are halfway through painting the living room and it is time to break for lunch, there is need to clean the paintbrush. Just put it in a plastic bag and it will remain wet and ready to use when you return. If you are planning to finish next weekend, put the bag-covered brush in the freezer. Defrost it next weekend and you will be ready to start again.

Contain paint overspray If you have a few small items to spray-paint, use a plastic bag to control any overspray. Just place one item at a time in the bag, spray-paint, and remove it to a spread-out newspaper to dry. When you have finished, throw away the bag to make cleaning up fast and easy.

PLASTIC BOTTLES...

...around the house

Make a foot warmer Fill a 1 or 2 litre drink bottle with hot – but not boiling – water, then sit down and roll it back and forth under your feet.

Make a bag or string dispenser Cut off the bottom and top ends of the bottle and screw it upside down inside a kitchen cabinet or under a shelf. Put washers under the screw heads to keep them from pulling through the plastic. Fill it with recycled bags (squeeze the air out of them first) and pull them out as needed. Make a string dispenser the same way, using a 1 litre bottle and letting the cord out of a hole in the bottom.

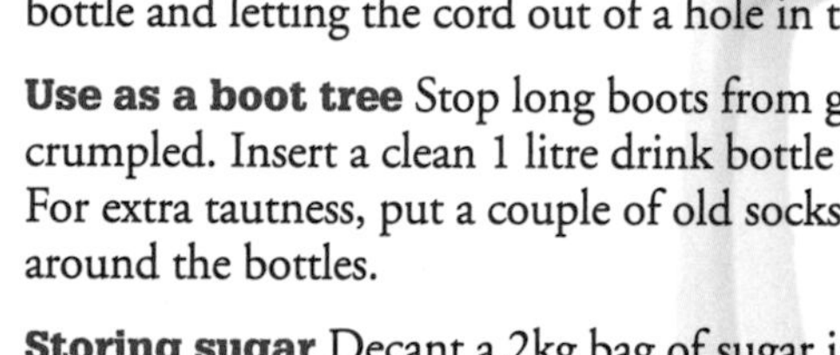

Use as a boot tree Stop long boots from getting crumpled. Insert a clean 1 litre drink bottle into each boot. For extra tautness, put a couple of old socks or towels around the bottles.

Storing sugar Decant a 2kg bag of sugar into a clean, dry 4 litre plastic bottle with a handle. The sugar is far less likely to harden and stick together and the handle will make pouring much easier.

Cut down on water when you flush If you have an older toilet that uses a lot of water for each flush, save money on water bills by filling an empty 1 litre soft drink bottle with water and placing it in the toilet cistern to reduce the amount of water used in each flush.

Cut out a toy carryall Make a simple holder for construction bricks by cutting a large hole in the side of a clean 4 litre plastic milk bottle with a handle. Cut the hole opposite the handle.

Make a dog chew Dogs love the crunchy texture of plastic. Remove labels and caps and let your dog munch on a bottle.

Fashion a funnel Cut a clean milk bottle with a handle in half across its midsection. Use the top portion (with the spout and handle) as a funnel for easy pouring of paints, rice, coins and other materials.

...away from home

Make a scoop or boat bailer Cut a clean plastic 2-litre bottle with a handle diagonally from the bottom so that you have the top three-quarters of the bottle intact. You now have a handy scoop that can be used for everything from

TIP* SAFE ROTARY CUTTER

Cutting plastic containers can be a tricky, dangerous business – especially when you use a sharp kitchen knife. But you can greatly minimise the risk by using a rolling cutter knife from a craft shop. Be careful as these knives use razor sharp blades, but they make life much easier when it is time to cut into a hard plastic container.

removing leaves and other debris from your gutters, to cleaning out a cat litter tray and cleaning up after your dog. Use it to scoop dog food from the bag, spread sand or salt on pavements or driveways in winter or bail water out of a boat (keep the cap on for this last application).

Keep a cooler cold Fill a few clean plastic milk cartons with water or juice and keep them in the freezer to use when transporting food in a cooler. As well as keeping food cold, you can drink the water or juice as it melts. Keep a few frozen bottles in your freezer if you have extra space; a full freezer actually uses less energy and can save money on your electricity bill. When filling a bottle, leave a little room at the top for the water to expand as it freezes.

Use for emergency road kit in winter Keep a couple of clean 4-litre bottles with handles filled with sand or cat litter in the trunk of your car. You will be prepared to sprinkle the material on the road surface to add traction under your wheels if you need to get moving on a slippery road. The handle makes pouring easier.

...in the garden

Make a watering can If you don't have a watering can, make one from a clean 4 litre juice, milk or bleach bottle with a handle. Drill about a dozen tiny (1.5mm) holes just below the spout of the bottle on the side opposite the handle. Or carefully punch the holes with a skewer or ice pick. Fill it with water, screw the cap on and start sprinkling.

Create a drip irrigator for plants During dry spells, a good way to get water to the roots of plants is to place several drip irrigators around the garden. You can make them from clean 4 litre juice or detergent bottle. Cut a large hole in the bottom of a bottle, then drill two to five tiny (1.5mm) holes in or around the cap. Bury the closed bottles upside down about three-quarters submerged beneath the soil near the plants you need to water and fill with water through the hole on top. Refill as often as needed.

PLASTIC BOTTLES...

Mark your plants Make identity tags for plants by cutting vertical strips from a couple of clear 4 litre water bottles. Make the strips the same width as a seed packet but double the length. Fold each strip over an empty seed packet to protect it from the elements and staple it to a strong stick or chopstick.

Feed the birds Take a clean 2 litre juice or milk bottle and carve out a large opening. Then make a small hole to insert a sturdy twig or dowel for a perch. Poke a hole in the middle of the cap and suspend it from a tree with a piece of string or monofilament fishing line. Fill it up to the opening with birdseed.

Secure garden netting If you are constantly having to re-stake loose netting or plastic lining over a flower bed, place large water-filled plastic bottles around the corners to keep the material in place.

Use as a portable rubbish bin or harvesting basket Cut a large hole opposite the handle of a large container and loop the handle through a belt or rope on your waist. Use it to collect debris you encounter as you mow the lawn or stroll through the garden. You can also make a basket for harvesting berries, cherries and other small fruits or vegetables.

Space seeds Use an empty soft drink bottle as a guide. Find the distance that the seed company recommends between seeds and then cut off the tapered top of the bottle so that its diameter equals that distance. Firmly press the bottle, cut edge down, into the soil and place a seed in the centre of the circle it makes. Line up the bottle so that its edge touches the curve of the first impression and press down again. Plant a seed in the centre and repeat until you've filled up all the rows.

Isolate weeds when spraying herbicides When using herbicides to kill weeds, to isolate the weed you want to spray, cut a 2 litre plastic bottle in half and place the top half over the designated weed. Then direct the pump's spraying wand through the opening in the top of the bottle and spray. After the spray settles down, pick up the bottle and move on to your next target.
WARNING You should always wear goggles and gloves when spraying any chemicals in the garden.

Set up a garden sprayer Keep children cool with a homemade garden sprayer. Just cut three 2.5cm vertical slits in one side of a clean 2 litre soft drink bottle. Or make the slits at different angles so the water will squirt in different directions. Attach the nozzle of a hose to the bottle top with gaffer tape (make sure it is fastened on tight). Turn on the tap and let the fun begin.

Build a fly and wasp trap Do flies, wasps and midges swarm around you every time you set foot in the garden? Use an empty 2 litre soft drink bottle to make an environmentally-friendly trap for them. First, dissolve 100g sugar in 100ml water in the bottle. Then add 200ml cider vinegar and a banana skin (squash it up to fit it through). Screw on the cap and give the mixture a good shake before filling the bottle halfway with cold water. Cut or drill a 2cm hole near the top of the bottle and hang it from a branch close to where the insects seem especially active. When the trap is full, throw it away and replace it with a new one.

...for the DIY-er

Build a paint bucket Cut a large hole opposite the handle of a clean 4 litre container. Pour in the paint so that it is about 2cm below the edge of the hole and use the edge to remove any excess paint from the brush before you lift it. You can also cut containers in half and use the bottom halves as disposable paint buckets when several people are working on the same job.

Store your paints Keep paints clean and fresh in plastic containers. Use a funnel to pour the paint into a clean, dry milk or water container and add a few marbles (they help mix the paint when you shake the container before your next paint job). Label each container with a piece of masking tape, noting the paint manufacturer, colour name and the date.

Use as workshop organisers Are you always searching for the right nail to use for a particular chore or for a clothes peg, picture hook or small fastener? Bring some organisation to your workshop with a few plastic containers. Cut out a section near the top of each container on the side opposite the handle. Use the containers to store and sort all the small items that slip through the cracks in the workbench. The handle makes it easy to carry the organiser to where you are working.

Use as a level substitute Make sure that a shelf you are about to fix is straight even if you don't have a spirit level on hand. Fill a 1-litre soft drink bottle about three-quarters full with water. Replace the cap, then lay the bottle on its side. When the water is level, the shelf will be too.

Make a weight for anchoring or lifting Fill a clean, dry 4 litre bottle with a handle with sand and put on the cap. You now have an anchor that is suitable for holding down a painting cloth, securing a shaky patio umbrella or steadying a table for repair. The handle makes it easy to move or to attach a rope. Or use a pair of sand-filled bottles as exercise weights, varying the amount of sand to meet your lifting capacity.

Plastic lids

Stop a sink or bath If the plug has disappeared, but you need to stop the water in a sink or bath, here is a stopgap solution. Place a plastic lid over the drain. The vacuum created keeps the water from draining away.

Keep the fridge clean Drippy bottles and leaky containers can create a horrible mess on the shelves of a fridge. Make coasters from plastic lids to keep things clean. Place the lids under food containers to stop any potential leaks. If they get dirty, you can wash them off easily, while the fridge shelves stay free from sticky mess.

Use as kids' coasters When you are entertaining a crowd of children and want to make sure your tabletops survive, give them plastic lids to use as coasters. Write their names on the coasters so they won't get their drinks mixed up.

Use as coasters for plants Plastic lids are the perfect water catcher for small houseplants. One under each plant will help to keep watermarks off the furniture.

Scrape non-stick pans Unfortunately food often sticks to so-called non-stick pans. Though using steel wool to get it off is not advisable, try scraping off the mess with a plastic lid which shouldn't scratch the surface.

Separate frozen hamburgers Prepare homemade hamburgers for a barbecue in advance. Season the meat as desired and shape it into patties. Place each patty on a plastic lid. Then stack them up, place in a plastic bag, and freeze. When the grill is fired up, you will have no trouble separating the pre-formed hamburgers.

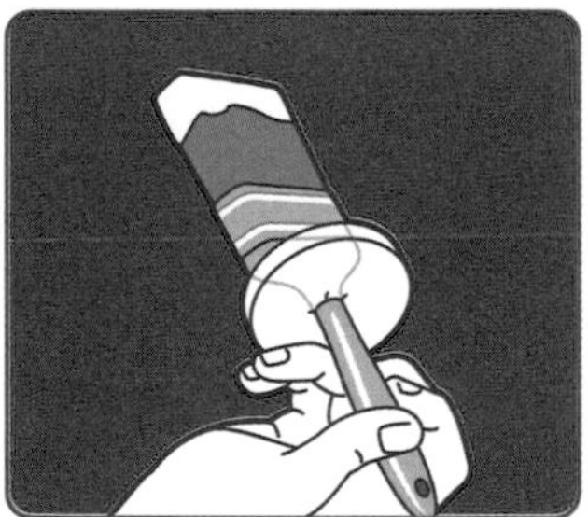

Prevent paintbrush drips If you are concerned about getting messy paint drips all over yourself while you are touching up a repair job on the ceiling, try this trick. Cut a slot in the middle of a plastic lid. The kind of plastic lid that comes on catering size tins is the perfect size for most paintbrushes. Insert the handle of the paintbrush through the lid so that the lid is on the narrow part of the handle just above your hand. The lid will catch any paint drips. Even with this shield, always be careful not to put too much paint on your brush when you are painting overhead.

Close a bag When you have run out of twist ties but need to take a bin bag out of the house, take a plastic lid, cut a slit in it, gather the top of the bag and thread it through. The bag will be completely sealed and ready for disposal.

Plastic tablecloths

Make a shower curtain A colourful tablecloth can make an attractive shower curtain to match your bathroom. Punch holes about 15cm apart and 1.25cm from one edge of a hemmed tablecloth. Insert shower curtain rings or loop strings through the holes and loosely tie to the curtain rod.

Make a high-chair drop cloth It is par for the course for a baby to get more food on the floor than in his or her mouth. Catch the debris and protect your floor by spreading a plastic tablecloth under the high chair.

Collect leaves Save bending at leaf-raking time. Don't pick the leaves up to put them in a wheelbarrow to transport them to the kerb or leaf pile. Just rake the leaves onto an old plastic tablecloth, gather up the four corners and drag the tablecloth to the kerb or pile.

Plungers

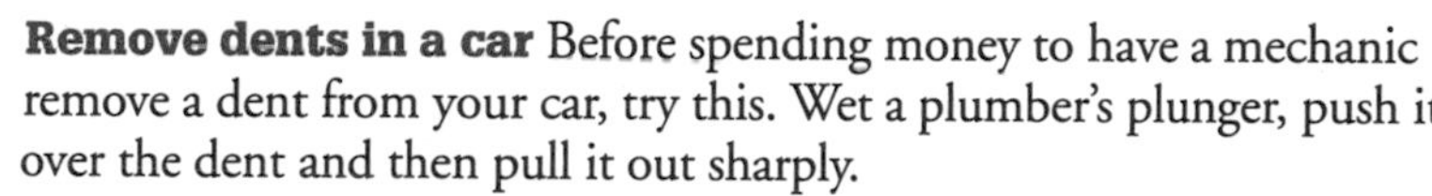

Remove dents in a car Before spending money to have a mechanic remove a dent from your car, try this. Wet a plumber's plunger, push it over the dent and then pull it out sharply.

Catch chips when drilling ceiling Before you use a drill to make an overhead hole, remove the handle from a plunger and place the cup over the shank of the drill. The cup will catch falling chunks of plaster, cement or brick.

Use as an outdoor candleholder If you are looking for a place to put an insect-repelling citronella candle, plant a plunger handle in the ground and put the candle in the rubber cup.

Polystyrene foam

Keep nail varnish smooth When applying nail varnish, a polystyrene pellet or a small chunk cut from a block of foam packaging placed between each finger or toe will help to spread them apart and keep the polish unblemished until it can dry.

Make your own protective pellets If you'd like to use foam chips to post some fragile items, but all you have got is sheets or blocks of foam, not pellets, just break up what you have into pieces small enough to fit in a blender and pulse it on and off to shred the foam into perfect packing material.

Hold treats for freezing and serving To prepare a quantity of ice-cream cones in advance, cut a foam block to a size that will fit flat in your freezer. Cut holes just large enough and close enough to hold cones so they won't touch, fall over or poke through the bottom. Fill the cones and slip them into the waiting holes. Then pop the whole thing into the freezer ready for serving at a moment's notice.

TIP* RECYCLING FOAM PELLETS

Even with lots of creative reuse, sometimes polystyrene packing pellets just come in faster than they go out again. If you have got more than you can handle, remember that packing and shipping businesses may accept clean pellets for reuse. Call to confirm before you bring them in.

Make a buoyant tray for a swimming pool Polystyrene foam is nearly unsinkable. Use the scraps from a building project to make a drinks holder or tray that will float in the pool:

- To make a drink-can holder, cut two pieces to the size you want the finished holder to be, then cut holes the same size as a drink can in one piece. Glue the piece with holes on top of the other piece, using a glue gun.
- To make a tray with a rim, just glue small strips of foam that are at least 2.5cm high around the edge of a larger tray-size section of the material.

Make a swimming float A sharp kitchen knife is all you need to cut a scrap of polystyrene insulation into a float to use when practising swimming strokes.

Help shrubs withstand winter Sometimes shrubs need a little help to survive winter. Leftover sheets of polystyrene foam insulation are perfect for the job. They're rigid, waterproof and block wind and road salt. Here are two ways to use the material:

- To give moderate protection, cut two polystyrene foam sheets and lash them together to form a 'tent' over the plant. To hold the pieces in place, drive bamboo garden stakes through the bottom of each piece and into the ground.
- For more substantial protection, fit pieces of foam together so that you can box in the plants on four sides. Put a stake inside each corner and join the pieces with gaffer or packing tape.

Plants in containers that overwinter outdoors are more likely to survive with polystyrene protection too.

* Potatoes

Extract salt for soup Did you go a bit overboard when salting the soup? Just cut a few potatoes into large chunks. Throw them into the soup pan while it is still on the stove. When they start to soften, in about 10 minutes, remove them and the excess salt they have absorbed. Save them for another use, such as potato salad.

Remove stains on your hands Your favourite carrot soup is simmering on the stove – but you have the orange hands to show for it. Otherwise hard-to-remove stains on hands from peeling carrots or handling pumpkins will come straight off if you rub your hands with a potato.

Remove a broken lightbulb If you are changing a lightbulb on the lamp on your bedside table and it breaks off in your hand, leaving the stem still inside. Unplug the lamp, then cut a potato widthwise and place it over the broken bulb. Twist and the rest of the lightbulb should come out easily.

Remove tarnish on silverware If you are serving high tea with all the silverware to make it a special occasion and you have run out of silver polish, boil up some potatoes. Remove from the water and save them for another use. Place the silverware in the remaining potato water and let it sit for an hour. Then remove and wash. The tarnish should be gone.

Keep ski goggles clear You can't keep a good lookout for trees and other skiers through snow goggles that fog up during a downhill descent. Rub raw potato over the goggles before you get on the ski lift and the ride down should be crystal clear.

End puffy morning eyes Everyone hates waking up in the morning and looking at a tired face and puffy eyes in the mirror. Applying slices of raw, cold potatoes to your eyes will quickly get rid of the puffiness.

Lure worms in houseplants When worms are crawling in and out of the roots of your favourite houseplant and the roots are suffering, slice raw potato around the base of the plant to act as a lure for the worms. They'll crawl up to eat and you can grab them and throw them out into the garden.

Make a decorative stamp Forget expensive rubber stamps – potato can provide the right medium for making your own stamp for decorating festive cards and envelopes. Cut a potato in half widthways. Carve a design on one half. Then start stamping as you would with a wooden version.

Feed new geraniums A raw potato can give a fledgling geranium all the nutrients it could ever desire. Carve a small hole in a potato. Slip a geranium stem into the hole. Then plant the whole thing, potato and all.

Hold a floral arrangement in place If you have a small arrangement of flowers that you'd like to stabilise but have no green floral foam on hand to stick the flower stems into, use a large baking potato. Cut it in half lengthways and place it cut side down. Poke holes where you want the flowers and then insert the stems.

Restore old, beat-up shoes If old shoes are just too scuffed to take a shine anymore, but they don't have holes, and are so nice and comfy that you don't want to throw them away, before you get rid of them, cut a potato in half and rub your old shoes with the raw potato. After that, polish them and they should come out nice and shiny.

Make a hot or cold compress Potatoes retain heat and cold well. The next time you need a hot compress, boil a potato, wrap it in a towel and apply to the area. Refrigerate the boiled potato if you need a cold compress.

{ SCIENCE FAIR }

DEMONSTRATE THE POWER OF AIR PRESSURE

Grasp a plastic straw in the middle and try to plunge it into a potato. It will crumple and bend, unable to penetrate the potato. Now grasp another straw in the middle, but this time, put your finger over the top. The straw will plunge right into the tuber. When the air is trapped inside the straw, it presses against the straw's sides, stiffening the straw enough to plunge into the potato. In fact, the deeper the straw plunges, the less space there is for the air and the stiffer the straw gets.

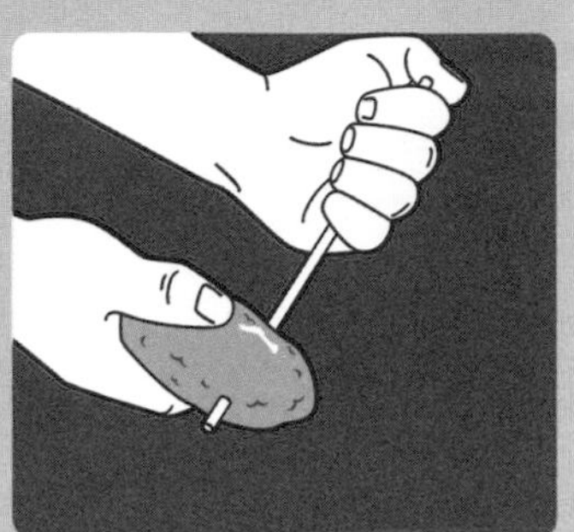

Pots and pans

Catch draining engine oil There is no need to buy an oil-collecting tray. When it is time to change the oil in your car engine, just place an old 5 litre or larger pot beneath the drain plug.

Create an instant birdbath You can quickly provide feathered visitors to your garden with a place to refresh themselves. Just set an old pan on top of a flowerpot and keep it filled with water.

Use as a large scoop Leave those 20kg sacks of fertiliser and grass seed in the garden shed and use a pan to carry what you need to the place you are tending. A small pan with a handle also makes a terrific boat bailer or dog-food scoop.

Make an extra grill If you have a big party or barbecue planned and the grill is not big enough to handle all those burgers, sausages, steaks and hot dogs, improvise a second grill by building a fire in an large old pot. Cook on a wire cake rack placed over the pot. After you are finished, put the pot's cover on to put out the fire and save the charcoal for another outdoor cooking session.

Rubber bands

Secure casserole lids When you hand somebody a lovingly prepared casserole dish to carry in the car, make sure that you secure the top to the base with a couple of thick, strong rubber bands to avoid the possibility of spillage.

Keep thread from tangling To prevent threads getting tangled in your sewing box, just wrap a rubber band around each spool to keep the thread from unravelling.

Anchor a cutting board Do you find yourself chasing your cutting board around the worktop when you are chopping up vegetables? Give the board some traction by putting a rubber band around each end.

Reshape your broom There is no need to discard a broom because the bristles are splayed with use. Wrap a rubber band around the broom a few centimetres from the bottom. Leave it for a day or so and the bristles should get back in line.

Childproof kitchen and bath cabinets Temporarily childproof bathroom and kitchen cabinets that you don't want visiting children to get into. Just wrap the bands tightly around pairs of handles.

Stop a sliding spoon To stop a wooden spoon slipping into the mixing bowl, wrap a rubber band around the top of the handle. It will catch the spoon before it falls and stop you from having to fish it out of the mixture.

Thumb through papers with ease Don't lick your finger. Wrap a rubber band around your index finger a few times the next time you need to shuffle papers. Don't make it too tight or you'll cut off circulation to your fingertip.

Extend a button If a top shirt button is a little too tight, put a small rubber band through the buttonhole, then loop the ends over the button to give yourself a little breathing space.

Use as a bookmark Paper bookmarks work well until they slip out of the book. Instead, wrap a rubber band from top to bottom around the part of the book you have already read. You won't lose your place, even if you drop the book.

Cushion a remote control To protect furniture from scratches and nicks, wrap a wide rubber band around both ends of the television remote control. You'll be protecting the remote too; it will be less likely to slide off a table and get damaged.

Secure bed slats Do the slats under your mattress sometimes slip out? Wrap rubber bands around their ends to make them stay in place.

Tighten furniture casters The casters on furniture legs can become loose with wear. To tighten up a caster, wrap a rubber band around the stem and reinsert.

Gauge your liquids Slip a rubber band around the liquid containers in your workshop to indicate how much is left and you will always know at a glance.

Wipe your paintbrush Every time you dip a paintbrush into a tin of paint, you wipe the excess against the side of the tin. Before you know it, paint is dripping off the side and the little groove around the rim is so full of paint that it splashes everywhere when you go to hammer the lid back on. Avoiding all this mess is easy. Wrap a rubber band around the can from top to bottom, going across the middle of the can opening. Now, when you fill your brush, you can just tap it against the rubber band and the excess paint will fall back into the can.

Get a grip on drinking glasses Does arthritis make it difficult for you to grasp a drinking glass securely, especially when it is wet with condensation? Wrap a couple of rubber bands around the glass to make it easier to grip. This works well for children as well as their small hands sometimes have a hard time holding a glass.

DID YOU KNOW?

The first rubber band was patented in 1845 by Stephen Perry, who owned a rubber manufacturing company in London.

A key ingredient in making rubber bands is sulphur. When it is added to the rubber and heated – a process known as vulcanisation – it makes the rubber strong and stretchy and prevents it from rotting. The process of making rubber bands is surprisingly similar to making a loaf of bread. First the dry ingredients are mixed with natural rubber. The resulting friction and chemical reaction heats and partially vulcanises the rubber. The rubber is cooled, then rolled out like bread dough. It is extruded into a long tube, and the tube is heated to finish the vulcanisation. Then it is rinsed, cooled and sliced into bands.

Get a grip on twist-off tops The tops on most beer bottles these days are supposed to be twist-off, but some still have sharp little crimps from the bottle-opener days that can really dig into your hand. Wrap the top in a rubber band to save the pain. The same trick works well for smooth, tough-to-grip bottle tops too.

Make a holder for your car visor Snap a couple of rubber bands around the sun visors on your car to make a handy place to slip parking receipts, directions and maybe even a favourite CD.

*Rubber flip flops

Remove pet hair Slip a rubber flip flop onto your hand and rub carpets and rugs in the direction of the pile. The pet hair will form into balls that can then be vacuumed up. This works well on upholstery, too, including car seats.

Stop that banging door Cut a piece of rubber from an old flip flop and use it to keep a door wedged open on a breezy day.

Prevent rattling windows If you can't sleep whenever the wind blows because older sash or casement windows rattle in their frames whenever it is windy, cut slivers of rubber from an old flip flop and wedge them between the window and the frame.

Keep furniture steady Stop the wobbles in a wonky table by cutting a piece of old flip flop to shape and gluing it beneath the offending leg.

DID YOU KNOW?

The design of flip-flops was inspired by the traditional woven or wooden soled 'zori' used by the Japanese. They were first used as beach wear in New Zealand in the 1930s, where they became known as 'jandals' or 'Japanese sandals'. They were first made from rubber and plastic in the 1950s and Maurice Yock patented the design in New Zealand in 1957.

Flip flops are known by a wide range of different names. In India, a similar kind of shoe is known as a chappal. In the USA, they may also be called beach walkers, zories or go-aheads, while in Australia, they are known as thongs or pluggers. In South Africa the common name for flip flops is 'slops'.

Rubber jar rings

Keep rug from slipping If you have a rug that tends to skate across a polished wooden floor, keep it in place by sewing a rubber jar ring or two in each corner on the wrong side of the rug.

Play indoor quoits What else can you do to keep fidgety young children happily occupied on a rainy day? Turn a stool or small table upside down and let them try to toss rubber jar rings over the legs.

Protect tabletops Protect tabletops from scratches and watermarks by placing a rubber jar ring under vases and lamps.

 Salt see page 268

 Salt shakers

Cut back on sugar You can cut back on sugar but still keep your sweet tooth happy if you fill a salt shaker with sugar. For sugar-restricted diets, use the sugar shaker as an alternative to dipping into the sugar bowl and sprinkle just a small amount lightly over food.

Use for flour-dusting Baking can be a messy job, so make at least one part of it tidier by putting flour into a large salt shaker. It is perfect for dusting cake tins. Keep it neat and close to hand in the cupboard with all your other ingredients for baking.

Use to apply dry fertiliser If you use dry fertiliser, try putting it in a salt shaker to use when fertilising seedlings. It gives you lots of application control so you can prevent fertiliser from burning tender young plants.

TIP* COLOURED SALT

To bring a little unexpected fun to the dinner table, try coloured salt. Put a few tablespoons of salt into a plastic sandwich bag and add a few drops of food colouring. Work it gently with your fingers to mix and let dry in the open bag for about a day. Cut a hole in the corner of the bag to pour the festive salt into the shaker. As a bonus, the coloured salt makes wonderful homemade glitter.

...around the house

Remove residue from a vase Once a beautiful bouquet has wilted, the souvenir it leaves behind is not the sort of reminder you want: deposits of minerals on the vase interior. Reach inside the vase, rub the offending ring of deposits with salt, then wash with soapy water. If your hand won't fit inside, fill the vase with a strong solution of salt and water, shake it or brush gently with a bottle brush, then wash. This should clear away the residue.

Clean artificial flowers You can quickly freshen up artificial flowers, whether they are made of silk or synthetic fabric, by placing them in a paper bag with 50g salt. Give the bag a few gentle shakes and the flowers will emerge crisp and bright.

Hold artificial flowers in place Salt is an excellent medium for keeping artificial flowers fixed in an arrangement. Fill a vase or other container with salt, add a little cold water and arrange the artificial flowers. The salt will solidify and the flowers will stay in place.

Keep wicker looking new Untreated wicker furniture often yellows with age and exposure to sun and the elements. To keep the natural tone, scrub the item with a stiff brush dipped in warm salt water. Let it dry in the sun. Repeat this process every year or two.

Make brooms last for longer A new straw broom will last longer if you soak the bristles in a bucket of hot, salty water. After about 20 minutes, remove the broom and let it dry.

Clean a fireplace with ease When you are ready to turn in for the night but the fire is still glowing in the hearth, douse the flames with salt. The fire will burn out more quickly, so you will end up with less soot than if you let it smoulder. Cleaning is easier, too, because the salt helps the ashes and residue to gather into piles so they can be swept up easily.

Make your own brass and copper polish When exposure to the elements dulls brass or copper items, there is no need to buy specialist cleaning products. To shine candlesticks or remove green tarnish from copper pans, make a paste by mixing equal parts salt, flour and vinegar. Use a soft cloth to rub the paste over the item, then rinse with warm, soapy water and buff back to its original shine.

Remove wine from a carpet Red wine spilled on a light-coloured carpet seems like a disaster. But it doesn't need to be. While the red wine is still wet, pour a little white wine or mineral water onto it to dilute the colour. Then clean the spot with a sponge and cold water. Sprinkle the area with salt and wait for about 10 minutes. Then vacuum up the residue and wait for the carpet to dry.

Clean grease stains from rugs or carpets Greasy marks on a rug or carpet can be hard to see, but they're not impossible to remove if you treat them correctly. Mix up 1 part salt to 4 parts methylated spirits and rub it over the grease stain, being careful to rub in the direction of the rug's natural nap.

Remove watermarks from wood Watermarks from damp glasses or bottles left on a wooden surface are very unattractive. Make them disappear by mixing 1 teaspoon salt with a few drops of water to form a paste. Gently rub the paste onto the ring with a soft cloth or sponge and work it over the spot until it is gone. Then restore the lustre of the wood with furniture polish.

Restore a sponge Hand sponges and mop sponges usually become horribly filthy long before they are really worn out. To restore sponges to a pristine condition, soak them overnight in a solution of about 50g salt per litre of water.

DID YOU KNOW?

Salt may be the key to life on Mars. Thanks to Mars missions, scientists have confirmed two things about the Red Planet. There's lots of ice and lots of salt. Of course, life as we know it requires water. And while temperatures on Mars are either too high or too low for fresh water, the presence of salt makes it possible that there is life-sustaining salt water below the planet's surface.

SALT...

...around the house

Keep windows and windscreens frost-free Salt greatly decreases the temperature at which ice freezes. Keep the windows in your home frost-free by wiping the outside with a sponge dipped in salt water, then letting them dry. In the winter, keep a small cloth bag of salt in the car. When the windscreen and other windows are wet, rub them with the bag. The next time you go out to your car, the windows won't be covered with ice or snow.

Deodorise your trainers Trainers and canvas shoes can get pretty smelly, especially if you wear them without socks in the summer. Cut down the odour and soak up the moisture by occasionally sprinkling a little salt into the shoes.

Relieve stings, bites and nettle rash Salt can help to reduce the pain of bee stings, mosquito bites and nettle rash:

- If you've been stung by a bee, immediately wet the sting and cover with salt. It will lessen the pain and reduce the swelling. If you are allergic to bee stings, you should get immediate medical attention.
- For relief from an itchy mosquito bite, soak the area in salt water, then apply a coating of vegetable oil.
- If you've blundered into a patch of stinging nettles, relieve the itching by soaking in hot salt water.

Make a scented air freshener Perfumed air fresheners can be expensive and the smell is often synthetic. Here is a wonderful way to make your room smell delightful at any time of year. Layer rose petals and salt in a pretty jar with a tight-fitting lid. Remove the lid to release the perfume and freshen the room.

End the ant parade If ants are beating a path to your larder, intercept them by sprinkling salt across the door frame or directly on their paths. They will be discouraged from crossing this barrier.

DID YOU KNOW?

The world's leading salt producer is the USA. In 2002 the US produced 43.9 million metric tons of salt. China was second, with 35 million metric tons. Other nations producing significant amounts of salt were Germany, with 15.7 million metric tons; India, with 14.8 million metric tons and Canada, with 13 million metric tons.

Give goldfish a parasite-killing bath The next time you take a goldfish out of its tank to change the water, put it in an invigorating saltwater bath for 15 minutes (no longer) while you clean the tank. Make the bath by mixing 1 teaspoon plain (non-iodised) salt into a litre of fresh water. As with tank water, you should let tap water sit overnight first to let the chlorine evaporate before submerging fish in it. The salt water kills parasites on the fish's scales and absorbs electrolytes. Don't add salt to the fish's tank, though. Goldfish are freshwater fish and should not spend a lot of time in salt water.

Clean a fish tank To remove mineral deposits from hard water in a fish tank, rub the inside of the tank with salt, then rinse the tank well before reinstalling the fish. Use only plain, not iodised, salt.

Repel fleas in pet habitats If your dog enjoys his kennel or bed, it is likely that fleas do too. Keep fleas at bay by washing down the interior walls and floor of the kennel with a solution of salt water every few weeks.

...in the kitchen

Freshen your waste disposal Is your waste disposal unit emitting an unpleasant smell? Freshen it up with salt. Pour in 100g salt, run the cold water, and start the disposal. The salt will dislodge stuck waste and neutralise any odours.

Clean greasy iron pans Grease can be hard to remove from iron pans, because it is not water-soluble. Sprinkle salt in the pan before you wash it and it will absorb most of the grease. Then wipe off the grease and salt and wash as usual.

Remove baked-on food You can remove food that has been baked onto pans or serving plates by lifting it with a pre-treatment of salt. Before washing, sprinkle the stuck-on food with salt. Dampen the area, let it sit until the salt lifts the baked-on food, then wash it away with soapy water.

Soak stains off enamel pans You can run out of elbow grease trying to scrub burned-on stains off enamel pans. Instead, soak the pan overnight in salt water. Then boil salt water in the pan the next day. The stains should lift straight off.

Keep oven spills from hardening The next time food bubbles over in the oven, don't give it a chance to bake on and cool. Throw some salt on the drips while it is still liquid. When the oven cools, you will be able to wipe up the spill with a cloth. The same technique works for spills on the hob. The salt will remove unpleasant smells as well, and if you would like to add a sweet scent, you can mix a little cinnamon in with the salt.

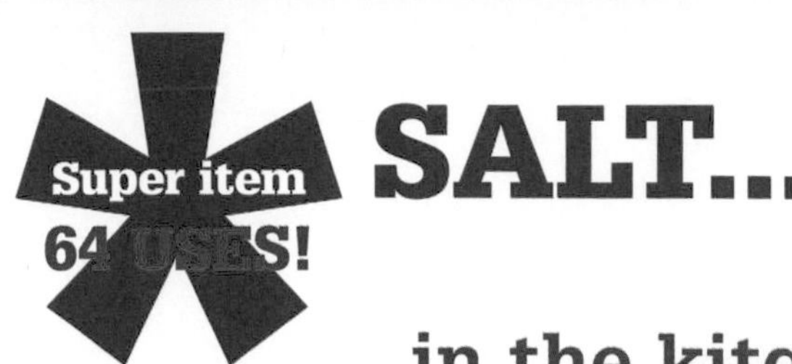

SALT...

...in the kitchen

Scrub off burned milk Burned milk is one of the toughest stains to remove, but salt makes it a lot easier. Wet the burned pan and sprinkle it with salt. Wait about 10 minutes, then scrub the pan. The salt will absorb the burned-milk smell too.

Clean discoloured glass Have the dishwasher and a good scrub failed to remove stubborn stains from glassware? Mix a handful of salt in a litre of vinegar and soak the glassware overnight. The stains should wipe off in the morning.

Clean a cast-iron wok No matter how thoroughly you dry them, cast-iron woks tend to rust when washed in water. Instead, when you have finished cooking, but while the wok is still hot, pour in about 50g salt and scrub it with a stiff wire brush. Wipe it clean, then apply a light coating of sesame or vegetable oil before putting it away. Don't clean a wok with a non-stick coating in this way, as it will scratch the finish.

Remove lipstick marks from glassware Lipstick smudges on glassware can be hard to remove, even in the dishwasher. That is because the emollients designed to help lipstick stay on your lips do a good job of sticking to glassware as well. Before washing wine glasses or tumblers, rub the edges with salt to erase lipstick stains.

Clean away messy dough Here is a way to make short work of cleaning up after you've rolled out dough or kneaded bread. Sprinkle the floured worktop with salt and you can neatly wipe away everything with a sponge.

Brighten up cutting boards After washing cutting boards and breadboards with soap and water, rub them with a damp cloth dipped in salt. The boards will come out lighter and brighter in colour.

{ KIDS' STUFF }

MAKE YOUR OWN CRAFT DOUGH

Make a craft dough that can be made into detailed ornaments, miniature food and dolls. In a bowl, slowly stir 200g salt into 200ml boiling water. After the salt dissolves, stir in 400g white flour. Turn the dough out onto a work surface and knead until smooth. If the dough is still sticky, add flour by the tablespoon until it is pliant. It should be easy to shape into balls, tubes, wreaths and other shapes. When they are finished, you can air-dry your creations or bake them in a 110°C/gas mark ¼ oven for up to 2 hours; the time depends on thickness. Or microwave on High for 1-2 minutes. Apply paint, then protect and shine with clear nail polish or varnish.

Revive overcooked coffee Before you throw out a stewed brew of coffee, try adding a pinch of salt to a cup to restore the flavour.

Erase tea and coffee stains Tea and coffee leave stubborn stains on cups and in pots. You can easily scrub away these rings by sprinkling salt onto a sponge and rubbing in little circles across the ring. If the stain persists, mix white vinegar with salt in equal proportions and rub with the sponge.

Clean the fridge After removing the food and the wire shelves from the fridge, mix up a handful of salt in 4 litres of warm water and use it with a sponge to clean the inside of the fridge. The mixture isn't abrasive, so it won't scratch surfaces. And you won't be introducing chemical fumes to a place where you keep food.

Shine a teapot spout Teapots with seriously stained spouts can be cleaned with salt. Pack the spout with salt and let it sit overnight or for at least a few hours. Then run boiling water through the pot, washing away the salt to reveal the old sparkle. If the stain persists, treat the rim with a cotton bud dipped in salt.

Prevent grease from splashing Add a few dashes of salt to the pan before starting to fry fatty foods such as bacon and sausages that can splash. You won't have to clean grease off the hob.

Shell hard-boiled eggs with ease Is there a secret to peeling hard-boiled eggs without breaking the shell into dozens of tiny pieces? There is: just add a teaspoon of salt to the water before placing the eggs in it to boil.

Make perfect poached eggs You know it is possible to keep the whites intact when you poach eggs – you've had them in a restaurant. But no matter how careful you are, the whites always diffuse into the water when you poach eggs at home. Here is the secret that restaurant chefs use. Sprinkle about ½ teaspoon salt into the water just before you put in the eggs. This helps to 'set' the whites in a neat package. A dash of vinegar also helps and improves the taste of the eggs too.

Test an egg's freshness If you are in doubt about the freshness of your eggs, add 2 teaspoons salt to 200ml water and gently place the egg in the cup. A fresh egg will sink. An old one floats.

Wash spinach more easily Fresh spinach leaves are an ideal health food, but their curving, bumpy surface makes it difficult to wash away all the dirt that collects in the crevices. Wash spinach leaves in salted water: the dirt is driven out along with the salt in the rinse water and you should get away with a single rinse.

SALT...

...in the kitchen

Keep salad crisp When you need to prepare leafy salad in advance for a dinner party, lightly salt the salad immediately after you prepare it and it will remain crisp for several hours.

Prevent mould on cheese Cheese is much too expensive to throw away because it has a touch of mould. Prevent it from getting mouldy in the first place by wrapping the cheese in a napkin soaked in salt water before storing it in the fridge.

Revive shrivelled apples Give apples a face-lift by soaking them in mildly salted water to make the skin smooth again.

Stop cut fruit from going brown To ensure that fresh-cut fruit for a desert looks appetising when you serve the dish and that cut apples and pears don't go brown, soak them briefly in a bowl of lightly salted water.

Use to whip cream and beat eggs The next time you whip cream or beat eggs, add a pinch of salt first. The cream will whip up more lightly. The eggs will beat more quickly and take in more air and will firm up better when you cook them.

Keep your milk fresh Add a pinch of salt to a carton of milk to help it stay fresh longer. This tip works for cream as well.

Speed up cooking time When you are in a hurry, add a pinch or two of salt to the water you are boiling food in. This makes the water boil at a higher temperature so the food you are cooking will require less time to finish.

Pick up spilled eggs If you have ever dropped an uncooked egg, you will know how messy it is to clean up. Cover the spill with salt. It will draw the egg together and you can easily wipe it up with a sponge or paper towel.

DID YOU KNOW?

The concentration of salt in the human body is nearly a third of the concentration found in seawater. This is why blood, sweat and tears are so salty. Many scientists believe that humans, as well as all animals, need salt because all life evolved from the oceans. When the first land dwellers crawled out of the sea, they carried the need for salt – and a bit of the supply – with them and passed it on to their descendants.

DID YOU KNOW?

One of a number of words that salt has added to our language is salary. It comes from the Latin word salarium, which means 'salt money' and refers to that part of a Roman soldier's pay that was made in salt or used to buy salt, a life-preserving commodity. This is also the origin of the phrase 'worth one's salt'.

Extinguish grease fires Keep a box of salt next to the cooker. If a grease fire erupts in a grill pan or frying pan, throw salt on it to extinguish the flames. Never pour water on a grease fire; it will cause the grease to splatter and spread the fire. Salt is also the solution when barbecue flames from meat drippings get too high. Sprinkling salt on the coals will quell the flames without causing a lot of smoke and cooling the coals as water does.

...in the laundry

Make a quick pre-treatment If you drop a spot of grease onto your clothes when eating out, you can't get it out with water but you can stop the stain from ruining your clothing. Quickly rub salt over the spot to absorb the grease. When you get home, wash the garment as usual.

Remove perspiration stains Salt is the secret to getting rid of stubborn yellow perspiration stains on shirts. Dissolve 4 tablespoons salt in a litre of hot water. Then just sponge the garment with the solution until the stain disappears.

Set the colour in new towels The first two or three times you wash new coloured towels, add 200g salt to the wash. The salt will set the colours so the towels will remain bright for longer.

Clean your iron's metal soleplate No matter how careful you are while ironing, certain substances melt onto the iron, forming a rough surface that is difficult to remove and may leave dirty marks on your clothes. Salt crystals are the answer. Turn the iron onto high. Sprinkle table salt onto a piece of newspaper on the ironing board. Run the hot iron over the salt and you should iron away the bumps.

SALT...

...in the garden

Stop weeds in their tracks The weeds that pop up in the cracks of a garden path or patio can be difficult to eradicate. But salt can do the job. Bring a solution of about 200g salt in 400ml water to the boil. Then pour directly onto the weeds to kill them. Another equally effective method is to spread salt directly onto the weeds or unwanted grass that appear between patio bricks or blocks. Sprinkle with water or wait until rain does the job for you.

Rid the garden of snails and slugs Hungry slimy creatures are not good for your plants. But there is a simple solution. Take a container of salt into the garden and put a ring of salt around your plants. Salt is lethal to soft-bodied animals and they shouldn't attempt to breach the salt 'defences'.

Clean flowerpots without water To clean out a flowerpot so that you can reuse it without washing the pot in water, just sprinkle in a little salt and scrub off the dry dirt with a stiff brush. This method is especially useful if your potting shed is not near a water source.

...in the bath

A pre-shampoo dandruff treatment The abrasiveness of ordinary table salt works well for scrubbing out dandruff before you wash your hair. Take a salt shaker and shake some salt onto your dry scalp. Then work it through your hair, giving your scalp a massage. You should find you have worked out the dry, flaky skin before you start to shampoo your hair.

Give yourself a salt rubdown. Try this trick to remove dead skin particles and boost your circulation. While you are still in the bath or just after, when your skin is still damp, give yourself a massage with dry salt. Ordinary salt works well; the larger sea salt crystals also do the job.

DID YOU KNOW?

Salt was surely the first food seasoning. Prehistoric peoples got all the salt they needed from the meat that made up a large portion of their diet. When humans began turning to agriculture as a more reliable food source, they discovered that salt, probably taken from the sea, gave vegetables a salty taste they craved. As the millennia passed, salt gradually made life more comfortable and certain as people learned to use it to preserve food, cure hides and heal wounds.

Open drains blocked with hair It is difficult to keep hair and shampoo residues from collecting in the drain of the bath and blocking it. Dissolve the mess with 200g salt, 200g bicarbonate of soda, and 100ml white vinegar. Pour the mixture down the drain. After 10 minutes, follow up with 2 litres of boiling water. Run the hot-water tap until the drain flows freely.

Remove spots on bath enamel Yellow spots on an enamel bath or sink can be reduced by mixing up a solution of salt and turpentine in equal parts. Using rubber gloves, rub away the discoloration and then rinse thoroughly. Don't forget to ventilate the bathroom.

Condition your skin Instead of using bath salts which contain colourings and a host of additional ingredients, dissolve 200g table salt in the bath and soak as usual. Your skin will be noticeably softer. For a real treat use sea salt which comes in larger chunks and can be found in health food stores and most supermarkets.

Freshen your breath the old-fashioned way Manufactured mouthwash can contain food colouring, alcohol and sweeteners. Instead, use a recipe Grandma used and your breath will be just as sweet. Mix 1 teaspoon salt and 1 teaspoon baking soda into 100ml water. Rinse and gargle.

Sand

Protect and store garden tools Garden tools are meant to last longer than perennials, so keep them clean and protected from the elements. Fill a large (10-15 litre) bucket with builder's sand (available at builders' merchants) and pour in about a litre of clean motor oil. Plunge spades, hoes, rakes and other tools into the sand a few times to clean and lubricate them. To prevent rust, you can also leave the tool blades in the bucket of sand for storage. A large coffee can filled with sand and a little motor oil will give the same protection to secateurs and trowels.

Clean a narrow-necked vase Once a colourful bouquet is dead, it is time to thoroughly clean the vase. If the opening is too narrow for your hand, put a little sand and warm, soapy water in the vase and swish gently. The sand will do the work of cleaning the residue inside for you.

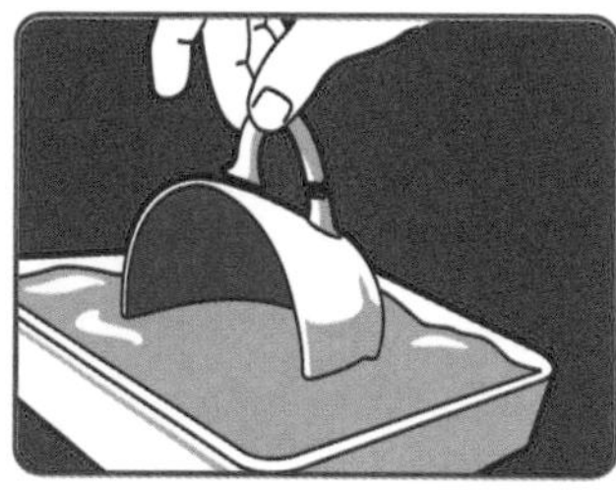

Hold items while gluing Repairing small items, such as broken china, with glue would be easy if you had three hands, one for each piece along with one to apply the glue. Since you only have two hands, try this. Stick the biggest part of the item in a small container of sand to hold it steady. Position the large piece so that when you set the broken piece in place, the piece will balance. Apply glue to both edges and stick on the broken piece. Leave the mended piece and the sand will hold it steady until the glue dries.

Carry in the car for traction A bag of sand in the boot of the car is good insurance against getting stuck or spinning out from a parking spot in icy weather. Take a clean margarine tub as well, to use as a scoop. For those with rear-wheel-drive vehicles, a bag or two of sand will also give you some extra traction.

Sandpaper

Remove pilling on sweaters If you are fighting a losing battle with the fuzz balls on your sweaters, a little sandpaper will handle them. Use any grade and rub lightly in one direction.

Remove scorches on wool Take some medium-grade sandpaper to any small scorch spots on woollen clothing. The mark left by a careless spark will be less noticeable with some light sanding around the edges.

Hold pleats while ironing If you like to keep pleats perfect, keep some fine or medium-grade sandpaper alongside the iron. Put the sandpaper under the pleat to hold it in place while you iron in a sharp fold.

Roughen slippery leather soles New shoes with slippery soles can send you flying, so take a little sandpaper and a little time to sand across the width of the soles and roughen up the slick surface. It is easier than taking new shoes to a repair shop to have new rubber soles put on.

Sharpen sewing needles Think twice before throwing out a used piece of fine sandpaper; the unused edges or corners are perfect for tucking into a sewing box. Running your sewing needles through sandpaper a few times or twisting them inside a folded piece of sandpaper, will keep them sharp.

Sharpen scissors Do your scissors cut less than crisply? Try cutting through a sheet of fine sandpaper to finish off the edge and keep every cut clean and sharp.

Remove ink stains and scuff marks from suede A little fine-grade sandpaper and a gentle touch will help to minimise an ink stain or small scuff mark on suede clothing or shoes. Afterwards, bring up the nap with a toothbrush or nailbrush. It may avoid an expensive trip to the dry cleaner.

Use to deter slugs Stop slugs from getting into potted plants by placing used sanding discs under the bases of pots, making sure the sandpaper is wider than the pot base.

Remove stubborn grout stains Sometimes a bathroom abrasive cleaner is just not abrasive enough. Get tough on grout stains with fine-grade sandpaper. Fold the sandpaper and use the folded edge to sand in the grout seam. But be careful not to sand the tiles and scratch the finish.

Open a stuck jar If you are having a hard time opening a jar, take a piece of sandpaper and place it grit side down on the lid. The sandpaper should improve your grip enough to twist off the lid.

Make an emery board If you don't have an emery board handy the next time you need to smooth your nails, use a piece of ultra-fine sandpaper instead.

{ KIDS' STUFF }

MAKE A DESIGNER T-SHIRT

You or a junior artist can make a beautiful one-of-a-kind T-shirt. Get the child to use crayons to draw a simple, bold design on the rough side of a sheet of sandpaper. Lay the T-shirt on the ironing board and slip a sheet of aluminium foil inside, between the front and back of the shirt. Place the sandpaper onto the T-shirt, design side down. Using an iron on the warm setting, press the back of the sandpaper in one spot for about 10 seconds and then move on to the next spot until the entire design has been pressed. Let the shirt cool to set the design, wash on a cool setting, then hang up to dry.

SANDWICH & FREEZER BAGS...

...around the house

Freeze a facecloth for a cold pack It is hard to predict when you will need a cold compress for a burn, teething pain or another bump or scrape. Be ready; freeze a wet facecloth in a sandwich or freezer bag. Get it out of the freezer the next time someone needs a cold pack.

Display baby teeth If a child has lost a first tooth and wants to show it off, place the tooth in a sealable plastic bag. It can be easily displayed and you won't have to worry about the tooth getting lost.

Make baby wipes for pennies You could buy expensive pre-moistened baby wipes or purchase cheap ones in bulk and hope they don't dry out before you use them. Or you can make your own wipes by placing soft paper towels in a sealable bag with a mixture of 1 tablespoon gentle antibacterial soap, 1 teaspoon baby oil and 75ml water. Use enough of the mixture to make the wipes damp, but not completely drenched.

Mould soap scraps into a new bar Slivers of soap are almost impossible to use when they get too small – but if you are feeling really frugal, start collecting them in a sealable plastic bag. When you have several (ideally of the same colour and fragrance), place the bag in a pan of warm, but not boiling, water. Watch the soap pieces melt and pour the mixture into a small mould. When it is cool, turn it out and you will have a new bar of soap.

Protect a padlock When the weather is cold enough to freeze padlocks on an outdoor shed or garage, placing a sandwich bag over the lock will stop it from getting frozen.

Feed the birds Mix some birdseed together with peanut butter in a sealable plastic bag. Seal the bag and mix the ingredients by kneading the outside of the bag. Then place the mixture in a small net bag or spread it onto a pine cone. Attach to a tree to make a delicious winter treat for garden birds.

...in the kitchen

Store grated cheese Pasta or pizza always tastes better with a dash of freshly grated Parmesan cheese. But who wants to bother with getting the grater out every time you want that taste? Instead, take a wedge of Parmesan, grate it all at once, and then double bag it in two self-closing bags to keep it completely fresh.

Make a piping bag Piping bags can be cumbersome, expensive and hard to clean. Instead, place the food you want to pipe, be it devilled-egg mix or cake icing, into a sealable bag. Push out the air and close the top. Snip off a corner of the bag to the size you want – start conservatively – and you are ready to begin squeezing.

Dispose of cooking oil Don't clog the kitchen drain with used cooking oil. Instead, wait for it to cool, then place it in a plastic bag. Throw the bag into the bin.

Colour biscuit dough without staining your hands Experienced bakers know what a mess hands can be after colouring dough. Place the prepared dough in a bag, add the drops of food colouring and squish it around until you get a uniform colour. You can use the dough at once or put it in the freezer so it is ready to use when you need it next.

Stop ice crystals on ice cream It is annoying to open up a container of ice cream from the freezer to find crystals forming on the frozen dessert. Place the half-full ice-cream container in a sealable bag and no crystals will form.

{ KIDS' STUFF }

MAKE COLOURED PASTA

Dyed dry pasta in different shapes and sizes is great for getting children's creative juices flowing. They can use it to make string jewellery or to decorate a picture frame or pencil holder. To dye the pasta, put a handful of pasta in a sealable plastic bag. Add several drops of food colouring. Next squirt in a few drops of methylated spirits. Seal the bag. Shake it up so the colouring dyes the pasta. Spread the pasta out on foil to dry.

SANDWICH & FREEZER BAGS...

...in the kitchen

Soften hard marshmallows If you store them for too long, once-fluffy marshmallow puffs can become as hard as rocks. Warm some water in a pan. Place the marshmallows in a sealable plastic bag, seal and place in the pan. The warmth will quickly soften them up.

Melt chocolate without a mess Melting chocolate in a microwave or double boiler leaves you with a messy bowl or pan to wash. Use a mess-free method instead. Warm some water in a pan (do not boil). Place the chocolate you want to melt in a sealable freezer bag. Seal and place the bag in the pan. In a few moments, you have melted chocolate, ready to bake or decorate with. You can even leave the bag sealed and snip off a bottom corner of the bag to pipe the chocolate onto a cake. When you are finished, throw the bag away.

Grease a cake tin If you are never quite sure how to handle butter or margarine when greasing a cake tin or biscuit tray, place a sandwich bag over your hand, scoop up a small amount of butter or margarine and start greasing the tin.

Use as children's gloves Helping hands are always welcome in the kitchen. But if they are little hands that will leave dirty fingerprints all over the place, place small sandwich bags over their hands before they start 'helping' you make chocolate chip cookies or cupcakes.

Make a funnel That most handy of kitchen tools, the funnel, can easily be replicated with a small sandwich bag. Fill the bag with the contents you need funnelled. Snip off the end and transfer into the required container. Then just throw away the bag when the funnelling is complete.

Keep a fizzy drink from going flat If you can't finish a fizzy drink in one go, zip the opened bottle or can into a large self-closing bag. It should help to keep the fizz intact until you are thirsty again.

{ KIDS' STUFF }

PLAY A PUDDING GAME

This is a fun and delicious activity to try when you are outdoors. Pour a small box of instant pudding mix (such as Angel Delight) into a sealable plastic bag and add the amount of milk required. Seal it up and then seal that bag into another sealable bag. Now you are ready to play football. Toss the bag around until it is mixed and the pudding forms. Open the first bag and remove the second bag. Pour the pudding into plastic dishes or tubs.

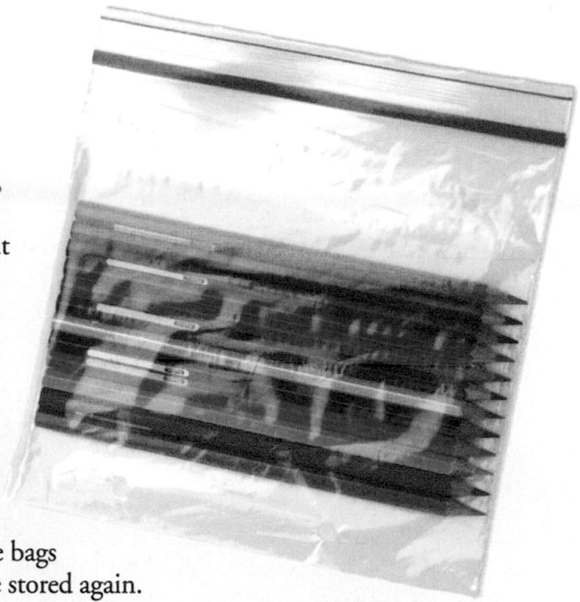

...for storing things

Make a pencil bag Do your children have trouble keeping track of their school pencils, pens and rulers? Puncture three holes along the bottom edge of a sealable freezer bag so it will fit in a three-ring binder and they can zip their supplies in and out of the bag.

Save your sweaters When storing winter sweaters, don't just put them in a box without protection. Ensure that each sweater is completely clean and dry, then place it in a sealable plastic bag and seal. They will be clean and moth-free when the cold weather rolls around again. Save the bags for next spring when the sweaters need to be stored again.

Protect your fragile breakables If a precious family heirloom, a statue, a vase or a trinket needs some extra padding when it is being put into storage, place it gently in a self-closing bag, close the bag most of the way, blow it up with air, then seal it. The air forms a protective cushion around the memento.

Create a sachet If your drawers sometimes smell musty, a small sealable bag can be an easy solution. Fill the bag with potpourri – for example, flower petals with a few crushed fragrant leaves and a couple of drops of aromatic oil. Punch a number of small holes in the bag. Then place in the drawer. Your drawers should soon smell fresh again.

Mothproof a wardrobe with cedar Fill a sealable bag with cedar chips (you may be able to get these at a pet shop for use as bedding for a mouse, gerbil or hamster). Zip it closed, then punch several small holes in it. Hang the bag in your wardrobe and the cedar smell will deter moths.

...out and about

Hold spare clothes When you are in the middle of toilet training a young child or need to be ready for accidents at mealtime, put a change of clothes for your son or daughter into a sealable plastic bag and keep it in the boot of the car. It will be easily to hand the next time you need to find them something else to wear.

Create a beach hand cleaner If you are sitting on the beach and it is time for lunch, before you start to eat, you need to get the sand off your hands. Baby powder in a sealable plastic bag is the key. Place your hands in the bag, then remove them and rub them together. The sand will be gone.

SANDWICH & FREEZER BAGS...

...out and about

Carry detergent for washing If you are planning a visit to a friend's holiday cottage and think you will be doing a few loads of washing while you are there, pre-measure some detergent into a sealable bag that you can pour it out when you need it.

Cure car sickness The last thing you need in the car is a child being sick. Make a child feel better and avoid the potential mess by placing a few cotton wool balls in a sealable plastic bag. Squirt in two drops of lavender oil. If motion sickness strikes, the child can open the bag and take a few whiffs of the oil.

Carry wet washcloth for cooling off When you are off on a long journey on a hot and sticky day, use a sealable bag to carry a few wet facecloths that have been soaked in water and lemon juice so that everyone can refresh their hands and face.

Store dirty clothes If you are away from home and a child spills chocolate ice cream down a light-coloured shirt, the stain will be much easier to remove if you can keep it from drying out before you get home. Change the item and spray the stain with stain remover, if you have a small bottle handy or just soak in water if you don't. Then seal the shirt in a sealable plastic bag and it will be ready for the wash when you get home.

Apply insect repellent to your face It can be difficult to apply insect repellent to your face without squirting yourself in the eyes or getting it on your hands. Instead, put some cotton wool balls into a plastic bag, squirt in the bug spray, seal and shake. You can now use the cotton wool balls to apply the insect repellent.

Use as a portable water dish If you take the dog with you on a long country walk, bring along some water for him in a sealable plastic bag. You can carry it in your rucksack and when you take a break, just hold the bag open while the dog has a refreshing drink.

Keep your valuables dry and afloat A capsize in a canoe or sailing dingy is nothing more than a soaking, unless you suddenly realise that your car keys and mobile phone are now submerged at the bottom of the lake. Avoid this disaster by putting valuables in a sealable bag. Blow air into it before you seal the bag so it will float. A sealable bag is perfect for keeping valuables dry by the seaside as well.

...in the bathroom

Organise your make-up Many of us have too much make-up. Ill-advised eye shadow and samples of powder and blusher fill our make-up cases. The trouble is, there are only a few cosmetics we really use every day. Put the favourites into a sealable plastic bag so you don't have to spend time hunting around for them every morning.

Make a bath cushion If you want to luxuriate in a hot bath complete with bubbles and champagne, here is a perfect, cheap accessory to make your bath experience complete: Blow up a large sealable plastic bag to make a comfortable cushion to rest your head on during your soak.

Clean a set of dentures Instead of soaking dentures in a glass, put your teeth and their cleaner in a sealable plastic bag before you go to bed at night. They will be clean and ready to use in the morning.

Shampoo

Lubricate a zip If a zip gets stuck, don't tug at it until it breaks. Put a drop of shampoo on a cotton bud and dab it onto the zip. The shampoo will help the zip to slide free and any residue will come out in the next wash.

Resize a shrunken sweater You can often bring a 'downsized' sweater back to full size again with baby shampoo and warm water. Fill a basin with warm water, squirt in some baby shampoo, and swish once with your hand. Lay the sweater on top of the water and let it sink on its own and soak for 15 minutes. Gently take your sweater out without wringing it and put it in a container, then fill the sink again with clean water. Lay the sweater on top and let it sink again to rinse. Take the sweater out, place it on a towel, and roll the towel to take out most of the moisture. Lay the sweater on a dry towel on a flat surface and gently start to reshape it. Come back to the sweater while it is drying to reshape a little more each time. Your patience should be rewarded with a full-size sweater.

Wash houseplant leaves Houseplants get dusty, but unlike furniture they need to breathe. Make a soapy solution with a few drops of shampoo in a pot of water, immerse a cloth and wring it out and wipe the dusty leaves clean.

Clean your car The grease-cutting power of shampoo works for washing a car as well. Use about 50ml shampoo to a bucket of water and sponge the car as usual. Use a dab of shampoo directly on a rag or sponge for hard-to-remove spots.

Lubricate stubborn nuts and bolts Do you have a nut and bolt that won't come apart? If a spot lubricant isn't to hand or you have run out, try a drop of shampoo. Let it seep into the threads and the bolt will be much more cooperative.

Revitalise leather shoes and handbags Bring life back to leather shoes and handbags with a little shampoo and a clean rag. Rub shampoo into worn areas in circles to clean and bring back the colour of your accessories. It will protect your shoes from salt stains as well.

DID YOU KNOW?

The word 'shampoo' was first used in the 18th century and derives from the Hindi word, champna, meaning 'to massage'. The earliest shampoos in the UK were made by boiling soap in water with fragrant herbs to make a cleansing solution for the hair. Kasey Hebert, a Londoner, is thought to have been the first actual manufacterer of shampoo; he sold bottles of 'shaempoo' in the streets near his home.

In Indonesia, rice husks and rice straw were burned to create ash which was then mixed with water to create a lather for cleaning the hair. The solution was very drying so coconut oil was then applied to the hair to add back moisture.

DID YOU KNOW?

Martha Matilda Harper was one of the pioneers of the idea of personal grooming and pampering as an experience that could be marketed and sold to a willing audience, rather than as simply a part of the personal grooming that took place in the home. She emigrated from Canada to the USA as a young girl, bringing with her a recipe for a hair 'tonic' (shampoo). Eventually she went from making her tonic in a shed to opening her own shop, where she offered the Harper Method. She encouraged wealthy women to leave their homes for a luxurious salon experience where their hair would be washed and dressed and they would be pampered by professionals.

Remove sticking plasters painlessly You don't have to brace yourself for pain when removing a plaster. Rub just a drop of shampoo on and around the plaster to let it seep through the air holes and it will come off easily.

Revitalise your feet Give your feet a pick-me-up while you sleep. Rub a little shampoo all over your feet and put on a light pair of cotton socks. When you wake up, your feet will feel smooth and silky.

Remove eye make-up You can't beat no-tears baby shampoo for a good-value eye make-up remover. Put a drop on a damp cotton wool pad to gently remove the make-up, then rinse clear.

Have bubble bath Shampoo makes a nice and sudsy bubble bath. It is especially relaxing if you love the scent of your favourite shampoo and the bath will be easier to rinse out.

Substitute for shaving cream If you are travelling and forget to bring shaving cream, don't use soap to lather up. With its softening agents, shampoo is a much better alternative.

Clean grimy hands In place of soap, a little undiluted shampoo works wonders for cleaning stubborn or sticky grime from your hands. It even works well to remove water-based paint.

Remove hair spray from walls If you have been using hair spray to kill flies or you have just noticed hair spray deposits on the bathroom walls, use some shampoo. Put some on a wet sponge to clean.Then wipe off the suds with a clean, wet sponge. Shampoo is tailor-made to handle any build-up from hair products.

Clean the bath and taps When you need to clean the bath quickly before guests arrive, use the handiest item – your shampoo. It does a great job on soap scum because it rinses clean. You can also use it to buff chrome taps to a shine.

Use to wash delicates Shampoo makes a great cleanser for delicate clothing that needs handwashing. It foams up well with just a drop and you get two cleaning products for the price of one.

DID YOU KNOW?

Johnson & Johnson introduced the world's first shampoo made specifically for infants in 1955 – containing its now-famous No More Tears formula. The company has promoted its baby shampoo to be 'as gentle to the eyes as pure water'. But, in fact, like most baby shampoos, Johnson's contains many of the same ingredients found in adult formulations, including citric acid, PEG-80 sorbitan laurate and sodium trideceth sulphate. The lack of baby tears has less to do with the shampoo's purity than it does with its relatively neutral pH.

Clean brushes and combs Oils from skin and hair can build up on combs and brushes faster than you realise. And if you keep them in a handbag or pocket, they're accumulating dust and dirt as well. Clean them thoroughly with a bath of shampoo. First comb any loose hair out of the brush, then rub a little shampoo around the bristles or along the teeth of the comb. Put a small squirt of shampoo into a tall glass of water, let the comb and brush sit for a few minutes, swish and rinse clean.

Remove sticky substances from pet fur Has Rex or Fluffy stepped on something sticky or rolled in chewing gum? Rub a tiny amount of shampoo on the spot and gently draw out the sticky mess towards the end of the fur. Rinse with a wet cloth.

* Shaving cream

Use to clean hands The next time your hands get dirty when you are camping, save the water for cooking and drinking. Squirt a little shaving cream in your hands and rub as you would liquid soap. Then wipe your hands dry with a towel.

Prevent bathroom mirrors from fogging Before you take a shower, wipe shaving cream on the bathroom mirror. It will stop it from fogging up so you don't have to wait before putting on make-up or shaving after you get out of the shower.

Remove stains from carpeting When a child spills some juice on the carpet, blot the stain, pat it with a wet sponge, squirt some shaving cream on it, and then wipe clean with a damp sponge. Use the same technique for small stains on your clothes; shaving cream can remove the spot of breakfast you discover during a quick check in the bathroom.

Silence a squeaky door hinge A squeaky door hinge can ruin a child's peaceful nap. But with its ability to seep into nooks and crannies, dabbing a little shaving cream on the hinge will let you check on a baby undetected.

Sheets

Make a beanbag bull's-eye To diffuse youthful energy on a rainy day, draw a large bull's-eye on an old sheet. Tape the sheet to a wall and let children throw beanbags at it.

Use as a tablecloth When it is your turn to host the whole family at Christmas and you need to use every table in the house, but just have enough tablecloths, a patterned sheet will make an attractive festive table covering.

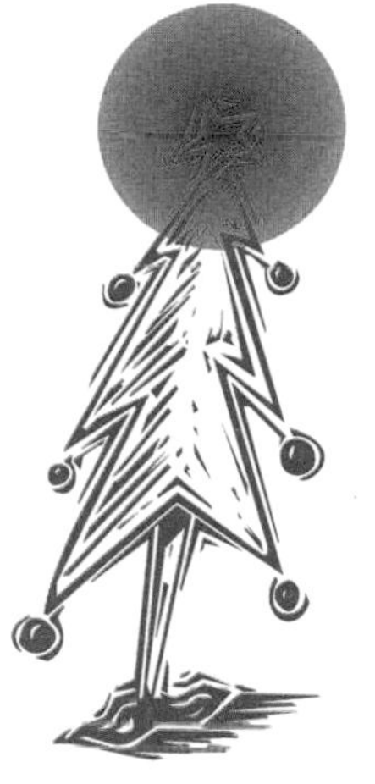

Repel deer from your garden Circle the garden with a cord set about 1 metre above the ground, then tie small strips of old white sheeting to it every 60cm; a tail-height flash of white is a danger sign to a deer.

Scoop up autumn leaves There is no reason to strain your back by constantly lifting piles of leaves into a wheelbarrow or bag. Just rake the leaves onto an old sheet laid on the ground. Then gather the four corners and drag the leaves to the kerb or leaf pile.

Wrap up an old Christmas tree After removing the decorations, wrap an old sheet around the tree so that you can carry or pull it out of the house without leaving a trail of pine needles.

Shoe bags

Bring order to a cleaning cupboard A pocketed hanging shoe bag is a brilliant organiser in a cleaning cupboard. Use the pockets to store sponges, scrubbing brushes and other cleaning utensils and even some bottles of cleaning products. It is also good for separating dusters and cleaning cloths so you will always have the right one for the job.

Tidy up an office area Free up some valuable drawer space in the office with an over-the-door shoe holder. Its pockets can store lots of supplies that you need to keep handy, like scissors, staples and markers. You can use the pockets to organise bills and other 'to do' items as well.

Banish clutter from the bathroom A shoe bag can keep lots of everyday bathroom items handy and tidy. Brushes, shampoo, hand towels, hair spray – almost everything can be stored at your fingertips instead of cluttering the shower or edge of the bath.

Organise a child's room A shoe bag hung over the bedroom door is a great way to help your children to organise their small toys. Whether your child likes dolls, dinosaurs or different-coloured building bricks, a shoe bag puts the toys on display and the children can keep them sorted themselves.

Keep car toys and games to hand Cut a shoe bag to fit the back of a car seat, fill it with toys, books and games and let children make their own choices for back seat entertainment.

Keep a bedroom tidily sorted Instead of lifting a hanger to get at a belt, or rummaging through a drawer for a scarf, try organising clothing accessories with an over-the-door shoe bag. The pockets can be used in the bedroom for keeping socks, gloves, scarves, ties and other accessories tidy and accessible.

*Shoe boxes

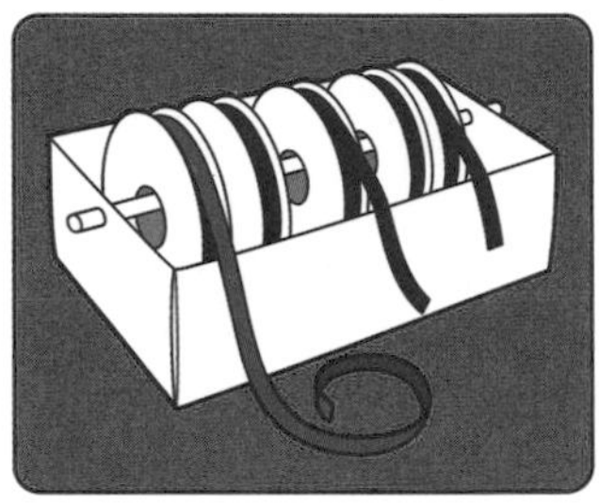

Make a gift ribbon dispenser Use a shoe box to make a ribbon dispenser so you always have a good selection to hand when you are wrapping presents.

1. Take a used broom handle or piece of a bamboo garden cane – anything you can use as a small dowel – and cut it a little longer than the length of the shoe box.
2. Cut two holes for the dowel, one in each short end of the box, at a height where a spool of ribbon slipped onto the dowel would spin freely.
3. Slip the ribbon spools onto the dowel as you poke it from one end of the shoe box through to the other. Once the dowel is in place, you can gaffer tape it at either short end to keep it from slipping out.
4. You could also cut holes along one long side of the shoe box for each spool of ribbon, and pull a little bit of each ribbon through the hole.

Get everything organised There are lots of ways shoe boxes can help you to get organised besides collecting old photos and receipts. Label the boxes and use them to store treasures, bank statements, pay slips, bills to be paid and other items you want to keep track of. For a neater appearance, cover the boxes with wrapping paper or any other decorative paper.

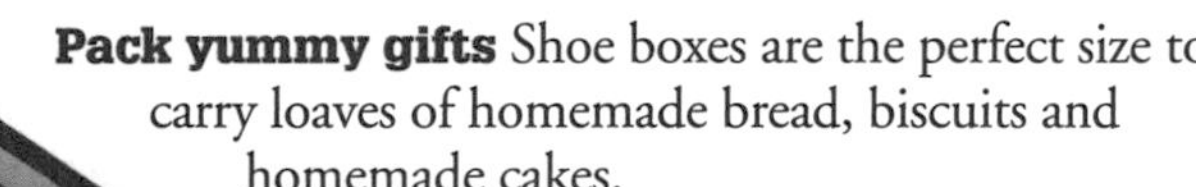

Pack yummy gifts Shoe boxes are the perfect size to carry loaves of homemade bread, biscuits and homemade cakes.

Use as a whelping box If your dog or cat is expecting puppies or kittens, reduce the risk of the mother rolling onto a newborn creature and smothering it by placing the puppies or kittens in a towel-lined shoe box while the others are being born.

 Shower curtains

Line cabinet shelves Don't discard old vinyl shower curtains or tablecloths. Turn them into easy-to-clean shelf liners instead. Simply cut to shelf size and set in place, using some rubber adhesive such as Copydex to hold them if you prefer. When they need cleaning, just wipe over with a damp sponge.

Make a protective apron When you are doing messy jobs around the house, wear a homemade apron made from an old shower curtain. Make a full-length apron, with a top as well as a skirt. Use pinking shears to cut the vinyl to size. Poke two holes at the top of the vest for cords or ribbons to tie around your neck and make two more holes in the sides so you can tie it around your waist.

Durable painting dustsheet Save an old shower curtain and use it as a protective cloth the next time you paint a room. The material is heavier and more durable than that used in the plastic dustsheets you can buy.

Protect the floor under a high chair Even the most well behaved babies leave a mess on the floor when they eat. Protect your floor or carpet by cutting a 1 metre square from an old shower curtain and placing it under the baby's high chair. You can use any leftover scraps to make additional bibs.

Cover picnic tables and benches When you are having a picnic, use an old shower curtain as a makeshift tablecloth. An extra shower curtain can be folded over a sticky or dirty picnic bench before you sit down to eat.

Protect a table when cutting fabric Next time you are cutting out a sewing pattern on the dining room table, put a shower curtain or plastic tablecloth under it before you cut. The scissors will glide more easily across the surface and you will protect the tabletop from an accidental nick.

DID YOU KNOW?

In the early 1920s, Waldo Semon, a rubber scientist, was none too thrilled when he first discovered polyvinyl chloride, commonly known as vinyl. He was trying to develop a new adhesive and it didn't stick at all. But Waldo was quick to recognise the material's potential and began experimenting with it, even making golf balls and shoe heels out of it. Soon vinyl products like raincoats and shower curtains reached the consumer. Today vinyl is the second-largest selling plastic in the world, used for everything from wallpapers, to roofing and cladding materials, plastic sheeting and countless other products.

Block weeds in mulched beds Old shower curtains will also come in handy next time you do any landscaping using a mulch such as gravel or bark chips. Place the curtain under the mulching material to prevent weeds from poking through.

Skateboards

Make a shelf Is your child an avid skateboarder? When he or she is ready for a new skateboard, turn the old one into a shelf for the bedroom. Support it on a couple of metal shelf brackets. You can remove the wheels or leave them on.

Use as a painter's scooter. Crawling along the floor to paint a skirting board can get very tedious. Borrow your child's skateboard and save your knees. Sit cross-legged on the skateboard and roll along with the paintbrush and can.

Soap

Loosen a stuck zip Rub a jammed zip loose with a bar of soap along the teeth. The lubricants in the soap will get it moving.

Unstick furniture drawers If you have a sticky drawer, rub the bottom of the drawer and the supports they rest on with a bar of soap.

Remove a broken lightbulb If a bulb breaks while it is still screwed in, don't chance nicks and cuts trying to remove it. First, turn off the power. Insert the corner of a large, dry bar of soap into the socket. Give it a few turns and the base will unscrew.

DID YOU KNOW?

Hanging a perfumed bar of soap has been touted as one way to keep deer off your property. But how long or how well soap works as a repellent depends on a number of factors, including the type of plant you are protecting and the location of the soap. However, some studies have shown that soap, especially tallow-based soap, will stop deer from making lunch out of your shrubbery.

TIP* HOMEMADE SOAP

Handcrafted soap makes a great gift and is easy to make. You need a solid bar of soap base (either glycerine or a vegetable base); soap moulds; a clean, dry can; a double boiler; food colouring and essential oil. Place the soap base in the can and put the can in a double boiler, which has water in the top as well as the bottom, and heat gently until it melts. To add colour, mix in food colouring. Spray a mould with non-stick cooking spray and fill it halfway with melted soap base. Add a few drops of essential oil and fill the rest with glycerine. Let it harden.

Lubricate screws and saw blades Lubricating with soap makes metal move through wood much more easily. Rub some soap on a handsaw blade for easier cutting and twist a screw into a bar of soap before screwing it in.

Say farewell to fleas If you have a flea infestation in the carpet, put a few drops of liquid soap and some water on a plate. Place the plate on the floor next to a lamp. Fleas love light – they will jump onto the plate and drown in the soap.

Deodorise a car If you want the car to smell nice, but are tired of tree-shaped pine deodorisers, place a little piece of your favourite-smelling soap in a mesh bag and hang it from the rearview mirror.

Mark a hem Don't buy marking chalk. A thin sliver of soap, like the ones left when a bar is just about finished, works just as well when you are marking a hem and the markings will wash straight out.

Make a pin holder Here is an easy-to-make alternative to a pincushion. Wrap a bar of soap in fabric and tie the fabric in place with a ribbon. Stick in the pins. As a bonus, the soap lubricates the pins, making them easier to insert.

Prevent cast-iron marks Rub the bottom of a cast-iron pot with a bar of soap before heating it over a sooty open flame and you won't get any dirty marks on the base during cooking.

Keep stored clothes fresh Pack a bar of your favourite scented soap when you store clothes or luggage. It will keep clothes smelling fresh until next season and prevent musty odours developing in your luggage.

Save those soap slivers When soap slivers get too small to handle, don't throw them away. Make a small slit in a sponge and put the slivers inside. The soap will last for several more washings. Or make a facecloth that is easy for children to hold by putting the soap slivers in a towelling sock.

Socks

Protect stored breakables Protect Grandma's precious vase or your china dog collection by wrapping it up. Slip the item into a sock to help to protect it from breaking or chipping.

Cover children's shoes when packing Before you pack trainers and other shoes into a child's suitcase, cover each one with an adult-size sock to protect the rest of the clothing.

Polish your car A big soft old sock makes a perfect hand mitt for buffing the wax on your car after you have cleaned it.

Keep hands clean when changing a tyre If you ever suffer a flat tyre on your way to a party or job interview, you will thank yourself for having the foresight to keep a pair of socks in the boot of the car. Put the socks on your hands while handling the tyre and they'll be clean when you arrive at your destination.

Protect floor surfaces The next time you need to move a heavy table or sofa across a smooth floor, put socks over the legs and it should slide about easily.

Store a pair of protective goggles Goggles won't fit in a glasses case, so put them into a sock to protect them from getting scratched. You can even nail or screw the sock to the wall or bench so you will always know where the goggles are.

Make a wash bag for delicate lingerie Protect your precious best underwear in the washing machine; slip them into a sock and tie the ends.

Use as cleaning mitts Save old or solo socks to use as cleaning mitts. Slip them on your hands and they are great for cleaning in tight corners and crevices.

Clean shutter and blind slats Don't waste money on expensive gadgets for cleaning the slats on a venetian blind. Just slip a sock over your hand and gently rub the dust off. You can use some dusting spray on the sock, if you like.

DID YOU KNOW?

Ginger has long been a traditional remedy for nausea, and recent scientific research has shown that ginger ale does work better than a placebo. Ginger ale was first made in Ireland in 1851, but it was not until 1907 that it was commercially marketed by a Toronto pharmacist named John McLaughlin. McLaughlin kept trying new formulas until he patented what is now known throughout the world as Canada Dry Ginger Ale. McLaughlin was one of the pioneers of the technology of mass bottling, which allowed customers to take fizzy drinks home in bottles, rather than drinking them at a soda fountain.

Clean rough plaster walls Use nylon socks instead of a sponge or cloth to clean rough plaster walls. They won't leave specks of lint as a cotton cloth would.

Wash small stuffed animals When your child's favourite stuffed toy needs a bath, slip it, and any other small stuffed animals into a sock and tie the end to prevent buttons, eyes and other decorative items from coming loose.

Protect a wall from ladder marks To prevent marks on a wall when you are leaning a ladder against it, place socks over the top ends of the ladder. Always make sure that someone is holding the ladder.

Soft drinks

Clean car battery terminals The acidic properties of fizzy drinks will help to eliminate corrosion from a car battery. Nearly all carbonated soft drinks contain carbonic acid, which helps to remove stains and dissolve rust deposits. Pour a soft drink over the battery terminals and let it sit for a while. Remove the sticky residue with a wet sponge.

Loosen rusted-on nuts and bolts Don't struggle with rusted-on nuts and bolts. A fizzy drink can help to loosen them. Soak a rag in the fizzy drink and wrap it around the bolt for several minutes.

Make cut flowers last longer Don't throw away the last drops of a bottle of soft drink. Pour about 50ml into the water in a vase full of cut flowers. The sugar in the drink will make the blossoms last longer. Note: If you have a clear vase and want the water to remain clear, use a clear drink, such as Sprite or 7-Up.

Clean the toilet Eliminate dirt and smells with a can of soft drink. Pour it into the toilet, let sit for an hour, then scrub and flush.

Keep drains from blocking If you have a slow drain and no drain cleaner in the house, pour a 2 litre bottle of cola down the drain to help to remove the blockage.

Get gum out of hair When a child gets gum in her hair, put the gummy hair in a bowl with some cola. Let it soak for a few minutes and then rinse.

Make a roast ham moist To make a ham juicier, pour a can of cola over the traditional ham recipe and follow the usual baking instructions.

Clean coins If coin collecting is your hobby, you can use cola to clean your hoard. Place the coins in a small dish and soak in cola for a brilliant shine. Don't do this with very rare and valuable coins.

Remove oil stains from concrete Here is an effective way to remove oil stains from concrete driveways and garage floors. Take a small bag of cat litter, a few cans of cola, a stiff bristle broom, bucket, liquid laundry detergent, bleach, eye protection and rubber gloves. Cover the stain with a thin layer of cat litter and brush it in. Sweep up the litter and pour cola to cover the area. Work the cola in with a bristle broom, and leave the cola for about 20 minutes. Mix 50ml laundry detergent with 50ml bleach in 4 litres warm water and use it to mop up the mess.

Sparkling mineral water

Make pancakes fluffier If you like pancakes to be fluffy, substitute sparkling mineral water for the liquid called for in the recipes. You'll be amazed at how light and fluffy they turn out.

Give plants a mineral bath Don't throw out leftover mineral water. Use it to water indoor and outdoor plants. The minerals in the water help green plants to grow. For maximum benefit, try to water your plants with sparkling mineral water about once a week.

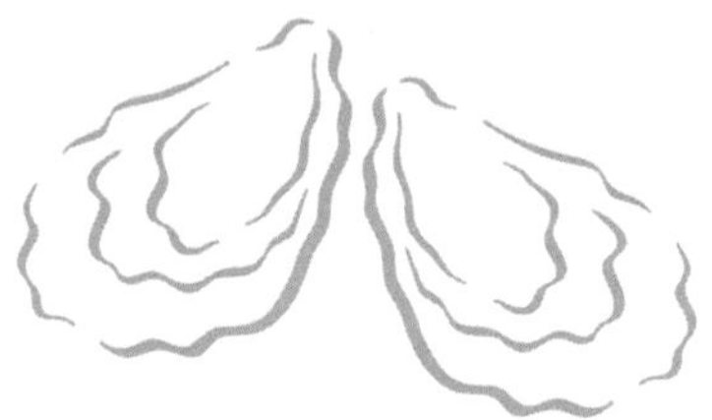

Help shell oysters If you love oysters but find removing them from their shells nearly impossible, try soaking them in sparkling mineral water before you open them. The oysters won't exactly jump out of their shells, but they will be much easier to open.

DID YOU KNOW?

Bubbling water has been associated with good health since the time of the ancient Romans, who enjoyed drinking mineral water almost as much as they liked bathing in it. Many Europeans now drink more than 100 litres of bottled water each year. It takes 1.3 million metric tons of carbon dioxide to provide all the fizz for the mineral waters and other drinks consumed annually in Europe.

Clean precious gems Soak diamonds, rubies, sapphires and emeralds in sparkling mineral water to give them a bright sheen. Simply place them in a glass full of sparkling mineral water and let them soak overnight.

Remove fabric stains Clean grease stains from synthetic knitted fabrics by pouring sparkling mineral water on the stain and scrubbing gently. Scrub more vigorously to remove stains on carpets or less delicate articles of clothing.

Clean a car windscreen Keep a spray bottle filled with sparkling mineral water in the boot of your car. Use it to help to remove bird droppings and greasy stains from the windscreen. The fizzy water speeds the cleaning process.

Restore hair colour If your blonde hair turns greenish when you swim in a pool with too much chlorine, don't panic. Rinse your hair with sparkling mineral water and it will change back to its original colour.

Tame your tummy Cold sparkling mineral water with a dash of bitters will work wonders on an upset stomach that is caused by indigestion or a hangover.

Clean worktops and fixtures Pour sparkling mineral water directly onto stainless-steel worktops, ranges and sinks. Wipe with a soft cloth, rinse with warm water and wipe dry. To clean porcelain fixtures, simply pour sparkling mineral water over them and wipe with a soft cloth. There is no need for soap or rinsing and the mineral water will not mar the finish. Give the inside of the fridge a good clean with a weak solution of sparkling mineral water and a little bit of salt.

Remove rust To loosen rusty nuts and bolts, pour some sparkling mineral water over them. The carbonation bubbles the rust away.

Eliminate urine stains When a child or pet has had an accident, blot up as much urine as possible, then pour sparkling mineral water over the stained area and immediately blot again. It will get rid of the stain and help to reduce the unpleasant smell.

Make cleaning cast iron simple Food tastes delicious when it is cooked in cast iron, but cleaning heavy pots and pans with a sticky mess inside is a pain. You can make cleaning easier by pouring some sparkling mineral water in the pan while it is still warm. The bubbly water will keep the mess from sticking.

Spices

Make a hair tonic Try a homemade tonic to enhance your natural colour and give it shine. For dark hair, use 1 tablespoon crumbled sage or 1 sprig chopped fresh rosemary or a mixture of 1 teaspoon allspice, 1 teaspoon ground cinnamon and ½ teaspoon ground cloves. For blonde hair, use 1 tablespoon chamomile. Pour 200ml boiling water over the herb or spice mix, let it steep for 30 minutes, strain it through a coffee filter and let it cool. Pour it repeatedly over your hair as a final rinse after shampooing.

TIP* TOOTHACHE AND OIL OF CLOVES

If you have a toothache, get to a dentist as soon as possible. Meanwhile, oil of cloves may provide temporary relief. Place a drop directly into the aching tooth or apply it with a cotton bud. But don't put it directly on the gums. Eugenol, an active ingredient in the spice oil, is a natural pain reliever.

Keep feet smelling sweet If you use sage only to make stuffing for a roast, then you have been missing out. Sage is great for preventing foot odour because it kills the odour-causing bacteria that grow on your feet in the warm, moist environment inside your shoes. Crumble a leaf or two into your shoes before you put them on. At the end of the day, just shake the remains into the bin.

Keep your Thermos fresh If you have just uncapped the Thermos bottle you haven't used for six months and it smells musty, place a whole clove inside the flask before putting the cap on to stop it from happening next time. A teaspoon of salt works too. Be sure to empty and rinse the Thermos before using it.

Scent your home What could be more welcoming than the smell of something delicious cooking? Instead of using commercial air fresheners, throw a handful of whole cloves or a cinnamon stick in to a pan of water and keep it simmering on the stove for half an hour. Or place a teaspoon or two of the ground spices on a baking sheet and place it in a 110°C/gas mark ¼ oven with the door ajar for 30 minutes. Either way, your house will have a delicious natural fragrance.

Keep woollens whole Woollen clothing can last a lifetime – if you keep the moths away. Preserve cold-weather clothing using sachets of cloves. Buy some small drawstring muslin bags at a health food store (or you can make your own) and fill each one with a handful of whole cloves. To prevent any transfer of oils or colour to clothes and to contain any spills, put the sachet in a small plastic bag, but don't seal it. Attach it to a hanger in your wardrobe or tuck one in your chest of drawers to protect your woollens from the attentions of hungry moths.

Stamp out silverfish These insects frequent places with lots of moisture, such as kitchens, bathrooms and laundry rooms. Hang an aromatic sachet containing sage or bay leaves on a hook in your bathroom and behind the washing machine or keep a few in decorative baskets along the skirtings.

Control insects in the garden Don't use harsh pesticides to control small-insect infestations outdoors. If ants are swarming on the garden path, add 1 tablespoon ground black pepper (or another strong-smelling ground spice, such as ground cloves or dry mustard) to 200g sifted white flour and sprinkle the mixture on and around the ants. They will vanish within the hour. Sweep the dry mix into the garden instead of trying to hose it off; water will just make it gooey.

Deodorise bottles for re-use To re-use wide-mouthed pickle jars and get rid of the pickle smell, add 1 teaspoon dry mustard to 1 litre of water, fill the jar and let it soak overnight. It will smell fresh by morning. This solution banishes the odour of tomatoes, garlic and other foods with strong scents.

Shield your vegetable garden For centuries, gardeners have used companion planting to repel insect pests. Aromatic plants such as basil, marigolds and sage are all reputed to send a signal to insects to go elsewhere, so try planting some near your prized vegetables. Mint, thyme, dill and sage are historic favourites near cabbage family plants (cabbage, broccoli, cauliflower and brussels sprouts) for their supposed ability to fend off cabbage-munching moths. Best of all, you can eat the savoury herbs.

DID YOU KNOW?

What is the difference between a spice and a herb? The basic guideline is this: if it is made from a plant's leaf, it is a herb; if it is made from the bark, fruit, seed, stem or root, it is a spice. Parsley and basil are typical herbs because we eat their leaves. Cinnamon (the bark of a tree) and pepper (the fruit of a vine) are considered spices. Salt, perhaps the most essential food enhancer of all but not a plant product at all is a seasoning – the word that describes anything used to flavour foods, regardless of its origin.

Keep ants at bay Flour, sugar and paprika can all fall prey to ants. Keep cooking essentials safe by slipping a bay leaf inside storage containers. If you are concerned about flour or sugar picking up a bay leaf flavour, tape the leaf to the inside of the canister lid. This trick works inside cabinets, too, where sachets of sage, bay, stick cinnamon or whole cloves will smell pleasant while discouraging ants.

Deter plant-eating animals Everyone knows that hot peppers make your mouth burn. So if animal invaders are attacking ornamental plants, the solution may be to make them too 'hot' for the animals. In fact, hot peppers are the basis for many commercial rodent repellents. Chop up the hottest pepper you can find and combine it with 1 tablespoon ground cayenne pepper and 2 litres water. Boil the mixture for 15-20 minutes, then let it cool. Strain it through cheesecloth, add 1 tablespoon washing-up liquid and pour it into a spray bottle. Spray vulnerable plants liberally every five days or so. The spray works best for rabbits, but may also deter deer, especially if used in combination with commercial products.

* Sponges

Keep your veggies fresh Moisture that collects at the bottom of the crisper in the fridge will make vegetables go off. Extend the life of fresh vegetables by lining the bins with dry sponges. When you notice that the sponges are wet, wring them out and let them dry before putting them back in the fridge. Every now and then, between uses, let them soak in some warm water with a splash of bleach to discourage the growth of mould.

Make flowerpots hold water longer If you find that houseplants dry out too quickly after watering, try this simple trick for keeping the soil moist longer when you repot them. Tuck a damp sponge in the bottom of the pot before filling it with soil. It will act as a water reservoir. And it will also help to prevent a gusher if you accidentally overwater.

{ KIDS' STUFF }

MAKE A CHILDREN'S GARDEN

Making seeds grow seems magical to young children. For an easy and renewable play garden with a minimum of mess, all you need is an old soap dish, a sponge, and seeds of a plant such as lobelia. Cut the sponge to fit the dish, add water until it is moist but not sopping and sprinkle the seed liberally over the top. Prop an inverted glass bowl over it until the seeds begin to grow. A bright window and a daily watering will keep it going for weeks.

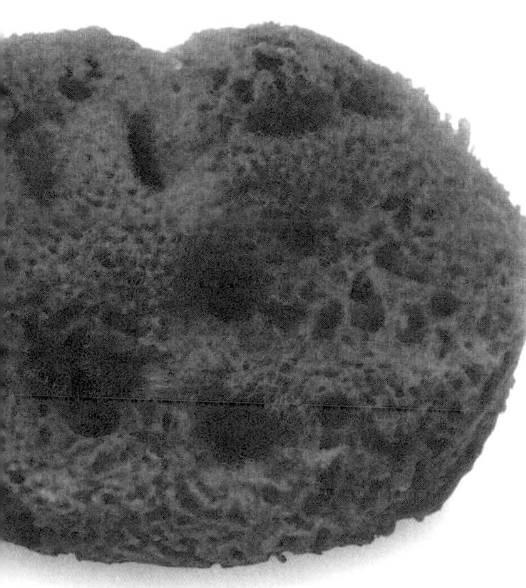

Make an 'unwelcome' mat for garden visitors Anyone who has ever cleaned a floor with ammonia knows that the smell of this strong, everyday household cleaner is overpowering. Throw browsing animals off the scent of ripening vegetables in a vegetable garden by soaking old sponges in your floor-cleaning solution and distributing them wherever you expect the next garden raid.

Sop up drips from soggy umbrellas When it has been raining, the family has been tramping in and out with umbrellas all day and your umbrella stand has only a shallow receptacle to catch drips, protect the hall floor from major flooding by placing a large sponge in the base of the stand. Even if you forget to squeeze it out, the sponge should dry on its own as soon as the weather clears.

Protect fragile items If you are posting or storing small, fragile valuables that won't be harmed by a little contact with water, sponges are a clever way to cushion them. Dampen a sponge, wrap it around the delicate item and use a rubber band to secure it. As it dries, the sponge will conform to the contours of your crystal ashtray or porcelain figurine. To unpack it, just dip the item in water again. You can even use the sponge again.

Stop soap getting slimy A shower is so refreshing in the morning, until you reach for the soap and are treated to the slimy sensation of a bar that has been left to marinate in its own suds. Your soap will last longer if you place a sponge on the soap dish. It will absorb moisture so the soap can dry out.

Lift lint from fabric To quickly remove lint and pet fur from clothes and upholstery, give the fabric a quick wipe with a dampened and wrung-out sponge. Just run your fingers over the sponge and the unwanted fluff will come off in a ball for easy disposal.

Spray bottles

Cool off in summer Whether you are jogging around the park, taking a breather between tennis matches, or just sitting out in the sun, a recycled spray bottle filled with water can make a refreshing summer companion. Use it to cool off during and after a workout or while sunbathing on the beach or in the garden.

Mist your houseplants Keep houseplants healthy and happy by using an empty trigger-type spray bottle as a plant mister. Clean the bottle by filling it with equal parts water and vinegar; don't use liquid soap, as you may not be able to get it all out, let the solution sit for an hour, and rinse it out thoroughly with cold water. Repeat if necessary. Then, fill the bottle with lukewarm warm water, and use it to frequently give your plants a soothing, misty shower.

Help with the laundry An empty spray bottle can always be put to good use in the laundry. Use clean, recycled bottles to spray water on clothes as you are ironing. Or fill a spray bottle with stain remover solution so that you can apply it to your garments without having to blot up drips.

Spray away garden pests Keep a few recycled spray bottles on hand to use around the garden. Here are two immediate uses:

- Fill one with undiluted white vinegar to get rid of weeds and grass poking out of cracks in concrete, as well as ants and other insects, but be careful not to spray it on the plants; the high acidity could kill them.
- For an effective homemade insecticide recipe that works on most slugs and snails, but won't harm plants, mix several cloves of crushed garlic, 50ml canola oil, 3 tablespoons hot pepper sauce and ½ teaspoon mild liquid soap in 4 litres of water. Pour some into your spray bottle and shake well before using.

Keep car windows clean Include a recycled spray bottle filled with windscreen cleaner in the boot of your car as part of a roadside emergency kit. Use it to clean off the car's headlamps, mirrors and windows whenever necessary. During the winter months, mix in ½ teaspoon antifreeze and you can spray it on to melt the ice on your windscreen or mirrors.

Squirt bottles

Stop cooking oil drips Fill a cleaned, recycled squirt bottle with olive oil or another favourite cooking oil. It is a lot easier to handle than a jar or bottle and you can pour precisely the right amount of oil over your salads or into a frying pan without having to worry about drips or spills.

Substitute for a baster If you can't find a kitchen baster, a cleaned squeeze bottle makes a good substitute. Simply squeeze out some air first, and use it to suck up the fat from roasts and soups. You can even use it to distribute marinades and drippings over meat.

Dispense condiments Recycled squirt bottles are good for storing condiments and other foods that are typically sold in jars, such as mayonnaise, salad dressing, jam and honey. In addition to having fewer sticky jars in the fridge or cupboard, you will also reduce the washing-up load by eliminating the need for knives or spoons. Make sure you give the bottles a thorough cleaning before using them again.

Clean out crevices A clean, empty squeeze bottle may be just the cleaning tool you need to get the dust out of the corners of picture frames and other tight spaces. Use it to give a good blast of air to blow out the dirt you can't otherwise reach.

Let children have a squirt party Fill up a few clean squeeze bottles with water, then give them to your children to squirt each other with in the garden on a hot summer day. It will keep them stay cool while they burn off some energy.

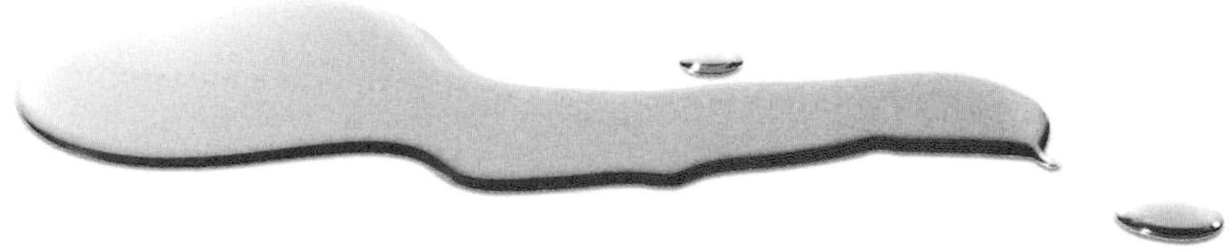

Steel wool

Scrub up filthy trainers If your trainers are bearing the brunt of too many treks or runs through the mud, some steel wool may keep them out of the dustbin. Moisten a steel wool soap pad and gently scrub away at stains and stuck-on grime. Wipe them clean with a damp sponge and you may be able to enjoy many more months of wear. (It is never a good idea to put trainers that you use for serious sport in the machine as it may cause them to fall apart.)

Sharpen a pair of scissors Sometimes you just need a small piece of a steel wool soap pad for a minor job. Cutting it in half with a pair or scissors will help to keep the scissors sharp while giving you the pint-size pad you need for your project.

Crayons begone A creative toddler has just made a work of crayon art on paper. Unfortunately, it is on the wallpaper. Use a bit of a steel wool soap pad to just skim the surface, making strokes in one direction instead of scrubbing in a circle and the wall should come clean.

Shoo heel marks away The black marks that rubber soles leave behind don't come off with a mop, no matter how hard you try. To rid a vinyl floor of smudges, gently rub the surface with a moistened steel wool soap pad. When the heel mark is gone, wipe the floor clean with a damp sponge.

Rebuff rodents Mice and rats are experts at finding every conceivable entrance into a house. When you discover one of their entry points, stuff it full of steel wool. Steel wool is much more effective than foam or newspaper because even dedicated gnawers are unlikely to try to chew through such a sharp blockade.

Keep garden tools in good shape Nothing will extend the life of gardening tools like a good clean at the end of each growing season. Use a piece of fine steel wool, saturate it with household oil such as WD-40 that you would use on a squeaky door hinge and rub the rust off garden shears, secateurs, spades, forks, hoes and anything else with metal parts. Wipe them clean with a dry rag, sharpen the blades and reapply a little oil before storing them for the winter.

TIP* NOT FOR STAINLESS STEEL

Steel wool may make stainless steel look better, but it scratches the surface and will ultimately hasten rusting. Most cutlery manufacturers caution against using any abrasive on stainless steel. The safest way to care for stainless steel is to wash with a sponge and mild soap and water.

Straws

Keep jewellery chains unknotted If you are not careful, fine chains on necklaces and pendants can get hopelessly tangled and kinked. To stop this from happening, run each chain through a straw cut to just under half the length of the chain and close the clasp before putting it away.

Give flowers needed height To perfect a flower arrangement where just a few of the flowers aren't tall enough, stick each of the too-short stems into plastic straws, trimming the straw to get the desired height and inserting them into the vase.

Get slow ketchup flowing Anticipation is great, but tomato ketchup that comes out of the bottle while your hamburger or cooked breakfast are still hot is even better. If the ketchup is recalcitrant, insert a straw all the way into the bottle and stir it around a little to get the flow started.

Improvise some foamy fun To make a cheap and easy game that will work even with a large group of children, cut the ends of some plastic straws at a sharp angle and set out a shallow dish of washing-up liquid diluted with a little bit of water. Dip a straw in the liquid and blow through the other end. All children love the piles of bubbles that result.

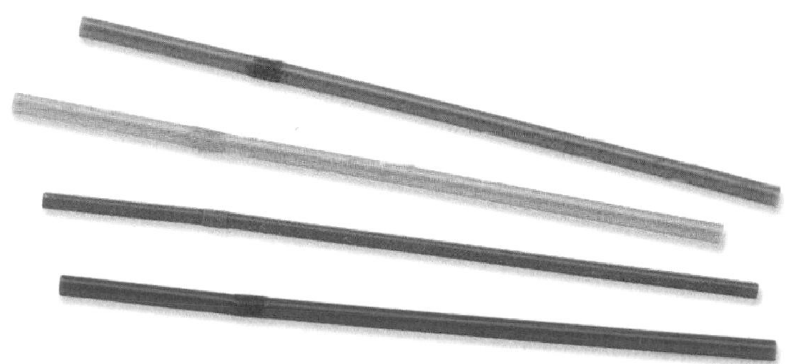

DID YOU KNOW?

It was the quest for a perfectly cold mint julep that led to the invention of the drinking straw. Mint juleps are served chilled and their flavour diminishes as they warm up. Holding a glass heats the contents, so the custom was to drink mint juleps through natural straws made from a section of hollow grass stem, usually rye. But the rye imparted an undesirable 'grassy' flavour. In 1888 Marvin Stone, a manufacturer of paper cigarette holders, fashioned a paper tube through which to sip his favourite drink. When other mint julep aficionados began clamouring for paper straws, he realised that he had a hot new product on his hands.

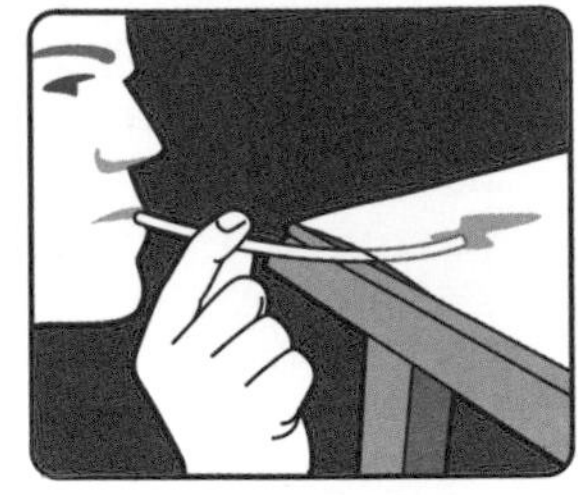

Fix loose veneer When the veneer on a favourite piece of furniture is coming away at the edges, although a dab of glue is a simple remedy, veneer can be very brittle and you may break off a piece by lifting it up. As a solution, cut a length of plastic drinking straw and press it to flatten it slightly. Fold it in half and fill one half with glue, slowly dripping the glue in from the top. Push the filled half gently under the veneer and gently blow in the glue. Wipe off any excess, cover the area with greaseproof paper and a wood block and clamp it overnight to dry.

Make a pull-toy protector Pull-along toys are perennial favourites of young children, but you can spend all day untying the knots that a toddler will inevitably put in the pull string. By running the string through a plastic straw (or a series of them), it should stay untangled.

Have seasonings, will travel Perhaps you are on a low-salt diet and need a low-salt alternative to use when dining out or you want salt and pepper to season your packed sandwich or salad just before you eat it. Straws provide an easy way to take along small amounts of dry seasonings. Fold one end over and tape it shut, fill it, and fold and tape the other end. If moisture may be a problem, use a plastic straw.

* String

Polish silverware more easily Polishing silver can be curiously satisfying – but it can be difficult to get a good result with intricate implements. Run a length of string through some silver polish and use it to get at the hard-to-reach spots between the tines of a fork.

Stop the sound of a dripping tap If a leaky tap is keeping you awake at night, you can silence it until a plumber arrives. Tie a piece of string to the fixture with one end at the point where the water is oozing out and the other end hanging down to the bottom of the sink. The water droplets will travel silently down the string instead of driving you to distraction.

Use as a straight-line guide Trimming a long hedge straight is a near-impossible feat unless you use a visual guide. Drive two stakes into the ground, one at each end of the hedge. Measure the height you want for the trimmed hedge, then run the string between the two stakes, tying it to each one at that exact height. As you clip away, cut down to the string line but no farther; the top of your hedge will be completely straight and true.

Outline garden features When you are planning a design for a new garden, lay white string on the ground to outline paths and beds. From an upstairs window or other high vantage point, you will be able to tell at a glance if borders are straight and whether the layout is working.

Measure irregular objects A cloth tape measure is the ideal tool for measuring odd-shaped objects, but you may not have one if you don't sew. Wrap a plain piece of string around the item instead, then hold it up to a ruler to get the measurement you need.

Plant perfectly straight rows It is harder than it looks to make straight garden rows freehand. String can be used in two ways to keep plants in line:

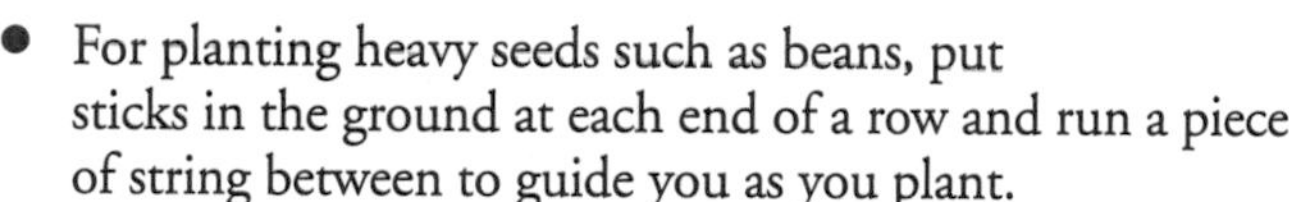

- For planting heavy seeds such as beans, put sticks in the ground at each end of a row and run a piece of string between to guide you as you plant.

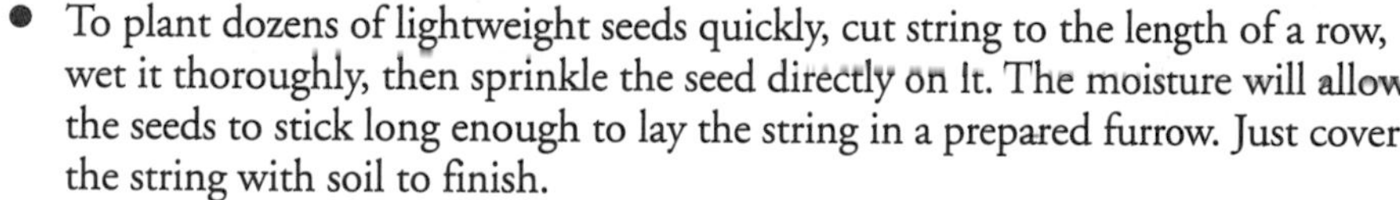

- To plant dozens of lightweight seeds quickly, cut string to the length of a row, wet it thoroughly, then sprinkle the seed directly on it. The moisture will allow the seeds to stick long enough to lay the string in a prepared furrow. Just cover the string with soil to finish.

Make wicks for watering plants To keep potted plants watered while you are away for the weekend, fill a large container with water and place it next to the plants. Cut several pieces of string so they are long enough to hang down to the bottom of the container at one end and be buried a few centimetres in the soil of the pots at the other. Soak the strings until they are completely wet and put them in position. As the soil begins to dry, capillary action will draw water from the reservoir to the pots through the strings.

Stop slamming doors When a slamming door is getting on your nerves, you can use string in two ways to control the way a door closes:

- A piece of light string tied to both sides of a door knob and running around the door edge will provide just enough friction to slow the door down and prevent a loud slam when it shuts.
- Use thicker rope in the same way to temporarily prop open a door that automatically locks when it closes or to make sure pets or small children don't get trapped in one room of the house.

Make a quick package opener Next time you are preparing a box for posting, take a second to make it easier for the recipient to open. Place a piece of string along the centre and side seams before you tape, allowing a tiny bit to hang free at one end. That way, the recipient will just need to pull the strings to sever the tape without having to resort to a sharp blade that might damage delicate contents. Do the same for packing boxes when you are moving house.

Sugar

Keep cut flowers fresh Make your own preservative to keep cut flowers fresh longer. Dissolve 3 tablespoons sugar and 2 tablespoons white vinegar per litre of warm water. When you fill the vase, make sure the cut stems are covered by 7–10cm of the prepared water. The sugar nourishes the plants, while the vinegar inhibits bacterial growth. You will be surprised how long the arrangement stays fresh.

Get rid nematode worms If your outdoor plants look unhealthy, with ugly knots at the roots, chances are they've been victims of an attack by nematodes. The nematode worm, nemesis of many an otherwise healthy garden, is a microscopic parasite that pierces the roots of plants and causes knots. You can prevent nematode attacks by using sugar to create an inhospitable environment for the tiny worms. Apply 2kg sugar for every 25m² of garden. Micro-organisms feeding on the sugar will increase the organic matter in the soil, thereby eliminating the nematodes.

Clean greasy, grimy hands To clean filthy hands easily and thoroughly, pour equal amounts of olive oil and sugar into the cupped palm of one hand and then gently rub your hands together for several minutes. Rinse thoroughly and dry. The grit of the sugar acts as an abrasive to help the oil to remove grease, paint and grime. Your hands will look and feel clean, soft and moisturised.

Make a non-toxic fly trap Keep the kitchen free of flies with a homemade fly trap that uses no toxic chemicals. In a small saucepan, simmer 400ml milk, 110g raw sugar, and 60g ground pepper for about 10 minutes, stirring occasionally. Pour the mixture into shallow dishes or bowls and set them around the kitchen, patio or anywhere that flies are a problem. They will flock to the bowls and drown in the sticky mixture.

Exterminate cockroaches If you hate using smelly, noxious pesticides as much as you loathe cockroaches, scatter a mixture of equal parts sugar and bicarbonate of soda over the infested area. The sugar will attract the cockroaches, and the bicarbonate of soda will kill them. Replace it frequently with a fresh mixture to prevent future infestations.

WARNING Keep the pesticide well away from pets and small children, as it is poisonous if ingested.

Soothe a burned tongue To relieve a tongue burned by a hot potato, pizza, coffee, tea or soup, sprinkle a pinch or two of sugar over the affected area. The pain should begin to subside immediately.

Keep desserts fresh You have used sugar to sweeten a cake mixture; now use it to keep the finished cake fresh and moist. Store the cake in an airtight container with a couple of sugar cubes, and it will stay fresh for days longer. You can also store a few lumps of sugar with cheese to prevent the cheese from going mouldy.

{ KIDS' STUFF }

MAKE YOUR OWN ROCK SWEETS

Make old-fashioned rock sweets with children, with no strings, paper clips, sticks or thermometers needed. Stir 500g sugar into 200ml hot water. Pour the syrup into several open dishes and set aside. Add a grain of sugar to act as a seed crystal in each container. Within days or weeks you should be able to collect glittering crystals of rock. Use a spoon to scoop it out, then rinse and dry the sweet before you eat it.

Surgical spirit

Clean bathroom fixtures Look in the medicine cabinet the next time you need to clean chrome bathroom fixtures. Pour some surgical spirit straight from the bottle onto a soft, absorbent cloth and clean the taps and other fixtures. There is no need to rinse as the alcohol will just evaporate. It does a superb job of making chrome sparkle, plus it will kill any germs in its path.

Remove hair spray from mirrors When you are using hair spray, some of it will inevitably end up on the mirror. A quick wipe with surgical spirit will whisk away the sticky residue and leave the mirror sparkling clean.

Clean venetian blinds Surgical spirit does a terrific job of cleaning the slats of venetian blinds. To make quick work of the job, wrap a flat tool such as a spatula in a cloth and secure it with a rubber band. Dip it in surgical spirit and start dusting backwards and forwards along each slat.

{ TAKE CARE }

Don't confuse denatured alcohol or methylated spirits with surgical spirit. Denatured alcohol is ethanol (drinking alcohol) to which poisonous and foul-tasting chemicals have been added to render it unfit for drinking. Often, the chemicals used in denatured alcohol are not ones you should put on your skin. Surgical spirit is made from chemicals that are safe for skin contact; the most usual solution is 70 per cent isopropyl alcohol and 30 per cent water.

Keep windows sparkling and frost-free Wash windows with a solution of 100ml surgical spirit to 1 litre water to prevent frost.

Dissolve frost on the windscreen If you'd rather be inside savouring your morning coffee for a little longer instead of scraping frost off the car windows in the winter, fill a spray bottle with surgical spirit and spray the glass. You will be able to wipe the frost straight off.

Prevent ring around the collar To prevent natural oil from your neck making a grimy line on a shirt collar, wipe your neck with surgical spirit each morning before you dress.

Clean a phone When a phone is getting a bit grubby, wipe it down with surgical spirit. It will remove the grime and disinfect the phone at the same time.

Remove ink stains If you have spilled ink on a favourite garment, try soaking the spot in surgical spirit for a few minutes before putting the garment in the wash.

Erase permanent markers If an artistic child has decorated your worktop with a permanent marker, don't worry if it is made from a non-permeable material such as plastic laminate. Surgical spirit will dissolve the marker back to a liquid state so you can just wipe it off.

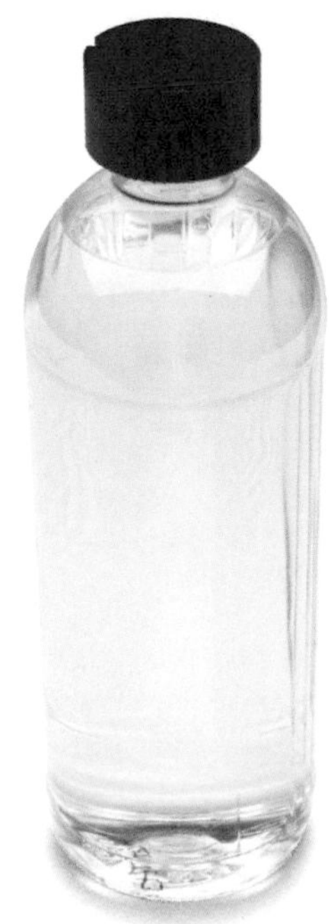

Remove dog ticks Ticks hate the taste of surgical spirit as much as they love the taste of your dog. Before you pull a tick off Fido, dab the creature with surgical spirit to make it loosen its grip. Then grab the tick as close to the dog's skin as you can and pull it straight out. Dab again with alcohol to disinfect the wound. This technique will work on people too.

Get rid of fruit flies The next time you see fruit flies hovering in the kitchen, take a fine-misting spray bottle and fill it with surgical spirit. Spraying the little flies knocks them out and makes them fall to the floor, where you can sweep them up. The alcohol is less effective than insecticide, but it is a lot safer than spraying poison around your kitchen.

Make a shapeable ice pack The problem with ice packs is they don't conform to the shape of the injured body part. Make a slushy, conformable pack by mixing 1 part surgical spirit with 3 parts water in a self-sealing plastic bag. The next time a sore knee acts up, wrap the bag of slush in a cloth and apply it to the area.

Stretch tight-fitting new shoes This doesn't always work, but it is worth a try. If new leather shoes are pinching your feet, try swabbing the tight spot with a cotton wool ball soaked in surgical spirit. Walk around in the shoes for a few minutes to see if they stretch enough to be comfortable.

* Sweet tins

Emergency sewing kit A small sweet tin is just the right size to hold a selection of needles, thread and buttons in your handbag or briefcase for on-the-spot repairs.

Store broken jewellery Don't lose all the little pieces of items of broken jewellery that you plan to have repaired one day. Keep the pieces together and safe in a small sweet tin.

Prevent jewellery-chain tangles Keep necklaces and chain bracelets separate and tangle-free in their own individual tins.

Keep earrings together To stop pairs of small earrings from getting separated, store them together in a little sweet tin and you won't have to hunt around to find a matching pair again.

Make a birthday treasure Decorate the outside of a small sweet tin, line it with felt or silk and insert a 1p piece or, if you can find one, a special commemorative coin from the birth year of a friend or relative.

Organise your sewing gear Use a small sweet tin to store snaps, sequins, buttons and beads in your sewing box. Label the lids or glue on a sample for easy identification of the contents.

Store workshop accessories Sweet tins are great for storing and organising by size, screws, nails, washers, tacks, fuses and other small items that might otherwise clutter up your workshop or get lost.

Store car fuses You'll always know where to find spare car fuses if you store them in a little sweet tin in the glove compartment of the car.

 Talcum powder

Keep ants away For an effective organic ant repellent, scatter talcum powder liberally around the foundations of your house and other known points of entry, such as doors and windows. Other effective organic repellents include cream of tartar, borax, powdered sulphur and oil of cloves. You can also try planting mint close to the foundations.

Fix a squeaky floor Don't let squeaky floorboards drive you crazy. Sprinkle talcum powder or powdered graphite between the boards. If that doesn't do the trick, squirt in some liquid wax to help to fill the gaps.

Remove bloodstains from fabric To remove fresh bloodstains from clothing or furniture, make a paste of water and talcum powder and apply it to the spot. When it dries, brush away the stain. Substitute cornflour or cornmeal if you have run out of talcum powder.

Get rid of greasy carpet stain A greasy stain can spoil the look of the most luxurious carpet. You can remove greasy stains from a carpet with a combination of talcum powder and patience. Cover the affected area with talcum powder and wait at least 6 hours for the talcum to absorb the grease. Then vacuum the stain away. Bicarbonate of soda or cornflour may be substituted for the talcum powder.

Get grease stains out of synthetics To delete greasy marks from synthetic fabrics such as polyester, sprinkle some talcum powder directly onto the spot and rub it in with your fingers. Wait 24 hours, and gently brush. Repeat as necessary until the stain is completely gone.

Loosen tangles and knots Don't break a fingernail trying to untie a knot in your shoelace. Sprinkle some talcum powder on the shoelaces (or any knotted cords) and the knots will pull apart more easily. Use talcum powder to help to untangle chain necklaces as well.

 Tape see page 314

 Tea see page 318

Tennis balls

Fluff up down-filled clothes and duvets Down-filled items like jackets, body warmers, duvets and pillows become flat and soggy when you wash them. You can fluff them up again by placing a couple of tennis balls in the tumble drier with the down items.

Sand curves in furniture Wrap a tennis ball in sandpaper and use it to sand curves when you are refinishing furniture. The tennis ball is just the right size and shape to fit comfortably in your hand.

Store valuables at the gym Here is a clever way to hide and store valuables when you are working out at the gym. Make a 5cm slit along one seam of a tennis ball and insert the valuables inside. Keep the ball in your gym bag among other sporting gear. But remember not to use the doctored ball next time you are out on the tennis court.

Park in the right place every time Make parking your car in the garage easier. Hang a tennis ball on a string from the garage ceiling so it will hit the windscreen just at the spot where you should stop the car. You will always know exactly where to park.

Massage your back Give yourself a relaxing and therapeutic back massage. Fill a long tube-shaped sock with a few tennis balls, tie the end and stretch the homemade massager around your back just as you would a towel after a shower or bath.

Massage sore feet For a simple but amazingly enjoyable and therapeutic foot massage, take your shoes off, place a tennis ball on the floor and roll it around under your feet.

Get a better grip on bottle caps If your hands are weakened by arthritis or other ailments, you probably have a difficult time removing twist-off bottle caps. An old tennis ball may help. Simply cut a ball in half and use one of the halves to enhance your grip.

{ SCIENCE FAIR }

TEACH CHILDREN ABOUT GRAVITY

Stand on a chair holding two tennis balls, one in each hand, and extend your arms so that they are at the same distance from the floor. Ask the children to observe as you release both balls at once. Did they hit the floor at the same time? Now repeat using a tennis ball and a much lighter table tennis ball. Again ask which will land first. Most will guess the heavier tennis ball, but they'll land at the same time because gravity exerts the same force on all objects regardless of their weight. Of course, if you try this with a ball and a feather, the kids will also learn that less dense objects fall more slowly due to air resistance.

TAPE...

...in the kitchen

Create a no-fly zone Make your own fly and pest strips that are free from toxic chemicals. Cover empty paper towel or toilet paper rolls with double-sided sticky tape and hang them in the kitchen or wherever else you need them.

Mark the start of a cling film roll Put a piece of clear tape on your finger, sticky side out and dab your finger on the roll of cling film until you find the edge. Use a short piece of tape to lift the edge and pull gently.

Prevent salt and pepper spills Many salt and pepper shakers, especially ceramic ones, have to be filled through a hole in the bottom. Before you refill one of these shakers, tape over the holes on top. The shaker won't spill when you turn it upside down to fill it. Also, remember to tape the tops when moving to a new home or even when you are transporting the shakers to and from a picnic.

Safely pick up glass shards Don't risk cutting yourself when picking up bits of broken glass. Hold a long piece of clear tape tightly at each end and use it to pick up the shards.

Keep your hands free at the supermarket Next time you go shopping for food, take some tape with you and use it to attach your shopping list to the handle of the shopping trolly. This will free both your hands and you won't keep mislaying or dropping the list.

...around the house

Find your favourite photo negative Before framing a favourite photograph, tape the negative to the back of the picture. If you ever want to make copies of the photo, you won't have to go searching through piles of old negatives to find the right one.

Make candles fit snugly Don't let wobbly candles spoil a romantic mood or cause a fire at a candlelit dinner. If the candles don't fit snugly into the holder, wrap a few layers of tape around the bottom edges until they slot in firmly.

Mark a phone number for quick reference Use transparent tape to highlight numbers in the phone book that you look up often. The tape will make the page easier to find and you will also be able to find the number easily without having to search the whole page.

Keep spare batteries handy Tape a set of extra batteries to the back of a wall clock. When the clock stops and you need to replace the batteries, they will be immediately to hand.

Code your keys Are you always groping around to find the right key when you get home in the dark? Wrap some tape around the top of your house key and you will be able to feel for the right key when it is too dark to see. Or if you have several similar-looking keys that you can't tell apart, colour-code them using tape of different colours.

Prevent jewellery tangles To keep fine chains from tangling when you are travelling, lay the chain along a piece of clear tape. Then place another piece on top to encase it. You can also use the tape trick to keep a pair of earrings from getting separated.

Contain grease stains on paper You may never be able to get rid of the grease spots on books or important papers, but you can keep them from spreading with a little help from some clear tape. Put a piece of tape over both sides of the spot to keep the grease from seeping through to other pages or papers.

Keep papers from blowing in the wind If you have to make a speech or accept an award at an outdoor event, bring a roll of clear tape with you. When it is your turn to talk, place some tape on the lectern, sticky side up, to prevent your papers from blowing away.

DID YOU KNOW?

Sellotape® dates back to 1937 when Colin Kininmonth and George Gray coated cellophane film with a natural rubber resin, to create a 'sticky tape' product, based on a French patent. They had seen this process carried out in France by a company called CIMA and obtained a licence to make it in the UK. When war broke out in 1939 the company made cellulose tape for sealing ration and first aid packs and a cloth tape for sealing ammunition boxes. They also made a product for covering windows to protect householders from breaking glass that was manufactured in sheet form.

Super item
30 USES!

TAPE...

Deter a cat from scratching Stop naughty cats and kittens from scratching furniture and carpets. Sprinkle some ground red pepper on a strip of tape and attach it to the areas you don't want them to scratch. They hate the smell and they will quickly get the message.

Keep flowers upright in a vase To keep cut flowers from sagging in their vase, crisscross several pieces of clear tape across the mouth of the vase, leaving spaces where you can insert the flowers. The flowers should look perky and fresh for a few extra days.

Make sewing easier Use clear tape to simplify your sewing – use it instead of pins. Hold a zip in place when you are making a garment. (You can sew through the tape and remove it when you have finished.) Keep badges, patches or name tags in place when sewing them onto shirts, uniforms or caps. Tape hooks, eyes and snaps to garments when sewing so they won't slip. Just pull the tape off when you have finished. Tape your pattern to the material and when you cut the pattern, you will have a reinforced edge.

End loose ends on spools of thread Put an end to time-wasting searches for loose ends of thread. Just tape the ends to the top or bottom of the spool when you have finished sewing and they will be ready to use next time you sew.

Remove lipstick from silk Why pay an expensive dry-cleaning bill to remove a lipstick spot from a silk scarf or dress when you can do it yourself for free? Just place a piece of clear tape (or masking tape) over the spot and pull it off. If you can still see some of the lipstick colour, sprinkle on some talcum powder or chalk and dab until the powder and the remaining lipstick disappear.

Clean a nail file Clean a nail file easily and effectively. Simply place a piece of clear tape over it, press and pull off. The tape will pick up all the dirt embedded in the surface of the file.

{ KIDS' STUFF }

THE BALLOON THAT JUST WON'T POP

Children will be delighted and amazed when you do this easy party trick at a birthday gathering. Secretly place a piece of transparent tape over an area of a blown-up balloon. When you are ready, get the children's attention and hold up the balloon in one hand and a pin in the other. For added effect, tell them to cover their ears. Pierce the balloon with the pin at the taped spot and remove it. The balloon will not pop! Then pop the balloon in another area. It's guaranteed to leave them laughing and scratching their heads.

...for the DIY-er

Keep picture-hook nails from damaging walls Before driving a nail into the wall, put a piece of masking tape on the wall at the site. This will prevent the paint from peeling off if you have to remove the nail.

Keep screws handy When doing repairs, place loose screws, nuts and bolts directly on to a piece of clear tape so they won't get lost. Stick double-sided tape on a workbench and use it to hold screws while you are working on a project.

Mend a broken plant stem Use clear tape to add support to a broken plant stem. Just wrap the stem in tape at the damaged area and leave the tape on until it mends. The taped plant will keep growing as long as moisture can continue to travel up the stem.

Make a seed strip Sprinkle some seeds on a piece of greaseproof paper and use your fingers to align them. After removing the excess, take a strip of clear tape and place it over the seeds. Bury the tape in the garden and you will soon have perfect rows of seedlings.

...for safety's sake

Make safety markers for a car emergency Make your own safety markers by wrapping strips of brightly coloured reflector tape around two large empty cans. Keep them in the boot of the car to use in an emergency.

Mark dark stairways Stop stumbling on poorly lit cellar or outdoor stairs or worrying about guests tripping and falling. Apply reflector tape along the edges of the steps and you will be able to see exactly where you are going.

Make pets visible at night Don't let your beloved family pet get hit by a car if it is out at night. Put reflector tape on its collar so drivers will be able to see it immediately in the dark.

...for the children

Secure a baby's bib Stop bits of food from getting under a child's bib by taping the edges of the bib to his or her clothes.

Makeshift child-proofing When visiting a home that isn't child-proofed, bring a roll of clear tape along too. Use it to cover electrical outlets as a temporary safety measure. Although it will not provide a lot of protection, it could give you the extra time you need to remove a child from a potentially hazardous situation.

Make multi-coloured designs Tape a few different-coloured markers or pencils together and let children draw multi-coloured designs. Be careful not to use too many, so the children can keep control of their drawings.

Super item

TEA...

...for health and beauty

Cool sunburned skin If you forget to use sunscreen and pay the price with painful sunburn, a few wet tea bags applied to the affected skin will take out the sting. This works well for other types of minor burns (such as those from a teapot or steam iron) too. If the sunburn is too widespread to treat this way, put some tea bags in your bath water and soak your whole body.

Reduce razor burn When you forget to replace a blunt razor blade before you start to shave and end up with razor burn and painful nicks and cuts, apply a wet tea bag to soothe the affected area.

Get the gray out Turn grey hair dark again without an expensive trip to the hairdresser or the use of chemical hair dyes. Make a natural dye using brewed tea and herbs. Steep 3 tea bags in 200ml boiling water. Add 1 tablespoon each of rosemary and sage (fresh or dried) and let it stand overnight before straining. To use, shampoo as usual and then pour or spray the mixture on your hair, making sure to saturate it thoroughly. Take care not to stain your clothes. Blot with a towel and do not rinse. It may take several treatments to achieve the desired result.

DID YOU KNOW?

Legend has it that tea originated some 5000 years ago with the Chinese emperor Shen Nung. A wise ruler and creative scientist, the emperor insisted that all drinking water be boiled as a health precaution. One summer day, during a rest stop in a distant region, servants began to boil water for the royal entourage to drink when some dried leaves from a nearby bush fell into the pot. As the water boiled, it turned brown. The emperor's scientific curiosity was aroused, and he insisted on tasting the liquid. It was just his cup of tea.

Condition dry hair To give a natural shine to dry hair, use a litre of warm, unsweetened tea (freshly brewed or instant) as a final rinse.

Tan your skin with tea Give pale skin a tanned appearance without exposure to dangerous ultraviolet rays. Brew 2 cups of strong black tea, let it cool and pour into a plastic spray bottle. Make sure your skin is clean and dry. Then spray the tea directly onto your skin and let it air-dry. Repeat as desired for a glowing tan. This will also work to give a man's face a more even tone after shaving off a beard.

Drain a boil Cover a boil with a wet tea bag overnight and it should have drained without pain by the time you wake up next morning.

Soothe nipples sore from nursing When breastfeeding a baby leaves your nipples sore, treat them to an ice-cold bag of tea. Just brew a cup of tea, remove the bag and place it in a bowl of ice cubes for about a minute. Then place the wet tea bag on the sore nipple and cover it with a nursing pad. Keep it under your bra for several minutes. The tannic acid in the wet tea leaves will soothe and help to heal the sore nipple.

Relieve your tired eyes Revitalise tired, achy or puffy eyes by soaking two tea bags in warm water and placing them over your closed eyes for 20 minutes. The tannins in the tea act to reduce puffiness and soothe tired eyes.

Relieve a baby's pain from an injection Is your baby's arm still painful from a recent inoculation? Try wetting a tea bag and placing it over the site of the injection. Hold it gently in place until the crying stops. The tannic acid in the tea will soothe the soreness. Try it on yourself the next time an injection leaves your arm sore.

TEA...

...for health and beauty

Soothe bleeding gums Your child's lost tooth has led to bleeding gums that are sore and feel horrible. To stop the bleeding and soothe the pain from a lost or recently pulled tooth, wet a tea bag with cool water and press it directly onto the site of the missing tooth.

Stop foot odour Put an end to smelly feet by giving them a daily tea bath. Soak your feet in strongly brewed tea for 20 minutes a day to cure offensive odours.

Make a soothing mouthwash To ease toothache or a mouth ulcer, rinse your mouth with a cup of hot peppermint tea mixed with a pinch or two of salt. Peppermint is an antiseptic and contains menthol, which alleviates pain on contact with skin surfaces. To make peppermint tea, boil 1 tablespoon fresh peppermint leaves in 200ml water and steep for several minutes.

...around the house

Tenderise tough meat Even the toughest cuts of meat will melt in your mouth after you marinate them in strong black tea. Place 4 tablespoons of black tea leaves in a pot of warm (not boiling) water and steep for 5 minutes. Strain to remove the leaves and stir in 100g brown sugar until it dissolves. Set aside. Season up to 1.5kg meat with salt, pepper, onion and garlic powder and place it in a large cast-iron casserole dish. Pour the liquid over the seasoned meat and cook in a preheated 160°C/gas mark 3 oven until the meat is tender (about 90 minutes).

Clean wooden furniture and floors Freshly brewed tea is great for cleaning wood furniture and floors. Boil a couple of tea bags in a litre of water and let it cool. Dip a soft cloth in the tea, wring out the excess and use it to wipe away dirt and grime. Buff dry with a clean, soft cloth.

Create 'antique' fashions Soak white lace or garments in a tea bath to create an antique beige, creamy or ivory look. Use three tea bags for every 2 cups of boiling water and steep for 20 minutes. Let it cool for a few minutes before soaking the material for 10 minutes or more. The longer you let it soak, the darker the shade you will get.

TIP* DYEING WITH HERBAL TEAS

Tea has been used to dye fabrics for a long time. It was first used to hide stains on linens. But you can also use herbal teas to dye fabric different colours and subtle hues. Try using hibiscus to achieve red tones and darker herbal teas like licorice for soft brown tints. Always experiment using fabric scraps until you obtain the desired results.

Give mirrors a shine To make mirrors sparkle, brew a pot of strong tea, let it cool and then use it to clean the mirrors. Dampen a soft cloth in the tea and wipe it all over the surface of the mirrors. Then buff well with a soft, dry cloth to get a streak-free shine.

Control dust from fireplace ash Keep dust from rising from the ashes when you clean out a fireplace. Before you begin cleaning, sprinkle wet tea leaves over the area. The tea will keep the ashes from floating around as you lift them out.

Perfume a sachet Next time you make a sachet to perfume a drawer or wardrobe, try using something a little more exotic than lavender or rose petals. What about trying the fragrant aroma of your favourite herbal tea? Just open a few used herbal tea bags and spread the wet tea on some old newspaper to dry. Then use the dry tea as stuffing for the sachet.

...in the garden

Give roses a boost Sprinkle new or used tea leaves (loose or in tea bags) around rosebushes and cover with mulch to give them a midsummer boost. When you water the plants, the nutrients from the tea will be released into the soil, encouraging growth. Roses thrive on the tannic acid that occurs naturally in tea.

Feed your ferns Schedule an occasional teatime for your ferns and other acid-loving houseplants. Substitute brewed tea when watering the plants. Or work wet tea leaves into the soil around the plants to encourage lush, luxuriant growth.

Prepare planter for potting For healthier potted plants, place a few used tea bags on top of the drainage layer at the bottom of the planter before potting. The tea bags will retain water and leach nutrients into the soil.

Enhance your compost heap To speed up the decomposition process and enrich the compost, pour a few cups of strongly brewed tea into the heap. The liquid tea will hasten decomposition and draw acid-producing bacteria, creating a desirable acid-rich compost.

TIGHTS...

...around the house

Buff your shoes Bring out the shine in freshly polished shoes by buffing them with a medium-length strip from a pair of old tights. It works so well, you may never want to use another method again.

Keep a hairbrush clean If you dread the prospect of cleaning out your hairbrush, here is a way to make the job much easier. Cut a 5cm strip from the leg section of a pair of tights, and stretch it over and around the bristles of your new (or newly cleaned) hairbrush. If necessary, use a hairgrip or a comb to push the tights down over the bristles. The next time the brush needs cleaning, simply lift up and remove the tights layer, along with all the dead hair, lint and dirt on top and replace it with a fresh strip.

Vacuum a fish tank If you have a wet-dry vacuum cleaner, you can change the water in your fish tank without disturbing the gravel and tank accessories. (you will still have to relocate the fish, of course.) Pull the foot of an old nylon stocking or pair of tights over the end of the vacuum's nozzle, secure it with a rubber band and you can start sucking out the water.

Wrap up wrapping paper Keep used rolls of wrapping paper from tearing and unravelling by storing them in tubes made by cutting the leg sections off old pairs of tights. (Don't forget to leave the foot section intact.) Or, if you have a number of used rolls, you can simply put one in each leg of a pair of tights and hang them over a hanger in the wardrobe.

Remove nail varnish If you can't find any cotton wool balls, moisten strips of recycled tights with nail varnish remover to take off your old nail varnish. Cut the material into 8cm squares and store several of them in an old plaster container or make-up bag.

Find lost small objects Have you ever spent hours on your hands and knees searching through a carpet for a lost gemstone, contact lens or another tiny, precious item? If not, count yourself among the lucky few. Should you ever be faced with this situation, cut a leg off an old pair of tights, making sure that the toe section is intact and pull it up over the nozzle of the vacuum cleaner hose. (If you want additional security, you can even cut off the other leg and slip that over as well.) Secure the stocking in place with a tightly wound rubber band. Turn on the vacuum, carefully move the nozzle over the carpet and you will soon find your valuable attached to the homemade filter.

Keep spray bottles unblocked If you recycle spray bottles to use with homemade cleaners or furniture polishes, you can prevent any potential blockages by covering the open end of the tube – the part that goes inside the bottle – with a small, square-cut piece of nylon tights held in place with a small rubber band. This works especially well for filtering garden sprays that are mixed from concentrates.

Substitute for stuffing Is your child's teddy bear, bunny or rag doll losing its stuffing? Get out a needle and thread and prepare the patient for an emergency 'transplant'. Replace the lost filling with narrow strips cut from clean, worn-out tights. Stitch the hole up securely and a complete recovery is guaranteed. This works well with deflated cushions too.

Take a citrus bath Make scented bath oil by drying and grinding up orange and/or lemon peel and then pouring them into the foot section of a recycled pair of tights. Put a knot about 2.5cm above the peel and leave another 15cm or so of tights above that before cutting off the remainder. Tie the stocking to a bath tap with the peel suspended below the running water. In addition to giving your bath a fresh citrus fragrance, you can also use the stocking to exfoliate your skin.

DID YOU KNOW?

Nylon, the world's first synthetic fibre, was invented at E. I. DuPont de Nemours, Inc., and unveiled on October 28, 1938. Instead of calling a press conference, company vice president Charles Stine chose to make the landmark announcement to 3000 women's club members at the New York World's Fair, introducing it with live models wearing nylon stockings. Stine's instincts were spot on. By the end of 1940, DuPont had sold 64 million pairs of stockings. Nylon had actually made its big-screen debut a year earlier, when it was used to create the tornado that lifted Dorothy out of Kansas in *The Wizard of Oz*.

TIGHTS...

...around the house

Hold mothballs or potpourri For an easy way to store mothballs in a wardrobe or to make sachets of potpourri to keep in your drawers, pour either ingredient into the toe section of a pair of recycled nylons. Knot off the contents, then cut off the remainder. If you plan to hang up the mothballs, leave several centimetres of material before cutting.

Make a ponytail scrunchy Why buy a scrunchy for a ponytail when you can easily make one for nothing? Cut a horizontal strip about 8cm wide across a stocking leg and wrap it a few times around the ponytail.

Use to hang-dry sweaters Avoid getting clothes peg marks on newly washed sweaters by putting an old pair of tights through the neck of the sweater and running the legs out through the arms. Then hang the sweater to dry on the clothes line by clipping the clothespegs onto the tights instead of the wool.

Organise a suitcase As any seasoned traveller knows, you can sqeeze more of your belongings into any piece of luggage by rolling up your clothes. To keep bulkier rolls from unwrapping, cover them in flexible nylon tubes. Cut the legs off a pair of old tights, snip off the foot sections and stretch the stockings over the rolled-up garmets for a neat and tidy suitcase

Bundle blankets for storage For an effortless and foolproof way to keep blankets and duvets securely bundled before they go into temporary storage, wrap them up in large 'rubber bands' made from the waistbands from your used pantyhose. You can reuse the bands year after year if needed.

Tie up boxes, newspapers, magazines If you run out of string (or need something stronger – perhaps for a large stack of glossy magazines), tie up bundles of boxes, newspapers and other types of recyclable paper goods using an old pair of tights. Cut off the legs and waistband to make the 'string'.

...in the kitchen

Secure rubbish bags How many times have you opened the kitchen bin to discover that the liner has slipped down (and that someone has covered it over with fresh rubbish anyway)? You can prevent such 'accidents' by firmly securing the bin bag or liner to your bin with the elastic waistband from a recycled pair of tights; tie a knot in the band to keep it tight. You can also use this method to keep rubbish bags from slipping off the edge of outdoor rubbish bins.

Dust under the fridge Catch the dust bundles that lurk underneath and alongside the fridge by rolling up a pair of old tights and attaching it with a rubber band to a coat hanger. The dust and dirt will cling to the nylon, which can easily be washed off before being called back for dusting duty.

Store onions in cutoff bundles Get the maximum shelf life out of onions by hanging them in nylon holders that provide the good air circulation they need to stay fresh. Place the onions one at a time into the leg of a clean pair of tights. Work the first one down to the foot section. Tie a knot above it and add the next one, repeating until finished. Cut off the remainder and then hang the stocking in a cool, dry area of the kitchen. You can easily remove the onions when required by snipping off each knot, starting from the bottom and working up.

Make a pot or dish scrubber Clean stains off nonstick cookware by making a do-it-yourself scrubbing pad. Crumple up a pair of clean old tights, moisten it with a bit of warm water and add a couple of drops of washing-up liquid. You can also make terrific scrubbers for dishes, as well as walls and other non-porous surfaces, by cutting off the foot or toe section, fitting it over a sponge and knotting off the end.

Make a flour duster Here is a simple way to dust baking pans and surfaces with exactly the right amount of flour. Cut the foot section off a clean old stocking leg, fill it with flour, tie a knot in it and keep it in the flour jar. Give your new flour dispenser a few gentle shakes whenever you need to dust flour onto a baking pan or prepare a surface for rolling out dough for breads or pastries.

Keep a rolling pin from sticking Getting pie dough to a perfect consistency is an art form in itself. Although you can always add water to dough that is too dry, it often results in a gluey consistency that sticks to your rolling pin. Avoid the hassle of having to scrape the rolling pin by covering it with a piece of nylon stocking. It will hold enough flour to keep even the soggiest pie dough from sticking to the pin.

DID YOU KNOW?

You have probably heard that you can temporarily replace a broken fan belt with a nylon stocking in an emergency. Well, don't believe it – it won't work! Pulleys in most vehicles require flat belts, not the rounded shape tights would give. Even on a V-belt pulley, they will fly off as soon as the engine starts. A much better idea is to replace a fan belt before it gets into bad condition.

TIGHTS...

...for the DIY-er

Apply stain to crevices in wood Getting wood stain or varnish into the corners and crevices of an unfinished bookcase or table can be a difficult task. Your brush just doesn't fit into them to give an even coating. Cut a strip from an old pair of tights, fold it over a few times, and use a rubber band to attach it to the tip of a wooden lolly stick. Dip the homemade applicator into the stain or varnish and you should find it easy to get into these inaccessible spots.

Test a sanded surface for snags Test how well you have sanded a wooden item for painting by putting it to the stocking test. Wrap a long piece of stocking around the palm of your hand and rub it over the wood. If the stocking snags onto any spots, sand them until you are able to freely move the nylon over the surface without it catching.

Clean a swimming pool Here is an effective way to skim the debris off the surface of a swimming pool. Cut a leg off a pair of tights and fit it over the pool's skimmer basket. It will catch tiny dirt particles and hairs that would otherwise get into and possibly clog the pool's filter unit.

Make a paint strainer Strain paint like a professional by using a nylon stocking filter to remove lumps from an old can of paint. Cut a leg off a pair of old tights, clip the foot off the leg and make a cut along the leg's length so that you have a flat piece of nylon. Then cut the leg into 30cm sections to make the filters. Stretch the nylon over a clean bucket or other receptacle and hold it in place with a rubber band or perhaps even the waistband from the pair of tights. Now slowly pour the paint into the bucket and it will come through free from lumps.

...in the garden

Stake delicate plants Give young plants and trees the support they need. Use strips of stocking to attach them to garden stakes. The nylon's flexibility will stretch as your seedlings or saplings fill out and mature – unlike string or twine, which can actually damage plant stalks if you tie it too tightly.

Cover a kids' bug jar Many children enjoy catching insects – and hopefully then releasing them. When making an insect jar for a child, don't punch holes in the jar's metal lid. It is much easier to cut a 15cm square from an old pair of tights and attach it to the jar with a rubber band. The nylon cover lets plenty of air enter the jar, and makes it easier to let insects in and out.

Prevent soil erosion in houseplants When moving a houseplant to a larger container, put a piece of nylon stocking at the bottom of the new pot. It will act as a liner to let excess water flow out without draining the soil at the same time.

Support melons Melons are not easy to grow in the UK. But you can help them along. Keep small melons such as cantaloupes off the ground and free of pests and disease by making protective sleeves for them from your old tights. Cut the legs off the tights. As the young melons start to develop, slide each one into the foot section and tie the leg to a stake to suspend the melon above the ground. The nylon holders will stretch as the melons mature, while keeping them from touching the damp soil, where they would be susceptible to rot or invasion by hungry insects and other garden pests.

Keep deer and foxes out of your garden If you have been catching deer and foxes on your property, put up a 'No Trespassing' sign they will easily understand. Fill the foot sections of some old tights with human hair clippings from a hairbrush or a local hairdresser or use dog hair collected after a brushing. Tie up the ends and hang them up where the deer tend to snack. They won't be back for more. The hair loses its scent after a while, so replace every four or five days.

Clean up after gardening Here are two recycling tips in one: save up leftover slivers of soap and place them in the foot section of an old nylon stocking. Knot it off, and hang it next to an outdoor tap. Use the soap-filled stocking to quickly wash off your hands after gardening and other outdoor work without worrying about getting dirt on door handles or bathroom fixtures inside the house.

Store flower bulbs in winter Stocking legs make terrific sacks for storing bulbs over the winter, since they allow air to circulate and so prevent mould and rot. Cut a leg off a pair of tights and place the bulbs inside, knot the end and stick ID tags on each 'sack' using a strip of masking tape. Hang them up in a cool, dry space and they will be ready for planting in the spring.

DID YOU KNOW?

Until the late 1950s, most women wore nylon stockings attacked to a suspender belt. Tights as we know them, with the legs fused to pants, were first produced in 1959 by the Gant company in the USA. Their popularity soared in the 1960s when the ubiquitous miniskirt made wearing stockings and suspenders virtually impossible as hemlines were too short to hide them.

Legend also has it that the doll maker Madame Alexander came up with the concept for tights in the early 1950s, when she started sewing tiny pairs of silk stockings onto her dolls' underpants to keep them from slipping down!

* Tomato juice

Deodorise plastic containers To remove an unpleasant smell from a plastic container, pour a little tomato juice onto a sponge and wipe it around the inside of the container. Then wash the container and lid in warm, soapy water, dry well and store them separately in the freezer for a couple of days. The container will be odour-free and ready to use again.

Rid a fridge of odours If a power failure has caused food to spoil in the fridge, get rid of the resulting smell in your refrigerator and freezer with the help of some tomato juice. After disposing of the spoiled food, thoroughly wipe the insides of the fridge and freezer with a sponge or cloth doused in undiluted tomato juice. Rinse with warm, soapy water and wipe dry. If any traces of the smell remain, either repeat the procedure or substitute vinegar for the tomato juice.

Restore the colour to blonde hair If you are a blonde who has ever gone swimming in a chlorine-treated pool, you know it can sometimes give your hair an unappealing green tint. To restore the blonde colour to your hair, saturate it with undiluted tomato juice, cover with a shower cap and wait 10-15 minutes. Then rinse thoroughly, shampoo and your hair should be back to its usual shade.

Relieve a sore throat For the temporary relief of sore throat symptoms, gargle with a mixture of 100ml tomato juice and 100ml hot water, plus about 10 drops of a hot pepper sauce.

DID YOU KNOW?

The ancient Chinese were apparently the first people to use toothbrushes, which they made with bristles from the necks of long-bristled pigs. William Addis is credited with producing the first mass-produced toothbrush in the UK in 1780. Toothbrushing did not become a two- or three-times-a-day habit for many people until after the Second World War when returning soldiers brought home their army-enforced hygiene habits. By then the DuPont company had invented the nylon bristle, which, unlike the natural bristles used earlier, dried completely between brushings and was resistant to the growth of bacteria. Nylon bristles are still used in most toothbrushes made today.

Toothbrushes

Remove tough stains Removing a stain that has soaked deep down into soft fibres can be hard. To remove deep stains, try using a soft-bristled nylon toothbrush, dabbing it gently to work in the stain-removing agent (bleach or vinegar, for example) until the stain is gone.

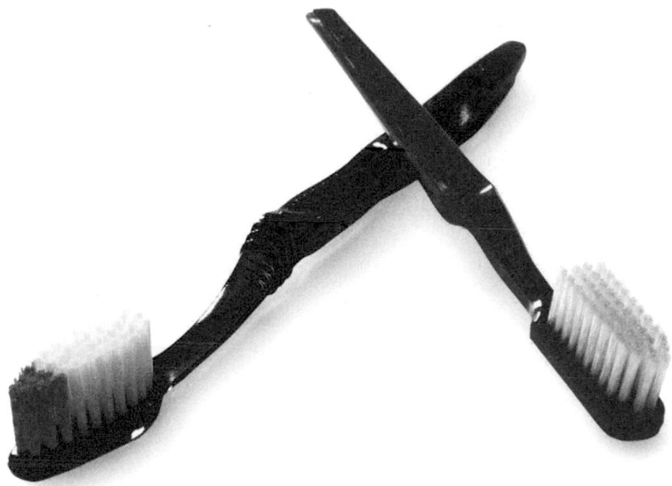

Use as all-purpose cleaners Don't throw out old toothbrushes. Instead, use them to clean a host of diverse items and small or hard-to-reach areas and crevices. Use a toothbrush to clean artificial flowers and plants, costume jewellery, combs, shower tracks, crevices between tiles and around taps. Also clean computer keyboards, can-opener blades and around hob burners. And don't forget the seams on shoes where the leather meets the sole.

Brush a cheese grater Give the teeth of a cheese grater a good brushing with a sterilised old toothbrush before you wash the grater or put it in the dishwasher. This will make it easier to wash and will prevent any blockages in the dishwasher drain by getting rid of bits of cheese or any other item you have been grating.

Clean silk from ears of corn Before cooking fresh sweetcorn, take an old toothbrush and gently rub down the ear to brush away the remaining clingy strands of silk. You won't have to brush them out from between your teeth after you have eaten the corn.

Clean and oil an electric grill A clean, soft toothbrush is just the right utensil to clean crumbs and grease from the nooks and crannies of an electric grill.

Apply hair dye When dyeing your hair at home, use an old toothbrush as an applicator. It is the perfect size.

Clean dirt from appliances Dip an old toothbrush in soapy water and use it to clean between appliance knobs and buttons and nameplates with raised lettering.

Toothpaste

Remove scuffs from shoes A little toothpaste does an amazing job of removing scuffs from leather shoes. Just squirt a small amount on the scuffed area and rub with a soft cloth. Wipe clean with a damp cloth. The leather will look like new.

Clean piano keys Has too much tickling of the ivories left them a bit dingy? Clean them up with toothpaste and a toothbrush, then wipe them down with a damp cloth. Toothpaste will work just as well on modern pianos that have keys made of plastic rather than real ivory.

Remove ink or lipstick stains from fabric When a pen has leaked in the pocket of a shirt, try this. It may or may not work, depending on the fabric and the ink, but it is certainly worth a try before consigning the shirt to decorating duty. Put white non-gel toothpaste on the stain and rub the fabric vigorously together. Rinse with water. If some of the ink has come out, repeat the process a few more times until you get rid of all the ink. The same process should also work for lipstick.

Brighten up canvas shoes Clean and whiten the rubber part of a pair of canvas shoes with non-gel toothpaste and an old toothbrush. After scrubbing, clean off the toothpaste with a damp cloth.

Clean the iron The mild abrasive in non-gel toothpaste is idea for scrubbing the sticky residue off the soleplate of an iron. Apply the toothpaste to the cool iron, scrub with a rag, then rinse clean.

Polish a diamond ring Put a little toothpaste onto an old toothbrush and use it to make a diamond ring sparkle. Clean off the residue with a damp cloth.

Deodorise baby bottles Baby bottles inevitably pick up a sour-milk smell. Toothpaste will remove the odour in no time. Just put some on a bottle brush and scrub away. Be sure to rinse thoroughly.

Prevent bathroom mirrors from fogging It is impossible to see your face clearly in a fogged-up bathroom mirror. Coat the mirror with non-gel toothpaste and wipe it off before you get in the shower. When you come out, the mirror won't have misted over.

Shine bathroom and kitchen chrome You can buy commercial cleaners with a very fine abrasive designed to shine up chrome, but if you don't have any, the fine abrasive in non-gel toothpaste works just as well. Smear on the toothpaste and polish with a soft, dry cloth.

DID YOU KNOW?

Ancient Egyptians used a mixture of ox-hoof ashes, burned eggshells, myrrh, pumice and water to clean their teeth. For most of history, tooth-cleaning concoctions were used mainly by the wealthy and included such alarming ingredients as salt, pepper, mint leaves, iris flowers, burnt bread, dragon's blood, cinnamon, and burnt alum. In 1850, Dr Washington Sheffield developed a formula we would recognise as toothpaste. He called it Dr Sheffield's Creme Dentifrice. His son, Dr Lucius Tracy Sheffield, observed collapsible metal tubes of paint and decided to use the same idea to make squeezable tubes of toothpaste. Fluoride was first added to toothpaste in 1914 but only became widely accepted in the 1950s.

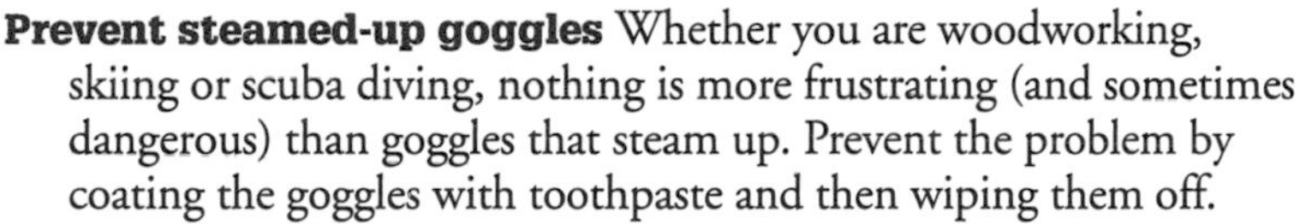

Prevent steamed-up goggles Whether you are woodworking, skiing or scuba diving, nothing is more frustrating (and sometimes dangerous) than goggles that steam up. Prevent the problem by coating the goggles with toothpaste and then wiping them off.

Clean the bathroom sink Non-gel toothpaste works as well as anything else to clean a bathroom sink. Squirt some into the sink, scrub with a sponge and rinse it out. As a bonus, the toothpaste will get rid of any smells emanating from the drain trap.

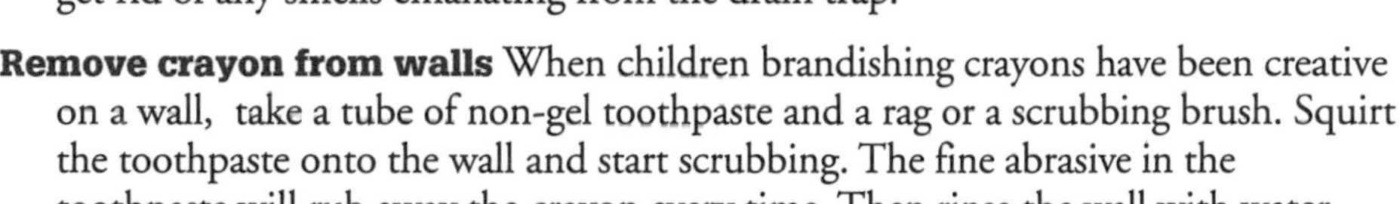

Remove crayon from walls When children brandishing crayons have been creative on a wall, take a tube of non-gel toothpaste and a rag or a scrubbing brush. Squirt the toothpaste onto the wall and start scrubbing. The fine abrasive in the toothpaste will rub away the crayon every time. Then rinse the wall with water.

Remove watermarks from furniture Even though you leave coasters around, some people just won't use them. To get rid of telltale watermark rings left by sweating drinks, gently rub some non-gel toothpaste on the wood with a soft cloth. Then wipe it off with a damp cloth and let it dry completely before applying furniture polish.

Remove tar Getting black tar on your feet at the seaside is annoying, but it is easy enough to remove. Just rub it with some non-gel toothpaste and rinse.

Clear up pimples Get rid of an offensive spot by dabbing a bit of non-gel, non-whitening toothpaste on the pimple. It should have dried up by morning. The toothpaste dehydrates the spot and absorbs the oil. This remedy works best on spots that have come to a head. But be careful as this remedy may be irritating to sensitive skin.

{TAKE CARE}

All toothpaste, including gels, contains abrasives. The amount varies, but too much can damage tooth enamel. People with sensitive teeth in particular should use a low-abrasive toothpaste. Ask your dentist which is the best toothpaste for you.

Remove smells from hands The ingredients in toothpaste that deodorise your mouth will work on your hands as well. If you have been preparing smelly food, wash your hands with toothpaste and the odour will be gone.

* Toothpicks

Mark cooking times on cuts of meat When all of your guests want their steaks cooked differently at a dinner or barbecue, keep track of exactly who wants what by using a series of different-coloured toothpicks to mark the steaks as rare, medium and well-done.

Stick through a garlic clove when marinading If you marinate foods with garlic cloves, stick a toothpick through the clove so you can remove it easily when you are ready to serve the food.

Keep pots from boiling over To stop a pot from boiling over on the hob, stick a toothpick, laid flat, between the lid and pan. The little space will allow enough steam to escape to prevent the pot from boiling over. This will also work with a casserole dish that is cooking in the oven.

Microwave potatoes faster The next time you microwave a potato, stick four toothpick 'legs' in one side. The suspended potato will cook much faster because the microwaves will reach the bottom as well as the top and sides.

Control your use of salad dressing Restrict your intake of calories from salad dressing. Instead of removing the foil seal when you open the bottle, take a toothpick and punch several holes in the foil. This will help to prevent too much dressing running out and make it last longer.

DID YOU KNOW?

- Buddhist monks used toothpicks as far back as the 700s and researchers have even found toothpick grooves in the teeth of prehistoric humans.
- Shakespeare mentions a toothpick in *Much Ado About Nothing.*
- In 1872 Silas Noble and J. P. Cooley patented the first toothpick-manufacturing machine.
- One cord of white birch wood, (also known as the toothpick tree) can make 7.5 million toothpicks.

Keep sausages from rolling around When cooking sausages, insert toothpicks between pairs to make turning them over easy and keep them from rolling around in the pan. They'll cook more evenly and will only need to be turned over once.

Mark the start of a roll of tape Instead of wasting time trying to find the beginning of some tape, just wrap it around a toothpick whenever you have finished using the tape and the start of the roll will always be easy to find.

{TAKE CARE}

Overusing toothpicks can damage tooth enamel and gums. If you have crowns or veneers, be extra careful to avoid breakage. Toothpicks also cause wear to tooth roots, particularly in elderly people whose gums have pulled away, exposing the roots.

Use to light candles When a candle has burned down and the wick is hard to reach, don't burn your fingers trying to use a small match to light it. Light a wooden toothpick instead and use it to light the wick.

Clean cracks and crevices To get rid of dirt, grime and cobwebs in hard-to-reach cracks or crevices, dip an ordinary toothpick in some alcohol and run it through the affected area. Also try this to clean around the buttons of your phone.

Repair a leaky garden hose If a garden hose springs a leak, don't go out and buy another one; just find the hole and insert a toothpick in it. Cut off the excess part of the toothpick. The water will make the wood swell, plugging up the leak every time.

Apply glue to sequins If you are working on a project that requires the gluing on of sequins, buttons, beads or other small items, squirt a little glue on a piece of paper and dip in a toothpick to apply small dabs of glue. You won't make a mess and you won't waste glue.

Make sewing easier Make sewing projects easier and complete them faster. Use a round toothpick to push fabrics, lace or gatherings under the pressure foot of the swing machine as you sew.

Repair small holes in wood When you have driven a nail into the wrong spot, dip the tip of a toothpick into PVA glue. Stick the toothpick in the hole and break it off. Sand the toothpick flush to the surface and you will never notice the repair.

Repair a loose hinge screw To fix a stripped hole on a door hinge, put some glue on the end of a toothpick and stick it in the hole. Break it off. Add one or two more toothpicks with glue until the hole is tightly filled, breaking each one off as you go. Re-drill the hole and screw the hinge back in place.

Repair a bent plant stem If the stem of a favourite plant has folded over, it is by no means doomed. Straighten the stem and support it by placing a toothpick against the stem and wrapping the toothpick on with tape. Water the plant and keep your eye on it. Depending on how fast it grows, the stem will regain its strength and you will need to remove the splint so you don't strangle the stem.

Foil cutworms Cutworms kill seedlings by encircling the stem and severing it. To protect seedlings, stick a toothpick in the soil about 60mm from each stem. This prevents a cutworm from being able to enclose the stem.

Touch up crevices in furniture The secret to touching up paint effectively is to use as little paint as possible, because even if you do have the right paint, what is in the can may not quite match faded or dirty paint on the furniture. Dip the end of a toothpick into the paint and use it to touch up just the crevice. Unlike a brush, the toothpick won't apply more paint than you need and you won't have to clean it.

* Twist ties

Organise electrical cords If the top of your computer desk looks like climbing plants have taken over or there is a thicket of wires behind the stereo system, tame the jungle of electrical wires by rolling each one up neatly and securing the extra length with a twist tie.

Make a trellis All you need are some twist ties and some plastic rings from four or six-packs of beer or soft drinks to make a trellis for climbing annuals such as sweet peas or morning glories. Just use the twist ties to join together as many of the rings as you want. Attach the trellis between two stakes, also using twist ties. You can even add sections to the trellis as the plant grows so that it looks like the plant is climbing on its own. At the end of the season, just roll the trellis up for storage and you can use it again next year.

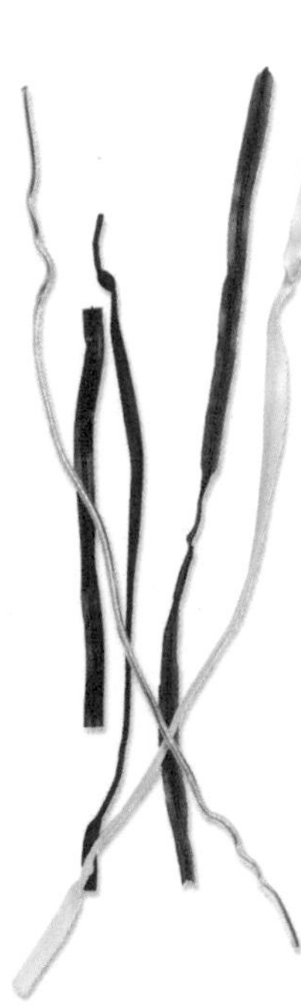

Tie up plant stems Twist ties are useful for securing drooping plant stems to a stake or holding climbers onto a trellis. Don't twist the ties too tight, because you might injure the stem and restrict its growth.

Temporarily repair a pair of glasses If your specs are slipping because a tiny screw that holds the earpiece has fallen out, secure the earpiece temporarily with a twist tie. Trim the edges off the tie to reveal just the centre wire. After you insert and tie it off, snip off the excess wire with scissors.

Use as an emergency shoelace When you don't have a replacement shoelace handy, try some twist ties. Use one tie across each opposing pair of eyelets.

Code your keys If there are several similar-looking keys on your chain, identify them with twist ties of different colours secured through the holes in the keys.

Hang Christmas tree ornaments. When Christmas tree ornaments have been in the family for generations, secure them to the tree with twist ties as extra insurance against breakages.

Make an emergency cuff link If you have packed a smart shirt with double cuffs to wear to a wedding, but forgot to pack cuff links, secure the cuffs with twist ties. Pull the ties through so the twist is discreetly hidden inside the cuff.

Bind loose-leaf paper Hold sheets of loose-leaf paper together by inserting twist ties in the holes.

Tyres

Protect vegetables Plant tomatoes, potatoes, aubergines, peppers or other vegetables inside tyres laid on the ground. The tyres will protect the plants from harsh winds and the dark rubber will absorb heat from the sun and warm the surrounding soil.

Make a paddling pool for children To make an impromptu paddling pool for toddlers, drape a shower curtain or other piece of waterproof material over the centre of a large lorry tyre and fill it with water.

Make a classic tyre swing A swing made from an old tyre is a timeless source of pleasure for children of all ages. To make one for the garden, drill a few drainage holes in the bottom of the tyre. Drill two holes for bolts in the top, bolt two chains or strong pieces of rope to the tyre, and suspend it by the chains from a healthy branch of a large tree. Put some wood chips or other soft material under and around the swing to cushion falls.

TIP* TYRE CHECKUPS

Spending 5 minutes a month to check your tyres can protect against avoidable breakdowns and crashes, improve vehicle handling, increase mileage and extend the life of your tyres.

Here are some guidelines:

- Check tyre pressure at least once a month and before going on a long journey.
- Don't forget to take a spare.
- Inspect for uneven wear on tyre treads, cracks, foreign objects or other signs of wear or damage. Remove bits of glass and other objects wedged in the tread.
- Make sure your tyre valves have caps.
- Do not overload your vehicle.

Umbrellas

Use as a drying rack An old umbrella makes a handy clothes drying rack. Strip off the fabric and hang the frame upside down from the shower rail. Attach wet clothing with clothes pegs. Your new drying rack will fold up easily for storage.

Clean a chandelier The next time you climb up to clean a chandelier or ceiling fan, bring an old umbrella with you. Open the umbrella and hook its handle on the fixture so that it hangs upside down to catch any drips or dust.

Cover picnic food To keep flies from feasting on a picnic place an old umbrella witht handle cut off over the dishes. It will shield your feast from the sun too.

Signal in a crowd The next time you and a friend go to a crowded event, carry a couple of identical brightly-coloured umbrellas. If you get separated, you can hold the umbrellas over your head and open them up to find each other in a flash.

Block plant overspray Houseplants always benefit from a misting with water, but walls don't enjoy being soaked as well. Place an open umbrella between the plants and the wall and give your plants a shower.

Make plant stakes If the wind has caught your umbrella, turned it inside out and ripped the fabric, before throwing it away, remove the ribs to make excellent supports for top-heavy garden plants, such as peonies.

Make an instant trellis Remove the fabric from an old umbrella and insert the handle into the ground to support climbing vines such as clematis. The umbrella's shape, covered with flowers, will look terrific in the garden.

Shield your seedlings If you thought you had waited long enough before planting your seedlings outside, but a killer frost is now forecast, sacrifice an old umbrella to save the seedlings. Open the umbrella, then cut off the handle. Place the umbrella over the seedlings to keep the frost away from them.

 Vanilla extract

Freshen up the fridge If an unpleasant smell is lingering in the fridge even after it has been thoroughly scrubbed, try wiping down the inside of the fridge with vanilla extract. To prolong the scent, soak a cotton wool ball or a piece of sponge with vanilla extract and leave it in the refrigerator.

Deodorise the microwave Is a strong fishy or spicy smell lurking in the microwave? Pour a little vanilla extract into a bowl and microwave it on High for 1 minute to get rid of the residual odour.

Neutralise the smell of fresh paint If you are not a fan of the smell of fresh paint, mix 1 tablespoon vanilla extract into the paint when you open it. The newly decorated house will smell as good as it looks.

Use as a perfume Put a dab of vanilla extract on each wrist; you will smell delicious and many people find the scent of vanilla very relaxing.

Repel bugs Almost everyone likes the smell of vanilla. But most insects hate it. Dilute 1 tablespoon vanilla extract in 200ml water and wipe the mixture on your exposed skin to discourage mosquitoes, flies and ticks.

Relieve minor burns If you've accidentally picked up a hot pan or been splashed with grease from a frying pan, use vanilla extract to give quick pain relief. The evaporation of the alcohol in the vanilla extract will cool the burn.

Sweeten the smell of your home Estate agents and property stagers who specialise in making homes appealing to buyers recommend this tip. Put a drop or two of vanilla extract on a lightbulb, turn on the light and your house will be filled with the appealing scent of fresh baking.

Vegetable oil

Help to remove a splinter When a stubborn splinter won't come out, don't keep poking at it. Instead soak it in vegetable oil. The oil should soften up your skin, perhaps just enough to be able to ease the splinter out with tweezers.

Remove labels and stickers Used jars, both plastic and glass, are always useful. But removing the old labels invariably leaves a sticky residue. Soak the label with vegetable oil and the label will slide off. It works well for sticky price tags as well.

Separate stuck glasses When stacked drinking glasses get stuck together, it seems like nothing you can do will separate them without breakage. But the solution is simple: just pour a little vegetable oil around the rim of the bottom glass and the glasses will pull apart with ease.

Smooth your feet Rub dry feet with vegetable oil before you go to bed and put on a pair of socks. When you wake up, they will be soft and smooth.

Prevent clippings from sticking to a mower The next time you turn over the lawn mower to remove stuck-on grass clippings, rub some vegetable oil under the housing and on to the blade. Next time, it will take a lot longer for clippings to build up again.

Control mosquitoes near a birdbath It is so satisfying to watch birds enjoying the garden bath you have provided. But unfortunately, still water can be a perfect breeding ground for mosquitoes. Floating a few tablespoons of vegetable oil on the surface of the water will help to keep mosquitoes from using the water and it won't bother the birds. But it is still important to change the water twice a week so that any insect larvae don't have time to hatch.

Season cast-iron cookware After washing and thoroughly drying a cast-iron grill pan or wok, use a paper towel to wipe it down with vegetable oil. Just leave a very thin layer of oil. It will prevent the pan from rusting and season it for the next time you use it.

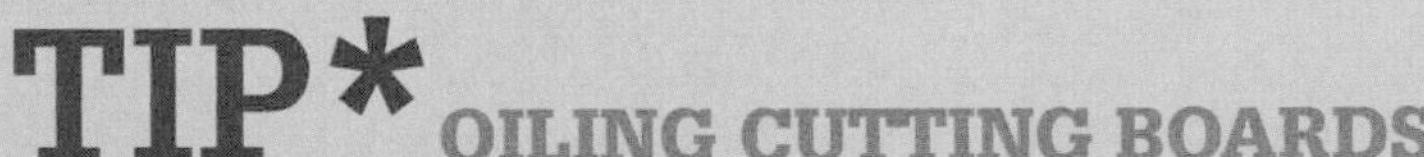

TIP* OILING CUTTING BOARDS

To restore and preserve dried-out wooden kitchen items such as cutting boards and salad bowls and tongs, use salad bowl oil – a special mineral oil that is safe to use near food, won't go rancid and is designed to protect wood that comes into contact with food. It is best not to use ordinary vegetable oil which will soak into dried-out wood and make it look much better, but never really dries and can get rancid after it has soaked into the wood.

* Vegetable peelers

Slice slivers of cheese or chocolate When you need cheese slivers that are thinner than you can cut with a knife or want to decorate a cake with fine curlicues of chocolate, use a vegetable peeler.

Sharpen a pencil When you've no pencil sharpener to hand, a vegetable peeler will do an excellent job of bringing your pencil to a point.

Soften hard butter fast When you need to soften cold, hard butter in a hurry – to use in a cake mixture for example – shave off what you need with a vegetable peeler. The butter will be soft in moments.

Renew scented soaps Ornamental scented soaps are a great addition to a toilet or guest bathroom because they make the room smell great as well as adding a decorative touch. But after a while, the surface of exposed soaps dries out, causing the scent to fade. To renew the scent, use a vegetable peeler to skim off a thin layer, revealing a new moist and fragrant surface.

VINEGAR...

...around the house

Remove dirt from computer equipment Computers, printers, fax machines and other office electronics will work better if they are clean and dust-free. Before you start cleaning, make sure that all the equipment is switched off. Mix equal quantities of white vinegar and water in a bowl. Dampen a clean cloth in the solution (never use a spray bottle; it is important not to get liquid on the circuits inside) then squeeze it out as hard as you can and start wiping. Keep a few cotton buds on hand for getting to build-ups of dirt in tight spaces (for example, around the keys of your keyboard).

Clean a computer mouse If you have a mouse with a removable tracking ball, use a 50/50 vinegar-water solution to clean it. First, remove the ball from underneath the mouse by twisting off the cover. Use a cloth, dampened with the solution and wrung out, to wipe the ball clean and to remove fingerprints and dirt from the mouse itself. Then use a moistened cotton bud to clean out the dirt and debris from inside the ball chamber (let it dry for a couple of hours before reinserting the ball).

Clean window blinds Make the job of cleaning slatted blinds considerably less torturous by giving them the 'white glove treatment'. Just put on a white cotton glove – the kind sold for gardening is perfect – and moisten the fingers in a solution made of equal parts white vinegar and hot tap water. Simply slide your fingers across both sides of each slat and prepare to be amazed. Keep a container of clean water nearby to periodically rinse the glove.

Clean chrome and stainless steel To clean chrome and stainless-steel fixtures, apply a light misting of undiluted white vinegar from a recycled spray bottle. Buff the item with a soft cloth to bring out the brightness.

TIP* BUYING VINEGAR

Vinegar comes in a surprising number of varieties: balsamic, Champagne, rice, and wine, not to mention bottle sizes. For household chores, however, plain distilled white vinegar is the best and least expensive choice, and you can buy it in large bottles to save even more money. Cider vinegar runs a close second in practicality and is also widely used in cooking and home remedies. All other types of vinegar should be used only with food.

Unblock and deodorise drains The combination of vinegar and bicarbonate of soda is one of the most effective ways to unblock and deodorise drains. It is also far gentler on your pipes (and your wallet) than commercial drain cleaners.

- To clear blockages in sink and bath drains, use a funnel to pour in 100g bicarbonate of soda followed by 200ml vinegar. When the foaming subsides, flush with hot tap water. Wait 4 minutes and flush again with cold water. As well as clearing blockages, this also washes away bacteria that can cause odours.
- To speed up a slow drain, pour in 100g salt followed by 400ml boiling vinegar, then flush with hot and cold tap water.

Get rid of the smell of smoke If you have recently burned a steak, or if a chain-smoking friend or relative has paid a surprise visit, remove the lingering smoky smell by placing a shallow bowl about three-quarters full of white or cider vinegar in the room where the smell is strongest. Use several bowls if the smell permeates the entire house. The smoky residue should be gone in less than a day. You can also quickly disperse the smell of fresh cigarette smoke inside a room by moistening a cloth with vinegar and waving it around.

Unglue stickers and price tags To remove a sticker or price tag from painted furniture or a painted wall, saturate the corners and sides of the sticker with full-strength white vinegar and carefully scrape it off (using an expired credit card or a plastic phone card). Remove any sticky remains by pouring on a bit more vinegar. Let it sit for a minute or two, and then wipe with a clean cloth. This approach is equally effective for removing price tags and other stickers from glass, plastic and other glossy surfaces.

Wipe away mildew When you want to remove mildew stains, try white vinegar first. It can be safely used without additional ventilation and can be applied to almost any surface: bathroom fixtures and tiles, clothing, furniture, painted surfaces, plastic curtains and many other items. To eliminate heavy accumulations of mildew, use it at full strength. For light stains, dilute it with an equal amount of water. You can also prevent mildew from forming on the bottoms of rugs and carpets by misting the backs with full-strength white vinegar from a spray bottle.

VINEGAR...

...around the house

{TAKE CARE}

- Do not apply vinegar to jewellery containing pearls or gemstones because it can damage their finish or, in the case of pearls, actually disintegrate them.
- Do not attempt to remove tarnish from antiques, because removing the 'patina' could diminish their value.

Give a shine to silver Make silverware, as well as pure silver bracelets, rings and other jewellery, shine like new by soaking in a mixture of 100ml white vinegar and 2 tablespoons bicarbonate of soda for 2-3 hours. Rinse in cold water and dry thoroughly with a soft cloth.

Polish brass and copper items Put the shine back into brass, bronze and copper objects by making a paste of equal parts white vinegar and salt or vinegar and bicarbonate of soda (wait for the fizzing to stop before using). Use a clean, soft cloth or paper towel to rub the paste into the item until the tarnish has gone. Then rinse with cool water and polish with a soft towel until dry.

Burnish a pair of scissors When scissor blades get sticky or grimy, don't use water to wash them off; you are far more likely to rust the fastener that holds the blades together, or the blades themselves, than get them clean. Instead, wipe down the blades with a cloth dipped in full-strength white vinegar and then dry off with a rag or towel.

Remove salt stains from shoes Ice, slush and snow are hard on shoes and boots, but the worst thing by far is the salt that is used to melt it. It leaves an unsightly white stain and can cause your footwear to crack and disintegrate if it is left on indefinitely. To remove it and prevent long-term damage, wipe fresh stains with a cloth dipped in undiluted white vinegar.

Clean piano keys Here is an easy and efficient way to get grimy fingerprints and stains off piano keys. Dip a soft cloth into a solution of 100ml white vinegar mixed in 400ml water, squeeze it out until there are no drips, then gently wipe off each key. Use a second cloth to dry off the keys as you move along, then leave the keyboard uncovered for 24 hours.

Remove old smells from lunch boxes and car boots Has your child's lunch box taken on the bouquet of week-old tuna? What about the musty old car boot? Stop holding your breath every time you open it. Instead, soak a slice of white bread in white vinegar and leave it overnight. The smell should be gone by morning.

Freshen a musty wardrobe or cupboard If a wardrobe or cupboard doesn't smell as fresh as you would like, remove the contents, then wash down the walls, ceiling and floor with a cloth dampened in a solution of 200ml each of vinegar and ammonia and 50g bicarbonate of soda in 4 litres water. Keep the door open and let the interior dry before replacing your clothes and accessories. If the smell persists, place a small tray of clean cat litter inside. Replenish every few days until the odour is gone.

DID YOU KNOW?

Taken literally, vinegar is nothing more than wine that's gone bad; the word derives from the French vin (wine) and aigre (sour). But, in fact, anything used to make alcohol can be turned into vinegar, including apples, honey, malted barley, molasses, rice, sugar cane and even coconuts. Vinegar's acidic, solvent properties were well known even in ancient times. According to one popular legend, Cleopatra is said to have wagered she could dispose of a fortune in the course of a single meal. She won the bet by dissolving a handful of pearls in a cup of vinegar ... and then consuming it.

Erase ballpoint-pen marks Dab some full-strength white vinegar on the marks using a cloth or a sponge. Repeat until the marks are gone.

Brighten up brickwork Here is an effortless way to clean a brick path or fireplace surround. Use a damp mop dipped in 200ml white vinegar mixed with 4 litres warm water, for bright, fresh brickwork.

Revitalise wood panelling Mix 450ml warm water, 4 tablespoons white or apple cider vinegar, and 2 tablespoons olive oil in a container, give it a couple of shakes, and apply to the panelling with a clean cloth. Let the mixture soak into the wood for several minutes, then polish with a dry cloth.

Restore a rug If your rugs or carpets are looking worn and dingy from too much foot traffic or an excess of children's building blocks, toy trucks and other miscellaneous equipment, bring them back to life by brushing them with a clean broom dipped in a solution of 200ml white vinegar in 4 litres water. The faded floor-coverings will look much brighter and you won't even need to rinse the solution away.

Remove carpet stains You can lift out a range of stains from a carpet with vinegar:

- Rub light carpet stains with a mixture of 2 tablespoons salt dissolved in 100ml white vinegar. Let the solution dry, then vacuum.
- For larger or darker stains, add 2 tablespoons borax to the mixture and use in the same way.
- For tough, ground-in dirt make a paste of 1 tablespoon vinegar with 1 tablespoon cornflour and rub it into the stain using a dry cloth. Let it set for two days, then vacuum.
- To make spray-on spot and stain remover, fill a spray bottle with 5 parts water and 1 part vinegar. Fill a second spray bottle with 1 part non-foaming ammonia and 5 parts water. Saturate a stain with the vinegar solution. Let it settle for a few minutes, then blot thoroughly with a clean, dry cloth. Then spray and blot using the ammonia solution. Repeat until the stain has gone.

VINEGAR...

...in the garage

Remove bumper stickers Saturate the top and sides of the sticker with undiluted distilled vinegar and wait 10-15 minutes for the vinegar to soak through. Then use an expired credit card to scrape it off. Use more full-strength vinegar to get rid of any remaining gluey residue. Use the same technique to detach stickers that your child has used to decorate the rear windscreen.

Clean windscreen wiper blades When a windscreen actually becomes more blurry after you turn on the wipers when it is raining, it usually means that the wiper blades are dirty. To clean them, dampen a cloth or rag with some full-strength white vinegar and run it down the full length of each blade a couple of times.

Keep car windows frost-free If you park your car outdoors during the winter, a simple way to keep frost from forming on the windows is by wiping (or, better yet, spraying) the outsides of the windows with a solution of 3 parts white vinegar to 1 part water. Each vinegar coating may last up to several weeks.

Clean carpets in a car A good vacuuming will remove sand and other loose debris from carpets, but it won't remove stains or ground-in dirt. Mix up a solution of equal parts water and white vinegar and sponge it into the carpet. Give the mixture a couple of minutes to settle in, then blot it up with a cloth or paper towel. This technique will also eliminate salt residue left on car carpets during winter months.

...for furniture care

Remove candle wax Candles create a romantic mood, but melted candle wax on the furniture may be an unwelcome consequence. To remove it, first soften the wax using a hair-drier on the hottest setting and blot up as much melted wax as you can with paper towels. Then remove what is left by rubbing with a cloth soaked in a solution made of equal parts white vinegar and water. Wipe clean with a soft, absorbent cloth.

{TAKE CARE}

Don't use vinegar on marble tabletops, worktops or floors. The acidity of vinegar can dull or even pit the protective coating and possibly damage the stone itself. Also, avoid using vinegar on travertine and limestone; the acid eats through the calcium in the stonework.

Give grease stains the slip Eliminate grease stains from a kitchen table or worktop by wiping them down with a cloth dampened in a solution of equal parts white vinegar and water. In addition to removing the grease, the vinegar will neutralise any residual odours.

Conceal scratches in wooden furniture To make a scratch much less noticeable, mix some distilled or cider vinegar and iodine in a small jar and paint over the mark with a small artist's brush. Use more iodine for dark woods; more vinegar for light shades.

Get rid of water rings on furniture To remove white rings left by wet glasses on wooden furniture, mix equal parts vinegar and olive oil and apply it with a soft cloth while moving with the wood grain. Use another clean, soft cloth to give a shine. To remove white water rings from leather furniture, dab them with a sponge soaked in full-strength white vinegar.

Wipe off wax or polish buildup When furniture polish or wax builds up on wooden furniture or leather tabletops, remove it with diluted white vinegar. To remove built-up polish from a piece of wooden furniture, dip a cloth in equal parts vinegar and water and squeeze it out well. Then, moving with the grain, clean away the polish. Wipe dry with a soft towel or cloth. Most leather tabletops will come clean simply by wiping them down with a soft cloth dipped in 50ml vinegar and 100ml water. Use a clean towel to dry off any remaining liquid.

Revitalise leather furniture If a leather sofa or easy chair has lost its lustrous finish, restore it to its former glory, by mixing equal parts white vinegar and boiled linseed oil (buy this ready boiled) in a recycled spray bottle. Shake it up well, and spray it on. Spread it evenly over the piece of furniture using a soft cloth, give it a couple of minutes to settle in, then rub it off with a clean cloth.

...in the kitchen

Refresh a refrigerator Vinegar is probably an even more effective safe cleanser for your fridge than bicarbonate of soda. Use equal parts white vinegar and water to wash both the interior and exterior of your fridge, including the door seal and the fronts of the vegetable and fruit crispers. To prevent the growth of mildew, wash the inside walls and the interiors of the crispers with some full-strength vinegar on a cloth. Also use undiluted vinegar to wipe off accumulated dust and grime on top of the fridge.

Steam-clean the microwave To clean a microwave, place a glass bowl filled with a solution of 50ml vinegar in 200ml water inside and heat the mixture for 5 minutes on the highest setting. Once the bowl cools, dip a cloth or sponge into the liquid and use it to wipe away stains and splatters on the interior.

TIP* VINEGAR AND FLOOR CLEANING

Damp-mopping with a mild vinegar solution is widely recommended as a way to clean wood, vinyl or laminate flooring. But, if possible, check with the manufacturer first. Even when diluted, vinegar's acidity can ruin some finishes and too much water will damage most wooden floors. If you want to try vinegar on your floors, use 100ml white vinegar mixed in 4 litres warm water. Start with a trial application in an inconspicuous area. Before applying the solution, squeeze out the mop thoroughly (or just use a spray bottle to moisten the mop head).

VINEGAR...

...in the kitchen

Clean china, crystal and glassware Put the sparkle back into glassware by adding vinegar to the rinse water or dishwater.

- To make glassware gleam, add 50ml vinegar to the dishwasher's rinse cycle.
- To rid drinking glasses of the cloudiness caused by hard water, heat up a pan containing equal parts white vinegar and water (use full-strength vinegar if your glasses are very cloudy), and let them soak in it for 15-30 minutes. Scrub them well with a bottle brush, then rinse clean.
- Add 2 tablespoons vinegar to the dishwater when cleaning crystal glasses. Then rinse them in a solution of 3 parts warm water to 1 part vinegar and allow them to air-dry. You can also wash delicate crystal and fine china by adding 200ml vinegar to a basin of warm water. Gently dunk the glasses in the solution and let them dry.
- To remove coffee stains and other discolorations from china, try scrubbing them with equal parts vinegar and salt, followed by a rinse in warm water.

Cut the grease Distilled vinegar is one of the best grease cutters around. It even works on seriously greasy surfaces such as the frying vats used in many food outlets. Here are other ways to put vinegar to good use in the kitchen:

- When you have finished frying, clean up grease splashes from the hob, walls, cooker hood, and surrounding worktop by washing them with a sponge dipped in undiluted white vinegar. Use another sponge soaked in cold tap water to rinse, then wipe dry with a soft cloth.
- Pour 3-4 tablespoons white vinegar into a bottle of washing-up liquid and shake. The added vinegar will increase its grease-fighting capabilities and give you more washing-up liquid for the money, as you will need to use less.
- Boiling 200ml vinegar in a frying pan for 10 minutes will help to keep food from sticking to it for several months at a time.
- Remove burned-on grease and food stains from stainless-steel cookware by mixing 200ml distilled vinegar in enough water to cover the stains (if they are near the top of a large pan, you may need to increase the vinegar). Let it boil for 5 minutes. The stains should come off with a light scrubbing.
- Remove blackened, cooked-on grease from a grill pan by softening it up with a solution of 200ml apple cider vinegar and 2 tablespoons sugar. Apply the mixture while the pan is still hot and let it sit for an hour or so. Then watch in amazement as the grime slides off following a light scrub.
- If a hot plate is looking more like a grease pan, wash it with a sponge dipped in full-strength white vinegar.
- Stop grease from building up inside the oven by wiping down the inside with a rag or sponge soaked in full-strength white vinegar once a week. The same treatment will get grease off the grates on gas cookers.

TIP* HOMEMADE WINE VINEGAR

Contrary to popular belief, old wine rarely turns into vinegar; usually a half-empty bottle just spoils due to oxidation. To create vinegar, you need the presence of *Acetobacter*, a specific type of bacteria. You can make your own wine vinegar, though, by mixing one part leftover red, white or rosé wine with 2 parts cider vinegar. Pour the mixture into a clean, recycled wine bottle and store it in a dark cupboard. It may taste as good, if not better, on a salad than an expensive wine vinegar from a delicatessen.

Disinfect cutting boards To disinfect and clean wooden cutting boards or a butcher's block worktop, wipe them with full-strength white vinegar after each use. The acetic acid in the vinegar is a good disinfectant, effective against such harmful bugs as *E. coli*, *Salmonella* and *Staphylococcus*. Never use water and washing-up liquid, because it can weaken the surface fibres of wood. To remove strong smells such as onion or fish from the wooden cutting surface, spread some bicarbonate of soda over it and then spray on undiluted white vinegar. Let it foam and bubble for 5-10 minutes, then rinse with a cloth dipped in clean cold water.

Deodorise a waste disposal unit Mix equal parts water and vinegar in a bowl, pour the solution into an ice cube tray and freeze it. Then simply drop a couple of 'vinegar cubes' down the waste disposal every week or so, followed by a cold-water rinse to keep it smelling fresh.

Wash out the dishwasher To keep a dishwasher operating at peak performance and remove built-up soap film, pour 200ml undiluted white vinegar into the bottom of the unit or in a bowl on the top rack. Then run the machine through a full cycle without any dishes or detergent. Do this once a month, especially if you live in a hard water area. Note: If there is no mention of vinegar in your dishwasher owner's manual, check with the manufacturer before trying this.

Clean a coffeemaker If your coffee consistently comes out weak or bitter, it is likely that the coffeemaker needs cleaning. Fill the decanter with 400ml white vinegar and 200ml water. Place a filter in the machine, and pour the solution into the coffeemaker's water chamber. Turn on the coffeemaker and let it run through a full brew cycle. Remove the filter and replace it with a fresh one. Then run clean water through the machine for two full cycles, replacing the filter again for the second brew. If you have soft water, clean the coffeemaker after 80 brew cycles and after 40 cycles if you have hard water.

Clean a tea kettle To eliminate lime and mineral deposits in a kettle, bring 600ml full-strength white vinegar to the boil. Boil for 5 minutes and leave the vinegar in the kettle overnight. Rinse out with cold water the next day.

VINEGAR...

...in the kitchen

Remove stains from pots, pans and ovenware Nothing does a better job than vinegar when it comes to removing stubborn stains on cookware. Here is how to put the power of vinegar to use:

- Get rid of dark stains on aluminium cookware (caused by cooking acidic foods) by mixing in 1 teaspoon white vinegar for every cup of water needed to cover the stains. Let it boil for a couple of minutes, then rinse with cold water.
- To remove stains from stainless-steel pots and pans, soak them in 400ml white vinegar for 30 minutes, then rinse with hot, soapy water followed by a rinse in cold water.
- To get cooked-on food stains off glass ovenware, fill with 1 part vinegar and 4 parts water, heat the mixture to a slow boil and let it boil at a low level for 5 minutes. The stains should come off with a light scrub once the mixture has cooled down.
- It may be non-stick, but no pot or pan is stainproof. For mineral stains on non-stick cookware, rub with a cloth dipped in undiluted, distilled vinegar. To loosen up stubborn stains, mix 2 tablespoons baking soda, 100ml vinegar and 200ml water and let it boil for 10 minutes.

Clear the air in the kitchen If the smell of yesterday's cooked cabbage or fish stew is hanging around the kitchen, mix a pan of 100ml white vinegar in 200ml water. Let it boil until the liquid is almost gone and the smell should disappear with it.

Refresh an ice cube tray If your plastic ice cube trays are covered with hard-water stains, or if it has been a while since they were cleaned, remove spots or disinfect the trays, by soaking them in undiluted vinegar for 4-5 hours, then rinse well under cold water and let them dry.

Trap fruit flies Make flytraps that can be used anywhere around the house by filling an old jar about halfway full of apple cider vinegar. Punch a few holes in the lid, screw it back on and place the jar where flies tend to gather.

DID YOU KNOW?

True balsamic vinegar comes only from Modena, in northern Italy, and is made from Trebbiano grapes, a particularly sweet white variety grown in the surrounding hills. Italian law mandates that the vinegar be aged in wooden barrels made of chestnut, juniper, mulberry or oak. There are only two grades of true balsamic vinegar, which typically sells for between £60 and £120 for a 100ml bottle: *tradizionale vecchio*, vinegar that is at least 12 years old, and *tradizionale extra vecchio*, vinegar that has aged for at least 25 years (some balsamic vinegars are known to have been aged for more than 100 years).

Make an all-purpose scrub for pots and pans Here is an effective scouring mix that costs a few pence and can be safely used on all metal cookware, including expensive copper pots and pans. Combine equal parts salt and flour and add just enough vinegar to make a paste. Work the paste around the cooking surface and the outside of the utensil, then rinse off with warm water and dry thoroughly with a soft dish towel.

Sterilise jars, containers and vases Do you dislike cleaning out mayonnaise, peanut butter or mustard jars to reuse them? Or worse, getting the residue out of a slimy vase, decanter or container? There is an easy way to handle these jobs. Fill the item with equal parts vinegar and warm, soapy water and let it stand for 10-15 minutes. If you are cleaning a bottle or jar, close it up and give it a few good shakes; otherwise use a bottle brush to scrape off the remains before giving it a thorough rinsing.

Clean a dirty Thermos To get a Thermos flask clean, fill it with warm water and 50ml white vinegar. If you see any residue, add some uncooked rice, which will act as an abrasive to scrape it off. Close and shake well. Then rinse and air-dry.

Make all-purpose cleaners For fast cleaning around the kitchen, keep two recycled spray bottles filled with these vinegar-based solutions:

- For glass, stainless steel and plastic laminate surfaces, fill a spray bottle with 2 parts water, 1 part distilled white vinegar and a couple of drops of washing-up liquid.
- For cleaning walls and other painted surfaces, mix 100ml white vinegar, 200ml ammonia and 50g bicarbonate of soda in 4 litres water and pour some into a spray bottle. Spray onto spots and stains as needed and wipe off with a clean towel.

Purge insects from your pantry or cupboards Are moths or other insects invading the pantry? Fill a small bowl with 300ml apple cider vinegar and add a couple of drops of washing-up liquid. Leave it in there for a week; it will attract the insects, which will fall into the bowl and drown. Then empty the shelves and give the interior a thorough wash with washing-up liquid or 400g bicarbonate of soda in 1 litre water. Discard all wheat products (breads, pasta, flour and similar) and wipe down cans of food before putting them back.

Tenderise meat and fish Soaking a lean or inexpensive cut of red meat in 400ml vinegar breaks down tough fibres to make it more tender – and also kills off any potentially harmful bacteria. You can also use vinegar to tenderise fish steaks. Let the meat or fish soak in full-strength vinegar overnight. Experiment with different vinegar varieties for added flavour or simply use apple cider or distilled vinegar if you intend to rinse it off before cooking.

Wash fruit and vegetables You can't be too careful when it comes to handling the foods you eat. Before cooking and serving fruit and vegetables, a good way to eliminate hidden dirt, pesticides and even insects, is to rinse them in 4 tablespoons apple cider vinegar dissolved in 4 litres cold water.

VINEGAR...

...in the kitchen

Make better boiled or poached eggs Vinegar does marvellous things for eggs. Here are the two most useful:

- When you are making hard-boiled eggs, adding 2 tablespoons distilled vinegar for every litre of water will keep the eggs from cracking and make them much easier to shell.
- When you are poaching eggs, adding a couple of tablespoons of vinegar to the water will keep your eggs in a tight shape by preventing the egg whites from spreading.

Remove strong smells from your hands It is often difficult to get strong onion, garlic or fish odours off your hands after preparing a meal. But you will find these scents are a lot easier to get rid of if you rub some distilled vinegar on your hands before and after you slice vegetables or clean fish.

Get rid of berry stains Use undiluted white vinegar on your hands to remove dark stains from berries and other fruits.

...in the medicine cabinet

Control dandruff To give dandruff the brush-off, follow up each shampoo with a rinse of 400ml apple cider vinegar mixed with 400ml cold water. Another method is to apply 3 tablespoons vinegar to your hair and massage it into your scalp before you shampoo. Wait a few minutes, then rinse it out and wash as usual.

Condition your hair Put the life back into limp or damaged hair by combining 1 teaspoon apple cider vinegar with 2 tablespoons olive oil and three egg whites. Rub the mixture into your hair, then keep it covered for 30 minutes using cling film or a shower cap. Then shampoo and rinse as usual.

Protect blonde hair from chlorine Keep golden locks from turning green in a chlorinated swimming pool by rubbing 50ml cider vinegar into your hair and letting it set for 15 minutes before diving in.

Use as an antiperspirant You don't need a roll-on or spray to keep underarms smelling fresh. Instead, splash a little white vinegar under each arm in the morning and let it dry. In addition to combating perspiration odours, using this method means that you won't get deodorant stains on your clothes.

DID YOU KNOW?

The world's only museum dedicated to vinegar, the International Vinegar Museum, is based in Roslyn, South Dakota, USA. It is run by Dr Lawrence J. Diggs, an international vinegar consultant also known as the Vinegar Man. You can visit him online at **www.vinegarman.com** The museum showcases vinegars from around the world, has displays on the various methods used to make vinegar, and even lets visitors sample different types of vinegars.

Soak away aching muscles If you have a sore back, a strained tendon in your shoulder or calf, or are feeling generally run down, adding 400ml apple cider vinegar to a bath is a great way to soothe away aches and pains or simply to take the edge off a stressful day. Adding a few drops of peppermint oil to the bath is also a great muscle relaxant and stress reliever.

Freshen your breath After you eat a lot of garlic or onions, a quick and easy way to sweeten your breath is to rinse your mouth with a solution made by dissolving 2 tablespoons apple cider vinegar and 1 teaspoon salt in a glass of warm water.

Ease sunburn and itching You can cool painful sunburn by gently dabbing the area with a cotton wool ball or soft cloth saturated with white or cider vinegar. (This treatment is especially effective if it is applied before the burn starts to sting.) The same technique will stop itching from mosquito and other insect bites.

Banish bruises Speed healing and prevent black-and-blue marks after a painful fall by soaking a piece of cotton gauze in white or apple cider vinegar and leaving it on the injured area for an hour.

Soothe a sore throat Here are three ways that you can make a sore throat feel better by using vinegar:

- Gargle with 1 tablespoon apple cider vinegar and 1 teaspoon salt dissolved in a glass of warm water; use several times a day if needed.
- For a sore throat as a result of a cold or flu, combine 50ml cider vinegar and 50ml honey and take 1 tablespoon every 4 hours.
- To soothe a cough and a sore throat, mix 100ml vinegar, 100ml water, 4 teaspoons honey, and 1 teaspoon hot sauce. Swallow 1 tablespoon four or five times a day, including one before bedtime.
  WARNING Children under a year old should never be given honey.

VINEGAR...

...in the medicine cabinet

Breathe easier Adding 50ml white vinegar to the water in a hot-steam vaporiser can help ease congestion from a chest cold or sinus infection. It is also good for your vapouriser as the vinegar will clear away any mineral deposits in the water tubes resulting from the use of hard water. Note: check with the manufacturer before adding vinegar to a cool-mist vaporiser.

Treat an active cold sore Quickly dry up a painful cold sore by dabbing it with a cotton wool ball saturated in white vinegar three times a day. The vinegar will quickly soothe the pain and swelling.

Make a poultice for corns and callouses This is an an old-fashioned, time-honoured method for treating corns and callouses. Saturate a piece of white or stale bread with 50ml white vinegar. Let the bread soak in the vinegar for 30 minutes, then break off a piece big enough to completely cover the corn. Keep the poultice in place with gauze or adhesive plaster and leave it on overnight. The next morning, the hard skin will be dissolved and the corn should be easy to remove. Older, thicker callouses may require several treatments.

Get rid of athlete's foot Quell the infection and quickly ease the itching from athlete's foot by rinsing your feet three or four times a day for a few days with undiluted apple cider vinegar. As an added precaution, soak socks or stockings in a mixture of 1 part vinegar and 4 parts water for 30 minutes before washing them.

Pamper your skin Using vinegar as a skin toner dates back to the time of Helen of Troy. And it is just as effective today. After you wash your face, mix 1 tablespoon apple cider vinegar with 400ml water as a finishing rinse to cleanse and tighten your skin. You can also make your own facial treatment by mixing 50ml cider vinegar with 50ml water. Gently apply the solution to your face and let it dry.

Fade age or sun spots Before you take any drastic measures to remove or cover up the brown spots on your skin caused by over-exposure to the sun or hormonal changes, try vinegar. Simply pour some full-strength apple cider vinegar onto a cotton wool ball and apply it to the spots for 10 minutes at least twice a day. The spots should fade or disappear within a few weeks.

Soften your cuticles You can soften the cuticles on your fingers and toes before giving yourself a manicure by soaking your hands or feet in a bowl of undiluted white vinegar for 5 minutes.

Make nail varnish last longer Nail varnish will have a longer life expectancy if you first dampen your nails with some vinegar on a cotton wool ball and let it dry before applying your favourite varnish.

Clean a pair of glasses When it is harder to see with your glasses on than it is with them off, they probably need a thorough clean. If your specs have glass lenses, applying a few drops of white vinegar and wiping them with a soft cloth will easily remove dirt, sweat and fingerprints, to leave them spotless. But you shouldn't use vinegar on plastic lenses.

Treat a jellyfish or bee sting If you have an encounter with a jellyfish, pouring some undiluted vinegar on the sting will quickly take away the pain and allow you to scrape out the stinger with a plastic credit card. The same treatment can also be used to treat bee stings. But using vinegar on stings inflicted by the jellyfish's cousin the Portuguese man-of-war is now discouraged because vinegar may actually increase the amount of toxin released under the skin.

WARNING If you have difficulty breathing or the sting area becomes inflamed and swollen, it is important to seek medical attention at once; you could be having an allergic reaction.

...in the bathroom

Wash mildew from shower curtains Clean mildew off a plastic shower curtain by putting it in the washing machine with a couple of dirty towels. Add 100g laundry detergent and 100g bicarbonate of soda to the load, and wash it in warm water on the machine's regular cycle. Add 200ml white vinegar to the first rinse. Before the machine goes into its spin cycle, remove the curtain and hang it up to dry.

Shine ceramic tiles If soap scum or water spots have dulled the ceramic tiles around your sink or bath, bring back the brightness by scrubbing them with 100ml white vinegar, 100ml ammonia and 50g borax mixed in 4 litres warm water. Rinse well with cool water and let the tiles air-dry.

Whiten tile grout Has the grout between the tiles of the bath or shower enclosure become stained or discoloured? Restore it to its original shade of white by using a toothbrush dipped in undiluted white vinegar to scrub away the dirt.

Clean the sink Put the shine back into a porcelain sink by scrubbing it with full-strength white vinegar, followed by a rinse with clean cold water. To remove hard-water stains from the bath, pour in 600ml white vinegar under hot running tap water. Let the bath fill up over the stains and allow it to soak for 4 hours. When the water drains out, you should easily be able to scrub off the stains.

DID YOU KNOW?

Recent research has shown that vinegar may be the most simple and inexpensive way to diagnose cervical cancer in women, in particular those living in impoverished nations. In tests conducted over a two-year period, midwives in Zimbabwe used a vinegar solution to detect more than 75 per cent of potential cancers in 10,000 women (the solution turns tissue containing pre-cancerous cells white). Although the test is not as accurate as a smear, doctors believe it will soon be an important screening tool in developing countries, where only 5 per cent of women are currently tested for this often fatal disease.

VINEGAR...

...in the bathroom

Shine up shower doors To leave glass shower doors sparkling clean and remove water spots, wipe them down with a cloth dipped in a solution of 100ml white vinegar, 200ml ammonia and 50g bicarbonate of soda mixed together in 4 litres warm water.

Disinfect shower door tracks Use vinegar to remove accumulated dirt and grime from the tracks of shower doors. Fill the tracks with about 400ml full-strength white vinegar and let it sit for 3-5 hours. (If the tracks are really dirty, heat the vinegar in a glass container for 30 seconds in a microwave first.) Then pour some hot water over the track to flush away the debris. You may need to use a small scrubbing brush or even a recycled toothbrush, to get rid of tough stains.

{TAKE CARE}

Combining vinegar with bleach or any other product containing chlorine, such as powdered bleach, may produce chlorine gas. Even in low concentrations, this toxic, acrid-smelling gas can cause damage to your eyes, skin, or respiratory system and high concentrations are often fatal.

Remove mineral deposits from a showerhead Wash away blockages and mineral deposits from a removable showerhead by placing it in a litre of boiling water with 100ml distilled vinegar for 10 minutes (use hot, not boiling, liquid for plastic showerheads). When you remove it from the solution, the obstructions should be gone. If you have a non-removable showerhead, fill a small plastic bag half full of vinegar and tape it over the fixture. Let it sit for about 1 hour, then remove the bag and wipe off any remaining vinegar from the showerhead.

Wipe down bathroom fixtures Don't just stop at the shower when you are cleaning with vinegar. Pour a little undiluted white vinegar onto a soft cloth and use it to wipe chrome taps, towel racks, bathroom mirrors, doorknobs and any similar fixtures. They will all come up gleaming.

Fight mould and mildew To remove and inhibit bathroom mould and mildew, pour a solution of 3 tablespoons white vinegar, 1 teaspoon borax and 400ml hot water into a clean, recycled spray bottle and shake it thoroughly. Then spray the mixture onto painted surfaces, tiles, windows or wherever you can see mould or mildew spots. Use a soft scrubbing brush to work the solution into the stains or just let it soak in.

Disinfect a toilet bowl Keep the toilet looking and smelling clean by pouring 400ml white vinegar into the bowl. Let the solution soak overnight before flushing. Including this vinegar soak in your weekly cleaning routine will also help to keep away the water rings that typically appear just above the water level in the toilet bowl.

Clean a toothbrush holder Remove grime, bacteria and caked-on toothpaste drippings from a toothbrush holder by cleaning the openings with cotton buds moistened with white vinegar.

Wash out a tumbler If several people in your home use the same tumbler to rinse after brushing their teeth, give it a weekly (or more regular if you prefer) cleaning by filling it with equal parts water and white vinegar or just full-strength vinegar and let it sit overnight. Rinse thoroughly with cold water before using.

...in the laundry

Soften fabrics, kill bacteria, eliminate static and much more There are so many benefits to be reaped by adding 200ml white vinegar to the rinse cycle of a washing machine that it is surprising that it isn't mentioned prominently in the owner's manual of every washing machine sold.

{TAKE CARE}

Keep cider vinegar out of the laundry. Using it to pre-treat clothes or adding it to wash or rinse water may actually create stains rather than remove them. Use only distilled white vinegar for laundering.

Here are the main ones:

- 200ml of vinegar will kill off any bacteria that may be present in a wash load, especially if it includes cloth nappies and similar items.
- 200ml of vinegar will keep your clothes coming out of the wash soft and smelling fresh, so you won't need to use fabric-softening liquids and sheets.
- 200ml of vinegar will brighten small loads of white clothes.
- Added to the last rinse, 200ml vinegar will keep clothes lint and static-free.
- Adding 200ml vinegar to the last rinse will set the colour of newly dyed fabrics.

Clean the washing machine An easy way to periodically clean out soap scum and disinfect a washing machine is to pour in 400ml vinegar, then run the machine through a full cycle without any clothes or detergent. If the machine is particularly dirty, fill it with very hot water, add 8 litres vinegar and let the agitator run for 8-10 minutes. Turn off the machine and let the solution stand overnight. In the morning, empty and run the washing machine through a complete cycle.

Stop reds from running Unless you have a fondness for pink-tinted clothing, take one simple precaution to prevent red or other brightly dyed washable clothes from ruining a light wash load. Soak new garments in a few cups of undiluted white vinegar for 10-15 minutes before their first wash. You should never have to worry about running colours again.

Brighten colours Add 100ml white vinegar to your machine's wash cycle to brighten up the colours in each load.

Make new clothes ready to wear Remove chemicals, dust, smells and stiff dressings from brand-new or secondhand clothes by pouring 200ml white vinegar into the washing machine the first time you wash them.

{ KIDS' STUFF }

MAKE A TIE-DYED T-SHIRT

Making tie-dyed clothing is great fun for children of all ages. Start with a few white T-shirts, then use as many colours as the cold dye selection in the craft shop will allow. (1) Dissolve each dye tin or sachet in 20ml vinegar in its own bowl or container. (2) Use rubber bands to twist the shirts into unusual shapes, then dip them into the bowls (remember to wear rubber gloves). (3) After drying, set the colours by placing an old pillowcase or thin tea towel over each shirt and ironing it with a medium-hot iron. Wait at least 24 hours, then wash each shirt separately.

1

2

3

4

...in the laundry

Whiten dingy cotton sports socks If it is getting increasingly difficult to identify the white cotton socks in your sock drawer, here is a simple way to make them so bright you can't miss them. Start by adding 200ml vinegar to 1.5 litres tap water in a large pan. Bring the solution to a boil, then pour it into a bucket and immerse the dingy socks. Let them soak overnight. The next day, wash them as you normally would.

Remove yellowing from light clothes To restore yellowed clothing, let the garments soak overnight in a solution of 12 parts warm water to 1 part vinegar. Wash them the following morning.

Soften blankets Add 400ml white vinegar to the washing machine's rinse water (or a bath or deep sink filled with water) to remove soap residue from both cotton and wool blankets before drying. This will also leave them feeling fresh and soft as new.

Flush out the interior of an iron To eliminate mineral deposits and prevent corrosion on a steam iron, give it an occasional cleaning by filling the reservoir with undiluted white vinegar. Place the iron in an upright position, switch on the steam setting and let the vinegar steam through it for 5-10 minutes. Then refill the chamber with clean water and repeat. Finally, give the water chamber a thorough rinse with cold, clean water.

Clean an iron's soleplate To remove scorch marks from the soleplate of an iron, scrub it with a paste made by heating up equal parts vinegar and salt in a small pan. Use a rag dipped in clean water to wipe away the remaining residue.

Sharpen your creases You will find the creases in freshly washed clothes will come out a lot more easily if you lightly spray them with equal parts water and vinegar before ironing. For truly sharp creases in trousers and smart shirts, first dampen the garment using a cloth moistened in a solution of 1 part white vinegar and 2 parts water. Then place a brown paper bag over the crease and start ironing.

Make old hemlines disappear To make the needle marks from an old hemline disappear for good, moisten the area with a cloth dipped in equal parts vinegar and water, then place it under the garment before you start ironing.

Erase scorch marks You can often eliminate slight scorch marks by rubbing the spot with a cloth dampened with white vinegar, then blotting it with a clean towel. Repeat if necessary.

Remove cigarette smell from suits If you find yourself in a situation where you get home with the lingering smell of cigarette smoke on a suit or dress, you can remove the odour without having to take your clothes to the dry cleaner. Just add 200ml vinegar to a bath filled with the hottest water your tap can muster. Close the door and hang the garments above the steam. The smell should be gone after several hours.

VINEGAR...

...in the laundry

Dull the shine in a skirt or trouser seat To get rid of a shiny seat on a dark skirt or trousers, brush the area lightly with a soft recycled toothbrush dipped in equal parts white vinegar and water, then pat dry with a soft towel.

Reshape woollens Shrunken woollen sweaters and other items can usually be stretched back to their former size or shape after boiling them in a solution of 1 part vinegar to 2 parts water for 25 minutes. Let the garment air-dry after you have finished stretching it.

Spray away creases In a perfect world, laundry would emerge from the tumble drier freshly pressed. Until that day, you can often get the creases out of clothes after drying by misting them with a solution of 1 part vinegar to 3 parts water. Once you are sure you haven't missed a spot, hang the garment up and let it air-dry. You may find this approach works better for some clothes than ironing; it is certainly a lot gentler on the material.

...for removing stains

Brush off suede stains To eliminate a fresh grease spot on a suede jacket or skirt, gently brush it with a soft toothbrush dipped in white vinegar. Let the spot air-dry, then brush with a suede brush. Repeat if necessary. You can also generally spruce up suede items by lightly wiping them with a sponge dipped in vinegar.

Release old stains Older, set-in stains will often come out in the wash after being pre-treated with a solution of 3 tablespoons white vinegar and 2 tablespoons liquid detergent in 1 litre warm water. Rub the solution into the stain, then blot it dry before washing.

Sponge out serious stains Cola, hair dye, ketchup and wine stains on washable cotton clothing should be treated as soon as possible (that is, within 24 hours). Sponge the area with undiluted vinegar and launder immediately afterwards. For severe stains, add 200-400ml vinegar to the wash cycle as well.

Get the rust out To remove a rust stain from cotton clothes, moisten the spot with some full-strength vinegar and then rub in a bit of salt. If it is warm outdoors, let it dry in the sunlight (otherwise a sunny window will do), then put it in the wash.

Clear away crayon stains Remove crayon marks from children's clothing by rubbing them with a recycled toothbrush soaked in undiluted vinegar before you put them in the washing machine.

Remove rings from collars and cuffs Give grimy collars and cuffs the boot by scrubbing the material with a paste made from 2 parts white vinegar to 3 parts baking soda. Let the paste set for half an hour before washing. This approach also works to remove light mildew stains from clothing.

DID YOU KNOW?

If you have just come across an old, unopened bottle of vinegar and wonder if it is still safe to use, the answer is an unqualified yes. In fact, vinegar has a practically limitless shelf life. Its acid content makes it self-preserving and even negates the need for refrigeration (although many people mistakenly believe in refrigerating open bottles). You won't see any changes in white vinegar over time, but some other types may change slightly in colour or develop a hazy appearance or a bit of sediment. However, these are strictly cosmetic changes; the vinegar itself will be virtually unchanged.

Pat away water-soluble stains You can lift out many water-soluble stains including beer, orange and other fruit juices, black coffee or tea and vomit from cotton clothing by patting the spot with a cloth or towel moistened with undiluted white vinegar just before placing it in the wash. For large stains, you can soak the garment overnight in a solution of 3 parts vinegar to 1 part cold water before washing.

Pre-treat perspiration stains To see sweat marks disappear from light-coloured shirts and t-shirts, pour a bit of vinegar directly onto the stain and rub it into the fabric before placing the item in the wash. You can also remove deodorant stains from washable shirts and blouses by gently rubbing the spot with undiluted vinegar before laundering.

Make pen ink disappear When a pen has leaked all over the front of a shirt, treat the stain by first wetting it with some white vinegar, then rub in a paste of 2 parts vinegar to 3 parts cornflour. Let the paste thoroughly dry before washing the item.

Soak out bloodstains Whether you nick yourself shaving or receive an unexpected scratch from a grumpy pet, it is important to treat stains on clothing as soon as possible; bloodstains are relatively easy to remove before they set but can be nearly impossible to wash out after 24 hours. If you can get to the stain before it sets, treat it by pouring full-strength white vinegar on the spot. Let it soak in for 5-10 minutes, then blot well with a cloth or towel. Repeat if necessary, then wash immediately.

VINEGAR...

...in the great outdoors

Use as insect repellent Here is an old army trick to keep away ticks and mosquitoes – essential if you are going camping or walking. Approximately three days before you leave, start taking 1 tablespoon apple cider vinegar three times a day. Continue using the vinegar throughout your trek and you may return home without a bite. Another time-honoured approach to keep gnats and mosquitoes at bay is to moisten a cloth or cotton ball with white vinegar and rub it over exposed skin.

Maintain fresh water when hiking Keep your water supply fresh and clean tasting when hiking or camping by adding a few drops of apple cider vinegar to your water bottle. It is also a good idea to use a half-vinegar, half-water rinse to clean out the water container at the end of each trip to kill bacteria and remove residue.

Make a trap to lure flying insects Keep gnats, flies, mosquitoes and other flying insects at bay by giving them their own VIP section in the garden when you are holding a garden party or barbecue. Place a bowl filled with apple cider vinegar near some food, but away from you and guests. By the end of the evening, most of the uninvited guests will be floating inside the bowl.

Give ants the boot Serve ants on your premises with an eviction notice. Pour equal parts water and white vinegar into a spray bottle. Then spray it around areas where you see the insects. Ants hate the smell of vinegar. It won't take long for them to move on to better-smelling quarters. Also keep the spray bottle handy for outdoor trips or to keep ants away from picnic or children's play areas.

Clean off bird droppings When birds have been using a patio or driveway for target practice, make the messy droppings disappear by spraying them with full-strength apple cider vinegar. Or pour the vinegar onto a rag and wipe them off.

DID YOU KNOW?

For a non-toxic alternative to commercial weed killers, vinegar is an ideal solution. In field and greenhouse studies, vinegar has been proven to be effective at killing several common weeds within their first two weeks above ground. The vinegar was hand-sprayed in concentrations varying between 5 and 10 per cent.

But that is old news to seasoned gardeners who've been using undiluted apple cider vinegar for ages to kill all kinds of weeds (and, regrettably, the occasional ornamental plant that grew too close to the target).

Clean outdoor furniture and decks It is hard to keep mildew at bay on wooden decking and patio furniture. But before you attack it with bleach, try a milder vinegar-based solution:

- Keep some full-strength white vinegar in a recycled spray bottle and use it wherever you see any mildew appear. The stains will wipe straight off most surfaces, and the vinegar will keep it from coming back for a while.
- Remove mildew from wooden decking and patio furniture by sponging them off with a solution of 200ml ammonia, 100ml white vinegar and 50g bicarbonate of soda mixed in 4 litres water. Keep an old toothbrush on hand to work the solution into corners and other tight spaces.
- To remove unpleasant smells and inhibit mildew growth on outdoor plastic furniture and patio umbrellas, mix 400ml white vinegar and 2 tablespoons washing-up liquid in a bucket of hot water. Use a soft brush to work it into the grooves of the plastic as well as for scrubbing seat pads and umbrella fabric. Rinse with cold water; then dry in the sun.

...in the garden

Clean a bird feeder Birds are innately discriminating creatures, so don't expect to see them flocking around a dirty, sticky or crusted-over feeder. Regularly clean feeders by thoroughly washing them in equal parts apple cider vinegar and hot water. Rinse well with cold water after washing, and air-dry them outdoors in full sunlight before refilling them with food.

Keep cut flowers fresh Everyone likes to keep cut flowers around for as long as possible, and there are several good methods. One way is to mix 2 tablespoons apple cider vinegar and 2 tablespoons sugar with the vase water before adding the flowers. Be sure to change the water (adding more vinegar and sugar) every few days to enhance the flowers' longevity.

VINEGAR...

...in the garden

Speed germination of flower seeds You can get plants with woody seeds off to a healthier start by scarifying them, that is, lightly rubbing them between a couple of sheets of fine sandpaper and soaking them overnight in a solution of 100ml apple cider vinegar and ½ litre warm water. Next morning, remove the seeds from the solution, rinse them off and plant them. You can also use the solution (minus the glasspaper treatment) to start many herb and vegetable seeds.

Eliminate insects around the garden If insects are feasting on the fruit and vegetables in your garden, try this simple, non-toxic trap. Fill a 2 litre soft drink bottle with 200ml apple cider vinegar and 200g sugar. Next, slice up a banana skin into small pieces, put them in the bottle, add 200ml cold water and shake it up. Tie a piece of string around the neck of the bottle and hang it from a low tree branch or place it on the ground, to trap and kill any investigating insects. Replace used traps with new ones as needed.

Encourage blooms on azaleas and gardenias A little bit of acid goes a long way toward bringing out the blooms on azalea and gardenia bushes, especially in a hard water area. Both bushes grow most successfully in acidic soils (with pH levels between 4 and 5.5). To keep them healthy and to produce more flowers, water them every week or so with 3 tablespoons white vinegar mixed in 4 litres water. Don't apply the solution while the bush is in bloom, as it may shorten the life of the flowers or harm the plant.

Test soil acidity or alkalinity To do a quick test for excess alkalinity in the soil in your garden, place a handful of earth in a container and then pour in 100ml white vinegar. If the soil fizzes or bubbles, it is definitely alkaline. Similarly, to see if the soil has a high acidity, mix the earth with 100ml water and 100g bicarbonate of soda. This time, fizzing would indicate acid in the soil. To find the exact pH level of your soil, have it tested or pick up a simple, do-it-yourself kit or meter.

Stop leaves from yellowing prematurely The sudden appearance of yellow leaves on plants accustomed to acidic soils, such as azaleas, hydrangeas and gardenias could signal a drop in the plant's iron intake or a shift in the ground's pH above a comfortable 5.0 level. Either problem can be resolved by watering the soil around the afflicted plants once a week for three weeks with 200ml of a solution made by mixing 2 tablespoons apple cider vinegar in 1 litre water.

Exterminate dandelions and unwanted grass If dandelions are sprouting in the cracks of your driveway or along the fringes of the patio, make them disappear for good by spraying them with full-strength white or apple cider vinegar. Early in the season, give each plant a single spray of vinegar in its mid-section, or in the middle of the flower before the plants go to seed. Aim another shot near the stem at ground level so the vinegar can soak down to the roots. Keep an eye on the weather, though; if it rains the next day, you will need to spray the weeds again.

{ SCIENCE FAIR }

COAT A NAIL WITH COPPER

Mix 100ml vinegar and ¼ teaspoon salt in a glass jar. Add 25 1p pieces to the solution and let them sit for 5 minutes. While you are waiting, take a large iron nail and clean it with some bicarbonate of soda applied to a damp sponge. Rinse off the nail and place it into the solution. After 15 minutes, the nail will be coated with copper, while the pennies will shine like new. This is a result of the acetic acid in the vinegar combining with the copper on the pennies to form copper acetate, which then accumulates on the nail.

Treat rust and other plant diseases Use vinegar to treat a host of plant diseases, including rust, black spot and powdery mildew. Mix 2 tablespoons apple cider vinegar in 2 litres water and pour some into a recycled spray bottle. Spray the solution onto affected plants in the morning or early evening (when it is cooler) until the condition is completely cured.

Clean lawn mower blades Grass, especially when damp, tends to stick on lawn mower blades after you have cut the lawn, sometimes with maggots or other insects hiding inside. Before you put a mower back in the shed, wipe down the blades with a cloth dampened with undiluted white vinegar. It will clean off leftover grass on the blades, as well as any pests hiding in the clippings.

Keep out four-legged creatures Some animals, including cats, deer, dogs and rabbits, can't stand the scent of vinegar even after it has dried. You can keep these unauthorised visitors out of the garden by soaking several recycled rags in white vinegar and placing them on stakes around your vegetables. Re-soak the rags about every 7-10 days to keep them working effectively.

...for pet care

Clean your pet's ears If you have noticed that your dog has been scratching his ears a lot more than usual lately, a bit of vinegar could give him some relief. Swabbing a pet's ears with a cotton wool ball or soft cloth dipped in a solution of 2 parts vinegar and 1 part water will keep them clean as well as helping to deter ear mites and bacteria. It also soothes minor itches from mosquito bites and similar.

WARNING! Do not apply vinegar to open lacerations. If you spot a cut in your pet's ears, seek veterinary treatment.

VINEGAR...

...for pet care

Keep cats away If you want to keep your cats out of the playroom or discourage them from using a favourite easy chair as a scratching post, sprinkle some full-strength distilled white vinegar around the area or onto the object itself. Cats don't like the smell of vinegar and will avoid it.

Get rid of a pet's territorial marks When a puppy or kitten is being toilet-trained it will often wet previously soiled spots. After cleaning up the mess, it is essential to remove the scent from the floor, carpet or sofa so that they don't continue to use them. And nothing does that better than vinegar:

- On a floor, blot up as much of the stain as possible. Then mop with equal parts white vinegar and warm water. (On a wood or vinyl floor, test a few drops of vinegar in an inconspicuous area to make sure it won't harm the finish.) Dry with a cloth or paper towel.
- For carpets, rugs and upholstery, thoroughly blot the area with a towel or some rags. Then pour a little undiluted vinegar over the spot. Blot it up with a towel, then reapply the vinegar and let it air-dry. Once the vinegar dries, the spot should be completely free from odour.

Add to pet's drinking water Adding a teaspoon of apple cider vinegar to a dog or cat's drinking water provides needed nutrients to its diet, gives it a shinier, healthier-looking coat and acts as a natural deterrent to fleas and ticks.

Directly protect against fleas and ticks To give your dog effective flea and tick protection, fill a spray bottle with equal parts water and vinegar and apply it directly to the dog's coat and rub it in well. You may have more trouble doing this with cats, because they really hate the smell.

...for the DIY-er

Wash concrete off your skin Even though you wear rubber gloves when working with concrete, some inevitably splashes onto your skin. Prolonged contact with wet concrete can cause skin to crack and may even lead to eczema. Use undiluted white vinegar to wash dried concrete or mortar off the skin, then wash with warm, soapy water.

Remove paint fumes Place a couple of shallow dishes filled with undiluted white vinegar around a freshly painted room to quickly get rid of the strong paint smell.

Degrease grates, fans and air-conditioner grilles Even in the cleanest of homes, air-conditioner grilles, heating grates and fan blades eventually develop a layer of dust and grease. To clean them, wipe with full-strength white vinegar. Use an old toothbrush to work the vinegar into the tight spaces on air-conditioner grilles and extractor fans.

Disinfect air-conditioner and humidifier filters An air-conditioner or humidifier filter can quickly become inundated with dust, soot, pet dander and even potentially harmful bacteria. Every ten days or so, clean the filter with equal parts white vinegar and warm water. Let the filter soak in the solution for an hour, then simply squeeze it dry before using again. If the filters are particularly dirty, let them soak overnight.

Keep the paint intact on a cement floor Painted cement floors have a tendency to peel after a while. Keep the paint stuck to the cement longer by giving the floor an initial coating with white vinegar before you paint it. Wait until the vinegar has dried, then begin painting. This same technique will also help to keep paint adhered to galvanised metal.

Peel off wallpaper Removing old wallpaper can be messy, but you can get it to peel off easily by soaking it with a vinegar solution. Spray equal parts white vinegar and water on the wallpaper until it is saturated and wait a few minutes. Then whip the softened paper off the wall with a wallpaper scraper. If it is stubborn, try carefully scoring the wallpaper with the scraper before you spray.

Slow drying of plaster To keep plaster pliable for a bit longer so that you can smooth it properly before it sets, add a couple of tablespoons of white vinegar to the plaster mix. It will slow down the drying process and give you the extra time you need for a perfect finish.

Revive your paintbrushes To remove dried-on paint from a synthetic-bristle paintbrush, soak it in full-strength white vinegar until the paint dissolves and the bristles are soft and pliable, then wash in hot, soapy water. If a paintbrush seems beyond hope, before you throw it away, try boiling it in 200-400ml vinegar for 10 minutes, followed by a thorough washing in soapy water.

Get rid of rust If you want to restore some rusty old tools that you have unearthed in the shed or picked up at a car boot sale, soak them in full-strength white vinegar for several days. The same treatment is equally effective at removing the rust from corroded nuts and bolts. And you can pour vinegar on rusted hinges and screws to loosen them up for removal.

Vodka

Make your own vanilla extract Here is an unusual homemade treat that takes only minutes to make. Take a dried vanilla pod (available at speciality food shops or online at *www.vanilla-pods.co.uk*) and slice it open from top to bottom. Place it in a glass jar and cover it with 150ml vodka. Seal the jar, and let it rest in a kitchen cabinet for 4-6 months, shaking it occasionally. Filter the homemade vanilla extract through an unbleached coffee filter or cheesecloth into a decorative bottle to make a great gift for a keen cook.

Clean glass and jewellery A few drops of vodka will clean any kind of glass or jewellery that has crystalline gemstones. So although people might look at you askance, you could dip a napkin into a glass of vodka to wipe away grime on your spectacles or dunk a diamond ring for a few minutes to get it sparkling again. But don't try this with contact lenses. Also avoid getting alcohol on any gemstone that is not a crystal. Only diamonds, emeralds and the like will benefit from a vodka bath.

Kill weeds in the garden For a quick and easy weedkiller, mix 30ml vodka, a few drops washing-up liquid and 400ml water in a spray bottle. Spray it on the weed leaves until the mixture runs off. Apply it at midday on a sunny day to weeds growing in direct sunlight, because the alcohol breaks down the waxy cuticle covering on leaves, leaving them susceptible to dehydration in sunlight. It won't work in shady spots.

DID YOU KNOW?

Essential to James Bond's Martini and so intrinsic to Russian culture that its name derives from the Russian word for water (voda), vodka was first made in the 1400s as an antiseptic and painkiller before it was drunk as a beverage. But what exactly is it? Classically, vodka starts as a soupy mixture of ground wheat or rye that's fermented (sugars in the grain are converted into alcohol by yeast), then distilled (heated until the alcohol evaporates and then condenses). Flavourings such as citrus were originally added to mask the taste of impurities, but are used today for enhancement and brand identification.

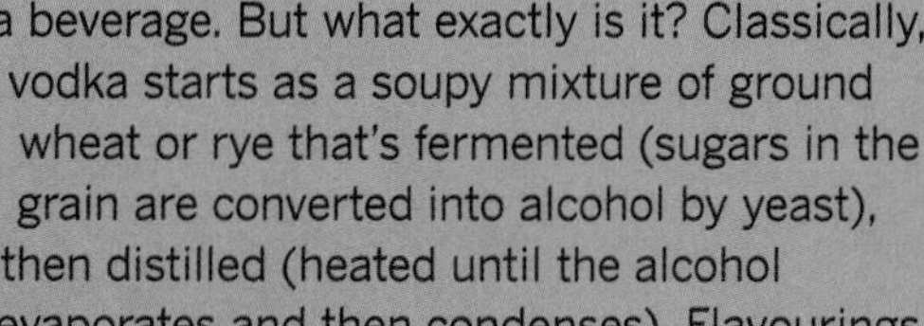

Use as a hygienic soak Vodka is an alcohol and like any alcohol, it kills germs. If you don't have ordinary surgical spirit on hand, use vodka instead. You can use it to soak razor blades that you intend to reuse, as well as to clean hairbrushes, toothbrushes and pet brushes, or on anything else that might spread germs from person to person or animal to animal.

Keep cut flowers fresh The secret to keeping cut flowers looking good as long as possible is to minimise the growth of bacteria in the water and provide nourishment to replace what the flower would have received had it not been cut. Add a few drops of vodka (or any clear spirit) to the vase water to give anti-bacterial action along with 1 teaspoon sugar. Change the water every other day, refreshing the vodka and sugar each time.

Wallpaper

Line drawers and shelves Wallpaper remnants can be an excellent substitute for shelf liner paper when used to line dresser drawers or cupboard shelves, especially designs with raised patterns or fabrics, which may add a bit of friction to prevent things from moving around. Cut the wallpaper to fit the space.

Restore a folding screen If you have an old folding screen that has become torn or stained over the years, give it a new look by covering it with leftover wallpaper. Use masking tape to hold the strips at top and bottom if you don't want to glue it on top of the original material.

Protect schoolbooks If your child goes through book covers on textbooks on a regular basis, make use of unused rolls of wallpaper, especially vinyl or coated papers. Book covers made of wallpaper are typically stronger than even traditional brown paper wrapping; they can hold their own against pens and pencils, and are much better at handling the elements.

Make a jigsaw puzzle What can you do with leftover wallpaper? Why not use a piece to make a jigsaw puzzle? Cut off a medium-sized rectangular piece of patterned wallpaper and glue it onto a piece of thin cardboard. Once it has dried, cut it up into a lots of curvy and angular shapes. It will give you or the children something to do on a rainy day.

Wax paper

Stop water spotting When guests are coming and you want every room of the house to look its best, keep bathroom fixtures spotless by rubbing them with a sheet of wax paper after cleaning them. They will deflect water droplets like magic – at least until the next cleaning.

Make a snow slide go faster As everyone knows, the more slippery the slide, the more fun it is. Keep children sliding fast and smoothly by crumpling a large piece of wax paper and rubbing it all over the slide surface.

WD-40 see page 370

* Window cleaning fluid

Slip off a stuck ring Spray a little window cleaner on your finger for lubrication and ease the ring off.

Remove stubborn laundry stains If washing with detergent isn't enough to get rid of tough stains such as blood, grass or tomato sauce, try a clear ammonia-based spray-on window cleaner instead. (It is the ammonia in the window cleaner that does the trick, and you need colourless cleaner to avoid staining the fabric.) Spray the stain with the window cleaner and let it sit for up to 15 minutes. Blot with a clean rag, rinse with cool water and wash again. A few tips:

- Do a test on a seam or other inconspicuous part of the garment to see if the colour runs.
- Use cool water and don't put the garment in the dryer until the stain is completely gone.
- Don't use this on silk, wool or fabrics that are blends of these materials.
- If the fabric colour seems changed after using window cleaner on it, moisten the fabric with white vinegar and rinse it with water. Acidic vinegar will neutralise alkaline ammonia.

Reduce swelling from bee stings Spraying some window cleaner on a bee sting is a quick way to reduce the swelling and pain. Be sure to remove the sting first. Flick it sideways to get it out – don't tweeze it – then spray. Use only spray-on window cleaner that contains ammonia and never a concentrated product. The small amount of ammonia does the work; beekeepers have known for years that a dilute solution of ammonia relieves strings.

Clean jewellery Use window cleaner to spruce up jewellery that is all metal or has crystalline gemstones, such as diamonds or rubies. Spray on the cleaner, then use an old toothbrush for cleaning. Don't do this if the piece has opaque stones such as opal or turquoise or organic gems such as coral or pearl. The ammonia and detergents in the cleaner can discolour porous stones like these.

DID YOU KNOW?

Will spraying window cleaner on a spot really help make it go away? Although the formula varies by brand, window cleaners generally contain ammonia, detergents, solvents and alcohol. This combination will clean, disinfect and dry out skin. So as long as you keep it out of your eyes and have no allergies to the ingredients, it probably will help to suppress spots.

WD-40...

...around the house

Treat your shoes Spray WD-40 on new leather shoes before you start wearing them regularly. It will help to prevent blisters by softening the leather and making the shoes more comfortable. Then keep the shoes waterproof and shiny by spraying them periodically with WD-40 and buffing gently with a soft cloth. To stop shoes from squeaking, spray WD-40 at the spot where the sole and heel join.

Clean and lubricate guitar strings To clean, lubricate and prevent corrosion on guitar strings, apply a small amount of WD-40 after each session. Spray WD-40 on a rag and wipe the rag over the strings rather than spraying directly onto the strings to prevent WD-40 from building up on the guitar neck or body.

Separate stuck glassware What can you do when you go to get a drinking glass and find two locked together, one stuck tightly inside the other? You don't want to risk breaking one or both by trying to pull them apart. Stuck glasses will separate with ease if you squirt some WD-40 on them, wait a few seconds for it to work its way between the glasses, and then gently pull the glasses apart. Remember to wash the glasses thoroughly before you use them.

{TAKE CARE}

- Do not spray WD-40 near an open flame or other heat source or near electrical currents or battery terminals. Always disconnect appliances before spraying.
- Do not place a WD-40 can in direct sunlight or on hot surfaces. Never store it in temperatures above 50°C or puncture the pressurised can.
- Use WD-40 in well-ventilated areas. Never swallow or inhale it (if ingested, call a doctor immediately).

Free stuck Lego blocks When your child's construction project comes to a halt because some of the plastic blocks are stuck together, use WD-40 to help to get them unstuck. Spray a little on the blocks where they are locked together, then wiggle them gently and pull them apart. The lubricant in WD-40 will penetrate into the fine seam where the blocks are joined. Wash them thoroughly afterwards.

Tone down polyurethane shine A new coat of polyurethane varnish can sometimes make a wood floor look too shiny. To tone down the shine and cut the glare, spray some WD-40 onto a soft cloth and wipe the floor with it.

DID YOU KNOW?

• In 1953 Norm Larsen founded the Rocket Chemical Company in San Diego, southern California, USA and, with two employees, set out to develop a rust-preventing solvent and de-greaser for the aerospace industry. On the fortieth try, they succeeded in creating a 'water displacement' compound. The name WD-40 stands for 'Water Displacement – 40th Try'.

• In 1958, a few years after WD-40's first industrial use, the company put it into aerosol cans and sold it for home use – inspired by employees who smuggled cans out of the plant to use at home.

• In 1962, when astronaut John Glenn circled the Earth in *Friendship VII*, the space capsule was coated with WD-40 and so was the Atlas missile used to boost it into space.

• In 1969 Rocket Chemical renamed itself the WD-40 Company after its renowned product.

Remove strong glue To remove super-glue from fingers, spray WD-40 directly onto the fingers and then rub your hands together until the fingers no longer feel sticky.

Remove a stuck ring When pulling and tugging does not get a ring off your finger, try WD-40. A short burst of WD-40 will get the ring to slide right off. Remember to wash your hands after spraying them with WD-40.

Free stuck fingers Use WD-40 to free a child's finger when he gets it stuck in a bottle. Just spray it on the finger, let it seep in, and pull the finger out. Always wash the hand and the bottle afterwards.

Loosen zips Stubborn zips on jackets, trousers, rucksacks and sleeping bags will run with ease again after you spray them with WD-40. Just spray it on and pull the zip up and down a few times to distribute the lubricant evenly over all the teeth. If you want to avoid getting the WD-40 on the fabric, spray it on a plastic lid; then pick it up and apply it with an artist's brush.

Get rid of cockroaches and repel insects Don't let cockroaches or other insects get the upper hand in your home.

- If you've had cockroach infestations in the past, keep a can of WD-40 to hand; a squirt kills them instantly.
- To keep insects out of the house, spray WD-40 on windowsills and frames, and door frames. Be careful not to inhale the fumes when you spray and do not do this at all if you have babies or small children at home.

Keep puppies from chewing Your new puppy is gorgeous, but it is chewing everything in sight. To keep puppies from chewing on telephone and television-cable lines, spray WD-40 on the lines. Dogs hate the smell.

Super item
58 USES!

WD-40...

...around the house

Keep wooden tool handles splinter-free No tools can last for ever, but you can prolong the life of wooden-handled tools by preventing splintering. To keep wooden handles from splintering, rub a generous amount of WD-40 into the wood. It will shield the wood from moisture and corrosive elements and keep it smooth and splinter-free for the life of the tool.

Unstick wobbly shopping-trolley wheels It may sound strange but you could take a can of WD-40 with you whenever you go food shopping. So when you get stuck with a sticky, wobbly wheeled shopping trolley, you can spray the wheels to reduce friction and wobbling. Less wobbling means faster shopping.

Remove chewing gum from hair It is one of an adult's worst nightmares: chewing gum tangled in a child's hair. You don't have to panic or run for the scissors. Simply spray the gummed-up hair with WD-40, and the gum will comb out with ease. Make sure you are in a well-ventilated area when you spray and take care to avoid contact with the child's eyes.

...for cleaning things

Remove scuff marks Tough black scuff marks on the kitchen floor can be quickly shifted if you spray them with WD-40. Use WD-40 to help to remove tar and scuff marks on all hard-surfaced floors. It won't harm the surface and you won't have to scrub nearly as hard. Remember to open the windows if you are trying to clean a heavily marked floor.

Clean dried glue Remove dried-on glue from virtually any hard surface with ease. Simply spray WD-40 onto the spot, wait at least 30 seconds, and wipe clean with a damp cloth.

Degrease your hands When you have finished working on the car and your hands are greasy and blackened with grime, use WD-40 to help to get them clean. Spray a small amount of WD-40 into your hands and rub them together for a few seconds, then wipe with a paper towel and wash with soap and water. The grease and grime will wash straight off.

Remove stickers You don't need a chisel or even a razor blade to remove old stickers, bumper stickers or clear tape. Just spray them with WD-40, wait about 30 seconds and wipe them away.

Remove stickers from glass Price tags and other stickers on a glass or mirror can be almost impossible to remove. When soap and water doesn't work and you don't want to ruin a fingernail or risk scratching delicate glass with a blade, try a little WD-40. Spray it on the sticker and glass, wait a few minutes, and then use a no-scratch spatula or acrylic scraper to scrape the sticker off. The solvents present in WD-40 will cause the adhesive to lose its stickiness.

DID YOU KNOW?

Around a million cans of WD-40 are sold every week and it can be found in 187 countries around the world. The secret recipe, which has had the same basic ingredients for more than 50 years, is known only by a handful of people within the WD-40 Company. A lone 'brew master' mixes the product at corporate headquarters in San Diego.

The latest innovation from WD-40 is the 'No Mess Pen'. It is designed to be used for small jobs around the home such as a squeaky drawer where using a spray can might be rather too messy. It is also highly portable – ideal if you need WD-40 on the move.

Clean your fridge When soap and water can't get rid of old bits of food stuck in and around the fridge, try WD-40. After clearing away food from the areas to be treated, spray a small amount of WD-40 onto each resistant spot. Then wipe them away with a rag or sponge. Make sure you wash off all the WD-40 before returning food to the fridge.

Wipe away tea stains To remove tea stains from worktops, spray a little WD-40 on a sponge or damp cloth and wipe the stains away.

Clean carpet stains Don't let ink or other stains ruin a carpet. Spray the stain with WD-40, wait a minute or two and then use a carpet cleaner or gently cleanse with a sponge and warm, soapy water. Continue until the stain is completely gone.

Remove tomato stains from clothes A fresh tomato looked so inviting that you couldn't resist biting into it and now your shirt or blouse has a big, hard-to-remove tomato stain. To remove stains caused by fresh tomatoes or tomato sauce, spray some WD-40 directly on the spot, wait a couple of minutes, and wash as usual.

Clean a toilet bowl You don't need a genie or a specialised product to clean filth and limescale from a toilet bowl. Use WD-40 instead. Spray it into the bowl for a couple of seconds and swish with a toilet brush. The solvents in the WD-40 will help to dissolve the gunk and limescale.

Condition leather furniture Keep a favourite leather chair or sofa in tip-top shape by softening and preserving it with WD-40. Just spray it on and buff with a soft cloth. The combination of ingredients in WD-40 will clean, penetrate, lubricate and protect the leather.

Pre-treat blood and other stains Spray some WD-40 directly on the bloodstains, wait a couple of minutes and then launder as usual. The WD-40 will help to lift the stain so that it will come out easily in the wash. Try to get to the stain while it is still fresh, because it will be harder to remove, once it has set. Use WD-40 to pretreat other stubborn stains on clothing, such as lipstick, dirt, grease and ink.

Super item
58 USES!

WD-40...

...for cleaning things

Clean a blackboard When it comes to cleaning and restoring a blackboard, WD-40 is ideal. Just spray it on and wipe with a clean cloth. The blackboard will look as clean and fresh as it did on the first day it was used.

Remove marker and crayon marks Have the children used your wall as if it was a big colouring book? Spray some WD-40 onto the marks and wipe with a clean rag. WD-40 will not damage the paint or most wallpaper (test fabric or more ornate wall coverings first). It will also remove marker and crayon marks from furniture and appliances.

...in the garden

Rejuvenate a barbecue grill To make a worn old barbecue grill look like new again, spray it liberally with WD-40, wait a few seconds, and scrub with a wire brush. Only use WD-40 on a grill that has cooled off completely.

Keep a shovel snow-free Make shovelling snow quicker and less strenuous by keeping the snow from sticking to your shovel and weighing it down. Spray a thin layer of WD-40 on the shovel blade, and the snow will slide straight off.

Protect a bird feeder To keep squirrels from taking over a bird feeder, spray a generous amount of WD-40 on top of the feeder. Squirrels will slide off the top.

Remove cat's paw marks Your cat may seem like a member of the family most of the time, but that is not what you'll be thinking about when you have to clean a host of paw marks off patio furniture or the bonnet of a car. To remove the paw marks, spray some WD-40 on them and wipe with a clean rag.

Keep animals off flowerbeds Animals just love to play in your garden, digging up favourite plants you've worked so hard to grow. But they hate the smell of WD-40. To keep the animals out and your flowers looking beautiful all season, spray WD-40 evenly over the flowerbeds one or twice over the course of the season.

TIP* THE LITTLE RED STRAW

'I've lost the red straw!' has been a common cry among countless users of WD-40 over the years. In response, the company introduced a notched cap, designed to hold the straw in place across the top of the can when not in use. Because the straw exceeds the width of the can by a substantial margin, the notch may be of little use to those with limited storage space. To save space, store the straw by bending it inside the lip of the can or simply tape it to the side as it was when first purchased. A snug rubber band will also work well.

Renew faded plastic furniture Bring colour and shine back to faded plastic patio furniture. Simply spray WD-40 directly on the surface and wipe with a clean, dry cloth. You will be surprised at the results.

Repel pigeons If pigeons and their droppings are keeping you from enjoying the view from your balcony, spray the entire area, including railings and furniture, with WD-40. The pigeons can't stand the smell and they will fly the coop.

Keep wasps from building nests Wasps love to build nests under the eaves. Mist some WD-40 under all the eaves of your house to deter their nest-building.

Kill thistles Don't let prickly weeds like thistles ruin your garden. Just spray some WD-40 on them and they will wither and die.

Remove dog mess from a shoe Cleaning dog mess from the bottom of a shoe with help from a can of WD-40. Spray some on the affected sole and use an old toothbrush to clean the crevices. Rinse with cold water.

...in the great outdoors

Waterproof boots and shoes Waterproof winter boots and shoes by giving them a coat of WD-40. It will act as a barrier so water can't penetrate the material. To remove salt stains spray WD-40 onto boots and shoes and wipe with a clean rag.

Remove old wax from skis and snowboards To remove old wax and dirt from skis and snowboards, spray the base sparingly with WD-40. Then scrape thoroughly with an acrylic scraper. Use a brass brush to clean the base more thoroughly and remove any oxidised base material.

Protect a boat from corrosion To protect a boat's outer finish from salt water and corrosion, spray WD-40 on the stern immediately after you have pulled it out of the water. The brief time it takes will save you from having to replace parts, and it should keep your boat looking like new.

Clean and protect golf clubs Protect and clean golf clubs by spraying them with WD-40 after each use. You can also use WD-40 to help to loosen the spikes on your golfing shoes.

WD-40...

...in the great outdoors

Keep flies off cows If flies are tormenting your cows, just spray some WD-40 on their backs. Flies hate the smell and they will stay clear. Take care not to spray any WD-40 in the cows' eyes.

Remove barnacles on boats Removing barnacles from the bottom of a boat is a difficult and odious task but you can make it easier and less unpleasant with the help of some WD-40. Spray the area generously with WD-40, wait a few seconds and then use a putty knife to scrape off the barnacles. Spray any remnants with WD-40 and scrape again. If necessary, use sandpaper to get rid of all of the remnants and corrosive glue still left by the barnacles.

Untangle fishing lines To loosen a tangled fishing line, spray it with WD-40 and use a pin to undo any small knots. Use WD-40 to extend the life of curled fishing lines. Pull out the first 3 to 6m of line and spray with WD-40 the night before.

Remove burrs To remove burrs from a horse's mane or tail without tearing its hair out (or having to cut off any hair) just spray on some WD-40. You will be able to slide the burrs out of the mane with ease. This trick will also work for dogs and cats with burrs or grasses stuck in their fur.

Protect horses' hoofs Winter horse riding can be painful for your horse if ice forms on its shoes. For protection during cold winter rides, spray the bottom of the horse's hoofs with WD-40 before you set out.

Spray on fishing lures Salmon fishermen spray their lures with WD-40 because it attracts fish and disguises the smell of humans that may scare them off and stop them from biting. You can increase the catch on a fishing trip by bringing a can of WD-40 along and spraying it on to lures or live bait before you cast your line. But first check local regulations to make sure the use of chemical-laced lures and bait is legal where you are fishing.

...for your health

Relieve arthritis symptoms For occasional joint pain or arthritis symptoms in the knees or other areas of the body, some people swear by spraying WD-40 on the affected area and massaging it in, believing it provides temporary relief and makes movement easier. For severe, persistent pain, consult a doctor.

Clean your hearing aid To give a hearing aid a thorough cleaning, use a cotton bud dipped in WD-40. Do not use WD-40 to try to loosen up the volume control (it will loosen it too much).

Relieve a bee sting For fast relief of pain from a bee or wasp sting, spray WD-40 directly on the bite site. It will soothe the pain at once.

DID YOU KNOW?

WD-40 is one of the few products with its own fan club. The official WD-40 Fan Club has more than 63,000 members and is growing. Over the years members have contributed thousands of unique and sometimes strange uses for the product. The strangest use of all occurred in Hong Kong where a python was caught in the suspension of a bus. Some WD-40 was used to remove the unfortunate serpent.

...in the garage

Stop insects from getting stuck on the car Spray some WD-40 on the grille and bonnet before going for a drive and most of the insects will slide straight off. The few that are left will be easy to wipe off later without damaging the finish.

Clean and restore a licence plate To help to restore a licence plate that is beginning to rust, spray it with WD-40 and wipe with a clean rag. This will remove light surface rust and will also help to prevent more rust from forming. It is an easy way to smarten lightly rusted plates and it won't feel greasy.

Remove stuck spark plugs To save time replacing spark plugs, spray WD-40 on to stuck plugs so they can be removed quickly and easily.

Remove 'paint rub' from another car If you return to a parked car to find that while you have been away, another vehicle has got a bit too close for comfort, leaving paint streaks on your car, you can remove the stains and restore the car's original finish, by spraying the affected area with WD-40. Wait a few seconds and then wipe with a clean rag.

Revive spark plugs When you can't get your car to start on a rainy or humid day, spray some WD-40 on the high tension leads before you try starting it up again. WD-40 displaces water and keeps moisture away from the plugs.

Clean oil spots from the drive If oil has leaked onto a concrete driveway, spray it with a generous amount of WD-40 and then hose it down with water.

TIP* DON'T OVERDO THE WD-40

When you need to apply tiny amounts of WD-40 to a specific area, such as the electrical contacts on an electric guitar, an aerosol spray is overkill. Instead, use the pen version or store a little WD-40 in a clean nail varnish bottle (with cap brush) and brush on as needed.

Yoghurt

Make moss 'paint' for the garden Wouldn't it be nice to simply paint some moss between the cracks of a stone path, on the sides of flowerpots or anywhere else you want it to grow? Put 200ml plain active-culture yoghurt into a blender along with a handful of moss and about 200ml water. Blend for about 30 seconds. Use a paintbrush to spread the mixture wherever you want moss to grow, as long as the spot is cool and shady. Keep misting the moss with water until it is established.

Make a facial mask You can give your face a quick boost with yoghurt.

- To cleanse your skin and tighten the pores, put some plain yoghurt on your face and let it sit for about 20 minutes.
- For a revitalising face mask, mix 1 teaspoon plain yoghurt with the juice from ¼ slice of orange, some of the orange pulp and 1 teaspoon aloe vera. Leave the mixture on your face for at least 5 minutes before rinsing it off.

Make play finger paint Mix food colouring with yoghurt to make finger paints and let children use their imagination. You can even turn it into a lesson about primary and secondary colours. For example, get children to put a few drops of yellow food colouring and a few drops of red in the yoghurt to make green finger paint. Or mix red and blue to produce purple.

Cure dog or cat flatulence If your dog or cat has been producing a lot of noxious gas lately, the problem may be a lack of the digestive bacteria that prevent gas and diarrhoea. The active culture in plain yoghurt can help to restore the helpful bacteria. Add 2 teaspoons yoghurt to the food for cats or small dogs weighing up to 6kg. Add 1 tablespoon for medium-sized dogs weighing 7-15kg. Add 2 tablespoons for large dogs weighing 16-38kg. Add 3 tablespoons for dogs larger than that.

Relieve sunburn For the quick, temporary relief of mild sunburn, apply cold plain yoghurt. The yoghurt adds much needed moisture and its coldness soothes at the same time. Rinse with cool water.

Z

* Zips

Secure your valuables Nothing ruins a holiday like reaching into your pocket and discovering it has been picked. To keep your wallet, passport and other valuables safe, sew a zip into the inside pocket of your jacket to keep items safe inside.

Make a sock puppet Create a cheerful sock puppet that will keep young children amused for hours. Just sew on buttons for the nose and eyes and some wool for hair and use a small smiling upturned zip to make the mouth.

Create convertible trousers Here's a great idea for hikers and bikers who like to travel light. Cut the legs off a pair of jeans or other comfortable trousers above the knee. Then reattach the legs using zips. You can zip off the legs when it gets warm and zip them back on for cool mornings and evenings. Besides lightening your load, you won't need to search for a place to change.

Keep your keys safe Have you ever lost your car keys in the sand at the seaside? Make sure it never happens again. Stitch a small zipped pocket – use matching terry towelling if you can – to one corner of the wrong side of your beach towel, just big enough for your keys, sunglasses and maybe a few coins.

Index

Bold entries and page numbers refer to main A-Z headings in text.
✱Indicates a Super Item.

A

B

C

D

E

F

G

H

L

M

Q

R

S

T

U

V

Where to source some of those

ordinary things

Although most of the items included in this book are humble and inexpensive, it is not always easy to find the generic products. The list below tells where you can buy such items – both locally, by mail order and via the internet. We have also given alternative names and where a number of different types are available we have indicated those that are best for 'extraordinary uses'.

Basters p61 Basters are generally widely available in department stores, specialist cookware shops and ironmongers. Go for a cheap, simple design with a plastic stem and a rubber bulb. To buy online, try **www.lakelandlimited.co.uk** tel 015394 88100 or **www.cookware.co.uk** tel 08700 707172, email info@professionalcookware.co.uk

Bicarbonate of soda p66-79 Supermarkets and ironmongers should stock bicarbonate of soda. Or try Wilkinsons with stores nationwide. The only firm that still manufactures bicarb is Dripak **www.dripak.co.uk** tel 0115 932 5165, e-mail sales@dripak.co.uk Other online sources include **www.soapbasics.co.uk** tel 01249 449039, email info@soapbasics.co.uk

Borax p83 Sources for borax are similar to bicarbonate of soda. Order it online from the manufacturer, **www.dripak.co.uk** tel 0115 932 5165, e-mail sales@dripak.co.uk

Bubble wrap p86 Most packaging supplies are simplest to order by mail or over the internet. All of the following will supply bubble wrap in various quantities. **www.thepackagingstore.co.uk** tel 0870 751 6660, email sales@thepackagingstore.co.uk **www.postpack.co.uk** tel 0870 264 3048 email sales@postpack.co.uk **www.indigoshop.co.uk** tel 01268 768 768 email sales@indigoshop.co.uk

Buckets p88 If you can't persuade a local deli or fast food restaurant to donate a large bucket or haven't been doing any DIY lately, you can get large sturdy buckets at most ironmongers or DIY superstores. Or try **www.screwfix.com** 0500 41 41 41, email online@screwfix.com **www.diytools.co.uk** tel 0151 709 8006 **www.euroffice.co.uk** tel 0800 316 3876

Candles p92 Supermarkets or ironmongers will stock basic candles. For online sources try **www.prices-candles.co.uk** tel 01234 264500, e-mail sales@prices-candles.co.uk or **www.thecandlecollection.co.uk** tel 0845 076 0084, email sales@thecandlecollection.co.uk

Car wax p104 Most car supplies shops and many garages stock car wax. You can buy it online at **www.halfords.com** or **www.eurochem.co.uk** tel 01938 555754, email support@eurochem.co.uk or **www.speeding.co.uk** tel 01482 648 688, email mal@speeding.co.uk or **www.fineautocare.com** tel 0845 3100 825

Cat litter p105 The most suitable kind of cat litter for the uses suggested here are the mineral based varieties. Most supermarkets and pet shops will carry a suitable product. An online source is **www.petplanet.co.uk** tel 0845 601 2765, email info@petplanet.co.uk

Chalk p107 Most educational or office suppliers or children's shops such as the Early Learning Centre will have plain chalk. Or try **www.mayfairstationers.co.uk** tel 0800 015 2310, email themayfair@mayfairstationers.co.uk or **www.officegiant.co.uk** tel 0800 731 7931, email sales@officegiant.co.uk

Charcoal briquettes p108 In the summer months these are available at most larger supermarkets and DIY stores alongside barbecue supplies. An online source is **www.barbecue-online.co.uk** tel 0800 662 663

Cheesecloth p109 Market stalls that carry fabric will often have a supply of cheesecloth, often at bargain prices. Ethnic fabric shops are also worth trying. Companies who will supply from online or telephone orders are: **www.aholt.co.uk** tel 020 7256 2222, email sales@aholt.co.uk and **www.whaleys-bradford.ltd.uk** tel 01274 576718 email info@whaleys-bradford.ltd.uk

Chest rub p110 The best known brand is Vicks VapoRub, available from pharmacists but many alternatives are also available from aromatherapy suppliers.

Chicken wire p111 Hardware stores and garden centres will carry chicken wire. For online sources try **www.prizepets.co.uk/Public/Wire_Mesh_and_Netting/7077.htm** tel 0845 226 1440 or **www.screwfix.com** tel 0500 41 41 41, email online@screwfix.com

Cooking spray p127 Most supermarkets stock cooking spray. Branded names include Spray n' Cook and Frylight.

Corks p128 If your wine drinking can't keep up with your need for corks – or all the bottles have screw tops or plastic corks, winemaking suppliers usually have a good stock of real corks. Online suppliers include **ww.easybrew.co.uk** tel 01425 479972, email info@easybrew.co.uk or **www.art-of-brewing.co.uk** tel 020 8397 2111 or **www.brewathome.co.uk** tel 01903 233832 email info@brewathome.co.uk

Cornflour p130 Most supermarkets and grocery shops stock cornflour. Manufacturers include Brown and Poulson or try supermarket own brands which can be exceptionally good value.

Cream of tartar p133 Supermarkets and grocery stores stock cream of tartar in the baking ingredients section. Brand names include Supercook.

Curtain rings p133 For the uses suggested in this book, simple brass rings or metal clip shower rings are the most suitable. Stockists of upholstery material will have a selection or try a department store such as John Lewis. Metal clip shower curtain rings which are particularly useful are available online at **www.plumbworld.co.uk** email customerservices@plumbworld.co.uk

Electrical tape p140 Also known as insulation tape, it is available from DIY stores and ironmongers. A good online source is **www.screwfix.com** 0500 41 41 41, email online@screwfix.com

Emery boards p141 Pharmacists stock emery boards alongside their manicure supplies. **www.manicure4u.co.uk** is an online supplier; tel 020 8998 1099, email sales@manicur4u.co.uk

Epsom salts p143 Pharmacies will generally keep epsom salts in stock. For online and mail order supplies try **www.baldwins.co.uk** tel 020 7703 5550, email sales@baldwins.co.uk

Foldback clips p153 Office and stationary supply stores such as Ryman and Viking keep a good range of foldback clips. You can order them online at **www.ryman.co.uk** tel 0800 801 901, email sales@ryman.co.uk or **www.viking-direct.co.uk** tel 0800 1971747

Gaffer tape p160-165 Try ironmongers and DIY stores for gaffer tape which is also known as duct tape and by its brand name, Duck Tape. For an online supplier, try **www.screwfix.com** 0500 41 41 41, email online@screwfix.com

Glycerine p166 Look for glycerine alongside hand lotions in a pharmacy or a craft shop that carries soap-making equipment. You can also purchase it online at **www.aromantic.co.uk** tel 01309 696900 email info@aromantic.co.uk

Hydrogen peroxide p173 Most pharmacists stock 3 per cent hydrogen peroxide. You can purchase it online at **www.detoxyourworld.com** tel 08700 113 119

Magnets p194 Ironmongers and DIY stores usually stock magnets. A huge range is available online at **www.uk-magnet.com** tel 0114 276 2264 email help@e-magnetsuk.com

Mouthwash p204 Available from most pharmacies and supermarkets. Check what you are planning to use the mouthwash for before buying; alcohol-based products are most effective for cleaning surfaces; specifically antiseptic varieties are more suitable for anything to do with your body.

Oven cleaner p222 Supermarkets and ironmongers will stock a variety of oven cleaners. Brand names include Cif, Mr Muscle and Oven Pride.

Petroleum jelly p240-243 Supermarkets and pharmacists will all keep Vaseline.

Plastic tablecloths p258 Don't choose plastic coated cotton – go for vinyl instead. Party shops will have cheap, but often highly decorative examples as do many market stalls that stock fabrics or kitchen supplies. Or go online at **www.tableclothsonline.co.uk** email sales@tableclothsonline.co.uk or **www.partydelights.co.uk** tel 0161 776 1133, email customercare@partydelights.co.uk

Spray bottles p302 Garden centres and DIY stores may have a selection of refillable plastic spray and squirt bottles. Online sources include **www.seton.co.uk** tel 0800 585 501, email sales@seton.co.uk **www.autojoy.co.uk** tel 01227 742593, email info@autojoy.co.uk **www.artfuldodgers.co.uk** tel 01254 207523, email info@artfuldodgers.co.uk

Surgical spirit p309 Ask for surgical spirit at a pharmacy; they will usually keep a cheap generic product. You can order it online at **www.stjohnsupplies.co.uk** tel 020 7278 7888, email customer-services@stjohnsupplies.co.uk

Vanilla extract p337 Find it in the baking aisle at most supermarkets. Brands include Supercook. Order online from **www.vanillaworks.co.uk** or **www.lakelandlimited.co.uk** tel 015394 88100

Wax paper p368 This is often referred to as waxed paper. You may find it with baking supplies in a supermarket. If not, obtain it from **www.lakelandlimited.co.uk** tel 015394 88100.

Editor Lisa Thomas
Art Editor Julie Bennett
Proofreader Barry Gage
Indexer Marie Lorimer
Cover digital manipulation Ian Atkinson
Writers Marilyn Bader, Serena Harding, Beth Kalet, Kathryn Kasturas, Michael Kaufman, Steven Schwartz, Anita Seline, Angelique B. Sharps, Delilah Smittle and Amy Ziffer
Photography Gary Ombler, Michal Kaniewski (Ad-Libitum)
How-to-illustrations © Bryon Thompson
Cartoons © Chuck Rekow

Reader's Digest Books

Editorial Director Julian Browne
Art Director Anne-Marie Bulat
Managing Editor Nina Hathway
Head of Book Development Sarah Bloxham
Picture Resource Manager Sarah Stewart-Richardson
Pre-press Account Manager Dean Russell
Product Production Manager Claudette Bramble
Production Controller Katherine Bunn

Origination Colour Systems Ltd

Printed and bound in China

Note The information in this book has been carefully researched and all efforts have been made to ensure accuracy and safety. Neither the authors nor Reader's Digest Association Limited assume any responsibility for any injuries suffered or damages or losses incurred as a result of following the instructions in this book. Before taking any action based on information in this book, study the information carefully and make sure you understand it fully. Observe all warnings and Take Care notices. Test any new or unusual repair or cleaning method before applying it broadly, or on a highly visible area or valuable item. The mention of any product or web site in this book does not imply an endorsement. All product names and web sites mentioned are subject to change and are meant to be considered as general examples rather than specific recommendations.

Extraordinary Uses for Ordinary Things was originated and first published by the editorial team of The Reader's Digest Inc., USA.

The UK edition was adapted and published by
The Reader's Digest Association Limited
11 Westferry Circus, Canary Wharf, London E14 4HE
www.readersdigest.co.uk

We are committed both to the quality of our products and the service we provide to our customers. We value your comments so please do contact us on **08705 113366** or via our web site at **www.readersdigest.co.uk**.

If you have any comments or suggestions about the content of our books you can contact us at **gbeditorial@readersdigest.co.uk**

Concept code US4655/IC
Book code 400-392 UP0000-1
ISBN 978 0 276 44410 4
Oracle code 250008876S.00.24